INTERNATIONAL AND COMPARATIVE POLITICS: A HANDBOOK

PHILIP M. BURGESS

Professor of Public Affairs
University of Colorado

JAMES E. HARF

Professor of Political Science
The Ohio State University

Executive Director,
Consortium for International
Studies Education

LAWRENCE E. PETERSON

Director of Program Services
Capitol University

INTERNATIONAL AND COMPARATIVE POLITICS: A HANDBOOK

wcb
Wm. C. Brown Publishers
Dubuque, Iowa

To James A. Robinson

The authors and publisher would like to thank the following authors and publishers for their permission to reprint materials:

Text on pages 9 and 10 is condensed from pp. 449–462 in *Approaches to the Study of Political Science,* edited by Michael Haas and Henry S. Kariel. Copyright © 1970 by Harper & Row, Publishers, Inc. Used by permission of the publisher.

Figure 2–3, p. 44, from Charles McClelland and Gary Hoggard, "Conflict Patterns in the Interactions among Nations," in James Roseneau (ed.), *International Politics and Foreign Policy,* Macmillan Publishing Co., Inc., © 1969. Reprinted by permission.

Figure 3–4, p. 72, from William D. Coplin, *Introduction to International Politics: A Theoretical Overview.* Reprinted by permission of the author.

Figure 3–5, p. 73, drawn from "The Calculus of Deterrence," by Bruce Russett, is reprinted from *Journal of Conflict Resolution,* vol. 7, no. 2, June 1963, p. 109, by permission of the publisher, Sage Publications.

Pp. 100 (ff), chapter four exercises: a portion of the material is from the code book for *French and German Elite Responses,* 1966, a multigraph published by Yale University; reprinted by permission of Professor Deutsch.

The scatter plot on p. 160 is reprinted by permission of Harper & Row, Publishers, Inc., from *Structure and Process in International Politics,* © 1973.

Figure 7–10, pp. 172–173, from B.J. Underwood et al., *Elementary Statistics.*

Library of Congress Catalog Card Number: 78–27113

ISBN 0–697–06793–9

Printed in the United States of America
10 9 8 7 6 5 4 3 2 1

CONTENTS

Chapter Three

Chapter Four

Chapter Five

Chapter Six

Chapter Seven

Conclusion

Appendix

PREFACE

This book originated from a series of mimeographed handouts first prepared for the students in a large introductory course in Contemporary International Politics at Ohio State University. The handouts were well-received by students, in large measure because they allowed the student to *apply* newly-acquired analytical skills to *problems* discussed in the course or derived from their readings. Problems included military spending and arms races, the impact and effects of foreign assistance programs, political alignments in the United Nations, processes of economic and political development, political and economic integration, etc. Hence, the handouts were transformed into what became the first of many "editions" of this book.

The pre-publication drafts were widely circulated and used in both undergraduate and beginning graduate courses, and the book's present form and content reflects the many suggestions and criticisms that were received from those who "field tested" the manuscript. While those who gave us valuable feedback should in no way be held responsible for that which follows, they deserve acknowledgment. Included in this group are J. David Singer and a team of graduate teaching assistants at the University of Michigan, where the book was used in an introductory course in world politics with more than 500 students. Pre-publication drafts were also tested by David Moore (now at New Hampshire) in the Social Science Division at the U.S. Military Academy at West Point, by Maurice East (now at Kentucky) in an introductory graduate level course at Denver's Graduate School of International Studies, and by ourselves in over a dozen courses at Ohio State during several years. In addition, William Liddle and his students gave us valuable comments, many of which we have used, after using a manuscript copy in an introductory course in comparative politics at Ohio State. Finally, pre-publication drafts have been used in the context of two professionally-oriented, inservice training programs in "Quantitative Policy Analysis" held at the Foreign Service Institute, and taught by Philip Burgess, James Harf, and Warren Phillips. Much was gained from comments, criticisms, and suggestions from the students and from the FSI staff, particularly John Bowling and Paul Kattenberg.

Particularly helpful individual comments and criticisms have been forthcoming over the past five years as the book evolved. Those giving us the benefit of their reactions include Richard Hofstetter (California State at San Diego); Charles Hermann, Richard Snyder, Warren Phillips, and John Kessel (Ohio State); James Rosenau (Southern California); William Coplin (Syracuse); David Singer (Michigan); Edward Azar (North Carolina); Ellen Pirro (Minnesota); John Gillespie (Indiana); Richard Merritt (Illinois); Robert Young (formerly of CACI); and Harold Guetzkow (Northwestern).

We have, in the following pages, illustrated major points with examples from extant research in comparative and international politics; hence, we acknowledge publishers for generally granting permissions to quote relevant materials. We are indebted to the Literary Executor of the late Sir Ronald A. Fisher, F.R.S., and to Dr. Frank Yates, F.R.S., and to Oliver and Boyd, Edinburgh, for permission to reprint figure 7.8 from their book, *Statistical Tables for Biological, Agricultural and Medical Research.*

Although it is sometimes difficult to assess the contributions of each author in a co-authored work, we believe that it is important to do so. While all three authors in this instance made contributions throughout the text, Burgess was primarily responsible for the first four chapters, Harf for the last three chapters and the appendix, and Peterson for the questions at the end of each chapter.

Finally, we are grateful to the extreme for the unusually competent (and, at times persistent) assistance that we have enjoyed from Ann Peterson, a Ph.D. candidate in Social Science Education; Evelyn Small and Janet Galchick, former Ph.D. students; and James Stoner, former undergraduate Political Science major. Without their insistence that this book be completed, we would undoubtedly be in the midst of another mimeographed edition. Others happy to see the manuscript finished include typists past and present: Sandy Nichols, Amy Fishbein, Barbara Bennett, Barbara Siegelman, Barbara Ottavi, and Nikki Lyons. Others who assisted at one time or another include Bruce Moon, David Hoovler, Michael Zavatsky, Robert Soppelsa, Raymond Lawton, Dennis Benson, Tom James, Richard Conway, Dan Grosh, Tom Waters, Wayne Stryjek, and Daniel Kennedy. Also, we owe much to the advice and assistance of Lawrence Mayer, formerly at Ohio State and now a professor in the Department of Statistics at Princeton.

Philip M. Burgess
James E. Harf
Lawrence E. Peterson

INTRODUCTION

You are about to begin an introduction to quantitative analysis in comparative and international politics. You may ask why a handbook should be prepared at all, particularly for an undergraduate course. There are several reasons. First, with a few partial exceptions,[1] no comparable handbooks exist which provide a broad introduction to basic principles and procedures in cross-national quantitative analysis. Similar books do exist in other disciplines,[2] and introductory books in statistics[3] and data processing[4] are abundant. But because of time limitations and conventional course structures, the use of these latter books is hardly possible in the context of most courses in international relations. They tend to be designed primarily for courses in research methods or data analysis, and their content is far removed from international or comparative politics. Thus, the first purpose is to provide a resource that is closely linked to the existing literature, with examples derived from international relations and comparative politics, and with techniques of data-making and data analysis that are most appropriate to research problems and substantive issues in the study of cross-national phenomena.

Second, the study of international politics and foreign policy has undergone radical change over the past decade. Early concerns with conceptual clarity and more explicit theorizing, evidenced first in the 1930s, were capped in 1948 with the publication of the first edition of Hans Morgenthau's *Politics Among Nations*. However, that book, now in its fifth edition, has been overtaken conceptually and methodologically by more recent advances. Trends in international relations research today are largely empirical, quantitative, and multivariate. The international relations student of fifteen years ago was self-consciously theoretical as compared to today's advanced student who is often self-consciously empirical—evidencing too little regard for theory.[5]

Historically, teaching materials lag far behind advances in research. This is not only true in international relations. Irish and Prothro's text on American government lagged behind research advances in American politics and political behavior by at least a decade. Samuelson's landmark text in economics was published nearly fifteen years after the Keynesian revolution had become the established paradigm for U.S. economic policy. Early attempts to approach international relations in the tradition of the sciences to supplement the tradition of the humanities were stillborn—in large part owing to the absence of an adequate data base.

That data base, however incomplete and *ad hoc*, has now been substantially developed,[6] yet few books exist that will give the beginning student an ability to understand, evaluate, and—most importantly—*to do* quantitative research in international relations. The material in this handbook will permit you to acquire knowledge of the operations of quantitative analysis so you can better understand and evaluate books like Bruce Russett's *Trends in World Politics*, David Singer's *Quantitative International Politics*, or Roger Cobb and Charles Elder's *International Community*, or articles collected in anthologies such as James Rosenau's two volumes entitled *International Politics and Foreign Policy*, Louis Kriesberg's *Social Processes in International Politics*, or Richard Merrit and Stein Rokkan's *Comparing Nations*.

The presentation of quantitative materials should be neither intimidating nor awesome. With just a little effort, you will find that the explicit and standardized methods or "rules of evidence" of quantitative research can be easily and quickly grasped, and that the products of quantitative research—once its basic operations are understood—are probably more easily comprehended than the products of non-quantitative research. The primary purpose of this handbook is not to induce you to become quantitative researchers. Rather, its aim is to make you more comfortable with ideas, concepts, and policy appraisals and recommendations that are examined, explored, probed, and investigated by quantitative methods—something we are all increasingly encountering.[7]

The principles and techniques of quantitative research are not bound to particular disciplines or fields. They should be learned as a set of logical operations and procedures for dealing with information or distributions of data. In the ideal curriculum, students in political science would acquire these analytical skills early and quickly in their undergraduate careers—just as today's liberal arts student is usually required to acquire primitive language skills and display verbal and writing skills. But these ideal conditions do not exist in many departments.[8] Also, much of what is learned about quantitative research in departments of political science is not as useful to the student in international relations as it is to the student in political behavior and other subfields of political science. For example, students of international relations are typically dealing with a known population (e.g., *all* nations in the international system or *all* nations in the Latin American area) and not with samples such as studies of voting behavior within a society. Hence, problems of data collection and data analysis are often quite different from the usual problems encountered by other political and social scientists.

The third reason for presenting the material in this handbook is to acquaint you with some of the elementary skills required for data collection, data storage and retrieval, and data tabulation and analysis. You will be encouraged to manipulate data and interpret the results not to make you a researcher in international relations, but rather so that you will learn the principles of science and the operations of quantitative analysis more thoroughly and quickly by actually *doing* elementary research than by *reading about* how it is done. Consequently, the exercises at the end of each chapter are designed to encourage you to engage in some elementary analysis. They are predicated on our commitment to *learn by doing* and on our hope that some of you will be stimulated and encouraged by the experiences of discovering knowledge.

Moreover, the style of quantitative research represented in many of the examples and exercises is not necessarily a style to which we are committed or that we would promote or encourage others to adopt. Indeed, there are many compelling reasons why the quantitative analysis of international politics might move away from simple hypothesis-testing and elaborate statistical operations performed on data of questionable quality. On the other hand, the research *skills* that are presented in the following pages are prerequisites for engaging in or understanding the products of alternative research *styles* and commitments that lean more to the simulation of social systems or to the design of future systems.[9] For example, the basic Forrester model examines the interacting effects of continued exponential growth of population, industrialization, food production, pollution, and the consumption of nonrenewable natural resources. If you want to be capable of critically appraising reviews[10] of this model, then you will need to acquire the ability to read charts and graphs—one of the basic skills covered in the following pages.

Finally, the material in this handbook is presented because of an increasing commitment to an empirical, design-oriented policy science among political and social scientists. Even though the analytical skills developed from this manual will help you to understand much contemporary writing about international politics and foreign policy, knowledge of the present trends toward quantitative analysis of policy problems is desirable. Students educated in the liberal arts should be exposed to the skills that will give them the capacity to be critical and informed consumers of public policy appraisals and recommendations that are based on rigorous and systematic social and political analysis.[11] In order to appraise public policy, you have to have some reliable and explicit methods for observing and evaluating *trends*. You need to have the skills necessary to identify the *conditions* that have sustained those trends and to evaluate the probability that observed trends will continue or will change. If you are going to make recommendations for the future (or evaluate those of others), you have the responsibility to appraise accurately the basic social forces at work in the present.

Also, if you have strong ideas about how the world "ought to be," then you can use these methods of political analysis not only to ascertain where we are now but also to estimate the likely consequences of our policy recommendations.[12] If you assume that knowledge itself affects the values we affirm, then quantitative methods of analysis can assist us in thinking through and designing policy proposals that have their source in deep-rooted normative concerns that we all hold with respect to national and international politics. In short, you must be able to assess with some rigor the probable consequences of our recommendations for policy if you are to make effective, compassionate, and responsible action recommendations; to become promoters; or to critically evaluate the recommendations of others.

In conclusion, the laboratory exercises at the end of each chapter are designed to give you first-hand, direct experiences with the substance and procedures of systematic political research. They will introduce you to some very basic ideas and concepts about how political data can be generated and analyzed in order to answer questions of interest. The lab will also require you to face and resolve some fundamental considerations of research design, and will provide an occasion for you to use modern data processing equipment (such as the key punch machine and counter-sorter) for recording, manipulating, compiling, and analyzing political and social data.

The techniques designed for review in the lab sessions are only a few among those available in the "kit of tools" of the political analyst. Moreover, the point of view or philosophy of research presented in this text is only one of several points of view currently followed in a pluralistic discipline such as political science.[13] We hope you will appreciate both the advantages and limitations of the approach introduced here, and that this text will stimulate a desire on your part to learn

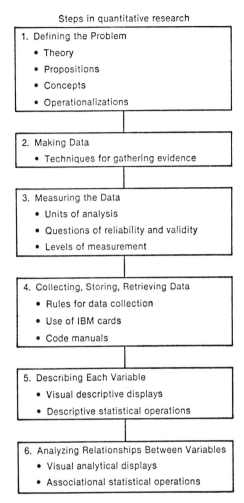

Steps in quantitative research

1. Defining the Problem
   - Theory
   - Propositions
   - Concepts
   - Operationalizations

2. Making Data
   - Techniques for gathering evidence

3. Measuring the Data
   - Units of analysis
   - Questions of reliability and validity
   - Levels of measurement

4. Collecting, Storing, Retrieving Data
   - Rules for data collection
   - Use of IBM cards
   - Code manuals

5. Describing Each Variable
   - Visual descriptive displays
   - Descriptive statistical operations

6. Analyzing Relationships Between Variables
   - Visual analytical displays
   - Associational statistical operations

Steps in quantitative research

more about the research philosophy and analytical techniques. Furthermore, we hope and expect that you will be better prepared to understand subsequent courses in political science (such as public opinion, legislative behavior, political decision-making, etc.). The research procedures in this text lie at the foundation of much that is known in these areas. And finally, we hope that you will assume a more creative and critical posture in relation to discussions surrounding critical issues of public policy, such as policies related to fuel and energy consumption or cost-benefit analyses of foreign area military bases.

The text is organized according to the basic steps of quantitative analysis. Each chapter corresponds to a basic step in researching a problem (with chapters 6 and 7 covering the final sixth step), and the appendix provides a comprehensive sample data set which may be used to practice the techniques and skills taught in the book. The following figure outlines these basic steps.

NOTES

1. For example, Ellen Pirro (1972) has developed a more specialized and sharply focused workbook of exercises, and Ted Gurr (1972) has provided an excellent, brief, and well-written introduction to analytical issues in cross-national analysis.

2. For examples in geography and psychology, see Yeates (1968) and Hergenhahn (1970). In the area of political behavior, see Benson (1969).

3. See Downie and Heath (1965) for a typical elementary introduction to statistics. We strongly recommend Zeisel (1968) for a stimulating and unusually readable guide to the use of quantitative language in social research. See Palumbo (1969) for an introductory statistics text closely linked to the political science literature. The most useful basic reference book for the beginning student in quantitative analysis is, in our judgment, Garson (1971).

4. On techniques and methods of data processing, consult an excellent treatment by Janda (1969).

5. See for elaboration, Singer (1968), Burgess (1970), and Palmer (1970). For an excellent summary of an earlier tradition in international relations, consult Dougherty and Pfaltzgraf (1971).

6. For a general discussion of the development of international and cross-national data bases, see Rokkan (1962), Bisco (1970), and Cutler (1974).

7. Even the study of history and the humanities has been deeply affected by the application of mathematical techniques to data analysis and by the revolution in computer technology. See Edmund A. Bowles' collection of readings on computers in humanistic research (Bowles, 1967). On the impact of computers in the social and behavioral sciences, see Borko (1962), and on the role of computers in foreign policy studies, see Bobrow and Schwartz (1968).

8. Indeed, they do not exist in many graduate level curricula, although the better graduate departments appear to be more demanding in this regard. See Luttbeg and Kahn (1968), or Lasswell (1963).

9. For a basic introduction to social systems simulation, consult Raser (1969). A more recent example of simulation applications in the social sciences can be found in Guetzkow (1972). A good example of a social system design orientation can be found in Boguslaw (1965). For a basic introduction to design theory notions, see Bellman (1967), or Simon (1969).

10. For example, see Passell, Roberts, and Ross (1972).

11. For an elaboration of the uses of quantitative analysis in problem-solving and goal-setting, see Lerner and Lasswell (1951), or Lasswell (1963;1972); see

Bauer's treatment of "social indicators" (1966), or the use of program-planning and budgeting techniques reviewed by Hitch (1965). See Wilcox et al. (1972) for a general bibliography on social indicators and see Lyden and Miller (1972) for a collection of major source papers on program budgeting. See Churchman (1968) for a basic, extremely well-written, nontechnical introduction to systems analysis.

12. These points are discussed under a variety of labels—such as "technology assessment," "social forecasting," and "evaluation research." On these points, see Rivlin (1971), Duncan (1969), and Rossi and Williams (1972). These issues are also widely discussed in the emerging literature on the "policy sciences." See, for example, Lasswell (1972) and Dror (1971).

13. For examples of this pluralism, consult the papers collected in Knorr and Rosenau (1969). It is our view that the "debates" between the "yea-sayers" and the "nay-sayers" with respect to the role of science in the study of international politics is not very productive and tends quickly to boredom. Hence, we want to recognize the views of others while affirming our own and suggest: (1) that the role of science in the study of individuals and social groups is an issue over which reasonable men can disagree, and (2) that ultimately the work of all will be appraised by what it achieves, *by what we are able to do* with the knowledge acquired by whatever methods.

Chapter One

THE DEVELOPMENT OF EMPIRICAL THEORY

This chapter focuses on the first step in quantitative analysis. It introduces you to the meaning and function of theory in the study of international relations. It reviews by way of example some current theoretical orientations that characterize contemporary research in international politics and foreign policy. It covers the role of the empirical proposition or hypothesis in scientific research, including a detailed discussion of variables and the relational statements that link variables one to another.

Because much of the literature of political science is "pre-operational" (lacking variables which have clear and reproducible definitions), insightful observations by political analysts and scholars must often be translated into new and less ambiguous terms. Verbal clarity is the first requirement if the assertions about politics and societal relationships are to be subjected to systematic observation and study. Consequently, one of the first skills to be learned by the social scientist is to construct empirically meaningful scientific statements. These empirical statements may be the result of observation or intuition; come from an inventory of existing literature; or be deduced from existing social or political theory. Therefore, the chapter begins with theory and its building block, the proposition. It concludes with a discussion of the strategies for constructing propositional inventories, relating the proposition back to the earlier discussion of theory.

THEORY AND INTERNATIONAL RELATIONS

The development of a science of international relations requires an understanding of the close relationship that exists between imagination or insight on the one side, and social theory, methodology, and systematic data analysis on the other. Subsequent chapters deal with *methodology* (the public and reproducible procedures that a scientist uses to observe his environment, and generate data); and with *analysis* (the analytical, statistical, mathematical, and modeling techniques that a scientist uses to describe data and to discover and/or represent relationships between or among elements in his environment and to establish the strength and direction of those relationships). For the present, however, we will be concerned with *theory*, that is, the general orientation that a scientist has toward the environment, toward data, and toward the classes of variables and major concepts that will be used to understand the social arena commonly labeled "international relations."

The following pages emphasize *empirical theory* (theory used to organize facts). Two other types of theory, *prudential* and *normative*, are identified in contrast to empirical theory. *Prudential theory*, also known as *design* or *policy theory*, is defined as theory used to guide action; and *normative theory*, also known as *philosophical theory*, is defined as theory in the sense of a statement of desirable ends.[1] Though we are interested in normative and prudential theory as well as empirical theory, we shall emphasize empirical theory. In the following sections, theory will be discussed from the viewpoint of the *scope* of the theoretical effort— the extent to which we are working with broad-gauged, general theories or narrow-gauged, partial theories—in contrast to its *purpose* or application (for policy or scientific purposes).

BROAD-GAUGE THEORIES

The term *theory* has a number of meanings for social scientists. For some, theory means a set of interrelated propositions; for others, it refers to a very broad frame of reference or general orientation. For example, some theories suggest that it is more productive to examine the gross characteristics of a polity (such as its level of economic development or its form of government), since these characteristics condition or otherwise lead to certain forms of behavior. By contrast, others encourage us to examine the behavior of individual decision-makers and their place in the network of organizational communications if we want to understand or anticipate the behavior of nations in the international system.

These *broad-gauge* or "metatheories" serve to identify classes of variables (such as national attributes or the motivations of decision-makers). However, broad-gauge theories do not typically provide us with a set of interrelated propositions that link these variables in a form that says, for example, "the more developed a nation is, the greater the likelihood it will seek alliances, avoid war, or expand its world-wide commercial or diplomatic contacts." This latter kind of concise empirical statement will be referred to later as a *proposition*. For the present, it is important to keep in mind only that broad-gauge theory is represented by more general statements about "how things work" in the political world.

Theories also involve major *organizing concepts*. In international relations there is a wide range of organizing concepts from major theoreticians. Some of the more common concepts include Arnold Wolfer's *billiard ball* model of the international system; John Herz's concept of territorial *permeability* which traces the development of the nation-state system; and Ernst Haas' concept of *spillover* which describes the process of international integration.[2] Charles McClelland and Morton Kaplan have developed important ideas around the concept of *system transformation* processes; George Liska (1962) has developed the notion of *multiple equilibrium* and applied it to the study of international relations; and the concept of the *decision-making process* developed by Richard Snyder and his colleagues has had a profound effect on the way a generation of researchers has conceptualized and studied foreign policy and the policy making process.[3]

Research in international relations has emphasized the development of a rich inventory of broad-gauge theories—due in part to the absence of an adequate data base that would support extensive systematic empirical research. This view is elaborated by Heinz Eulau in his wide-ranging review of research in political science. Eulau observes that there appears to be an inverse relationship between theorizing, as an independently creative activity, and the empirical accessibility of the theorized phenomena. "I find that the most exciting theoretical work . . . now being done falls into the range of problems traditionally of interest to the student of international relations—precisely the area where access to behavioral data is perhaps difficult to come by. On the other hand, theorizing has been sluggish in problem areas where empirical research is relatively easy—for instance, the study of elections and voting behavior."[4]

Michael Haas has written a notable and unusually concise essay that slices through the voluminous and highly specialized literature in the field of international relations. He assesses contemporary international relations theory in relation to seven major broad-gauge or "metatheoretical" orientations. This effort is probably one of the most coherent statements of the *range* of theoretical perspectives found in the contemporary study of international relations.[5] Although Haas' essay on international relations theory deserves to be read directly, we will, with some slight modifications, use Haas to characterize the inventory of metatheoretical orientations that are dominant today:

1. *Cognitive rationalism:* Cognitive rationalism examines the public justifications and private objectives that underpin a decision-maker's behavior. A cognitive rationalist is not concerned so much with psychological motivations as he is with the manifest reasons for behavior that are derived from an examination of concerns that emerge from the deliberations over issues. Key concepts are goal, reason, issue, event, means, dispute, and many legal terms. The cognitive rationalist orientation, typical of diplomatic historians, is represented among political scientists by Herman Finer and Allen Whiting.

2. *Power theory:* Power theory is linked to cognitive rationalism. It examines the behavior of the state by reference to its capabilities and to the process of rational calculation where the desire to maximize power is viewed as the dominant motive. Major concepts are struggle, interest, preservation, power, capabilities, balance of power, ideology, sovereignty, security, and nationalism. Major contributors to the contemporary literature are Hans Morgenthau, Raymond Aron, Inis Claude, John Herz, Klaus Knorr, Harold Sprout, and Robert Strausz-Hupe.

3. *Decision-making:* Decision-making analysis conceives state action as an outcome of a decision process in which the *role* assumed by the decision-maker (his sphere of competence in a decision structure, his place in a communications net, and his motivations) is postulated as the most significant factor. Key concepts are surprise, deliberation, perceived threat, authority structure, decision latitude, participation in decision-making, feedback, competitive role demands, informal channels, socialization, and perceptual selectivities. Decision-making structures have been examined by Richard Snyder, James Robinson, Dean Pruitt, Charles Hermann, and Glenn Paige. Chadwick Alger, Richard Brody, James Rosenau, and Charles McClelland have reported research on communications patterns. Motivational variables have been researched by Robert North, Ole Holsti, and Dina Zinnes.

4. *Strategy theory:* Strategy theory, which also has roots in decision-making theory, involves a more analytically rigorous form of capability analysis embedded in power theory. It is concerned with the *evaluation* of alternatives in terms of payoffs and explicit as well as tacit bargaining processes. Major concepts include payoff, threat, perception, image, negotiation, saddle point, utility, zero-sum, and cooperation. Major contributors have been Richard Brody, John Raser, Thomas Milburn, Anatol Rapoport, Thomas Schelling, and Kenneth Boulding.

5. *Communications theory:* Communications theory, taking account of the social and cultural context within which decision processes occur, examines the flow of

persons, goods, and messages across political boundaries looking for recurring and sustained patterns of interaction or isolation. Major concepts include transaction, integration, mobilization, value compatibility, spill-over, responses, load, and case. Major contributors who have adopted a communications theory orientation include Karl Deutsch, Hayward Alker, Bruce Russett, Amitai Etzioni, Ernst Haas, Werner Levi, Richard Merritt, and Donald Puchala.

6. *Field theory:* Field theory examines those factors and characteristics of a polity that serve to condition or otherwise lead toward various forms and levels of behavior. Major concepts are dimension, factor, distance, asymmetry, attribute, cluster, pattern, and space. Major contributors have been Quincy Wright, R. J. Rummel, Michael Haas, Steven Brams, the Feierabends, Rauol Naroll, and Raymond Tanter.

7. *System theory:* System theory, the most generic and inclusive metatheory, examines the structure and function of the international system as a whole with the expectation that propositions confirmed in biological and physical systems can be confirmed in social systems. Major concepts are input, output, environmental exchange, homeostasis, performance, transformation, stimuli and response, and channels for action. Major contributors from the systems perspective have been Morton Kaplan, Charles McClelland, David Singer, Richard Rosecrance, and Karl Deutsch. Structural-functional analysis has been employed by Chadwick Alger, Michael Haas, George Liska, David Singer, George Modelski, Michael Brecher, James Rosenau, and others as an alternative strategy to applying systems theory in the study of international relations.

MIDDLE-GAUGE THEORIES

Theories that lie between the broad-gauge orientations just reviewed and the working hypotheses or propositions that are reviewed in some detail below are typically called *middle-gauge theories.* Middle-gauge theories are constituted by a set of hypotheses or propositions. These propositions are related to one another by implication or by deduction, so that Proposition 1 (P_1) implies Proposition 2 (P_2) or such that Proposition 3 (P_3) may be deduced from the relationship between P_1 and P_2. For example, consider the so-called compatibility theory of alliances which suggests that nations seek alliances with those other nations with whom they share certain common interests or ideology, or with whom they share similar political or economic institutions.[6] From this compatibility theory, we might develop the following propositions about inter-nation alliances:

P_1 The greater the ideological similarities among nations in alliance, the greater the cohesion of the alliance.

P_2 Alliances among autocratic states rely more on ideology as a means of achieving alliance cohesion, while alliances among democratic states rely on a prospect of gain as the major force in achieving cohesion.

Note that while both propositions P_1 and P_2 suggest that a compatible ideology is an important factor determining alliance cohesion, proposition P_2 suggests that the form of government characterizing the nations in alliance is an important *intervening* factor influencing the impact of compatible ideologies on the cohesion of an alliance. As a consequence, we are able to deduce the following proposition:

P_3 The weight of the factors influencing the cohesion of an alliance is significantly affected by the compatibility of the governmental structures of the nations in alliance.

While all three of these propositions remain to be proved or confirmed,[7] the example should serve to demonstrate the way in which we build middle-gauge theory. Compatibility theory has no pretensions to be a general theory of alliances. It simply identifies some classes of variables (such as ideology, political and economic institutions, cultural features such as religion and language) and states a relationship, that is, the empirical expectation that these features of nations will be similar or at least compatible in cohesive and stable alliances. From this middle-gauge theory we are then able both to induce and deduce additional researchable hypotheses.

NARROW-GAUGE THEORIES

So far in this chapter we have been talking about theories, hypotheses, and propositions without defining what we mean. When we turn to the lowest level of theory (narrow-gauge theories) we are working with the building blocks of theories—propositions. Recall that we suggested earlier that theory is sometimes defined as a set of interrelated propositions. Now it is appropriate to state more clearly what we mean by the term *proposition*.

As we attempt to apply scientific methods of political and social analysis, it is necessary to express observations, insights, or hunches about the way things work in a social system in terms that have empirical meaning. In short, we have to be able to express relationships among the many factors that constitute political reality in a clear and unambiguous way.

An empirical proposition is a sentence that expresses an empirically meaningful relationship. Take, for example, the statement, "Nations either go to war or remain at peace." This statement expresses a formal proposition, *not* an empirical proposition. A formal proposition, such as this, has no relation to observations or experience and does not, therefore, express a meaningful empirical relationship. Formal propositions are either tautologies (as above) or contradictions.

By contrast, an *empirical proposition* depends on observations or evidence for its verification. Consider, for example, the proposition, "Nations with highly developed economic capacities tend to interact more with each other than with less developed nations." Unlike the formal proposition stated earlier, the truth value of the empirical proposition is in question, can be explored by empirical investigation, and can be tested against empirical evidence or observations.[8] The formal proposition, by contrast, was self-evidently true.

For our purposes here, we are concerned only with empirical propositions. However, because many of the empirical propositions encountered in the literature of comparative and international politics will be of little use in building middle-gauge theories, we should briefly review and dispose of them. Among these are the vague proposition, the global proposition, and the trite proposition.

The *vague proposition* is too general to permit a test of its truth value. Consider, for example, Hans Morgenthau's proposition that "Whatever the ultimate aim of international politics, power is always the immediate aim."[9] The term *power* is much too general for testing. The *global proposition* is one which on its face admits of too many exceptions or one the referents of which are too broad to justify the commitment of research resources for testing. Illustrative of this type is the following proposition extracted from the writings of the noted geopolitician, Nicholas Spykman, "Who controls the Rimland rules Eurasia; who rules Eurasia controls the destinies of the world."[10]

The *trite proposition*, by contrast, states the obvious. An instance of this type of proposition is found in the statement of Kenneth Thompson and Roy Macridis that "Some nation-states and their political leadership are likely to resort to violence more readily than others."[11] However, we must be alert to the obvious proposition, for after examination, some turn out to be not so obvious. Second, it is often possible to find rival or competing obvious propositions, for example, propositions that state exactly the opposite conclusions (not infrequently within one person's work!). Third, obvious propositions often can be converted to significant propositions. As an example, if the above proposition from Thompson and Macridis indicated the characteristics of nations or leadership that leads to the propensity for violence, then it might be worth further examination and research. If the proposition were converted to read, "Nation-states whose political leadership is unaccountable are more likely to resort to violence than are nations whose leadership is accountable to other political and social groups . . ." then we would have created an interesting empirical proposition that relates political accountability (or open and closed polities) to the propensity for violence—a proposition with a long history of emphasis in political theory.

CHARACTERISTICS OF THE PROPOSITION

Because the primary purpose in this chapter is to provide an overview of the process of theory-building and to introduce the role of the empirical proposition (or hypothesis) in scientific research, it is important to examine more closely the components of a proposition.

We stated earlier that an empirical proposition states a relationship between two or more variables. For our purposes here, a variable will be considered as a characteristic, concept, or abstraction, created by the analyst. Moreover, the variable can be specified and measured and its value varies or changes. Variables may refer to aspects of human behavior (trusting, aggressive, skillful, hostile) or to attributes of the nonhuman physical or social environment (isolated, contiguous, wealthy, large, powerful).

Variables can be defined in at least two ways: one way is to define them conceptually by specifying as clearly as possible the meaning of the variable. This type of variable definition is usually called a *nominal definition*. Consider, for example, the nominal definition of "integration" used by Deutsch: "the attainment, within a territory, of a 'sense of community' and of institutions and practices strong enough and widespread enough to assure, for a 'long' time dependable expectations of 'peaceful change' among its population."[12]

A more demanding and scientifically useful definition of a variable is the *operational definition*. When we operationally define a variable (operationalize), we define it in terms denoting the procedure(s) we use to measure it. For example, when we say that "Developed nations interact more with each other than with less developed nations," we have a proposition that might be stated more concisely as follows:

P_1 The *frequency of interaction* is higher AMONG *economically-developed nations* than BETWEEN *developed and less developed nations*.

Now we are faced with the problem of operationalizing the major variables in the proposition (italicized above). While "everybody knows" what we mean by *inter-*

action and *economic development*, most would, if asked, give nominal definitions that would elaborate in considerable verbal and anecdotal detail what they mean by *economic development*. Recalling, however, that an operational definition is one which defines the variable by the procedures used to measure it, we might want to consider the following operational definitions:

> *Economic development:* All nations identified as "less developed" by the United Nations Conference on Trade, Aid, and Developed (UNCTAD) will be "less developed." All others will be identified as "economically developed."

> *Interaction:* Interaction will be defined by UN records of the flow of mail between nations. Nations that exchange mail at rates exceeding the global average will have "high interaction"; nations that exchange mail below the global average will have "low interaction."

While many may object to these operational definitions of economic development and interaction, they are clear, unambiguous, standardized, explicit, and reproducible by others.[13]

We use operational procedures to define variables because they permit other researchers to replicate our research. When others repeat research procedures we use and get the same results, this serves to strengthen the level of confidence in our own findings and thereby to establish more securely and build upon the knowledge we have obtained. The replication of research and analysis by different observers and analysts is possible only if they are able to reach inter-subjective agreement about the precise meaning or definition of key terms and variables. The demand for inter-subjective agreement on the meaning of key terms and the methods of observation is what is meant when the scientist says he uses objective procedures. The objective procedures used by the scientist to define his terms and make his observations (i.e., to "operationalize" his methods) are contrasted with the preoperational subjective or impressionistic procedures used by the nonscientist.

Before moving on, let's examine another example of operationalizing a proposition. Take the proposition, "Nations that are unstable internally are hostile in their external behavior."[14] The key variables here are "internally unstable" and "external hostility." Before we can test this proposition (by gathering evidence to confirm or disconfirm it), we must operationalize the key variables. For example, we might operationalize "internally unstable" by noting the frequency of assassinations, or by measuring the average tenure of office of a government or administration. Or we might combine both of these operational indicators of instability in order to create an index of instability.

External "hostile" behavior might be operationalized by computing the ratio of friendly to unfriendly public pronouncements by key foreign policy officials, or by noting the frequency of wars initiated by the countries under examination. And, again, we might combine these two (or other) measures to create an index of external hostility.[15] Now, having operationalized the variables, we are ready to make empirical observations (to collect data) in order to confront the proposition with data or evidence in order to assess its truth value (i.e., the extent to which confidence in the empirical statement is justified or warranted).

THE CLASSIFICATION OF VARIABLES

Propositions are formed by a relational statement linking two or more variables. For the present, let's examine the variables by noting their function in a proposition. Classified functionally, we obtain three different kinds of variables:

1. Independent variables.
2. Intervening variables.
3. Dependent variables.

An independent variable (IV) is the factor that presumably explains, accounts for, or determines the behavior under investigation. The conventional symbol for the IV is "X." A dependent variable (DV) refers to the behavior we are observing and which we want to explain or account for. The conventional symbol for the DV is "Y."

Let's return to the proposition "Internally unstable nations are more hostile in their external behavior." The behavior that interests us, the variable or behavior that we want to explain or account for, is external hostility. Thus, external hostility is the *dependent variable*. We have hypothesized that external hostility is "caused" by, related to, or otherwise associated with internal instability. Thus, domestic instability is the *independent variable*. But what if our research does not confirm our hypothesis? We might then simply have a "bad" hypothesis, one whose truth value is low.

Or we might find an *intervening variable* operating. For example, where the hypothesis is not confirmed (i.e., where internal instability is not found to be associated with external hostility), we may find in all those cases that the nations are dictatorships. We might then discover that authoritarian regimes have a greater capacity to insulate themselves from the domestic pressures that are operating including instability. Thus, we would have identified an intervening variable (in this case, the "responsiveness" or "accountability" of the political elite to the demands of the people) that affects systematically the strength and direction of the relationship between the independent (sometimes called the "causal" or "determinate") variable and the dependent (or "resultant") variable. In short, an *intervening variable* is a link between those factors treated as explanations (IV) and the behavior to be explained (DV). An intervening variable is sometimes viewed as an additional independent variable or as a *control variable*. However, this moves us beyond the examination of simple two variable (or *bivariate*) relationships into the more exciting arena of *multivariate* relationships. In the meantime, it can be noted that as a control, the intervening variable may be designated by X' (read "X prime") or by X_1 (read "X subscript").

The analyst always attempts to identify an independent variable that explains, accounts for, or is associated with change (or variance) in the value or behavior of the dependent variable. To the extent that variation in the IV is associated with variance in the DV, we have *explained variance*; the remainder is *unexplained variance*. A high percentage of unexplained variance simply means we must search elsewhere for explanations of the behavior that interests us.[16]

THE CLASSIFICATION OF PROPOSITIONS

We will classify propositions according to the type of relational statement that is used to link the variables in the proposition. Recalling that independent variables are designated by the symbol "X" and dependent variables by the symbol "Y," we can identify four basic types of propositions:

Anatomical propositions where X has the characteristic Y.

Consequential propositions which state that Y is determined by or a consequence of X.

Correlational propositions which state that X and Y are associated, and that they exhibit covariation in their values. They vary together; for example, as one increases, the other increases.

Null propositions which state that variation in X has no relation to variation in Y.[17]

Keeping in mind these elementary considerations of propositions, variables, and relational statements, and maintaining the distinction between empirical and normative, and empirical and formal statements, it is useful to identify more clearly the four basic types of propositions that are typically encountered in the literature in comparative and international politics. Note that each of the following propositions can be located in the set of relational statements identified above. Once the basic propositional types are fully understood, you should return to the more exhaustive and discriminating propositional types suggested by Zetterberg in footnote 17.

X Has the Characteristic Y

March and Simon have called this type of descriptive statement a "simple qualitative anatomical" proposition.[18] The *anatomical proposition*, found throughout the literature in political science, does *not* establish a relationship between two or more variables. Some examples of the anatomical proposition might be:

1. In choosing policies, decision-makers do not select from among all the possible alternatives, but from the alternatives that are visible to them.[19]

2. An actor, or more precisely, the decision-making apparatus of an actor, has a capacity for storing experience.[20]

3. In national crises, the principal decision-making group will tend to vary in size from twelve to fifteen officials.[21]

Or consider the following anatomical propositions developed by Christensen to characterize the *technologically more advanced* nations (TMA's) and the *technologically less advanced* nations (TLA's).[22]

TLA Nations

1. Over half the human family lives in Asia.
2. Most of the world's people are non-white.
3. Most of the world's people are non-Christian.
4. Most people live in rapid population growth areas and are members of large families.
5. Most people make their living as farmers and craftsmen and depend heavily on hand and animal labor.
6. Most of the world's people are poor in terms of money income.
7. Most people are very poorly fed.
8. Most people are sick and in need of medical care.

9. Most people are illiterate and only about one in three knows the bare rudiments of reading and writing.
10. The nations in which most people live depend very little on trade and many of them depend on only a few specialized exports.
11. Most people live under new, relatively inexperienced, and, in many cases, unstable governments.

TMA Nations

1. Most people are white, Christian, and live in mid-latitude areas of North America, Europe, and the Soviet Union.
2. Most people live in rapidly growing towns and cities.
3. Most people live at levels of nutrition and health that are far above minimum standards and average longevity is half again as large as it is in the less developed nations.
4. Most people have incomes that are large enough to provide much more than a bare minimum level of living.
5. Economic systems are completely commercialized and depend on high rates of production and consumption of all kinds of goods and services.
6. People and nations exist at a high level of interdependence and economic vulnerability.
7. People are governed by experienced, mature governments that are elected by and generally responsive to an informed electorate.
8. Literacy rates are high and people are informed about conditions in their own country and in others as well.
9. R & D programs, the accumulation of wealth, and other successes have brought the most difficult and change-fraught problem: automation and the cybernation revolution.

While these kinds of anatomical propositions are not by themselves useful for empirical theory, they may contribute to theory-building in a number of ways: (1) they serve as statements of prior (antecedent) conditions under which certain relationships among other variables may be expected; (2) they may suggest other propositions that can be obtained by the process of conversion (i.e., they have a *heuristic* value);[23] and (3) they may serve as components of other propositions. Because anatomical propositions have basic descriptive qualities, they are easily identified in most of the literature that you will read.

If X, Then Y

This kind of proposition might be called a *consequential proposition* because it implies that X is both a necessary and a sufficient condition for Y, or that Y is *always* a consequence of X. Examples of consequential propositions include:

1. If there is an awareness of a discrepancy between ideal and actual behaviors, then subordinate administrators will behave in the direction of the ideal when they know they are being observed by superiors.[24]
2. If nations have collaborated previously, then they will be more likely to develop attitudinal and transactional ties (converted from Cobb and Elder).[25]
3. If a nation feels it can hold its own unilaterally, it will avoid membership in an alliance.[26]

Proposition #1 above is an example of converting an anatomical proposition (e.g., "subordinates are aware of discrepancies between actual and ideal behaviors") into a consequential proposition. A consequential proposition implies a *causal* relationship.

The More X, the More Y

This type of proposition is called a *positive correlational proposition*. Its obverse, of course, may be also stated, *the less X, the less Y*. Examples of this type of proposition include:

1. The more a supranational structure promotes the common interests of its members, the more responsive its members will be to the supranational structure.[27]

2. The greater the crisis, the greater the interdepartmental collaboration.[28]

3. The more the consonance between the ideology of the elite and the masses, the more stable the society and the more consistent its behavior.[29]

4. The more absolute the weapons in the hands of the two super-powers, the more likely for the smaller powers to use violence, as long as the two powers are in disagreement.[30]

5. The greater the volume of substantively varied issues that are fed into the world political system, the better are the chances for growth of consensus upon one procedural law of mankind.[31]

6. The more intergovernmental collaboration, the higher the level of transactional exchange among states.[32]

7. The lower the level of crisis, the less a leader will solicit the advice of subordinates.[33]

The More X, the Less Y

This type of proposition may be called *negative correlational proposition*. As with the above, this proposition may be stated, *the less X, the more Y*. Some examples include:

1. In a crisis, the greater the revocability of a costly commitment, the smaller the decisional unit.[34]

2. The greater the ratio of substantive to procedural consensus among the founders of a new political system, the less adaptable it is to new problems.[35]

3. The more successful a regional organization, the lower the probability of establishing a wider organization.[36]

4. The greater the number of defense pact commitments among major powers, the less the severity of war.[37]

X Has No Relation to Y

This type of proposition is called a *null proposition*. More commonly it is referred to as the *null hypothesis*. A null hypothesis is implicit in each of the foregoing propositions because each could be transformed to a null hypothesis. The foregoing hypotheses, however, are distinct from the null hypothesis because they are *directional hypotheses*, that is, they state the direction of the expected findings. The *null hypothesis*, by contrast, suggests that no relation between variables will be found and consequently begs for disconfirmation, but not in a preferred direction. Examples of null propositions could be developed from each of the preceding propositions. In addition, however, null propositions are also found in the literature. Consider, for example, the following:

1. Internal development has no effect on the patterns of interaction between states.[38]

2. Cultural homogeneity will not significantly influence the pattern of interaction between two nations.[39]

3. Geographic conditions do not appear to play a significant role in alliance-making or the formation of diplomatic or economic coalitions.[40]

PROPOSITIONAL INVENTORIES

Once you have acquired the facility to identify the four basic types of propositions just reviewed, it is possible to construct inventories of propositions that are susceptible to empirical testing and verification. It is by this process of empirical investigation that the analyst is able to accumulate by his or her own efforts and those of others an increasing stock of information about the theory (or theories) from which the propositions are derived. As the level of confidence in the theory itself increases over time and with many experiments or tests, the analyst can increasingly rely on deductions from the theory rather than on empirical tests and experiments.[41]

In the meantime, it will be necessary to test propositions derived from theory. Hence, the analyst needs to be aware of methods for developing inventories of propositions to serve as subjects of empirical investigations. The construction of propositional inventories involves *extracting* clearly stated propositions from verbal or symbolic presentations or *converting* sentences vaguely suggestive of a proposition into a sentence that expresses the variables and their relationships more clearly and directly. Thus, it is possible to *propositionalize by extraction* or to *propositionalize by conversion*. In building inventories of propositions both methods are employed.

The utility of propositional inventories for these purposes is well-established. First, the propositional inventory can be used to summarize the current state of research. For example, Berelson, Lazarsfeld, and McPhee present an inventory of propositions about electoral behavior to summarize their study of voting behavior. James March and Herbert Simon use the propositional inventory both to organize and to index their study of organizations. Roger Cobb and Charles Elder present eighteen basic propositions referencing processes of international integration and link them to relevant theoretical material and research findings. Finally, James Robinson's appraisal of the research on crisis decision-making is summarized by an inventory that includes statistical assessments of the truth-value of the propositions cited.[42]

Second, propositional inventories are undertaken to stimulate further ideas and new research. Even though all research should extend scientific horizons by improving our capacity to generalize about political and social phenomena, the particular advantages of gathering, classifying, and storing propositions for future research are unique. Classic models in this regard are found in the broad-ranging review of the literature on national and international decision-making by Richard Snyder and James Robinson, and in the systematic integration and evaluation of propositions from the voluminous and widely scattered literature on small group behavior put together by Irwin Altman and Joseph McGrath.[43]

Third, a propositional inventory is a useful technique to make explicit the generalizations of an analyst so that his or her ideas can be logically and systematically analyzed. For example, Lewis Coser derives sixteen propositions from the work of Georg Simmel to clarify and elaborate contemporary theory of the functions of social conflict, and Robert Dahl inventories the propositions implicit in James Madison's writings to facilitate a more rigorous and formal analysis of "Madisonian Democracy" and democratic theory. By contrast, Anthony Downs summarizes his own work on the theory of democratic decision-making in the form of an inventory of twenty-five testable propositions derived from his economic theory of democracy. Glenn Paige concludes his study of the Korean War decision with a systematic inventory of relevant propositions from the decision-making scheme. And Robert North and his colleagues reference twenty-nine explicit propositions to summarize their findings from extended studies of the 1914 crisis leading to the outbreak of World War I.[44]

Finally, the propositional inventory is useful for revealing gaps in knowledge and research and for identifying competing assertions as evidenced by the review of research on human behavior by Bernard Berelson and Gary Steiner, by the previously-cited work on integration by Cobb and Elder, by Altman and McGrath's review and assessment of studies of small groups, and by Richard Brody's simulation study of the systemic effects of nuclear diffusion on the polarity of the international system.[45]

Two interesting and productive strategies are available in constructing such inventories of propositions. One involves the extraction (or conversion) of *competing* or *rival* propositions. In its most minimal form, a search would be made for rival propositions that state "the more X, the more Y," versus "the more X, the less Y," or a search for "X varies with Y" versus "X does not vary with Y," etc. Such inventories are useful in a variety of ways: (1) a sample of the literature can be assessed for consistency, both between authors and within a sample of the writings of any one author; (2) it may be possible to show that both relationships are plausible and that neither is transparently obvious; (3) if these propositions are subjected to empirical tests or other forms of evidence, the researcher is obliged to consider all evidence, some of which will undoubtedly tend to disconfirm one of the hypotheses; and (4) the strategy of building inventories of rival propositions stimulates thought about the conditions which are necessary and/or sufficient to confirm the rival hypotheses, thereby aiding the development of causal propositions.

A second strategy involves the construction of inventories of *interrelated propositions*.[46] In its minimal form, a search will be made for propositions containing related variables: "the more X, the more Y," plus "the greater X' (read "X prime"), the smaller C," plus "the fewer the occurrences of C, the more Y will occur." The search, therefore, is made for relations between or among principal variables in *different* propositions. The usefulness of the strategy of interrelated propositions is the opportunity it gives for building middle-gauge theory about political processes and behavior. Because of the nature of social science research (i.e., the requirement to frame questions in operational/testable terms), there is a tremendous need for synthesizing the volumes of potentially related findings.

As a general rule, the inventories of *rival* or *competing propositions* may be useful for analyzing the pre-operational (or "traditional") literature, while the inventory of interrelated propositions might have more payoff for analyzing and integrating the operational (or "social science") literature.[47] However, it is important to note that it is not sufficient merely to search for competing or concordant propositions. Let's take the following example from the literature on alliances.[48]

In the alliance literature it is possible to identify a number of middle-gauge theories. One formulation, advanced by William Riker is derived from the theory of games and built upon the "size principle." Professor Riker's theory predicts that potential members of an alliance will form *minimum winning coalitions* that include just enough members to control the decision about the distribution of a "payoff" or gain. Although Riker's work has been impressively supported by well-designed experimental studies, the situational conditions in which the theory is embedded impose critical constraints on the likelihood of obtaining empirical confirmation as the theory is applied to the domain of international politics. For example, the theory postulates a "zero-sum" condition (that is, a situation where one player "wins" only what another player "loses"—like in poker) where information is complete with respect to the intentions as well as the "weight" or power of other potential coalition members. Consequently, its utility to students of international politics may be severely limited.

Providing sharp contrast to the work of Riker, Mancur Olson and Richard Zeckhauser have applied the economic theory of public goods to alliances, deriving a proposition that is directly contrary to Riker's theory of minimum winning coalitions. They argue that joint action undertaken to secure "public goods" (i.e., benefits or payoffs, that, once secured, are jointly available to all and are indivisible —that is, their consumption by one member does not reduce the amount available to others) will lead to "grand coalitions" where the attempt will be made to induce the participation of as many potential members as possible.

Thus, we obtain two competing propositions about the size of an alliance. Riker suggests that *potential members of an alliance will tend to form minimum winning coalitions*. Olson and Zeckhauser suggest that *potential members of an alliance will tend to form grand coalitions*, i.e., coalitions as large as possible.[49]

The contradiction between the propositions derived from the size principle of Riker and Olson's theory of public goods is only apparent, however, for Riker is postulating the formation of coalitions in situations where payoffs are zero-sum (i.e., where the consumption of the payoff or benefits by one member of a coalition reduces by that amount the benefits available to other members) while Olson is postulating a "public good" payoff (i.e., a situation where the magnitude or the amount of the payoff available to all is not reduced as it is consumed by one or more).[50] In short, predictions from Riker and Olson are mediated by situational factors, and the nature of the payoff: where public (or indivisible) goods are produced, inclusive, grand coalitions will form; where private (or divisible) payoffs are sought, exclusive or minimum winning coalitions will form. Here we have a clear example of why it is not sufficient merely to search for competing or concordant propositions, for some attention must be given to the higher order theoretical structure under which the middle-gauge propositions are subsumed. Moreover, the postulated conditions in which the competing (or concordant) propositions are said to operate must also be assessed.[51]

The problem of evaluation, displayed in Figure 1.1, is much more subtle than might be implied by a simple search for rival and concordant propositions. For example, it is precisely because the competing propositions from Olson and Riker would be entered in cell D in Figure 1.1 that their contrary predictions are "uninteresting." What *is* interesting and important is the assessment in a concrete political context of the *conditional statements* that surround each of the competing propositions in order to determine whether the postulated conditions are, in fact, found in the "real life" or natural context. Examined this way, it appears that Professor Riker's theory of minimum winning coalitions derived from the theory of

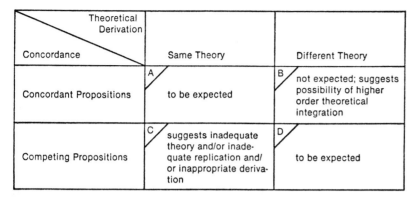

Concordance \ Theoretical Derivation	Same Theory	Different Theory
Concordant Propositions	A / to be expected	B / not expected; suggests possibility of higher order theoretical integration
Competing Propositions	C / suggests inadequate theory and/or inadequate replication and/ or inappropriate derivation	D / to be expected

Figure 1.1   *Comparative assessment of propositions*

N-person, zero-sum games involves conditional requirements (not the least of which are the zero-sum condition and the divisible nature of the payoff) that may be less appropriate to processes of coalition formation in international politics than are those postulated by Professer Olson's theory of collective action derived from the economic theory of public goods.[52]

SUMMARY

In this chapter we have introduced ideas about the role of theory in scientific research and the process of theory-building—examining in some detail the empirical proposition, the building block of scientific empirical theories. Because a number of theorists, methodologists, and philosophers of science would cut finer distinctions among different terms we have introduced, it should be noted that we have used the term proposition more or less interchangeably with *generalization* or *hypothesis*. A proposition is considered as a term referencing a class of empirical statements that ranges from the *tentative hypothesis* (i.e., an informal "hunch" about empirical phenomena derived from intuition, the viscera, or from prior research) to *scientific laws* (i.e., well-established or verified generalizations that describe the way the world or some aspect of it works). Somewhere in between these extremes are found *strong hypotheses, principles*, and *theories*. The criteria for locating a given statement on this continuum include: (1) the degree or level of verification, and (2) the presence or absence of exceptions. A proposition, therefore, states a fact (or facts), relationship between facts or variables, or relationships between concepts. Relational terms in propositions usually state the presence (or absence), direction, strength (or magnitude), and form of empirical covariation, and propositions are usually contained in declarative sentences, such as Hans Morgenthau's proposition that "the permanency of an alliance (varies directly with) the limited character of the interests it serves."[53] Keeping in mind the close relationship that exists between theory, data, and analysis, we will turn in the next two chapters to the major data generation techniques and to the problems of observation and measurement in social science research. In the meantime, it should be remembered that one of the primary purposes of empirical investigation is to broaden and strengthen the store of accumulated knowledge in the form of verified theory that will tell why things happen as they do in international politics and foreign policy or from which we can develop expectations about the future behavior of men and institutions in the international environment. It is primarily through the development and refinement of increasingly general and generalizable theories of human and social behavior that the investments in empirical investigations can be aggregated and justified. Theory, in short, serves as a "general store" for the best knowledge available.

EXERCISES

1   Identify the type of proposition:

_____ A.   "The implication is that the greater the quantity of military aid, the greater the civilian and competitive political institutions . . ." (Wolf, 1967, p. 94, extracted).

_____ B.   Up to the atomic age, an increase in air warfare has decreased the relative security of the territorial state (Herz, 1957, p. 487, converted).

_____ C.   "The greater the number of nations that possess the capability of launching a nuclear strike, the greater the probability there will be a strike" (Brown and Real, 1960, p. 25, extracted).

_____ D.   "If the diffusion of nuclear weapons continues unchecked, the structure of international relations will be profoundly altered" (Kissinger, 1961, p. 240, extracted).

_____ E.   "Opinion-makers are those who by virtue of their position of leadership in the society, have direct access to the impersonal channels" (Rosenau, 1961, p. 28, extracted).

_____ F.   The more economic aid per capita, the lower the level of political development (Wolf, 1967, p. 120, converted).

2   Convert the following statements into propositions:

A   "Some countries, possessing relatively developed economies and extensive resources, have been able to absorb vast amounts of American aid with corresponding benefit, while smaller amounts of aid can disrupt the economy and corrupt the bureaucracies of others" (Montgomery, 1962, p. 12).

B   "A political system that makes it difficult for the government to continue appropriate responses may threaten the world with its erratic actions or may doom itself to a gradually disintegrating position in international politics" (Waltz, 1967, p. 279).

C "Non-alignment and neutralism are international policies inspired largely by domestic concerns. By the same token, they are political policies largely motivated by economic needs and interests" (Liska, in Toma and Gyorgy, 1967, p. 420).

3 Identify the independent and dependent variables in the following propositions:

A If there is a breakdown in the accustomed norms within a society, there will be a tendency toward political extremism and violence (Scott, 1967, p. 25, extracted).

I.V. _____

D.V. _____

B The weaker the cross pressures among the members of the international system, the greater the threat to systems stability (Russett, 1965, p. 89, converted).

I.V. _____

D.V. _____

C "The greater the volume of substantively varied issues that are fed into the world political system, the better are chances for the growth of consensus upon one procedural law of mankind" (Spiro, 1966, p. 196, extracted).

I.V. _____

D.V. _____

D "Other things being equal, a coalition will become more stable to the extent that decision-making is centralized, i.e., the coalition is hierarchically organized" (Snyder, 1961, p. 70, extracted).

I.V. _____

D.V. _____

4 Operationalize the variables in the following propositions:

A The larger the military program, the less democratic the regime (Wolf, 1967, p. 95, converted).

Independent variable·

Dependent variable:

B The higher the level of economic development of a nation, the greater the degree of political competitiveness (Wolf, 1967, p. 25, converted).

Independent variable:

Dependent variable:

C "The most advanced countries tend to be those which have had the fewest revolutionary changes" (Reischauer, 1967, p. 89, extracted).

Independent variable:

Dependent variable:

D The higher the economic rate of development, the weaker the stability of the social system (Wolf, 1967, p. 31, converted).

Independent variable:

Dependent variable:

E "Authoritarian regimes generate relatively large demands for military assistance" (Wolf, 1967, p. 94, extracted).

Independent variable:

Dependent variable:

5 Supplementary exercises:

A Generate four or five propositions for *each* of the four types of propositions. This will be very easy for some (e.g., the anatomical proposition) and more difficult for others (e.g., the consequential proposition). Nevertheless, do your best to generate sixteen to twenty propositions. Indicate whether the proposition is *extracted* or *converted*. *Extracted propositions* should be surrounded by quotation marks with author, title, and page number given. *Converted propositions* should be stated without quotes and supplemented by a quote of the passage from which you converted the propositions. Follow the same citation rules as for the extracted proposition.

B Select two of the most interesting, theoretically important, or policy-relevant propositions from your inventory and specify the key variables in each proposition. Suggest operational definitions for each of the variables.

NOTES

1. On these distinctions, consult Riemer (1962), and McClelland (1966).

2. On these points, see Wolfers (1959), Hertz (1962), and Haas (1964).

3. See McClelland (1966), Kaplan (1957), Liska (1962), and Snyder, Bruck, and Sapin (1962).

4. See Eulau (1962, p. 37).

5. Although a number of assessments of the present state of theory have been published in recent years, Haas' essay is by far the most useful, for he ties his review to a number of stakes: to the history of theory in the social sciences as well as to the history of political science, to the nature of theory, and to generic processes in theory development. Interested students should also consult reviews of theoretical developments in IR by Palmer (1970), Burgess (1970), Holsti (1970), Platig (1966), Knorr and Verba (1961), Lasswell (1958), Kaplan (1968), Rosenau (1961; 1969). The inventory of metatheoretical orientations is from Michael Haas and Henry S. Kariel, "International Relations Theory," *Approaches to the Study of Political Science*, Chandler Publishing Co., 1970.

6. For a review of the components of alliance theory, see Russett (1968). For a review of propositions on alliance, see Burgess and Moore (1972).

7. Normally, the words "proof," and "to prove," are avoided. Our aim is to try to "disprove" our hypotheses or propositions. If we fail, then we can have confidence in the truth value of the propositions we have tested. The accepted terminology for discussing the process of verifying propositions uses the term "confirm." Thus, we use the terms "confirm" and "disconfirm" to discuss the status of propositions, since these terms imply a *continuous process* of attempting to "prove" or "disprove" hypotheses. In short, *one never "proves" his hypothesis; he only fails to disconfirm it.* The greater the number of failures to disconfirm a given hypothesis, the more confidence we can have in its truth value.

8. By "truth value" we mean the extent to which the empirical statement can be or has been verified. In other words, can we find evidence to support or otherwise give us confidence that the empirical statement is "true" or the conditions under which it is "true"?

9. Morgenthau (1962, p. 27).

10. See Spykman (1944, p. 43).

11. See Thompson and Macridis (1967, p. 12).

12. See Deutsch (1957, pp. 5–7).

13. For a comprehensive treatment of the operationalization of variables and index construction in the social sciences, see Lazarsfeld and Rosenberg (1955), especially Section I, pp. 19–108.

14. This proposition, stated one way or another, can be found in much of the literature of international relations. See Waltz (1959, p. 81).

15. Consider the following examples of criteria for developing operational measures of conflict behavior from Tanter (1966):

   "Measures of Conflict Behavior." With respect to the methods and goals of this study, any act or occurrence chosen to index conflict behavior must: (1) be capable of empirical delimitation; (2) be an act or occurrence of sufficient interest to be generally reported—that is, data must be available; (3) be applicable to all countries (e.g., "colonial violence," if made a measure, would not be applicable to those countries without colonies) if spurious factors are not to result; (4) be as diverse as possible to cover the greatest possible range of conflict behavior; and (5) be an act of or within, or an occurrence with respect to, seven or more countries (this is to prevent the correlations from being dependent on too few such happenings and,

therefore, to reduce the role of aberrations on what are meant to be general conclusions).

On the basis of these criteria, nine measures of domestic and thirteen measures of foreign conflict were chosen for this study. The domestic conflict measures and a brief definition of the conflict act or occurrence are as follows:

1. *Number of assassinations:* any politically motivated murder or attempted murder of a high government official or politician.

2. *Number of general strikes:* any strike of 1,000 or more industrial or service workers that involves more than one employer and that is aimed at national government policies or authority.

3. *Presence or absence of guerrilla warfare:* any armed activity, sabotage, or bombings carried on by independent bands of citizens or irregular forces and aimed at the overthrow of the present regime.

4. *Number of major government crises:* any rapidly developing situation that threatens to bring the downfall of the present regime—excluding situations or revolt aimed at such an overthrow.

5. *Number of purges:* any systematic elimination by jailing or execution of political opposition within the ranks of the regime or the opposition.

6. *Number of riots:* any violent demonstration or clash of more than 100 citizens involving the use of physical force.

7. *Number of revolutions:* any illegal or forced change in the top government elite, any attempt at such a change, or any successful or unsuccessful armed rebellion whose aim is independence from the central government.

8. *Number of anti-government demonstrations:* any peaceful public gathering of at least 100 people for the primary purpose of displaying or voicing their opposition to government policies or authority, excluding those demonstrations of a distinctly anti-foreign nature.

9. *Number of people killed in all forms of domestic violence:* any deaths resulting directly from violence of an intergroup nature, thus excluding deaths by murder and execution.

The measure of foreign conflict definitions are as follows:

1. *Number of anti-foreign demonstrations:* any demonstration or riot by more than 100 people directed at a particular foreign country (or group of countries) or its policies.

2. *Number of negative sanctions:* any nonviolent act against another country—such as boycott, or withdrawal of aid—the purpose of which is to punish or threaten that country.

3. *Number of protests:* any official diplomatic communication or governmental statement, the purpose of which is to complain about or object to the policies of another country.

4. *Number of countries with which diplomatic relations severed:* the complete withdrawal from all official contact with a particular country.

5. *Number of ambassadors expelled or recalled:* any expelling of an ambassador from, or recalling for other than administrative reasons an ambassador to, a particular country. This does not involve expulsion or recall resulting from the severance of diplomatic relations.

6. *Number of diplomatic officials of less than ambassador's rank expelled or recalled:* replace "ambassador" by "officials of lesser . . . rank" in above definition.

7. *Number of threats:* any official diplomatic communication or governmental statement asserting that if a particular country does or does not do a particular thing it will incur negative sanctions.

8. *Presence or absence of military action:* any military clash of a particular country with another and involving gunfire, but short of war as defined below.

9. *Number of wars:* any military clash for a particular country with another and in which more than .02 percent of its population are militarily involved in the clash.

10. *Number of troop movements:* any rapid movement of large bodies of troops, naval units, or air squadrons to a particular area for the purpose of deterring the military action of another country, gaining concessions, or as a show of strength.

11. *Number of mobilizations:* any rapid increase in military strength through the calling up of reserves, activation of additional military units, or the de-mothballing of military equipment.

12. *Number of accusations:* any official diplomatic or governmental statement involving charges and allegations of a derogatory nature against another country.

13. *Number of people killed in all forms of foreign conflict behavior:* the total number of deaths resulting directly from any violent interchange between countries.

16. When "unexplained variance" is low, it means that changes in the value of the independent variable account to a large degree for changes in the value of the dependent variable. However, this finding does *not* mean that *other* independent variables could not be found that would also "explain" a high degree of variance in the dependent variable. In other words, *a dependent variable like external hostility may be strongly associated with more than one independent variable.*

17. This list of four basic types of relational statements is derived from Paige (n.d.) and from a more extensive inventory of relational statements suggested by Zetterberg (1963), who identified the following types of relational statements that link X and Y. Relational statements, according to Zetterberg, may be:

1. *reversible* (if X then Y; if Y then X)

2. *irreversible* (if X, then Y; if Y, then no conclusion about X)

3. *deterministic or consequential* (if X, then always Y)

4. *stochastic* (if X, then probably Y)

5. *sufficient* (if X, then Y regardless of anything else)

6. *coextensive* (if X, then also Y)

7. *sequential* (if X, then later Y)

8. *contingent* (if X, then Y, but only if X')

9. *necessary* (if X and only if X, then Y)

10. *substitutable* (if X then Y; but if X' then also Y).

18. March and Simon (1958, p. 8).

19. Scott (1967, p. 91).

20. Scott (1967, p. 88).

21. Paige (1968, p. 286).

22. Christensen (1967).

23. The process of converting propositions into researchable empirical questions is discussed in more detail later on in this chapter.

24. Paige (1963, p. 11).

25. Converted from Cobb and Elder (1970, p. 48).

26. Morgenthau (1962, pp. 181–82).

27. Converted from Russett (1965, pp. 30–32).

28. Paige (1968, p. 290).

29. Scott (1967, p. 55).

30. Converted from Thompson and Macrides (1967).

31. Spiro (1966, p. 196).

32. Converted from Cobb and Elder (1970, p. 50).

33. Paige (1968, p. 290).

34. Paige (1968, p. 286).

35. Spiro (1966, p. 119).

36. Guetzkow (1967, p. 64).

37. Singer and Small (1968, pp. 277–281).

38. Cobb and Elder (1970, p. 44).

39. Cobb and Elder (1970, p. 40).

40. K. J. Holsti (1972, p. 111).

41. The propositional inventory is also a useful strategy when higher order theories are not involved. For example, the analyst in a policy setting might extract propositions from position papers or from public testimony for a variety of purposes:

    1. to clarify and make more precise the kinds of arguments or assumptions being made, or

    2. to explore empirically the truth value of essentially empirical, though theoretical statements.

    For example, the analyst may want to examine empirically "trend statements" or "conditions statements" typically found in policy papers that are simply stipulated by the writers, "Because The European Community has been increasingly insensitive to U.S. influence, . . ."

42. On these points, see Berelson, et al. (1954), March and Simon (1958), Cobb and Elder (1970), and Robinson (1970).

43. See Janda (1968), Altman and McGrath (1966, esp. pp. 40–46), and Snyder and Robinson (1961).

44. See Coser (1956), Simmel (1955), Dahl (1956), Downs (1957), Paige (1968), and North, et al., (1960).

45. See Berelson and Steiner (1964, esp. p. 662), Cobb and Elder (1970), Altman and McGrath (1966), and Brody (1963).

46. W.I.B. Beveridge (1957, p. 98) has pointed out—implying the need for inventories of interrelated propositions—that ". . . facts obtained by observation or experiment usually only gain significance when we reason to build them into the general body of knowledge." He quoted Darwin's admonition that "Science consists of grouping facts so that general laws or conclusions may be drawn from them."

47. This need to integrate propositions and findings is manifested by the "annual reviews" in the social sciences, such as *Advances in Experimental Social Psychology.* Even political science has progressed sufficiently to warrant *Political Science Annual.* Perhaps the most ambitious example of an effort to inventory hypotheses and research findings is found in Berelson and Steiner's (1964) efforts with findings related to human behavior.

48. This example is taken from the inventory of propositions on alliances by Burgess and Moore (1972, pp. 78–80).

49. On these points, see Riker (1962), Olson (1965), and Olson and Zeckhauser (1966).

50. For example, if the benefit or payoff to members of an alliance is in the form of territory, then the payoff would be *zero-sum* since the assignment of territory to

one member of an alliance would reduce by the amount so assigned the territory available to others. By contrast, if the payoff were in the form of an international agreement to a six-mile (rather than a 200-mile) limitation on "territorial waters," then the gain of 194 miles for "international waters" would constitute a *public good* whose use by one member would not, practically speaking, reduce the amount available to others.

51. Game theory assumes that the distribution of payoffs will be proportionate to the relative contribution that each member makes to the resource base of the winning coalition. When payoffs are indivisible, however (the case with public goods) then the redistribution of the payoff to the members of winning coalitions is not at issue, for each member is able to consume as much as he wants of the resulting payoff. Consequently, many empirical conditions fail to conform to the postulates of game theoretic perspectives.

52. On these points, consult Olson (1965, pp. 5–52 and especially 39–40); Zetterberg (1963, especially chapters five and six); Kelly (1968); and Dubin (1969). See also Riker's treatment (1962) of the predictions derived from his "size principle" that are discordant with those derived from Down's (1957) "economic theory of democracy."

53. Morganthau (1962, p. 186).

Chapter Two

DATA IN INTERNATIONAL RELATIONS

Chapter 1 discussed the types of theories and empirical propositions, how to propositionalize, and *why* it is sometimes useful to construct propositional inventories. Here, some of the problems and issues involved in gathering information about the concepts which we will use in testing propositions about international politics and foreign policy will be addressed.

After a proposition has been developed, evidence must be adduced as the second step in quantitative research. This chapter is divided into five sections—each one devoted to a technique or method appropriate for generating data to be used as evidence. Aggregate data analysis, simulation, content analysis, events data, and roll call analysis will each be examined in terms of the data they produce and the positive and negative values associated with each technique. Each method for generating data will be illustrated by examples drawn from published research in international and comparative politics. While the section discussions are not sufficiently detailed to permit you to become proficient in the application of these techniques, they will yield a foundation of knowledge that will facilitate your understanding of the use of these techniques when you encounter them in your reading. Moreover, the section discussions will provide the basis for you to move to the more specialized literature cited throughout this chapter for learning more about methodologies of special interest.

MAJOR TECHNIQUES FOR DATA GENERATION

After selecting an interesting empirical proposition and operationally defining the variables in the proposition, the analyst begins the search for data that can be used to test the truth value of the empirical relationship alleged by the proposition. Often, however, the data will not be readily available. This dilemma contrasts sharply with the advantages enjoyed by other social scientists—for example, economists. Consequently, the analyst must design new methods or apply existing methods for generating the evidence or data needed to test the proposition, i.e., to examine its "fit" with reality and to assess the conditions under which confidence in the trust value of the proposition is warranted.

It is important to remember that conceptual and theoretical issues are related to, but different from, methodological issues. Broad-gauge conceptual orientations reviewed in chapter 1 such as Snyder's decision-making approach or Rummel's field theory, are frameworks that serve to guide the development or derivation of empirical propositions. Although broad-gauge theories and conceptual frameworks suggest important *classes* of data that are appropriate, they do not tell us exactly what kinds of data to reference.

For example, Snyder's decision-making framework includes a large number of propositions about the behavior of individuals. So if you use the decision-making framework, you will need to generate data from observations of individuals—their perceptions, their role in a bureaucratic hierarchy, or the process by which they were recruited and socialized. Consider Rummel's field theory. Here, propositions cover the behavior of collectivities of individuals, i.e., of nations. Hence, if we take a field theory orientation, we need to generate data from the observations of nations —their size, their level of economic development, their political system style, and measures that tell whether Nation A and Nation B are more or less similar with respect to these attributes. This is what Rummel calls "attribute distance."

In other words, the general class of data needs will be largely determined by the conceptual orientation you use to make sense out of world politics. The conceptual or theoretical framework will tell you, first of all, whether you want data on the attributes or behavior of individuals, groups, or even larger collectivities. The ability to identify *classes* of data, however, still leaves open the specific kinds of observations we will want or be required to make.

Let's say we know we want data on individuals. Or be even more specific—data on the *perceptions* of individuals. Now we know the class of data (individuals), but we still have wide latitude in selecting among alternative data generation techniques for the purpose of observing, measuring, and recording the individual perceptions that we're interested in. For example, personal interviews with individual decision-makers could be used. We could also systematically examine the speeches or other writings of key decision-makers. Or, we could talk to informed people who know them well and ask them how a particular individual views the world, and so on. In short, the alternatives available are limited only by our imagination and inventiveness (assuming we have unlimited time and unlimited resources).

In other words, methods of data generation are the means through which information and experience are transformed into data or evidence appropriate to test the propositions that are thought to explain how some part of the empirical world works. The selection of data is constrained only by broad-gauged orientation toward the problems being examined, suggesting whether we want data on individuals, on interactions among individuals, on collectivities, or on interactions among collectivities (or some combination of these analytical units).

It is also important to keep in mind that certain types of data are more appropriate than others for certain kinds of questions or analytical units. For example, survey data are particularly well-suited to questions that require evidence on the variation in individual opinions, attitudes, or expectations. By contrast, simulation techniques are particularly well-suited to the study of complex social processes. Moreover, it should be noted that different techniques may be combined. For example, we may use the indepth interview or questionnaire in the framework of a simulation experiment—providing perceptual or attitudinal data on the participants in the simulation. Or attitudinal data from surveys may be used in constructing simulations designed to forecast how different groups of people or different voting blocs will react to a hypothetical situation.

In short, the analyst has a variety of options available as he begins to narrow down and to specify more concretely the specific data requirements in the context of his theoretical or policy interest.

Typical methods for generating data include social surveys, indepth interviews, sociometric techniques (evaluating the frequency and quality of interaction among individuals), participant-observation, expert panels, content analysis, roll call analysis, and simulation. Major methods for generating data that have been used extensively in the study of international relations are described briefly below. In subsequent sections, five of them are elaborated in some additional detail.

1. *Content analysis*, the systematic study of the content of print or electronic media, has been used to generate data from simulations, historical documents, newspaper editorials, television and radio broadcasts, and international treaties in order to guage perceptions, intensities of commitments, and changes in the salience of or "attention" given to people, places and things.

2. *Opinion surveys* have been used for examining mass as well as elite opinions and attitudes. Opinion surveys in international relations are typically undertaken either to assess the linkages between public opinion and foreign policy-making; to estimate the distribution of opinions with respect to some issue; or to assess the pattern of commitment or adherence to some belief system. Elite surveys have been conducted to profile opinions on issues with respect to generational differences, location in a bureaucracy, assessment of elite-mass cleavages, or examination of the impact of events on opinions.

3. *Simulations and laboratory experimentation* involve the representation of selected aspects of a social system under controlled conditions. They are employed for a number of distinct research purposes: to examine the logic, the consistencies, and the implications of verbal theories of international relations (what is typically called the sensitivity testing of theories); to serve as more complex environments for operationalizing variables in middle-gauge theories; to re-create conditions and social dynamics that will facilitate the projection of trends into the future; to explore experimentally theories cast at the level of individual behavior; and to explore alternative futures—i.e., to design social systems that have never existed in order to see if and how they work.

4. *Roll call analysis* is employed to study the voting behavior of individuals and groups (or "voting blocs") in legislative and quasi-legislative assemblies such as the U.S. Congress, the U.N. General Assembly, the International Labor Organization (ILO), and other international organizations with deliberative functions. Roll call analysis has been used by international relations scholars and analysts to delineate different voting groups, to assess the political cohesion or level of agreement within different voting groups, to develop measures that indicate the political or policy orientations of different groups, and to explore linkages between social structures (e.g., the way committees are organized) in legislative (assemblies) and political behavior (e.g., voting).

5. *Aggregate data*[1] largely involve the secondary analysis of economic and social accounting data typically collected and published by national governments, or rediffused through international agencies such as the United Nations *Demographic Yearbook*, or through academic efforts represented by the *World Handbook of Political and Social Indicators* or the *Cross-Polity Survey*. Aggregate data have been used to explore middle-gauge theoretical interests derived from broader orientations toward field theory and communications theory (to examine cross-polity transactions of goods, persons, and messages; to delineate international regions; to establish trends in the international distribution of values; and to link the foreign behavior of nations to the attributes by which the nations can be characterized).

6. *Events data* is the observation of words and deeds exchanged between nations. Events data are frequently included under discussions of aggregate data, but are probably more usefully examined as a separate category for a number of reasons. First, an in-

creasing number of people have recently been drawn to events data research and may not be simultaneously working with aggregate social accounting data. Second, events data are typically collected by the researcher and not, unfortunately, by governmental agents. Events data have been used to explore models of civil violence; to measure foreign policy behavior and outcomes; to appraise relations between pairs of nations (i.e., *dyadic* relations) and relations among major actors in the international system as a whole by observing the frequency of different classes of events (e.g., threats and protests); by scaling event interactions according to dimensions like conflict (hostile—friendly), support (strong—weak), and affect (positive—negative); and by examining event cycles (e.g., cooperation and conflict cycles).

There are, to be sure, a number of variations in these techniques for generating data—in the ways they are applied and the research problems to which they are addressed. Although these six are the most significant, other techniques for data generation have been employed and should be noted, for they may well become increasingly important as time goes on.

Chadwick Alger has developed novel applications of the method of participant-observation for studying political behavior in the United Nations and in other international organizations.[2] Participant-observation, as the name implies, involves the researcher "on the inside looking around" rather than "outside-looking." It is the oldest among the methods of social observation. Participant-observation, however, requires the researcher to maintain and refine his capacity for observing and recording a social process while being a part of it. The advantage of the participant-observer is his ability to develop a detailed and contextually-rich portrait of the social process he is observing. The disadvantage is the private or nonreproducible quality of the data that are obtained by participant-observation and the relative absence of controls over the tendency in all research to see what you want to see. As we have pointed out in chapter 1, science places a high value on public and reproducible knowledge, so the reliability of participant-observer data is often suspect. Hence, participant-observation, like other social science techniques for generating data, is best used in combination with alternative kinds of data that can be used to corroborate, refine, or call into question the knowledge or findings recorded by the participant-observer.

Another noteworthy method for generating cross-national data and data about phenomena that are otherwise difficult or impossible to observe directly is the method of the *expert panel*.[3] Expert panels involve asking knowledgeable people to reach a consensus with respect to their best judgment or estimate about the value that is to be given to some variable. For example, expert panels have been used by researchers to categorize the political systems of nations as Open or Closed or Democratic or Authoritarian. Expert panels have been used to develop assessments of the role of the legislature in domestic policy-making—important knowledge to have for many, but difficult to measure by more objective techniques.[4] Similarly, the University of Missouri's Freedom of Information Center has used the expert panel to develop an annual measure of world press freedom on a country-by-country basis.

One more recent application of the method of the expert panel deserves special mention. Reference here is to the work by the RAND Corporation led by Norman Dalkey and Olaf Helmer who developed the Delphi technique which provided the data base for the subsequent publication of *Social Technology and Studies in the Quality of Life*.[5] The Delphi technique is used for the forecasting of time-related future events. Delphi involves repeated consultations among the informed people who together constitute the Delphi panel. Each consultation or iteration is designed to elicit the best judgment of each expert as to when a specific event, goal, or achievement is likely to occur.

Delphi is an important innovation in social analysis for at least two reasons. First, it provides a systematic way to take full advantage of the tremendous store of wisdom, insight, and specialized knowledge that people carry around in their heads as a consequence of life's experiences. Second, a Delphi panel is typically *not* brought together in a face-to-face situation. Rather, the panelists are sent questionnaires or other appropriate instruments and are asked (1) to record their best judgments, and (2) to make explicit the reasons why they make those judgments. Hence, both the participants and their responses remain anonymous so that the judgments expressed will be more immune to distortions that are an inevitable consequence of face-to-face confrontations. For example, inhibitions might result if a low-status panelist held views that were at odds with a high-status participant.

When the initial responses of each panelist are returned to the Delphi director, they are assembled and sent back to the participants (again preserving anonymity). Participants are then invited to reconsider their judgments in the light of the insights of other panelists. At this point, the panelist may revise his or her forecast *or* may defend it further—despite the views of the others on the panel. The revised estimates and extended elaborations are once again returned to the Delphi director, assembled, and sent out again to the panelists. After repeated cycles or iterations, a consensus generally begins to emerge from the intuitions of the informed and experienced witnesses who constitute a Delphi panel, and who in the process clarify their own thinking as the final forecasts are made. Experience with Delphi suggests that final decisions will tend to converge as the range of the original estimates is narrowed in response to new information and in response to repeated confrontations with convincing arguments that are unbiased by leadership styles, personal idiosyncracies, and other potential sources of distortion that tend to surface in the dynamics of small group problem-solving.

Participant-observation and variations on the method of the expert panel are interesting and promising techniques for generating data of interest to students of comparative and international politics. However, in the following sections we will limit our more detailed review to five more commonly-used data generation techniques—in relation to the different kinds of behavior, units of observation, and units of analysis that are of interest to social scientists. Thus, for example, we find that surveys are used to develop evidence on the attitudes of individuals; participant-observation and sociometric techniques for observing interaction among individuals; aggregate data for measuring the attributes of collectivities; and simulation techniques used to observe the dynamics of social system behavior. First, however, we want to draw a distinction between the units of *analysis* and units of *observation*; and between attribute space and behavior space by way of introduction to aggregate data.

AGGREGATE DATA

Aggregate Data and the Concept of Behavior Space

It is useful to make the distinction displayed in Figure 2.1 between units of analysis (referring to the individual or collectivity whose behavior we are trying to explain), and its behavior and/or attribute space (referring to the position of a unit on a continuum that is defined by a set of values characterizing or measuring behavior

Units of Analysis \ Attribute Space	wealth	power	skill	size
international system				
IGO'				
nation				
government				
interest group				
individual				

Figure 2.1   The relationship between units of analysis and attribute space

at some point in time). Thus, we might say that our unit of analysis—the nation state—occupies a position in the top 10 percent of all nations ranked according to wealth. The values that we use to locate the position of the nation need not be quantitative in the strict sense of the term. They merely need to permit us to order or rank different units in relation to each other, allowing us to say, for example, that a specific nation is "higher," "more conservative," "less aggressive," "richer," etc., than some other nation.

While we can establish as many gradations ("wealth," "aggressiveness," etc.) as we want, our analytical purpose is to specify the position of the nation (the unit of analysis) in the attribute space (wealth) relative to its own past location—or, as displayed in Figure 2.2, in relation to other nations. In this regard, it is important to note that at any given point in time, a nation can occupy one and only one position in a multi-dimensional behavior or attribute space. That is, a nation may have one and only one value with respect to economic development, size, power, well-being, etc. However, as we move backward in time or look to the future, it should be equally clear that a nation could (indeed, probably would) change the position it occupies in some multi-dimensional behavior space. Hence, one of the primary purposes of science is to develop the theory, data, and analysis techniques that will allow us to forecast the location of an individual, an aggregate of individuals, or a collectivity in some future behavior or attribute space.

Kenneth Boulding has expressed the scientific relevance of thinking about the relation between units of analysis (or behavioral unit) and behavior space. Boulding explains that:

> The history of a behavior unit is the record of the positions it has occupied at successive moments of time. We can think of a position as a single frame of movie

Nation as Unit of Analysis \ Attribute Space	Wealth	Power	Skill	Size	Security
Nation A	High	High	Low	High	Medium
Nation B	Medium	Low	High	Low	Low
Nation C	Low	Low	High	Low	Medium
Nation D	High	High	High	Low	High

Figure 2.2   The location of nations in a multi-dimensional attribute space

reel. The history, then, is the successive frames of the reel. History, however, stops at the present; all possible future positions of the behavior unit are what we mean by its behavior space. Back from the present, the history of the behavior unit unfurls as a single reel; forward from the present, there is not a single reel but a great many different possible future reels. It is this set of future positions that comprises the behavior space. There is not an infinite number of such reels because the set of potential positions is limited by the existence of laws. A law is a stable relationship between positions at different dates. Thus, if we have a body falling in a vacuum under a constant acceleration of 32 feet per second, the law of its movement tells us that there is only one possible place for it to be at each moment. It will have fallen 16 feet by the end of the first second, 64 feet by the end of the second second, and so on. This is an extreme case in which there is only a single set of future positions. In the case of complex systems like human and social systems, we cannot define the future positions uniquely. Nevertheless there are limits. I am sure I shall not be on the moon tomorrow, I am pretty sure I shall not be in New York, and, in fact, I am pretty sure I shall be right here where I am today, which is where I plan to be. There is a possibility, however, that my plans might change—the death of a relative, an urgent matter of business, and so on. I might be able to range these possible futures in order of their present likelihood, starting with the highly probable and going down to the impossible. This is the usual form of laws in social science.[7]

Thus, as Boulding suggests, we study the present and past location of units in a behavior space in order to try to establish probabilistic empirical laws or expectations that will allow us to understand the process by which a unit moves from one value to another in its attribute or behavior space. It is hoped that this increasing understanding will permit us to predict or forecast its future movement, "starting," as Boulding says, "with the highly probable and going down to the impossible."

Although this process of relating units of analysis to attribute or behavioral variables operates in all areas where we are trying to establish scientific empirical theories, we have included this discussion in our introduction to aggregate data because it is here that you'll most likely encounter the explicit use of the term *behavior space* or the phrase *the behavior space of nations*.

Aggregate data come in large numbers and in great variety, referencing a broad set of attributes that characterize an analytical unit. The most typical type, used in research in international politics and foreign policy, is aggregate social and economic accounting data. Social accounting data refer to those data typically collected in national census reports and in the process of monitoring the performance of an economic system—sometimes called national account statistics. For example, economic accounting data include gross measures of wealth (e.g., Gross National Product), monetary stability (e.g., the rate of inflation), or economic development (e.g., GNP per capita); social accounting data include measures of well-being or health (e.g., hospital beds per 1000 population), safety (e.g., crime statistics), enlightenment (e.g., literacy rate), skill (e.g., high school educated as a proportion of the total population), and so on for all major categories of human values.

Normally, these data are collected for purposes seemingly far removed from the interests of the student of international relations. For example, national census reports are used primarily to reapportion legislative districts; to reallocate resources; to facilitate the appraisal of policy (for example, measuring the impact of past policies on the distribution of values in a society); or to provide an information base to facilitate and guide national, regional, or local policy-making. However, as we shall see, economic and social accounting data are now widely used as surrogate measures for concepts of interest to students of international relations. The process of re-analyzing data that were collected by others for their own purposes is known as *secondary analysis*. This is an important term to remember because much of what we do in quantitative international politics involves secondary analysis.

Before reviewing some of the research using aggregate data, it may be useful to distinguish between aggregated and integral measures of the attributes of national or subnational units—although both measures usually are included under aggregate data. *Aggregate measures* are based on the aggregation or summing of observations or measures of the attributes of individual members of a collectivity (e.g., a national or group). Thus, for example, a polity's enlightenment or education can be obtained by estimating the number of adults in society who are able to read, then dividing that value by the total population, giving us a percentage. An *integral measure*, by contrast, characterizes the polity or collectivity itself (independent of its members). For example, the number of political parties in a country might be used as an integral measure of political pluralism or political competition inasmuch as it is not derived by examining the attributes of individuals. By contrast, a more typically used measure of competition is the distribution of votes among parties, which is an aggregate measure because it depends on the aggregation of individual attributes (in this case, the percentage of individuals voting for one party or another).

In much cross-national research, integral measures are probably underused. They are not as exciting as many aggregate measures because they have lower scaling properties (usually nominal or ordinal characteristics) and consequently they are not as susceptible to higher forms of statistical analysis.[8] But, you should not shy away from using integral measures (for example, the number of political parties; the existence of a state religion, an air force, or a coastal patrol capability; the age or duration of the constitution of the civic order, etc.). In fact, the methods and techniques of analysis that are applied in many aggregate data studies are probably good examples of analytical overkill, that is, the use of excessively sophisticated techniques of statistical analysis on data of very poor quality.

Aggregate Data Research

In addition to reports of national social accounting statistics issued by individual nations and by the United Nations, students of comparative and international politics have access to a number of published handbooks and compendia containing aggregate data. In addition you have access to a variety of data on punch cards and/or computer tape, archived by the International Relations Archive (IRA) of the Inter-University Consortium for Political Research (ICPR).[9] The most widely used data collections published in a conventional format include *The World Handbook of Political and Social Indicators* and the *Cross-Polity Survey*. Also considerable research has been generated from the data collected by the Dimensionality of Nations (DON) project, and the data are accessible through the ICPR on punch cards or tape.[10] Other publications for your general use in aggregate political and social accounting data include:

- *Hammond's Standard World Atlas*, published by the Hammond Company.
- *Yearbook of Labor Statistics*, published by the International Labor Organization.
- *Direction of Trade*, published by the International Monetary Fund.

- *Europa Yearbook*, published by Europa Publications.
- *General Telegram Statistics*, and *General Telephone Statistics*, both published by the International Telecommunications Union.
- *International Travel Statistics*, published by the International Union of Office Travel Organizations.
- *Commercial Atlas and Marketing Guide*, published by Rand McNally.
- *Statesmen's Yearbook*, published by MacMillan.
- *Demographic Yearbook* and *UNESCO Yearbook* and *Treaty Series*, all published by the United Nations.
- *Worldmark Encyclopedia of Nations*, published by Harper and Row.
- *Yearbook of International Organizations*, published by the Union of International Associations.

As this brief listing suggests,[11] the range of aggregate data available is very impressive. Nonetheless, as pointed out later on in this section, there are a number of problems associated with collections of aggregate data for the purposes of comparative cross-national research. First, however, let's review some of the research findings where variables are operationalized by reference to aggregate data.

R. J. Rummel and his associates have discovered that the great variety and number of attributes by which nations are described using social and economic accounting data (e.g., the number of hospital beds, miles of railroads and highways, GNP, cultural factors such as language and religion, etc.) can all be reduced to a few basic *dimensions* or *factors* (e.g., from 236 variables down to 3 or 4 underlying dimensions) that effectively group similar nations and differentiate dissimilar nations.[12] Rummel's findings also suggest that international behavior is structured—not random—behavior. Hence, the tools of science can be used to discover the underlying patterns that give structure and predictability to the international behavior of nations.

With respect to similarities, Rummel found that from his original large pool of variables only a few dimensions or factors are required to summarize the underlying relationships among the variables. These independent clusters of variables or underlying factors appear to be related to a few independent characteristics of a nation, including its size, level of economic development, domestic political orientation or style, Catholic culture, domestic conflict, and its foreign conflict.

In another study using aggregate data from the *World Handbook*, Bruce Russett examined 54 social and cultural variables for 82 countries. Russett found that they could be reduced to five independent dimensions: size, level of economic development, Communist influence, Catholic culture, and the characteristics of the agricultural system (intensive or extensive).[13]

Russett then developed a measure of socio-cultural distance, discovering five major regions of socio-cultural homogeneity: (1) Afro-Asia, (2) Western Community, (3) Latin America, (4) Semi-developed Latins, and (5) Eastern Europe. However, membership in these new empirical (as contrasted with areal) groups reveals some insights and a few surprises. For example, both Japan and Israel appear in the Western Community and not in the Afro-Asian group. Similarly, Turkey is found in the Afro-Asian—not the Western Community or Eastern Europe grouping. The Philippines emerges as a Latin American, not an Asian nation. By contrast, Yugoslavia remains in the Eastern European grouping, even though many popular images might place it elsewhere. In short, Russett found that the classification of nations according to standard geographic regions cannot be reproduced if we classify these same nations according to socio-cultural criteria. In other words, important differences exist between a geographic definition of a region and a socio-cultural definition of a region—though most of us tend to confound the two in everyday language. Hence, a close examination of Russett's work allows us to assess the extent to which nations that share a geographic location also share basic socio-cultural characteristics. Russett's findings fail to support a number of the assumptions typically made by those who study conventionally-defined areas.

Problems with Aggregate Data

Even though aggregate data may be readily available through a large number of sources, it is important to be aware of some of the problems that are typically encountered. First, very often the figures reported are inaccurate. For example, the figures presented may be biased or distorted so as to reflect positively on the reporting nations. Also, the sampling or other data gathering techniques used by the collecting agencies may be weak or inappropriate, thus generating considerable error—sometimes called source error.[14]

Another problem is that the data often lack comparability. Nations frequently employ different methods for defining and measuring the attributes (variables) they are reporting. Several examples will serve to illustrate this problem. The Soviet Bloc, for instance, does not report a GNP value, but instead uses a Net Material Product (NMP) measure which is not immediately comparable to the more familiar Gross National Product (GNP) used by capitalist countries. Similarly, the variable "Percentage Illiterate Age 5 to 19 of Population" from a UN source permits only limited comparability among the reporting nations. Indeed, an examination of the footnotes reveals that some nations report from "puberty to 21," others in a "selective sample age 12–15," and others use various years other than the 5–19 criterion. Finally, the problem of comparability is found in almost all labor statistics. The UN's *Yearbook of Labor Statistics* cites over 100 qualifying footnotes, one for each of the sovereign nations in 1963, with respect to the variable "non-agricultural workers as a per cent of the total economically active population."

Another major problem with aggregate data is that of missing data. On some attributes, many nations do not report figures. This problem is particularly acute with respect to less developed countries in Africa, Asia, and Latin America. In other words, missing data tend *not* to be randomly distributed (which would create fewer problems in analysis), but rather appear to be systematically related to important characteristics of certain identifiable nations, such as less developed nations. Hence, those using aggregate data in cross-national analyses must carefully estimate the distortions that may occur as a consequence of the nonrandom pattern of missing data.

When using aggregate data, one should be sensitive to the need to select sources of high reliability and exhaustive coverage of the cases and variables of interest. When more than one source is used for a single variable, source reliability can be checked by computing the differences in scores (e.g., GNP estimates) between sources on variables and cases where there is overlap in reporting. In short, the use of aggregate data is not without its limitations and pitfalls, but, as we shall see, this warning holds for all data sources and data generating techniques. That is why studies should incorporate more than one method of data generation, that is, the use of multi-method approaches to analysis.

EVENTS DATA

The Use of Events Data

Events data are used as indicators of the behavior of nations, or to monitor the performance of the international system (e.g., similar to social indicators used in domestic political systems to monitor increases or decreases in crime, etc.). Although interest in events data has appreciably increased in recent years, the systematic collection and analysis of events data have a long history. As early as the 1930s Quincy Wright (1942) was systematically collecting data on international wars. During the 1950s and 1960s, a number of scholars were systematically mining sources such as *Facts on File, Deadling Data,* and the *New York Times Index,* for data on threats, protests, diplomatic expulsions, domestic violence, riots, strikes, and assassinations as indicators of violence and conflict.

The aggregation of events as an indicator of the performance of a social system is not, of course, novel. Indeed, we are exposed daily to aggregate events data that help us to assess the robustness of the stock market (the Dow-Jones averages), the relative strength of political parties (voting data), the dangers of holiday travel (auto death statistics), and the skill of a favorite quarterback (through his week-by-week completion record). Under the influence of researchers like Charles McClelland and Robert North, a number of students of international relations began to work to add diplomacy and other forms of inter-nation behavior to the list of issue areas monitored by the daily aggregation of events data. The work that has emerged in recent years, however, evidences much more concern for the multiple components of an event. Although the definition of an event varies from researcher to researcher, nearly all are concerned with some aspect of the communications process—given a classic formulation by Lasswell: "Who says what to whom through what channels with what effects." Hence, events monitoring usually involves coding the actor or initiator of an event and the target or the recipient of the activity. Although actors and targets tend to be nation-states, some researchers include inter-governmental organizations as well as intra-governmental agencies or departments in their observations. An event is also recorded by the verbal or physical activity that characterizes it, and according to the time when it occurs. The activity may range from a simple statement of approval of some prior action by another government or to the declaration of war.

In a short monograph that provides an excellent introduction to events data research, Azar (1970) identifies two approaches to the organization of events data: the categorization approach and the measurement approach.[15]

The Categorization Approach

The work of Charles McClelland and his World Event/Interaction Survey (WEIS) project is one of the most notable examples of the categorization approach, where the effort is made to classify events into types or categories. McClelland begins with a distinction between event interactions and transactions. Transactions refer to the constant and routine exchange of goods and services such as foreign trade, tourist travel, book transactions, and diplomatic representation. Event interactions, by contrast, reference the extraordinary official arts of governments that are individually reported in public accounts as manifestations of nonroutine international conduct. It is only with this latter class of behavior that McClelland and his associates are concerned (McClelland, 1968a; 1968b; 1969; 1970).

The WEIS approach categorizes the worldwide external performance characteristics of all actions citing the *New York Times* as the sole source of the data. The world event survey orders the actions and responses of nations into 63 primary categories that form a cooperation-conflict continuum ranging from "praise" to "military engagement." The 63 primary event categories may be collapsed into 22 more general classes of behavior that may then be referenced by 6 basic behavior types, as displayed in Figure 2.3.

The Measurement Approach

Those who take the measurement approach to events data not only locate events in predetermined categories of theoretical and empirical interest, they also attempt to assess the quantity of conflict, cooperation, hostility, or friendship that each event manifests. If we examine Azar's Middle East Cooperation-Conflict Events Analysis (MECCA) project, the contrast between the measurement and categorization approaches will be clearer.

First, the MECCA project does not collect events data for all nations. Rather, it collects data on thirty-five actors and targets, including both domestic and international events. Second, the MECCA project attempts to scale or weigh the events that occur by reference to contextual factors or the location of the event in a sequence of events. For example, the MECCA project might not give the same weight to a threat that was issued in the context of high levels of tension as it would to a threat issued in the context of reduced tensions between the actor and the recipient. In other words, the measurement approach not only locates events in categories, but assumes that the meaning or significance "same" overt physical or verbal activities (i.e., events) will vary with the situation. Thus, the MECCA project has developed a 13-point scale for measuring the quantity of cooperation or

Cooperation		Conflict	
Behavior Types	*Action Types*	*Behavior Types*	*Action Types*
	approve	verbal	reject
verbal	promise	conflict—	protest
cooperation	agree	defensive	deny
	request		
	propose		accuse
		verbal	demand
		conflict—	warn
cooperative	yield	offensive	threaten
action	reward		
	grant		demonstrate
participation	comment	conflict	reduce relationship
	consult	action	expel
			seize
			force

*Figure 2.3 The major WEIS event categories**

---

* From McClelland and Hoggard (1969, pp. 714–15).

conflict in a given event. Figure 2.4 displays the typical events that are found at each point on the MECCA scale.

Research Using Events Data

The WEIS and MECCA projects are mentioned here because they point up differences among those who are doing events data research. Others are developing innovative events data designs that include (1) coding the internal sources of the event in actor's government (East, Hermann, and Salmore); (2) developing comprehensive event typologies—one of the more promising developments (Leng and Singer); and (3) examining in detail event sequences (Corson). However, most events data research is only beginning to move to the analysis stage, given the considerable time required to generate data. Among the findings that do exist, however, are those described by McClelland and Hoggard (1969). The analysis of WEIS data show that the distribution of participation in the international system— like the distribution of other values noted above in our discussion of aggregate data —is highly skewed. That is, the 20 most active participants were found to contribute nearly 70 percent of the total volume of reported acts, with the U.S. and the USSR prominent as both originators and recipients of interaction. Second, they found that the highly organized and routine flow of international politics is primarily cooperative and collaborative in character and that conflict does not appear to dominate international politics. Rather, they found "an approximate balance of three general classes of behavior: cooperation, conflict, and participation" (p. 724).

It should be noted that there are a number of methodological debates among those using events data regarding the selection of data sources. Some researchers tend to rely on a single source—like the *New York Times* or *Deadline Data*— while others consult multiple sources on the grounds that reliance on single sources introduces unacceptable bias owing to the differences in attention among newspapers to different areas of the world. While some research suggests that the volume of events from source to source may not have unacceptable variance, we know very little about the more important issue, namely, the comparability among sources by

C	1	Nations A and B merge to form a new nation-state.
O	2	Nations A and B establish a regional organization among
O		themselves.
P	3	Nation A extends economic aid to Nation B.
E	4	Nations A and B establish a friendship agreement among
R		themselves.
A	5	Nation A receives support for its internal and/or external
T		policies.
I	6	Nations A and B communicate regarding issues of mutual
O		concern.
N	7	Nation A experiences limited internal political difficulties.
C		
O	8	Nation A makes a protest directed against Nation B.
N	9	Nation A increases its military capabilities.
F	10	Nation A encounters domestic politico-military violence.
L	11	Nation A initiates subversion in Nation B.
I	12	Nations A and B engage in limited war activities.
C	13	Nation A engages in an all-out war against Nation B.
T		

Figure 2.4 Typical events on the MECCA project scale*

---

* Edward Azar, "Analysis of International Events," *Peace Research Reviews* IV, 1970, Peace Research Institute, Dundas, Ontario.

the proportion of event types. Hence, we may expect to find that regional or local news organs like *Asian Recorder* or *Al-Ahram* may report a higher proportion of some event types than world news sources such as the *New York Times* or *Le Monde*. There are a number of other problems using events data. Data collection, the training of coders, and the development of data storage retrieval routines are critical intellectual as well as management problems. If a measurement monitoring and ensuring approach is used, the problems of inter-coder reliability are increased substantially.[16]

CONTENT ANALYSIS

Content Analysis in International Relations

Given the obvious importance of verbal and written communications in politics, it should hardly be surprising to find considerable effort devoted to developing systematic techniques for analyzing the content of these communications. Content analysis is a data-making technique whereby characteristics of the sender (or encoder) of a communication, characteristics of the communication itself, and the effects of a communication on the receiver (or decoder) are systematically analyzed by studying key words and phrases contained within the context of the message unit. Content analysis has been used as a method for inferring national symbols (goals, aims, and inclinations) and for developing insights into the attitudes or predispositions of key decision-makers from the content of their oral and/or written statements.

One of the most extensive studies using content analysis was the Revolution and Development of International Relations (RADIR) project, conducted during the early 1950s at Stanford University. Editorials from one leading newspaper of the United States, Great Britain, France, Germany, and the Soviet Union were analyzed over the period 1890 through 1949 (Pool, 1952). The data were used to trace the changing foci of attention and attitudes in each of the above countries during the 60-year period. Illustrative of the findings are the following (cited in Holsti, 1968):

1. Hostility to the outside world seems to be very much a function of insecurity. Those nations which have at any given moment dominated the world scene have generally said little that was adverse to prestige papers in the other power. The insecure or unsatisfied powers, on the other hand, have generally had editorials full of hostile judgment of foreign states (Pool, 1951, p. 62).

2. Two main trends in the modern world are: (a) a shift in the center of attention, in which traditional liberalism is being replaced by proletarian doctrines; and (b) a growing threat of war and a corresponding increase in nationalism and militarism (Pool, 1952a, p. 84).

More recent studies in international relations using the content analysis technique are the Stanford studies of the 1914 case (Holsti, North, Brody, 1968), an analysis of John Foster Dulles' belief system (Holsti, 1962) and an analysis of the perceptions of decision-makers in the Cuban missile crisis (Holsti, Brody, North, 1964). Illustrative of the findings from these studies are the following:

1. The tendency of the Dual Alliance to respond at a level of violence higher than the Triple Entente was consistent with the former's more hostile perception of the environment (Holsti, et al., 1969, p. 157).

2. Dulles' image of the Soviet Union was preserved by associating decreases in his perceived hostility with decreases in Soviet capabilities (Holsti, 1969, p. 547).

3. In the Cuban missile crisis, both sides tended to perceive rather accurately the nature of the adversary's action and then proceeded to act at an "appropriate" level; that is, as the level of violence or potential violence in the adversary's actions diminished, perceptions of these actions increased in positive affect, and the level of violence in the resulting policies also decreased (Holsti, et al., 1969, p. 688).

There are several ways in which content analysis can be undertaken. These include frequency counts of communications, frequency counts of themes within communications, and the intensity of themes found within communications.

Frequency of communication involves the simple counting of the number of messages sent, inches of column space used in newspapers, or the number of minutes used on radio or TV. An illustrative finding is the following from Zinnes (1966, p. 477): "The frequency of interaction within the bloc will be greater than the frequency of interaction between blocs."

Frequency of themes involves analyzing the units of communication for the presence or absence of specified themes and then determining the frequency with which these themes occur. Thematic content analysis generates the following kinds of findings: "There is a positive relationship between perception of threat and perceptions of unfriendliness" (Zinnes, 1966, p. 476), and "There is a positive relationship between X's expression of hostility to Y and Y's perception of threat" (Zinnes, 1966, p. 476).

Intensity of themes involves attaching weights to or "scaling" statements so as to obtain measures of the degrees of hostility and/or friendliness. An example of weighting themes is found in Zinnes' (1966, p. 481) study in which a scaling procedure was employed that assigned each unit a weight from one to twelve, indicating the level of hostility contained in the message.

Holsti (1968, p. 114) points out several advantages to the use of content analysis in international political research. First, because so much of the work done by political scientists involves the analysis of documents, content analysis (through the use of structured and explicit coding procedures) helps control the subjective biases of the individual members of a research team while at the same time allows for the analysis of large amounts of data. Second, because data are often inaccessible to the researcher (e.g., verbal interactions among those in the foreign policy-making community), public policy statements must be relied upon since the researcher cannot obtain admission to high level policy-planning sessions. Third, content analysis is useful when the theory that is being subjected to confirmation involves the nature of the language itself. Cross-cultural studies of values and/or attitudes, for example, often employ content analytic techniques to control for semantic differences among languages. Also, content analysis can be used to identify the authors of statements or other written words.

There are, however, certain problems associated with the use of content analysis. One problem is the question whether it is possible to make inferences about antecedent factors thought to influence the content of statements. These antecedent variables are usually characteristics of the psychological makeup of the decision-maker that are thought to relate to the content of any statements made by the decision-maker and/or situational or contextual attributes of the decision-maker's role or the environment in which decisions are made (Holsti, 1962; Brody, 1963; Snyder, et al., 1962). In response to this, two points can be made. First, verbal exchange constitutes much of the "stuff" of verbal exchange politics. Regardless of whether a decision-maker means what he or she says, what is said is important to the perception and implementation of policy. Second, what is said may not be as important as the motivations or factors that condition the content of the statement. The latter point is important in the debate of whether role requirements (e.g., the Secretary of State) weigh more heavily in conditioning the statement or whether the individual personality (e.g., John Foster Dulles) has more influence on the behavioral pattern (Rosenau, 1969).

The Coding of Content

One of the major problems with content analysis as a data-making technique is that the interpretations of researchers can and often do differ. The statement, "Although we disagree with the policies of X, we will support their course of action," might be interpreted by two different coders as "anxious submissive" (meaning we disagree, but we *have* to go along) or "cooperative" (meaning we will support your policy). In content analysis, therefore, if a researcher is going to obtain reliable data, he must attain a high level of intersubjective agreement on the coding categories. This goal is facilitated through the use of a clearly explicated coding guide in which coding categories are mutually exclusive and exhaustive and coding decision rules are explicit, thereby minimizing the possibility of inter-coder disagreement.

SIMULATION AND GAMES

The Laboratory in International Relations

Simulation and gaming are laboratory techniques for the study of social processes and social systems. Although the terms *simulation* and *games* are used interchangeably in political science, some people attempt to distinguish between them. One basis for such distinction is the ratio of manual to computer activity (Dawson, 1962). The term *games* or *gaming* is used to designate those activities that consist largely of interactions among human participants; *simulation* by contrast, is used to designate those activities involving human participants with a machine dimension designed to represent some central features of a social system. Using the criterion of machine involvement, three types of games have emerged in the study of international relations.

All-human games, used primarily to probe alternative strategies in complex interaction situations and to gain insight into the process and outcomes likely to emerge in different real world problem areas, employ human participants interacting with each other and with a team of judges who pass on the realism of their actions as surrogate decision-makers. An example of an all-human game is the MIT Political-Military Exercise (PME) (Speier and Goldhemer, 1959; Bloomfield and Whaley, 1965; and Giffin, 1965).

Human-machine games or simulations are models in which selected elements of the environment (e.g., subnational groups or elements of an international system) has been programmed reflecting the adequately developed elements of international theory, leaving those areas and levels of theory that are ambiguous or undeveloped to be represented by human participants. Examples are the Inter-Nation Simulation (Guetzkow, et al., 1963) and the World Politics Simulation (Coplin, 1968).

All-machine simulations are models in which all variables and interaction are represented in computer programs. Human participation occurs only with respect to creating and manipulating the modeled system. An example is the Technological, Economic, Political, Evaluation Routine (TEMPER), developed originally by the Raytheon Corporation and now used by the Joint War Games Agency and the Industrial College of the Armed Forces.

Distinctions among simulations might also be made by referencing the level of abstraction. The all-human games emphasize very concrete international political situations. The selection of the nations depends on the political and/or diplomatic problem under investigation, for example, the Berlin crisis or Mideast crisis. Participants in these games play decision-making roles found in the referent nations, acting in the gaming situation in a manner similar to the way they feel the referent world counterparts would respond to the situation being gamed.

A simulation, on the other hand, is a more formal model of a referent system. For example, some simulations attempt to represent symbolically the major contextual factors that constrain decision-makers when they select courses of action in the international system. Interactions among these factors are generated by the decision-making behavior of participants and by programmed relations which together determine the consequences of the decisions made by the participants. Simulation typically uses prototypic decision-making roles and prototypic nations, i.e., roles and nations that are abstracted from referent world roles and nations— roles such as "central decision-maker" (for prime minister, president, etc.), and "Amra" (to represent all large, developed, open polities). The use of prototypes (rather than "de Gaulle" or "Russia") focuses the attention on the typical political functions and processes, inducing the participants to react to role responsibilities rather than to bootleg their own assumptions about how a particular referent world decision-maker would respond.

Simulation is an operational representation of the central features of reality, involving a replication or model of a more complex system. To simulate is to build an operating model of an individual or group process and to experiment with the behavior of this replication by the manipulation of variables (Schwartz, 1965, pp. 677–678). Simulation, therefore, can be thought of in terms of samples. It is necessary to include in the model the samples of those relationships and variables which are thought to affect behavior in the referent system. This means that simulation requires a theory of how relationships change under specific conditions. Simulation is built on theory; it is not a substitute for theory (Verba, 1964, p. 496). In the first part of this section, we have used the term simulation to refer to all games that contain a complex environment in which individual or system behavior is studied. In the second part of this section we will discuss another type of game—the simple two-person or bargaining game used to study conflict and bargaining behavior.

Some recent studies using simulation demonstrate the areas in which simulation has been used as a data-making technique. These include a study of the systemic effects of the proliferation of nuclear weapons (Brody, 1963), a study of the effects of certain types of benefits produced by an organization on the cohesion and effectiveness of associational groups (Burgess and Robinson, 1969), and a comparison of the hostile behavior of decision-makers in a simulate and historical environment (Zinnes, 1966). Representative findings are as follows:

1. "Four key elements of the pre-spread system are different after the spread of nuclear capabilities: (1) threat external to the bloc is reduced; (2) threat internal to the bloc is increased; (3) the cohesiveness of the bloc is reduced; and (4) the bipolarity is fragmented. All of these add up to a step level change in the 'cold war system'" (Brody, 1963, p. 745).

2. "In summary, the evidence obtained from the perceptual data indicates that the presence of private benefits increases cohesion among the members of a coalition and results in higher ratings of coalition effectiveness by its constituent members" (Burgess and Robinson, 1969, p. 213).

3. "The five relevant hypotheses . . . have shown in both simulate and historical data that a decision-maker's perception of a hostile environment is a function of two presumably independent factors: the international alliance structure and the extent to which the decision-maker has received hostile communications" (Zinnes, 1966, p. 494).

Advantages and Limitations of Research on Simulates

Several advantages have been identified as being associated with the use of simulation as an experimental technique (Guetzkow and Jenson, 1966; Schwartz, 1965; Singer, 1965; and Verba, 1964). Though models exist, the study of some areas of international relations is constrained by the fact that situations of critical interest have not yet happened and/or happened so rarely that data are not available to confirm hypotheses drawn from the model. Simulation allows the researcher to generate data that can be used to explore these hypotheses (Verba, 1964, p. 500). Moreover, the simulator can construct a model or build competing models that explain variation in particular outcomes and then explore the behavior of the model in the laboratory or on a computer even if the situation has not yet occurred in the referent system (Brody, 1963). Variables operating in international political relations often are not susceptible to simple and direct manipulation. However, in the laboratory or on the computer, the researcher has the capacity to manipulate variables where in real life it would be either impossible, undesirable, unethical, or dangerous (Dawson, 1962).

Additionally, it must be recalled that certain trade-offs exist between field and laboratory research methods. Confirmation of hypotheses in the field can be highly ambiguous because controlling for the effects of other variables is difficult (Campbell, 1969). Whereas in the laboratory, the researcher has the ability to control extraneous factors if he exercises the appropriate techniques in his design. In short, increased control and insight into causality is usually purchased with decreased richness and realism otherwise found in the field research situation. However, direct methods of observation and data collection are often difficult in international relations. The international system is a complex interaction with many stimuli and many responses. Sometimes the very identification of decision-makers is difficult, as is the behavior the researcher chooses to observe (Verba, 1964, p. 500).

One of the values of the scientific method is the ability to replicate research so as to determine the consistency of the results showing causal links. Laboratory simulations provide the means to replicate a design such that the independent effects of variable on an outcome can be ascertained with a higher level of confidence (Burgess and Robinson, 1969). An historical event can be replicated in a laboratory (even replication) and subjected to intensive analysis to determine the relationship among the factors inducing the event (Zinnes, 1966; and Hermann and Hermann, 1967).

There are, however, several problems with simulation that bear serious consideration. These problems are: (1) model construction; (2) realism; (3) validity; and (4) the meaning of research results. Model construction refers to design and theoretical problems in the area of constructing the model, particularly the inclusion of significant variables. Realism refers to the nature of the game and the participants. Validity refers to model-referent correspondence. And the meaning of results is the all-important consideration of the contribution simulation can make to the understanding of international affairs.

Model Construction. The problem here for the researcher is to represent the important relationships and dimensions of the referent system in the simulate model. Models by definition are oversimplifications, reductions, or samples of the referent system, and in the process of oversimplifying the referent system, certain features are distorted and other complex features and relationships may be excluded. Simulation may or may not replicate major features of the referent system, depending upon the particular model and the definition of problems that guided the development of the model. Yet to deny its utility by saying it is not a realistic representation is to deny the use of all models in the social sciences. Rather, we must ask whether the model excludes elements or relationships that are significant to the operation of the particular system in which we're interested.

The Problem of Realism. Some authors distinguish between two forms of realism in simulation (Thorelli and Graves, 1964, p. 14). Objective realism requires that the variables and problems selected be theoretically and empirically meaningful. Subjective realism demands that the simulation models have the appearance of reality and/or probability for the participants, sometimes called face validity. The problem of reality is essentially a design or model building problem. It is not impossible to make the laboratory exercise a realistic one for the participants, and thereby increasing the subjective realism. But an important question in this regard is, can the actions of a participant in a laboratory situation be any less real than the actions of the participant in a non-laboratory situation? The problem of objective realism—or validity—is an empirical issue and should be viewed as such when evaluating a simulation method.

The Problem of Meaning. What can simulation as a data-making technique contribute to our knowledge of international affairs? Various contributions of simulation as a data-making technique have been listed. Some feel that given the current level of development or state of the art, simulation is primarily useful as a technique for the discovery of variables and the exploration of hypotheses, sometimes referred to as simulation's "hueristic" value (Singer, 1965). Others (Verba, 1964) note that simulation can add an important link between theory and the referent world. A model can be designed under the assumption that the theory is correct and then be used to explore the implications of the theory in the laboratory or on the computer (Verba, 1964; Milstein and Mitchell, 1969). These implications can then be used as hypotheses for subsequent referent or field analysis. Others suggest using the simulate to study analytic structures found in international relations as well as in other social arenas, such as communications or coalition processes (Burgess and Robinson, 1969; Brody, 1963).

The problem of evaluating the meaning of research using simulation as a data-making technique can be partially resolved by the distinction between research on simulates and research in simulated environments. For example, Singer (1967) developed a computer simulation of a disarmament inspection system to assess the sensitivity of the inspection proposals to reveal efforts that might be made to develop weapons clandestinely. In this case the simulate facilitated the researcher's efforts to explore the way a complex system would operate under different conditions. Here the research was focused on the operation of the system itself. By contrast, the research by Burgess and Robinson uses a simulated environment within which they executed a traditional experimental design. Their research asks what happens to an associational group producing public goods as that group begins to produce different benefits for its members. As the authors themselves state:

> The emphasis in the research reported here, however, is on the use of simulation for hypothesis-testing, for examining under the controlled conditions of the laboratory, the relationship between properties in a theory and those factors which account for variance in the behavior of complex systems (Burgess and Robinson, 1969, p. 218).

Research *in* a simulated complex environment allows the researcher to test hypotheses drawn from his theory under controlled conditions. He must then gather similar data from the referent system and if the same results obtain under richer conditions over which the researcher exercises less control, then he has more confidence in his results.

ROLL CALL ANALYSIS

The Study of Voting Behavior

Roll call analysis has been used as a data-making technique in international relations to study national voting behavior and coalition behavior in international organizations, particularly the United Nations. As Anderson, et al. (1966, p. 4) point out, *roll call* is a term which has come to be associated with all votes that are a matter of public record with respect to the positions taken by the individuals casting the vote. With respect to the United Nations, roll call analytic techniques are used to describe and delineate voting patterns for nations on those votes that are a matter of public record on issues of some policy or analytical significance. Representative findings from roll call analysis applied to the United Nations are as follows:

1. The "Latin American caucusing group" turned out to consist of three identifiable voting blocs on colonial issues. Two of these blocs were rather closely aligned, but the third established a very different voting record. In fact, the principle division on colonial questions in the General Assembly as a whole also cut through the so-called Latin American caucusing group (Lijphart, 1963, p. 917).

2. Nevertheless, our analysis of the voting indicates that the African caucusing group does not present a completely united front on even African issues, though it does reach a high degree of cohesion on them. Moreover, its policy of confining itself primarily to African issues, gives the group a basis for negotiation in the Assembly (Hovet, 1963, p. 218).

3. In the first place, caucusing groups and blocs are to a considerable extent regional in character, which suggests that contacts and negotiations on a regional basis are fairly easily carried over into the United Nations, formulating what is a natural procedure which then can be carried out from both ends, so to speak (Hovet, 1960, pp. 113–114).

4. We can thus confirm our earlier interpretations that the East–West controversy is most clearly a contest between old Europeans and the Soviet bloc; that the North–South contest pits Africans, Arabs and Asians against the Soviet bloc and to a lesser extent against old Europeans; but these Africans, particularly the Casablanca states, oppose old Europeans on self-determination issues (Alker, 1964, p. 653).

Extrapolating from the purposes of roll call analysis listed by Anderson (1966), the application of roll call techniques in international relations provides the researcher with a technique for undertaking the following research tasks.

Roll call analysis provides the means for describing and measuring variation in the voting behavior of groups of nations. Examples of this are Hovet's analysis of African states in the United Nations (1963) and Hovet's earlier analysis of bloc politics in the United Nations (1960). The research task in this area is to determine which sets of nations have a high index of agreement on issues that come before the General Assembly of the United Nations. The sets of nations with high indices of agreement are, therefore, considered to constitute fairly cohesive voting blocs within the UN. Lijphart (1963) has used the following formula as an index of agreement between countries A and B.

$$IA = \frac{f + \frac{1}{2}g}{t} \times 100$$

In this formula, t equals the total number of votes under consideration, f equals the number of votes on which A and B were in full agreement, and g equals the number of votes on which they agreed only in part (one nation abstained). An index of agreement of 100 would indicate complete agreement between nations, and an index of 0 would indicate complete disagreement between nations. Using this formula, Lijphart (1963, p. 913) found that among the Europeans and Commonwealth nations, there were three voting blocs at the 95.5 percent level of cohesion. These were the Danish-Norwegian-Swedish bloc, and two interconnected blocs composed of Western European states and the English-speaking nations of the Commonwealth.

Roll call analysis provides a means for describing and measuring variations across issues which may arise in international assemblies. Examples of this type of analysis are found in Alker and Russett's work on world politics in the General Assembly (1967). These works utilize the statistical techniques of factor analysis to isolate underlying dimensions and/or major issues of conflict in the General Assembly voting. In his analysis of the United Nations General Assembly, Russett (1967) found that there were five major dimensions or issue areas around which voting behavior in the Assembly clustered. These were (1) a "Cold War" dimension, which accounted for 21 percent of the variance; (2) an "intervention in Africa" dimension, which accounted for 19 percent of the variance; (3) a "supranationalism" dimension accounting for 18 percent of the variance; (4) a "Palestine" dimension, accounting for 4 percent of the variance; and (5) a "self-determination" dimension, accounting for 4 percent of the variance. In another study, Alker and

Russett (1965) have shown that there are three major dimensions which can be identified over several sessions of the General Assembly. These are the "cold war," "colonial-self-determination," and "supranational" dimensions. These three issue areas account regularly and consistently for more than half of the variance in all roll call voting in the United Nations.

The third area where roll call analysis is useful combines the first two: *Roll call analysis facilitates the examination of complex relationships among voting blocs and issue areas in the General Assembly or in other international organizations.* Using factor analysis for data reduction, the following findings have been generated:

1. . . . those Asians and Africans sometimes identified in world politics by the term Afro-Asian neutralists . . . more often than not . . . vote with the Soviet Union on cold war and colonial questions (Russett, 1967, p. 74).

2. Casablanca, Arabs, and Brazzaville states took very different positions on Moslem questions (Palestine and West Irian); while on the supranationalist alignment the Soviet bloc and to a lesser extent Old Europeans opposed an Afro-Asian majority (Alker, 1964, p. 653).

This last research area represents a refinement of the first two. It attempts to locate national positions in relation to behavior in the General Assembly while controlling for the effects of issues.

Using Roll Call Techniques in Research

There are a number of considerations that must be taken into account when applying roll call analysis as a data-making technique. Anderson, et al. (1966) point out two problems that are associated with this method. First, roll call analysis cannot explain the *why* of the patterns that are determined to exist. In this respect, the roll call data-making technique is simply a method directed at discovering what patterns do exist, what issues underlie any given session in the UN, and/or what nations constantly vote together as blocs in the General Assembly. The technique, however, may give insight into competing explanatory constructs. In this regard, a roll call analysis may be very suggestive. For example, consider the following insight offered by Alker:

> Turning to the substantive conflicts in the Assembly, racial variables, economic development, colonial history, and American military alliances all influence policy positions . . . on self-determination. Trade and aid, as indicators of what might be best described as a two-way process of interdependence, rather than just "buying votes," help improve our understanding of the reasons for the Cold War membership alignments (Alker, 1964, p. 655).

These questions must be answered by other analytic techniques, but roll call analysis has suggested where we might begin probing for answers.

A second major problem is that of inferring from the voting behavior of nations to other behavior patterns of nations. Although nations in the General Assembly may find themselves in conflict over certain issues, they often find themselves in agreement in other issue-areas in international politics. For example, the Soviet Union and the United States are in conflict over many of the Cold War issues that come before the General Assembly, but share substantial agreement and cooperate very closely in matters that come before the International Atomic Energy Agency (Stoessinger, 1965, pp. 134–151). Therefore, great care must be taken not to assume automatically that relations that obtain between nations over issues in the

United Nations necessarily extends to those nations' interactions in other political arenas in the international system.

Roll call analysis in international politics has seen only rather limited use and has been applied primarily to the study of voting behavior within the United Nations, although there are roll call studies of the ILO, the European Assembly, and other international organizations. An additional area in which roll call techniques have been applied is in the study of foreign policy issues within national legislatures. Roll call analysis has proven itself a relatively economical and an extremely useful technique to understand international politics.

In this chapter we have described five principal methods of gathering information in comparative and international research. The generating of data represents the second major stage in the sequence of quantitative research. In the next stage we turn to a series of questions which we must ask of the data before proceeding to collect them.

EXERCISES

1 List three problems associated with the use of aggregate data in testing propositions.

2 A content analysis designed to measure the frequency of cooperative themes in governmental statements had an intercoder reliability of .33. Comment on the value of the research and the possible reasons for such a low intercoder reliability.

3 If a researcher were interested in investigating the proposition, "with many countries possessing nuclear weapons, the possibility of nuclear war obviously increases" (Kissinger, 1961, p. 242, extracted), what data-making techniques might be most appropriate and why?

4 Given the proposition "if the UN did not serve some national interest of the superpowers, it would be ignored by them" (Stoessinger, 1965, p. 171, extracted), what combination of data-making techniques would seem most appropriate?

5 In the library, examine rather closely the following data sources:

Required:	Optional:
Europa Yearbook	UN Demographic Yearbook
UN Statistical Yearbook	International Trade Statistics
UN Compendium of Social Statistics	Ginsberg's Atlas
Yearbook of Labor Statistics	World Energy Supplies
National Accounts Statistics	World Strength of the Communist Party
Statemen's Yearbook	Organization
Deadline Data	Facts on File
	Keesing's Contemporary Archives

A Write a brief evaluation of two of the *Required* data sources as a primary source of data. Describe their major strengths. What problems and constraints have to be faced in using each of them?

6 Evaluate the quality and usefulness of the following variables:

A Total land area in UN Demographic Yearbook.

B Female life expectancy at age 0.

C Agriculture workers as a percentage of total economically active population in UN Production Yearbook.

7 Being sure to make clear your recording unit, context unit, system of enumeration, and the decision rules for the coders, prepare a code manual or set of coding decision rules designed to:

A Show the ratio of the foreign affairs to domestic affairs in your local newspaper editorials.

B Appraise the position of your local newspaper along some dimension, such as hawk or dove, hard-line or soft-line, isolationist or internationalist, or some other theme of interest to you.

C Show the intensity of commitment to the theme selected for analysis in part B.

8 Refer to the following code guide:

CODE GUIDE

1.	Military Action	Any military clash for a particular country with another and involving gunfire.
2.	Troop Movement	Any rapid movement of large bodies of troops, naval units, or air squadrons to a particular area for the purpose of gaining concessions or as a show of strength.
3.	Troop Mobilization	Any rapid increase in military strength through the calling up of reserves, activation of other military units, or the de-mothballing of military equipment.
4.	Negative Sanction	Any nonviolent act against another country, such as boycott, withdrawal of aid, etc., the purpose of which is to punish that country.
5.	Threats	Any official diplomatic communication or governmental statement asserting that if a particular country does or does not do a particular thing, it will incur negative sanctions.
6.	Accusations	Any official diplomatic or governmental statement involving charges and allegations of a derogatory nature against another country.

A Identify the type of events in the following:

1. East Germany condemns China's views saying they were endangering the world Communist movement, 23 January 1963.

2. The USSR warned Communist China that a major split in the Communist movement would occur if Chinese attacks continued, 9 January 1963.

3. The USSR charged that the U.S. used poison gas in fighting the war in Vietnam, 9 March 1963.

4. Communist Chinese warned India that if its frontier soldiers create border disputes, the Indian government will be exposed, 27 May 1963.

5. India accused Communists of aggressive action in Indian territory, 11 October 1963.

6. Yemen-based U.A.R. planes attacked Saudi Arabian villages, June 1963.

7. U.S. suspended the shipments of arms and ammunition to Indonesia because of its opposition to Malaysia, 25 November 1963.

8. Indonesia charged that U.S. proposal to send ships to Indian Ocean was an attempt "to deter Indonesia" from its decision "to crush Malaysia," 19 December 1963.

9. Malaysia expanded its armed forces to counter Indonesia's policy of confrontation, 13 February 1963.

10. U.S. announces that the 7th fleet has begun taking precautionary measures in the Gulf of Siam, 22 April 1963.

B   With someone else in the class and using the following formula, calculate the index of inter-coder agreement on the ten events coded above.

$$\text{Inter-code agreement} = \frac{\text{number of coder agreements}}{\text{total number of coder decisions}} = \frac{(\qquad)}{(10)} =$$

9   Hovet (1963, p. 74) lists the following members of caucusing groups in the United Nations:

Scandinavian Group	*European Community Group*
Norway	Belgium
Denmark	Netherlands
Iceland	Luxembourg
Sweden	France
Finland	Italy

Alker (1964, p. 654) has found that a strong predictor of a nation's position on the East-West Dimension of conflict is whether or not it is a U.S. military ally. The following proposition might, therefore, be developed:

H_1 United States military allies will tend to agree more with the U.S. on those issues on which the U.S. and USSR vote against each other in the UN than those nations that are not U.S. allies.

A   Knowing that the European Community Group contains five members of
NATO and that the Scandinavian Group contains only three members of
NATO, which group would you predict to have the highest average index
of agreement with the U.S. on those issues that the U.S. and USSR
take opposing stands?

VOTING ISSUE / NATION	1	2	3	4	5	6	7	8	9	10	11	12	13	14	15	16	17	18	19	20	21	22	23	24	25	26	27	28	29	30	31	32	33	34	35	36	37
EUROPE																																					
Belgium	2	2	1	2	2	2	2	2	2	2	2	2	2	2	2	2	2	2	1	2	2	2	2	2	2	1	1	2	2	2	2	2	2	2	2	2	2
Luxembourg	2	2	1	2	2	2	2	2	2	2	2	2	9	2	2	2	2	2	9	9	9	9	9	9	9	9	9	9	9	9	9	9	2	2	2	2	9
Netherlands	2	1	1	2	2	2	2	2	2	2	2	2	2	2	2	2	2	2	2	2	2	2	2	2	2	1	2	2	2	2	2	2	2	2	2	2	2
France	1	2	2	2	2	2	2	2	2	2	1	1	2	2	2	2	2	1	1	0	2	2	2	2	2	2	2	1	2	2	1	2	2	2	2	1	2
Italy	2	2	1	2	2	2	2	2	2	2	2	2	2	2	2	2	2	2	1	2	2	2	2	2	2	2	1	2	2	2	2	2	2	2	2	2	1
SCANDINAVIA																																					
Norway	2	0	1	2	2	1	1	2	2	2	2	2	2	1	2	2	2	1	1	2	2	2	2	2	1	1	2	2	2	2	2	1	2	2	2	2	2
Sweden	2	0	1	2	2	1	1	2	2	2	2	2	2	1	2	1	2	1	1	2	2	2	2	2	1	1	2	2	2	2	2	2	2	2	2	2	1
Finland	2	0	1	2	2	1	1	1	2	2	2	2	1	1	1	1	1	1	2	2	2	2	2	2	1	2	2	2	2	2	1	2	2	2	2	2	2
Denmark	2	0	1	2	2	1	1	2	2	2	2	2	2	1	2	2	2	1	2	2	2	2	2	2	1	1	2	2	2	2	2	2	2	2	2	2	1
Iceland	2	1	1	2	2	1	2	9	2	2	2	2	2	9	2	2	2	1	2	2	2	2	2	2	1	1	2	2	9	9	2	2	2	9	9	2	2

This table shows data on 37 votes in the United Nations General Assembly on
which the U.S. and the USSR took opposing sides.

Code: 2 = vote with U.S.
       1 = abstain
       0 = vote with USSR
       9 = absent

B   Using the Rice-Beyle Index of Agreement, calculate the Index of Agreement
between each of the ten nations and the United States.

$$I.A. = \frac{f + \frac{1}{2}g}{t} \times 100$$

I.A. = Index of Agreement
   f = votes in agreement with U.S.
   g = abstentions
   t = total number of votes (absences should not be counted)

European Group	*Scandinavian Group*
Belgium _____	Norway _____
Luxembourg _____	Sweden _____
Netherlands _____	Finland _____
France _____	Denmark _____
Italy _____	Iceland _____
Average _____	Average _____

C   Was your prediction substantiated?

D   Do you feel the hypothesis is a valid one? Why?

NOTES

1. The student should be sensitive to the fact that the term *aggregate data* tends to be used by international relations scholars in a highly specialized way that may obscure its more generic technical meaning. Although we'll return to this point later, don't be surprised when you hear others use the term in its more generic sense referring to data from content analysis or from public opinion surveys.

2. See Alger (1966) for an account of his U.N. study; see also Miles (1968). For an overview and assessment of research in political science using the method of participant-observation, see Robinson (1970).

3. The *expert panel* should not be confused with the *panel method.* The former involves the pooling of observations from experienced observers; the panel method, by contrast, typically refers to a technique for generating longitudinal or time-series data from social surveys, i.e., data at different points in time on the attitudes and opinions of the *same* respondents.

4. Expert panels were used by Banks and Textor (1963) to locate nations in the proper category on many of the variables in the *Cross-Polity Survey* (see chapter 4). See also the work of Klingberg (1941), Jensen (1966), Teune and Synnestvedt (1965), Fitzgibbon (1967), and Kent (1969). Unfortunately, researchers in political science using expert panel methods have not yet produced a string of publications, a major source book, or a core of adherents sufficient to develop a firm set of guidelines for applying the panel methodology.

5. See Dalkey (1972, pp. 141–143) for a guide to literature assessing *Delphi* and *Delphi* applications and for literature on theories of group opinion, group problem-solving, and group value judgments that are the foundation of the *Delphi Technique.*

6. IGO refers to "intergovernmental organization." Note that the units of analysis are ranked from the bottom according to increasing levels of aggregation, i.e., each higher unit includes the elements of the lower.

7. Kenneth C. Boulding, *Conflict and Defense: A General Theory,* Harper & Row, Inc., 1962, p. 3.

8. On these points, see Galtung (1967), Bauer (1966), and Etzioni and Lehman (1967).

9. These data sets are discussed in detail in Burgess and Munton (1973) and are listed in chapter 4.

10. The World Handbook has two editions: see Russett, et al. for *World Handbook I* and Taylor, et al. for *World Handbook II.* Similarly, the *Cross Polity Survey* includes an edition referencing nations in the 1960s and a time-series edition that goes back to 1815. See Banks and Textor (1963) and Banks (1971). Data from the DON project are described in Rummel (1966).

11. Extensive listings of data sources relevant to the student of international politics can be found in Zawodny (1966), Merritt and Pyszka (1969), and Park (1968).

12. The beginning student will not find it easy to understand factor analysis the first time around. For the present, try the following: A research design with 236 (or even 50) variables is clearly unwieldy. Moreover, it is likely that a number of the variables will be measuring the same thing, or they'll be highly related—or inter-correlated. A factor analysis routine will identify clusters or groupings of variables that are highly related to each other, and these variables are said to form a "factor" or "dimension." Other clusters of related variables will be located, and another factor will thereby be created. Moreover, the factors will be independent of each other. Thus, having started with 100—or, in Rummel's case, 236—variables, factor analysis allows us to reduce the interrelated variables to a few

(say, five or ten) independent clusters or factors which can then be treated as variables. For an introduction to factor analysis, see Rummel (1967).

13. As would be expected, a large number of studies using aggregate data from the *World Handbook* have been undertaken. These studies have been reviewed by Russett (1968) and should be perused by the interested student.

14. See, for example, Russett, et al. (1964); Bergson (1953); Bauer (1966); and Morgenstern (1963) for discussions of the problems of source error in aggregate social accounting data.

15. The short monograph by Azar (1970) is one of the few published accounts that goes beyond a report of one's own research, and interested students are urged to read it. Other published accounts include McClelland (1968) and McClelland and Hoggard (1969). Most accounts, however, remain unpublished and are noted in the bibliography.

16. It should be noted that both McClelland and Azar have provided clear and visible accounts of their data quality control procedures and coder reliability experiments. Concern for these problems is unfortunately occasionally discounted by others.

Chapter Three

MEASUREMENT IN INTERNATIONAL RELATIONS

As pointed out in the previous chapter, the selection of one data generation technique rather than another may be influenced by a number of considerations. One of these is related to the unit whose behavior we are trying to explain or understand, for example, a nation, an IGO (intergovernmental organization), or an individual decision-maker. Therefore, one of the first considerations in thinking about measurement problems is the unit of analysis issue and the distinction that can be made between the object unit (the unit whose behavior we are trying to explain) and the subject unit (the unit whose behavior we are observing). Hence, in this chapter, we will present some of the more technical issues that the analyst must consider in the third research step when applying the tools of observation to the unit of analysis. These considerations—related to methods of observations—are essentially measurement issues. For example, after data have been generated to test a proposition, several questions remain to be asked. First, are the data reliable, that is, are measurements consistent over repeated observations? Second, are the measurements valid, that is, do the data accurately measure the phenomena under investigation? Another consideration is the level of measurement for each of the variables. Are they nominal, ordinal, interval, or ratio variables? This answer will determine the appropriate statistical technique to employ in the subsequent analyses. Finally, we will consider some different ways of conceptualizing a unit's behavior. Accordingly, this section will introduce the notions of contextual effects and structural effects as one way to conceptualize or think about the forces at work on some unit's behavior—a man or woman, a group, a nation, whatever. In the process of this discussion, we will review *aggregate measures*, *integral measures*, and *relational measures*. In designing your research or evaluating the research of others, these questions will constitute one basic set of criteria by which the quality of a research effort is to be judged.

UNITS OF ANALYSIS

As suggested previously, students of international politics focus their attention on a variety of behavioral units—nations, IGO's, regional political systems, individual decision-makers, even the entire global socio-political system. And if the objects of international relations research vary widely, so do the theories that are used to explain international political phenomena.

For example, some analysts try to understand international politics from theories about individual human behavior. These include theories of frustration-aggression, or others that are thought to account for the behavior of decision-makers or the attitudes of mass publics toward their own or the national symbols of other nations.[1] Other analysts examine global politics by looking at the characteristics of the nations themselves (its size, cultural characteristics, or level of economic development) without trying to account for the differences that exist among the personalities of the decision-makers or variations in the national character of different states.[2]

For an interesting case study that contrasts these two perspectives on international political behavior, compare the Stanford Studies on the outbreak of World War I noted earlier with the research by Robert North and Nazli Choucri on the same subject.[3] Recall that the Stanford Studies used a variation on the stimulus-response (SR) model from psychology to interpret data from the content analysis of official documents that were used to characterize the predispositions of the principal decision-makers in Austria, Germany, Great Britain, etc. Thus, the Stanford group observed the (verbal) behavior of individuals and "filtered" or interpreted their readings (or data) through the SR model from psychology. By contrast, North and Choucri used "capability analysis" to try to account for tensions among the nations in the Triple Alliance (Austria-Hungary, Germany, and Italy) and the Triple Entente (Great Britain, France, and Russia). Rather than measure the behavior of *individuals*, North and Choucri measured differences among the six *nations* with respect to their territorial size, diplomatic status, economic productivity, and military capability.

The point is not that one or another perspective is right or wrong. Indeed, the perceptive reader will have noted that Professor North is a principal investigator in both efforts. Rather, the point is that the analyst can approach the study of a problem in international relations from a variety of theoretical perspectives, each of which may require different kinds of data that will be developed from the observation of different behavioral units. Hence, the differences among analysts regarding what they study and whose behavior they theorize about, thereby raising the important *levels of analysis issue*, is one of the most fundamental considerations involved in social research.[4]

The levels of analysis issue is primarily concerned with the empirical unit that is selected for analysis. Distinctions among units are usually made according to some criterion, for example, by a rule of aggregation. If we think of individuals as one level of analysis and the global political system as another level of analysis, it is clear that groups of varying size exist between these two extremes. For example, we could examine cliques among individuals or we could look at larger groups such as political parties, voluntary associations, pressure groups, or nations.

In order to develop the basis for some useful distinctions, let's organize the different units of analysis in an arbitrary way, remembering that levels of unit aggregations can be displayed in a wide variety of ways. Let's examine a set constituted by six elements that would begin with (1) *intra-psychic units* (e.g., political attitudes measured by the psychologist's nationalism-internationalism scale); (2) *individual* units; (3) *groups* (including voluntary associations, political parties, coalitions, etc.); (4) *nations*; (5) multi-nation *regions*, that is, an analytic region such as an alliance (NATO or the Warsaw Pact) or a geographic region such as Asia; and (6) the *global polity* itself as a unit of analysis. Note that these distinctions among units are ordered from the level of least aggregation to the level of greatest aggregation.

The importance of distinguishing among units of analysis is extremely important because it directly affects the way we build and transmit knowledge about a unit's behavior. To illustrate this point, we'll refer to Figure 3.1, where units are ordered by levels of aggregation from smallest (F = intraphysic) to largest (A = global).[5]

OBJECT UNITS AND SUBJECT UNITS

Next, it is important to make an additional distinction—this time between the unit whose behavior we want to understand vis-a-vis the unit whose behavior we observe and measure. This distinction between the unit we observe and unit whose behavior we want to explain is important because they may not be the same units. For example, we may be interested in the foreign behavior of nations, but we might measure the behavior of decision-making elites by using elite interviews, a content analysis of elite speeches, or articles in elite publications.[6] Similarly, we might be interested in explaining the behavior of foreign ministers, yet the subject of investigation may be the differences in governmental structures (e.g., presidential or parliamentary systems) in which foreign ministers operate.[7] It is for this reason that we make the distinction between object units (the units whose behavior we are trying to explain) and subject units (the unit whose behavior we observe in order to understand the object unit). This is a very neat and useful distinction— one that is found in one form or another in nearly all the basic methodological literature in social science.[8]

STRUCTURAL AND CONTEXTUAL EFFECTS

The distinction is useful because it allows us to see clearly the differences between structural analysis and contextual analysis. Go back to Figure 3.1. Let's say we wanted to understand, explain, or forecast the foreign behavior of a nation. That is, assume our object of analysis is the nation—for example, to what extent is a nation

Subject units \ Object units	1 global	2 regional	3 nation	4 group	5 individual	6 intra-psychic
A global	▓					
B regional		▓				
C nation			▓			
D group				▓		
E individual					▓	
F intra-psychic						▓

Figure 3.1   A schematic representation of levels of analysis

likely to pursue cooperative or noncooperative strategies in its dealings with other nations? That decision (to try to forecast the foreign behavior of nations) puts us in column 3 where we find the nation located as "Object Unit."

Next, as we try to understand the foreign behavior of nations, we have six alternative subject units (rows A–F) whose behavior we can observe in order to try to understand why a nation manifests the foreign policy it does.

First, we might analyze the unit at its own level of analysis (i.e., its own level of aggregation). Note that the analysis of units at their own level is represented by the shaded diagonals in Figure 3.1, indicating that the object unit and the subject unit are the same. Or, alternatively, we can analyze our object unit (the nation) by examining subject units at either lower or higher levels of aggregation. When object units are analyzed by observing the behavior of higher level subject units (rows A and B) it is called *contextual analysis*. When object units are analyzed by observing subject units found at the same or at lower levels (rows C, D, E, and F), it is called *structural analysis*, and is related directly to philosophies of reductionism and constructionism.

Be sure to note that whether looking at structural variables or contextual variables, we are still concerned with explaining *national* behavior and whether it will be cooperative or noncooperative. Therefore, if we assume that our research interest is organized around the nation as the object unit, then regional and global units are contextual units (or variables) and political parties (row D) or individual decision-makers and their attitudinal structures are structural units (or variables).

However, if we organize our research question around the behavior of decision-making elite as the object unit, then the nation becomes a contextual unit (moving down column 4, note that measurements at the level of the nation would now be treated as contextual variables). Hence, whether a given subject unit has a contextual or structural effect on behavior depends entirely on what object unit we are studying.[9]

One other point should be made here: it is important to remember that a research design must hold constant the object unit—although it can shift subject units to the limits of the analytical space (e.g., in this scheme, rows A–F). In other words, we can take measurements or observations from any combination of structural or contextual variables once we have determined the object unit (the column we enter). However, we cannot shift object units, i.e., we cannot move along the columns in the context of a single research design.

Accordingly, it is important (1) to decide very early what your object unit is— whether you want to understand or forecast the behavior of individuals, decision-making elites, nations, alliances, or global political processes, and (2) to avoid shifting from one object unit to another. If a decision is made to examine the nation as the object unit, then it is still possible to examine the effects of alliances (row B) or the level of violence in the international system (row A) on national behavior.[10] You could also examine the relationship among decision-makers or the distribution of public attitudes and their subsequent effects on the behavior of nations.[11] But, regardless of the subject unit (or units) selected for observation and measurement, all of the inferences or findings will be linked to the nation—the unit whose behavior you are trying to explain.

It may be helpful to note here that much research and analysis in political science tends to examine *either* structural effects on object units *or* contextual effects on object units. Although trends in contemporary theory and research suggest that this tendency to examine only structural effects (e.g., public opinion and foreign policy) or only contextual effects (e.g., the impact of strategic considerations such as the balance of power on foreign policy) may be changing, much of the quantitative literature that you will encounter will evidence this more narrow orientation.[12]

Now, let's extend this discussion to some additional measurement considerations. Continue to assume for the purpose of illustration that our object unit is the nation. Contextual effects will usually be based on indicators for variables that describe relational measures—i.e., characteristics or variables that describe a unit's linkages with other units. For example, we might develop contextual indicators based on the number of IGO's a nation belongs to, a nation's volume of trade, or the number of nations to which a nation sends diplomatic representatives. In other words, contextual indicators give us a measure of a unit's connections with its environment.

Structural effects will be based on indicators for variables that describe or otherwise reference some quality or characteristic of the unit itself. Often structural effects are measured by aggregate data, that is, indicators that are simply the sum of individual characteristics or properties. For example, we might want to measure a nation's "level of economic development" by using an indicator that tells us the "percent of the working age population employed by the public sector." Or, we might measure the structural effect "level of economic development" by using an indicator that measures the "per capita Gross National Product" of the society. In both cases, we are using an aggregate measure. In the latter example, the aggregate measure is obtained by adding up (aggregating) the total product of goods and services produced by the society and dividing by the total population of the society.

Of course, we sometimes run into problems with simple aggregate measures. It is not uncommon to find that the process of aggregation conceals substantial inequalities in the way the value being measured is distributed among individuals. We may discover, for instance, that Sweden's per capita GNP is less than $1500, while per capita income in the U.S. may exceed $3000. However, a closer examination of the distribution of income among individuals may reveal that the U.S. has many more poor people than does Sweden, even after adjusting for the differences in the absolute size of their population. Hence, the aggregate measure of wealth has concealed that the U.S., which at the aggregate level appears to be twice as wealthy as Sweden, in fact has a disproportionately large segment of economically-deprived individuals compared to Sweden.

This problem of making inappropriate inferences from aggregate indicators back to individuals is called the *ecological fallacy*. Although the simple process of adding properties of individuals (e.g., their wealth) to obtain an aggregate measure may yield an indicator where the aggregate property corresponds closely to individual properties (e.g., the case of Sweden in the example), relationships or properties found at the aggregate level may not, in fact, be duplicated at the individual level (e.g., the case of the U.S. in the example). Hence, the appropriateness of using aggregate indicators depends very much on the quality of the data, the specific purposes of the analysis, and, most importantly, the unique distributional characteristics of the value being measured in a specific case.

Finally, structural effects may be measured by the use of indicators that describe properties of the unit as a whole, properties that are independent of individuals or groups within the unit (in this case, the nation). These kinds of measures are usually referred to as *global* or *integral indicators* because they are not derived from an aggregation of individual measures, i.e., they are not reproduced at the level of the individual. For example, we may want to characterize a nation's level of economic development using an indicator that profiles the national budget—by reference to a ratio of administrative costs to program costs. Or we might characterize the stability of a regime not by observing the "incidence riots and strikes" (an aggregate measure) but by noting "the number of years of continuous constitutional rule" (an integral measure not reproduced at the level of the individual).

STRUCTURAL AND CONTEXTUAL EFFECTS IN FOREIGN POLICY ANALYSIS

Now let's try to tie all these considerations together by reformulating and modifying some proto-theoretical ideas for the comparative study of foreign policy. A number of researchers (including Raymond Cattell, R. J. Rummel, and Jack Sawyer) reported findings suggesting that nations might be profitably viewed as object units which can be characterized by a few underlying characteristics—especially size, development, and political culture. By drawing on and reassembling this earlier work, it is possible to describe and classify nations by using three dichotomized characteristics (1) size, i.e., large and small; (2) level of economic development, i.e., developed and less developed; and (3) political accountability, i.e., open and closed. If these three dichotomized characteristics are nested, as displayed in Figure 3.2, we obtain eight nation types ranging from large, developed, open polities (Type A) to small, underdeveloped, closed polities (Type H).[13]

Elsewhere, Karl Deutsh, Lewis Edinger, and subsequently James Rosenau suggested that it was possible to identify five basic sources of foreign policy behavior: (1) idiosyncratic factors, (2) role factors, (3) governmental factors, (4) societal factors, and (5) systemic factors. Moreover, it was argued that the strength or impact of the source variables (or variable clusters, since each of the five could include a large number of variables) would vary in their effect on the foreign behavior of nations depending on the nation type of a given national actor.[14] For example, Rosenau suggests that

> . . . the potency of a systemic variable is considered to vary inversely with the size of a country (there being greater resources available to larger countries and thus lesser dependence on the international system than is the case with smaller countries), that the potency of an idiosyncratic factor is assumed to be greater in less developed economies (there being fewer of the restraints which bureaucracy

Large				Small			
Developed		Undeveloped		Developed		Undeveloped	
Open	Closed	Open	Closed	Open	Closed	Open	Closed

Nation Type   A   B   C   D   E   F   G   H

Figure 3.2 Eight basic nation-types

and large-scale organization impose in more developed economies), that for the same reason a role variable is accorded greater potency in more developed economies, that a societal variable is considered to be more potent in open polities than in closed ones (there being a lesser need for officials in the latter to heed non-governmental demands than in the former), and that for the same reason governmental variables are more potent than societal variables in closed polities than in open ones.[15]

Now, if we take this rather imaginative statement intended to help give coherence to the comparative study of foreign policy and reformulate it in terms of measurement considerations suggested above, we find that it combines structural and contextual effects within the framework of a single, coherent, conceptual statement. So, once again, we can see how a design for analysis can simultaneously examine both contextual and structural effects, that is, look at many different subject units (A–E from Figure 3.1) in trying to understand a nation's foreign behavior. In fact, it might be argued that the most exciting and promising research going on today combines structural and contextual variables in the framework of a single design.[16]

RELIABILITY AND VALIDITY

Once the analyst has selected the unit of analysis (the object unit whose behavior the analyst wants to explain) and developed a conceptual or theoretical statement that permits identification of the subject units (that is, the contextual and/or structural effects that will be observed and measured) other kinds of measurement problems have to be faced.

When political analysts properly use survey research techniques (e.g., interviews or questionnaires), simulation or other experimental techniques, content analysis, and other procedures for generating data, they are in effect making systematic, rigorous, and reproducible observations or measurements. Inasmuch as these techniques of observation or measurement are applied by other students to the same phenomena in an attempt to repeat the study and to confirm or disconfirm the findings, this exercise is called *replication*. When studies can be replicated, and when similar results are obtained, either by the original investigator or by others, the analyst can have a higher level of confidence in the findings that he or she has generated. And this process serves to describe, at least in part, what science is all about—the invention and application of standardized, visible, explicit, and repeatable investigative procedures.[17]

The analyst must be alert to two important considerations regarding the technique or tool of observation that is being used to give operational meaning to a variable. With respect to any measurement technique the analyst must ask,

1. Is it reliable?
2. Is it valid?

If an observation (interview, experiment, questionnaire, content analysis) is reliable, the same results should be reproducible, i.e., attainable time after time by the same investigator or by others. Thus, *reliability* refers to consistency among repeated observations.

For example, in manual content analysis, as pointed out in chapter 2, it is common practice to employ at least two coders to code the material being analyzed.

The level of agreement among these coders is called inter-coder reliability (or inter-coder agreement) and the analyst typically expects to have an agreement score greater than .70. Also, it is not uncommon for analysts to code a sample of their material twice in order to determine whether the same individual will make the same coding decisions, that is, assign the same item (e.g., a newspaper editorial or comment) to the same category (or theme) in a content analysis coding guide. The level of agreement between the coding decisions of the same individual at two different times is called *intra-coder reliability*. Assessments of intra-coder reliability are particularly important to make when the analyst is required to do all his own coding, for it provides at least one check on the reproducibility of his research techniques.[18]

Validity, by contrast, expresses the extent to which a test or observation measures what it is supposed or intended to measure. The question is not "Is a research technique valid?" but rather "For what is a given research technique valid?" In short, all research techniques are appropriate for some questions or set of questions. The crucial issue is whether a given research technique or procedure generates a measurement that is appropriate to the concept and variable under investigation.

The two concepts of reliability and validity can be demonstrated by reference to the pistol targets in Figure 3.3, where target A represents the concept of reliability. Even though there are no "bull's eyes," the gun (or, better, the person using it) has obtained reliable (or consistent) results. Target B, by contrast, represents the concept of validity where all the shots are in the bull's eye and Target C, as noted, represents observations that lack both reliability and validity.

It should be clear from these three examples that an observation technique may be reliable, though invalid (Target A), and that a valid research instrument is always reliable. Reliability therefore may be expressed as an association or relationship between two or more observations. Validity on the other hand, represents the relationship between an observation and some external criterion. Hence, it is possible to have reliability without validity, but it is not possible to have validity without reliability. It should also be understood that all measurements contain some error.

Let's examine briefly the concept of error. Considerable attention is given in the specialized literature to the problems of measurement error. Briefly, measurement error has four primary sources: (1) observer bias—for example, the influence that an untrained interviewer may have on the answers or responses given by a respondent in a survey; (2) design error—where the analyst is not measuring indicators that are relevant to the variables in his or her model or proposition, e.g.,

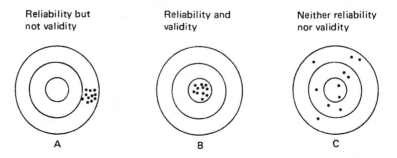

Figure 3.3 Reliability and validity, compared and contrasted

using "political assassination" as a single indicator of domestic violence; (3) imprecision—the variation obtained in the process of observation or measurement that is a result of the crudeness of our measuring instruments. For example, chapter 2 pointed out the reliability problems associated with cross-national comparisons of national social accounting statistics (recall the labor statistics and all the exceptions to the definition of employed); and (4) random error—the chance variation in observations, variations that are unsystematic and inevitable.

In chapters 5 and 6 (when we discuss data analysis), we will find that analytical techniques are available to control for, take account of, or to reduce error. However, for the present, it should be noted that most analytical techniques assume that imprecision is distributed randomly among observations or measurements (what we referred to previously as random error). Systematic error or imprecision, however, is much more difficult to handle and should always be avoided.[19]

LEVELS OF MEASUREMENT

Assuming we want quantitative data, and assuming we want to conform to the rules of evidence that have developed among social scientists, it is important to face the question of measurement, examine the rules, and take care not to violate them. Although it is sometimes asserted that the measurement of political and social phenomena is not possible, the detractor should take note of the many quantitative statements that are typically uttered by political and social scientists and commentators. Consider for example, statements such as, "Decentralized resource allocation or decision-making systems are more effective than centralized systems," or "Israel is more powerful than the Arab states combined." The words *more* and *combined* in the above empirical descriptive propositions presume the capacity to measure: *more* assumes qualitative measurement; *combined* assumes quantitative measurement.

Not all measurement is quantitative. Moreover, measurement involves more than simply assigning numerical values or labels to a thing, a property, or a characteristic. By the same token, not all numerical values suggest measurement. Think, for example, of telephone numbers, addresses, numbers on the jerseys of athletes, etc.

Qualitative measurement includes such commonplace exercises as categorizing or ranking. For example, when we speak of Democrats and Republicans, Protestants or Catholics, French or Russians, we are categorizing or classifying people by placing them in mutually exclusive categories. Or, when we talk about developed or underdeveloped nations or great powers and small powers, we are classifying nations by placing them in mutually exclusive categories. And when we engage in the process of creating mutually exclusive and exhaustive categories (or classification systems sometimes called *taxonomies*), we are, in fact, engaging in a form of qualitative measurement called *nominal scaling*.

Nominal scaling is the lowest or weakest level of measurement. It exists whenever numbers or other symbols are used to classify an entity—a person, a nation, a group, or some characteristic of an entity. For example, consider the effort by William Coplin (1971) to classify intergovernmental organizations (IGO's) according to their purpose and to the scope of their geographic interest (Figure 3.4). Coplin argues that with respect to scope, IGO's may have either regional or global interests. That is, he creates two mutually exclusive categories that include a value or designation for all IGO's, and the characteristics *global* and *regional* could be identified in any number of arbitrary yet meaningful ways—as an A and B, as 1 and 2, or as 1 and 5. In Figure 3.4, note that Coplin chose to use English words (alphabetic rather than numeric symbols) to denote his nominal categories. Similarly, the purpose of each IGO is denoted by four nominal categories: (1) social, (2) economic, (3) military, and (4) multi-purpose. Although English words are used to denote the nominal category into which each IGO falls, we could just as well use the numerical symbols 1 through 4 to achieve the same end. That is, we could use numerical rather than alphabetic symbols to identify the groups to which various objects or entities belong. Note, however, that the nominal scales for both scope and purpose are mutually exclusive and exhaustive—that is, no IGO can be both regional and global. Thus, according to Coplin, an IGO must be *either*

Organization	Scope	Purpose
African Development Bank	Regional	Economic
African Postal Union	Regional	Social
Arab International Tourist Union	Regional	Social
Arab Postal Union	Regional	Social
Asian Development Bank	Regional	Economic
Bank for International Settlements	Global	Economic
Central Treaty Organization	Regional	Military
Commonwealth Agricultural Bureau	Regional	Social
Council for Mutual Economic Assistance	Regional	Economic
Council of Europe	Regional	Multipurpose
Danube Commission	Regional	Economic
European Civil Aviation Conference	Regional	Social
European Coal and Steel Community	Regional	Economic
European Economic Community	Regional	Economic
European Free Trade Association	Regional	Economic
European Nuclear Energy Agency	Regional	Social
European Parliament	Regional	Multipurpose
Euratom	Regional	Social
Inter African Coffee Organization	Regional	Economic
Inter American Defense Board	Regional	Military
International Civil Aviation Organization	Global	Social
International Development Association	Global	Economic
International Coffee Organization	Global	Economic
International Cotton Institute	Global	Economic
International Exhibition Bureau	Global	Economic
International Finance Corporation	Global	Economic
International Monetary Fund	Global	Economic
International Wheat Council	Global	Economic
Latin American Free Trade Association	Regional	Economic
League of Arab States	Regional	Multipurpose
Nordic Council	Regional	Multipurpose
North Atlantic Treaty Organization	Regional	Military
Organization of American States	Regional	Multipurpose
Pan American Health Organization	Regional	Social
Southeast Asia Treaty Organization	Regional	Military
United Nations	Global	Multipurpose
UN Food and Agricultural Organization	Global	Social
UNESCO	Global	Social
Warsaw Treaty Organization	Regional	Military
World Health Organization	Global	Social

*Figure 3.4 Forty intergovernmental organizations classified by scope of interest and purpose**

* Figure from Coplin (1971, p. 165).

	Attacker Holds Back						Attacker Presses On — Defender Does Not Fight								Defender Fights		
	Iran	Turkey	Berlin	Egypt	Quemoy—Matsu	Cuba	Ethiopia	Austria	Czechoslovakia (1938)	Albania	Czechoslovakia (1939)	Rumania	Guatemala	Hungary	Poland	South Korea	North Korea
Pawn 20% + of Defender's Population	*						×	×			×	×			×		
Pawn 5% + of Defender's G.N.P.								×	×		×	×			×		
Formal Commitment Prior to Crisis	?	×			?	?	?	×	×	?	×	×		?	×		×
Defender Has Strategic Superiority	×	×	×		×		×	×	×	×	?			?	×		
Defender Has Local Superiority							×	×	?	?						?	?
Defender is Dictatorship				×	×		*							×			×
Pawn–Defender Military Cooperation	×	×	×	×	×	×			×		×	×	×		×	×	×
Pawn–Defender Political Interdependence	×	×	×	×								×	×		×	×	
Pawn–Defender Economic Interdependence	*	×	×	×	×	×	*									×	×

Key: × Factor present
? Ambiguous or doubtful
* Factor present for one defender

Figure 3.5 Presence or abuse of various factors alleged to make deterrent threats credible*

* Figure from Russett (1963).

global or regional (hence, the categories are mutually exclusive) and it *cannot* be something else (hence, the categories are exhaustive).

Similarly, consider a comparative study of deterrence by Bruce Russett (1963). First, he identifies the range of factors that many believe are related to successful deterrence. Then he examines these factors with respect to seventeen historical cases. As Figure 3 5 indicates, each factor is measured by means of a non-numerical symbol. Presence is denoted (x); absence (blank), presence for one party (*), or residual categories labeled "ambiguous or doubtful" are denoted by (?).

It is important to note, however, that a nominal value or symbol tells us nothing about the degrees of a trait or quality that we are measuring. It only tells us whether the trait is present or absent. Thus, Coplin's scope measure would not permit us to differentiate between larger regional groupings such as NATO and smaller groupings such as the Danube Commission. Russett's scheme will not give us any information on the relative strength of formal commitments, say, between Korea and Poland. In order to know something about degrees or qualities we must turn to a second kind of qualitative measurement, *ordinal scaling.*

Ordinal scaling permits us to make "more or less" statements about concrete or analytical categories that are exhaustive and mutually exclusive. An ordinal value is characterized by gross variations in magnitude or degree where the categories into which objects are placed are not only different from each other but where they also have some relation to each other. Hence, the use of ordinal scales not only enables us to say that an object or entity belongs in one or another category, but also that one category is larger, more difficult, higher, more preferred, etc., than another. In other words, where nominal scales only allow us to measure an object according to its place in some equivalent categories, an ordinal scale incorporates both the idea of equivalence and the notion of ranking or order among the categories.

Take, for example, the examination of guerilla wars since 1945 by Mueller (1969) where he attempts to assess the degree of outside assistance that was available to both the incumbents and the guerrillas. As Figure 3.6 shows, Mueller is able to measure much more than the presence or absence of outside support. Indeed, it may be inferred from Figure 3.6 that the level of outside support can be ranked and numbered according to a five-point ordinal scale: (1) none, (2) little, (3) considerable, (4) great, and (5) very great. Indeed, any numbers could be assigned so long as the order in ranks is preserved. The number 2 could designate none, the

Location	Period	Winner	Outside Support	
			Incumbent	Guerrillas
China	46–49	G	Great	None
Indonesia	45–49	G	Considerable	None
Indochina	45–54	G	Great	Considerable
Philippines	46–54	I	Great	None
Malaya	48–60	I	Great	None
Tibet	59–	I	Great	Little
So. Vietnam	58–	?	Very great	Great
Greece	46–49	I	Great	Great
Cyprus	54–59	G ?	Great	Considerable
Algeria	54–62	G	Great	Great
Israel	45–49	G	Great	Great
Iraq	61–66	G ?	Great	Little
Yemen	62–	?	Great	Great
Kenya	52–56	I	Great	None
Congo	64–65	I	Great	Great
Angola	61–	I	Great	Great
Colombia	48–58	I	Great	Little
Cuba	56–59	G	Great	Considerable
Venezuela	59–66	I	Great	Great
Guatemala	63–	?	Great	Considerable
Burma	48–50	I	Considerable	None
No. Korea	50–53	?	Great	Great
So. Korea	50–53	I	Great	None
Laos	60–62	G	Great	Great
Hungary	56–	I	Great	None

Figure 3.6   Guerrilla wars since 1945*

* John E. Mueller, *Approaches to Measurement in International Relations: A Non-Evangelical Survey,* © 1969, p. 8. Reprinted by permission of Prentice-Hall, Inc., Englewood Cliffs, New Jersey.

number 18 could designate little, and so on. In other words, an ordinal scale tells us nothing about the distance or intervals between the ranks or categories; it only tells us that one category is greater than or less than another.

Another example would be to rank order nations according to their authoritarian style—highly authoritarian, moderately authoritarian, etc., but because of the complexity of the authoritarianism concept and its measurement, we probably will not be able to say how much more authoritarian the top ranked nation is in comparison to the second ranked nation, and so on. Once again, ordinal values simply permit us to say that something is more or less than something else in another category.

For a more familiar example, consider the Gallup poll interviewer's attempt to discover the party identification of respondents. He or she will ask the respondents whether they consider themselves a Democrat or a Republican. Then the interviewer will follow up (or probe) by asking whether the respondents consider themselves a "strong" or "weak" partisan identifier. Consequently, the pollster generates five ranks of partisans: strong Democrats, weak Democrats, strong Republicans, weak Republicans, and a residual rank of Independents who identify with neither party. However, with respect to the variable partisan identification, the interviewer can only say that respondents were *more* or *less* (e.g., *strong* or *weak*) Democrats or Republicans. He or she can say nothing about the intervals (or distance) between the ranks. This latter involves a quantitative assessment.

Quantitative measurements are more difficult for social scientists to obtain but the attempt to construct valid quantitative measures promises (and in some instances has given) substantial payoffs for social analysis. The *interval scale* is a form of quantitative measurement which permits statements that reveal the distance (or intervals) between qualities or characteristics that are observed. An interval value is therefore characterized by measurement on a continuous scale that permits us to estimate the magnitude of the difference or distance between any two characteristics or observations of it. Because interval scales involve common and constant units of measurement, they can be added and subtracted.

For example, we can talk about domestic political instability (operationally defined as the annual frequency of assassinations) in ordinal terms simply by recording the frequencies of assassinations on a numbered scale or continuum, dividing the continuum in two (i.e.. dochotomize) and stipulating that those nations on one side of the dividing line are *more* stable than nations on the other side. Or we might say that nations on one side are stable; those on the other are unstable. Obviously, this is a very gross or imprecise ordinal measurement.

By contrast, if the absolute frequency of assassinations is maintained intact along with each nation's location on the continuum, we can make an interval statement because we can say that a nation with twenty annual assassinations stands in the same relation to a nation with ten annual assassinations as a nation with forty assassinations stands in relation to a nation with twenty. That is, with interval scales we not only have equivalences and relationships among the categories (as with nominal and ordinal scales respectively), but we also can know the distance between any two intervals. We *cannot* say that a polity with forty assassinations is four times more unstable than one with ten. We can, however, say that intervals between ten and twenty and between twenty and forty bear some functional relationship to the difference between the two magnitudes. That is, the interval ten (between ten and twenty above) and the interval twenty (between twenty and forty above) are meaningfully related in an empirical sense.

Recall the information read about attaching numbers to ordinal scales. It was said that the numbers used were inconsequential *as long as the rank order was preserved*. So it makes no difference whether "little," "great," and "very great" are denoted by 1-2-3 or by 5-30-80 as long as the order is preserved.[20] Interval scales, by contrast, denote empirical meaning to the intervals between the numbers. In the example above, 1-2-3 would mean that "very great" involved as much outside support beyond "great" as "great" involved beyond "little." Or, 5-30-80 would mean that "very great" involved twice as much outside support in relation to "great" (interval = 50) as "great" involved in relation to "little" (interval = 25). *Hence, the interval scale involves a common unit of measurement, the absence of an empirically meaningful zero point, and the ability to say that one object or entity has more or less of a given property or characteristic and how many units more or less.*[21]

Finally, we have *ratio scales* that include all the measurements allowed by the interval scale (adding and substracting distance, time, etc.), plus they allow us to multiply and divide. This is possible because, unlike the interval scale, *the ratio scale assumes a non-arbitrary zero point*; that is, a zero that does have empirical meaning (where a zero means that the object being measured has "none" of the characteristic being measured). Therefore, ratio scales tell us not only the absolute magnitude of intervals between any two objects on it (which we also get from the interval scale), but also the relative magnitude of differences between the objects. So, if we return to our political stability example, and assume that "no observed assassinations" means a complete absence of (or "zero") instability, then we can say that a nation with twenty annual assassinations is not only eighteen units more unstable than a nation with two, but that it is also ten times more unstable. A more realistic example might be reflected in a measure of war proneness that is operationalized by counting the number of wars a nation has been involved in since 1815. Here, a score of zero would be meaningful empirically because we could say that a nation involved in twenty wars has been four times more prone to war than another nation involved in only five wars. Similarly, if we are measuring the number of IGO's to which a nation belongs or the number of years of national independence, then we have additional examples of ratio scales, for in both cases "zero" is non-arbitrary, i.e., it is meaningful.

Thus, qualitative and quantitative measurements are ways of assigning numbers or values to objects or observations. To summarize, there are four levels of measurement: nominal, ordinal, interval, and ratio. Each is a higher level of measurement containing the properties of each lower level. One should be clear about the characteristics and properties of each level and should be careful to use the appropriate measurement level on the phenomena, objects, or entities under examination. As a footnote to this discussion of measurement, we can now note that *variables* can be classified according to levels of measurement. Recall from chapter 1 that we classified variables according to their *function* in a proposition. This mode of classification yielded three kinds of variables: the independent variable, the dependent variable, and the intervening variable. Classified according to levels of measurement, we obtain four kinds of variables that tell us about the qualities of that to which they refer (the *referent* of the variable).

1. *Nominal variables* suggest the presence or absence of a concrete or analytical property, such as "parliamentary system" or "war."

2. *Ordinal variables* suggest greater or lesser degrees of a property, such as "authoritarianism" or "outside support."

3. *Interval variables* suggest identifiable time or distance intervals between properties, such as the "level" of political instability.

4. *Ratio variables* suggest identifiable time or distance intervals between properties *plus* an identifiable, non-arbitrary zero point, such as "war proneness" measured by the number of wars a nation has been involved in.

In cross-national research, we frequently have to be satisfied with lower levels of measurement. That is, it is often not possible to obtain ratio and interval data. Therefore, we have to work with ordinal and nominal data, a condition that has major implications on the kinds of statistical analysis we are able to perform on our data. Or, even when we have what appear to be interval or ratio measures, the quality of the data may suggest to the cautious student that the data be collapsed, i.e., reduce the level of measurement to a lower level scale. For example, the *World Handbook of Political and Social Indicators* presents many data that appear to have interval and even ratio qualities. Yet, as the authors themselves point out, source error and measurement error are often so high (for example, GNP estimates may contain error ± 20 percent) that prudent use may suggest collapsing the interval level measures into ordinal categories such as "high," "medium," and "low."

Consider the following example. Using factor analytic techniques on ratio scale data, Taylor (1968) generated five major dimensions describing national attributes. Nations are then identified in relation to each factor and the resulting factor loadings are then collapsed into ordinal level measures (using a 5-point scale) to denote each nation's value in relation to each of the five factors (shown in Figure 3.7).

Another contribution to the cross-national political data base is found in the *Cross-Polity Survey*. Here the authors present profiles of the political characteristics of nations in nominal-ordinal categories only. For example, nations are ranked by population according to the categories "very large" (100 million and above), "large" (17–99.9 million), "medium" (6–16.9 million), and "small" (under 6 million). So, while we aspire to developing higher order measurements (interval or ratio), we frequently are forced by the crudeness of our measurement techniques and/or by scholarly and scientific caution to cast our measurements at the nominal or ordinal levels.

This chapter has focused upon the third basic step in the research process—procedures and problems associated with the measurement of your data: questions of reliability and validity, units of analysis, and levels of measurement. Once these questions have been solved, the researcher moves into the actual collecting of the data, the storing of the data, and the subsequent retrieving of this information.

Country	Component				
	I	II	III	IV	V
	Level of development	Size of country	Population density Agricultural intensity	Catholic, Latin American	Tempo of development
Japan	4	3	5	2	4
Korea	2	3	5	3	5
Taiwan	2	3	5	3	5
Philippines	2	4	4	5	4
Thailand	2	4	3	2	3
Malayan Fed.	2	4	4	3	4
Indonesia	1	4	4	1	1
Burma	2	4	3	1	2
India	1	5	4	1	3
Ceylon	3	2	4	3	4
Pakistan	1	5	5	2	4
Israel	4	3	3	3	5
Turkey	2	4	3	3	3
Cyprus	3	2	3	2	3
United Arab Rep.	2	3	4	3	4
Morocco	2	4	3	3	3
Nigeria	1	4	4	2	2
Congo (Leo.)	1	4	2	2	1
South Africa	3	3	2	3	3
Mauritius	3	2	4	4	4
Canada	4	5	2	4	4
United States	5	5	4	5	1
Mexico	2	4	2	3	4
Guatemala	2	3	3	4	3
Honduras	2	3	2	4	3
El Salvador	2	3	3	4	3
Nicaragua	2	3	2	4	3
Costa Rica	3	3	2	5	4
Panama	3	3	2	4	4
Cuba	3	3	3	4	3
Jamaica	3	1	3	4	3
Dominican Rep.	3	2	2	5	3
Puerto Rico	3	4	4	5	3
Columbia	3	4	2	4	3
Venezuela	3	3	1	4	4
Trinidad-Tobago	3	1	3	3	5
Cuyana	3	3	2	3	4
Brazil	3	4	1	4	4
Bolivia	2	3	2	3	2
Paraguay	2	3	3	4	3
Argentina	3	4	2	3	3
Chile	3	3	1	3	3
Peru	3	3	1	3	3
Ecuador	2	3	2	4	3
Iceland	4	3	1	2	4
Denmark	4	3	4	3	3
Norway	4	2	3	2	3
Sweden	5	3	3	2	2
Finland	4	3	3	2	2
Soviet Union	4	5	2	2	4
Poland	3	2	3	3	2
East Germany	4	2	4	1	2
Czechoslovakia	4	2	3	3	2
Hungary	3	2	3	2	2
Rumania	3	3	3	2	2
Bulgaria	3	2	3	2	2
Greece	3	3	3	2	2
Yugoslavia	3	3	3	2	3
Italy	3	2	3	3	2
Austria	4	2	3	3	2
Switzerland	4	2	4	3	3
West Germany	5	3	4	3	3

(continued)

Country	Component				
	I	II	III	IV	V
			Population density	Catholic,	
	Level of development	Size of country	Agricultural intensity	Latin American	Tempo of development
France	4	4	3	3	2
Luxembourg	4	1	3	2	1
Belgium	4	1	4	4	2
Netherlands	4	2	4	3	3
United Kingdom	5	3	4	3	3
Ireland	3	2	3	3	2
Portugal	3	2	3	3	1
Spain	3	2	3	3	3
Malta	3	1	5	4	4
Australia	5	4	1	1	5
New Zealand	4	4	2	3	4

Figure 3.7   *Country scale points on each component**

* Charles Lewis Taylor (ed.), *Aggregate Data Analysis: Political and Social Indicators in Cross-National Research*, © 1968 by Mouton & Co. and International Social Science Council.

EXERCISES

1   Give an example of a variable for each of the following levels of analysis.

global _____

regional _____

national _____

group _____

individual _____

intra-psychic _____

2   For the following hypotheses, list the object and subject units of analysis.

A   There is a high correlation between decision-makers' perceptions of hostility and the level of violence of their country's foreign policy actions.

subject unit _____

object unit _____

B   The more economically developed a nation, the greater its level of international activity.

subject unit _____

object unit _____

C   Socially progressive groups within a nation result in more war-like behavior by the nation than do those with traditional social groupings.

subject unit _____

object unit _____

D   The greater the amount of status discrepancy in the international system, the greater the level of international conflict.

subject unit _____

object unit _____

3   For each of the four hypotheses in question 2, indicate whether there is a structural or contextual effect in operation.

A _____   C _____

B _____   D _____

4   Consider the measurement of the concept "pro-United States attitude."
Construct situations where (A) reliability and (B) validity have been violated.

A   Reliability:

B   Validity:

5   Consider the variable "extent to which the regime is Communist." Construct
three sets of categories for this variable such that they represent nominal,
ordinal, and interval scales respectively.

A   Nominal:

B   Ordinal:

C   Interval:

6   Comment briefly on the measurement problems involved in a research design
in which the offensive military orientation of a nation was operationalized by
reference to total defense expenditures as a percent of GNP. Assume the data
were obtained by writing to national defense ministries.

7   Using GNP per capita, generate two measures of a nation's economic
development using an ordinal and then an interval scale.

8   Identify the scales used to measure the following variables.

_____A   The measurement of a nation's support for the international
system by referencing whether the nation belongs to the
UN or not.

_____B   The measurement of a nation's support for the international
system by referencing the year it joined the UN.

_____C   The measurement of a nation's support for the international
system by referencing the period in the organization's
existence that the country joined (e.g., 1945–50 =
period 1; 1951–55 = period 2; etc.)

_____D   The measurement of a nation's support for the international
system by referencing the total number of years it has been
a member of the UN.

NOTES

1. See the papers collected in two volumes by Zawodny (1966) on the role of "man in international relations" for examples of behavioral theories of international politics and foreign policy. The pages of the *Journal of Conflict Resolution* are also a useful source of this perspective.

2. Chapter 1 described this particular theoretical perspective as field theory. See, for example, Rummel (1966). See also the contributions of those noted in relation to systems theory—for example, Singer and Small (1968) or McClelland and Hoggard (1969). For a stimulating and well-written account of how these various perspectives or images are reflected in the thinking of philosophers and statesmen alike with respect to the causes of war and the conditions for peace, see Waltz (1959). Professor Waltz finds, for example, that some attribute war to the nature of man (e.g., St. Augustine, Martin Luther, Malthus, Bismarck, Reinhold Niebuhr, or the modern ethologists); others attribute war to social origins—the nature of society (e.g., Plate, Adam Smith, Jeremy Bentham, J. S. Mill, Woodrow Wilson, and most revolutionary doctrines); still others attribute war to the anarchic nature of the nation-state system itself (e.g., Thucydides, Machiavelli, Thomas Hobbes, Rousseau, Alexander Hamilton, Woodrow Wilson, Henry Kissinger, and most modern "strategy theorists," and "balance of power" proponents).

3. The Stanford Studies are referenced in the bibliography under North, et al. (1963). For the contrast, see North and Choucri (1968).

4. The levels of analysis issue was raised most explicitly in the context of research in international relations by J. David Singer (1961). The distinction between "action" analysis (or foreign policy) and "interaction" analysis (or international relations) also served as the major organizing criterion for the readings collected by James N. Rosenau and published by The Free Press (1961; 1969).

5. Figure 3.1 is modified from Eulau (1962, p. 15).

6. See, for example, the Stanford Studies on the outbreak of World War I cited in note 3 above. Or, see Singer's analysis of Soviet and American attitudes toward arms control and other foreign policy issues based on a content analysis of "elite publications" such as editorials from the *New York Times* and *Pravda* or articles from journals—e.g., the Soviet's *International Affairs* or the American's *Foreign Affairs* (Singer, 1964).

7. See, for example, the comparative study of the foreign policy process in presidential and parliamentary systems (Waltz, 1967) or the investigation of "summitry" as a diplomatic technique among leaders of different political blocs or among leaders with different international status or rank (Galtung, 1964).

8. For example, see Galtung (1967, Part One), Lazarsfeld and Menzel (1961), Selvin and Hagstrom (1963), Blau (1960), and Davis et al. (1961).

9. See East and Gregg (1967) for an example of a study that examines this question.

10. These measurements would, in this example, be treated as contextual effects. East and Gregg's contextual variables included foreign mail, technical assistance received, the number of bordering nations, etc.

11. These measurements would be considered structural effects. East and Gregg's structural variables included press censorship, telephones per capita, ethnic homogeneity, etc.

12. This is, indeed, one reason why the "man of wisdom" and the "arm chair theorist" frequently reject what they call the simplistic designs of his more systematical empirical bete noire. Although he would not use these terms, he knows that behavior—whether of nations or individuals—is always complicated and influenced by the interaction among both structural and contextual effects. However, neither the intuitionist nor the social scientist could handle these complex relationships with much rigor—certainly not the intuitionist owing to the inherent

limitations of human thought processing and not the social scientist owing to his often inadequate training, the absence of data (i.e., measurements), and overly-simple theories. However, things are rapidly beginning to change in this regard. Although the human brain has not evolved dramatically over the past twenty years, the social scientist does have better training, more data, and better social theory. These enhanced analytical capacities are beginning to be reflected in the quality theory and research in international politics and foreign policy.

13. In fact, this describes what was done by Rosenau (1966; 1970). For the background on which the Rosenau essay is based, see Cattell (1949), Rummel (1966), and Sawyer (1967).

14. See Deutsch and Edinger (1959) and Rosenau (1966).

15. Rosenau (1966, p. 47).

16. For elaboration, see Dogan and Rokkan (1969) and Lasswell (1963). For examples, refer back to notes 9, 10, and 11.

17. Singer (1968, p. 1). Reflect for a moment on the investigative norms, procedures, and other rules of evidence that are followed by the legal profession (say, Ralph Nader), the historian (say, Arthur Schlesinger), the journalist (say, Jack Anderson), or the investigative commentator (say Truman Capote). Then consider some other professions and the rules of evidence they use and are constrained by—e.g., auditors, accreditors, social workers, teachers, intelligence analysts, and so on. The norms of science are demanding with respect to the requirements that inferences be based on evidence that is both public and repeatable.

18. See North, et al. (1963).

19. For a useful inventory of the sources of error in experimental and quasi-experimental designs, see Campbell and Stanley (1963).

20. This is something of an overstatement. The results of analysis will be affected by whether one uses 1-2-3 or 5-30-80. The decision regarding the numerical values that should be attached to an ordinal scale depends on the analyst's substance knowledge, his or her best judgment regarding the importance of belonging to one rank or another. The judgment used will, of course, be arbitrary. But the rule of thumb that assigns 1-2-3 is just an arbitrary. So if you have some substantive reasons to assign 1-3-5 or 1-10-25 to ordinal categories, you should do it. On this point, see Tufte (1969).

21. A good example of an interval scale is the Georgian Calender where the birth of Christ stands as an arbitrary zero point. Another is the centigrade or Fahrenheit scale for measuring temperature where the difference between the two scales serves well to illustrate the arbitrary nature of the zero point (e.g., water freezes at $0°$ centigrade and at $32°$ F). Yet the intervals between the points on each scale are meaningful empirically—evidenced by the fact that the two scales can be functionally related by using the formula $F = 9/5 \ C + 32$. Using the distance between freezing and boiling as the range of the scale, each degree of $C = 1/100$ of the distance (between $0°$ and $100°$) and each degree of $F = 1/180$ of the distance (between $32°$ and $212°$).

Chapter Four

DATA COLLECTION, STORAGE, AND RETRIEVAL

After a data-making technique has been selected, it is necessary to collect and store the data in a systematic manner. This fourth basic research step involves, in addition to the steps outlined earlier, the processing of data prior to punching them on IBM cards for storage. Chapter 4 is addressed to three issues: (1) basic rules for data collection, (2) the format and use of an IBM card, and (3) the use of code manuals to transfer data to storage decks and to retrieve information for subsequent analysis.

DATA COLLECTION

Whenever data are processed several basic rules should be followed. First, if data are to be transferred from one form to another (for example, from a UN statistical source to an IBM code sheet), a quality control procedure should be instituted. Every transfer of a single digit from one page to another involves the possibility of error. For example, GNP expressed in millions of U.S. dollars for 116 nations in 1963 contains over 400 possible sources of error in the transfer of data from the source to the code sheet. The second basic rule in quality control procedures is that some person other than the original coder should check the coding by recoding a sample of the original material. This prevents systematic error that may find its way into the final analysis.[1]

There are three basic data processing steps: coding, transferring, and punching. Their routines are outlined as follows (Burgess and Peterson, 1969); manifest check points are denoted by an asterisk.

Processing Routines

A   *Coding*
  1. Code from original source onto temporary "transfer" code sheets, if required by logistics or computations.
  2. Perform all necessary computations on the data (e.g., calculate proportions, ratios, percentages, etc.).

B   *Transferring*
  1. Transfer data—or in the case of prior coding requirements (as in A.1 and/or A.2)—relocate data on "working" code sheets.

*2. Check original against working code sheets. *Note:* All coder reliability checks are to be undertaken by someone other than the original coder.

*3. Check all computations (i.e., recalculate all variables for all nations) and compare against working code sheets.

4. Transfer data from working code sheets onto IBM code sheets using the IRA identification sequence.

*5. Check IBM code sheets against working code sheets.

C *Punching*

1. Punch cards from IBM code sheets.

*2. List cards and check listings against IBM code sheets.

3. Repunch errors.

*4. Run new listing and check against original source.

5. Duplicate decks (1 master and 3 copies) and run three listings for archival records.

Steps A.1, A.2, and B.1 are required because most statistical sources are found in library reference rooms and are often not available to be checked out. Therefore it is often necessary to maintain two code sheets, transfer and working, in a procedure that permits the transfer of data from the source to the "working" code sheets. Transfer code sheets are generally legal size sheets of paper on which the variable name and country ID number are placed. Transfer code sheets are also used whenever any computations must be performed prior to entering the data records.

Steps B.2, B.3, B.5, C.2, and C.4 are self-explanatory in that they involve checking previously completed work. Step C.4 is perhaps the single most important in the data processing stage. The check of the data deck listing against the original source is the final opportunity to catch and correct coding errors. For this reason, two people (other than the original coders) check the listing against the original source independently. Moreover, it is important in this stage to ensure that those checking the listing against the original list of nations, should take the first nation in the original source and then check it against the listing of the data deck. This procedure corrects for the possibility that nation may have been overlooked in the original coding. If this kind of error has occurred, a check *from* the listing *to* the source would not correct it.

A number of standard procedures are applicable to all coding and collection of data:

1. Always write your initials on each coding form that you use. If subsequent problems arise, you will know who the original coder was.

2. Always take care to write legibly. To distinguish certain ambiguous symbols in the English alphanumeric system, the following rules apply:
    a. To distinguish 2 and Z, write the Z with a slash (Ƶ).
    b. To distinguish 1 and 7, write the 7 with a slash (7̸).
    c. To distinguish the letter O from zero, all letter O's should be written with a slash (Ø).
    d. Be very careful to distinguish between 4 and 9.

3. Any special or unusual coding decisions or circumstances should be noted clearly on the appropriate space on the coding form. Also any qualifications about the data mentioned in the source should be noted. For example, the source may indicate the value for a certain nation on a certain variable is an

estimate or is based on a secondary source. Such information must always be included on the coding form.

4. The source of the data should be identified on each coding form.

5. The measurement units used by the source reporting the data must be noted. For example, monetary units are often used as the report-in values. It should be noted if these units are dollars, rubles, kroner, francs, etc.

6. The definition of the variable, the basis on which the data are reported by the source, should be provided verbatim (although this may be done on a form other than the coding form).

7. The ID number for the analytic unit (nation, interview respondent, simulation participant, etc.) must be included on every collection form.

8. Code forms should be designed to retain maximum flexibility so that all potentially relevant data will be available at a later date if so desired.[2]

Figure 4.1 represents a code sheet for administrative, executive and managerial workers for one case, the United Kingdom. The sheet contains data for three variables: the raw number of workers, workers as a percentage of the economically active population, and the number of personnel per diplomat.

Step B.4 in data processing begins the procedure whereby the raw data are transferred to IBM cards prior to the manipulation and analysis stages of the research. The crucial point to be mentioned here is that a standardized format for data storage must be employed. By using a standardized format the researcher is able to retain for all variables such factors as variable source, year of source publication, year of data, and other desired information. An elaboration of the IRA standard identification sequence is found in the appendix.

The final step, C.5, is undertaken to prevent possible loss of data. Duplicate decks and listings should be stored in different places to minimize possibilities for such loss. If decks are lost, it is important to remember that the process will have to be repeated, a process that is very costly.

Although this particular outline for data processing is very rigid and designed for projects of a larger scale in which a large number of people are coding, the

---

CAPE DATA

NATION _____ United Kingdom _____ ID CODE _____ 111 _____

SOURCE: __ Yearbook of Labor Statistics, 1968 __ YEAR OF SOURCE __ 1968 __

YEAR OF DATA _____ 66 _____

ADMINISTRATIVE, EXECUTIVE AND MANAGERIAL WORKERS

__ 765,830 __   3.1
NUMBER   As % ECONOMICALLY ACTIVE POP.

                        __ 546 __
                ADMINISTRATIVE PERSONNEL
                    PER DIPLOMAT

                            CODER'S INITIALS __ JEH __

NOTES:

Figure 4.1 Sample code sheet

principles on which it is based apply to smaller projects. Regardless of the scope and size of a project, when aggregate data are being processed by a group, it is always advisable to institute rigid quality control procedures such as those described, particularly when the sample (or population) size is small. The researcher cannot control source error, but attention to the social situation in which coding is carried out, to monitoring routines, coder training, eyeballing data listings, double coding of all data, checking marginal distributions and other quality control routines, can prevent additional error resulting from otherwise loose and ad hoc data processing techniques.

THE IBM PUNCH CARD

The punch cards are used to store data, to manipulate data mechanically or electronically, to transfer data to computer tape, and to facilitate the statistical analyses of the data in order to develop conclusions with respect to the proposition under investigation. The benefits of using punch cards as a data handling medium are speed, convenience, neatness, accuracy, permanency, flexibility, and reproducibility.[3]

These benefits can be demonstrated by an example of a survey of foreign policy elites. If the respondents' answers to the questionnaires were stored in the form in which they were recorded, they would be hard to duplicate and would require considerable time to analyze on a question-by-question basis. The same mass of data could cheaply and efficiently be stored on machine readable Hollerith cards (the generic name for IBM cards). One 15″ × 7½″ box of cards has the capacity to store over 150,000 units of information and would store the total information obtained from most questionnaires.

An example of a standard punch card is provided in Figure 4.2. A punch card contains 80 columns and 12 punching positions or rows. Data are arranged in fields. If the number "one" in the first column represents a unit of data, it would be called a "one-column field." In Figure 4.2, the alpha representation "ABC" in columns eleven through thirteen and the number "567" in columns 6 through 8 each signify three-column fields. Similarly, in the student raw data deck found in the appendix, each of the first 72 columns represent single-column fields (72 variables), and columns 74–76 and 78–80 are three-column fields signifying the alpha and numeric code of the specified nation respectively. Figure 4.3 reveals the IBM card for the United States from this data set.

One other characteristic of a punch card is important. The top edge is called the twelve edge (for row 12) and the bottom edge is called a nine edge (for row 9). Because much of the auxiliary equipment (such as the countersorter and the lister, both of which will be described later) instructs the user to place the cards in the machine with a specific edge facing the card feeder, it is important to learn the names of the edges.

DATA MATRIX

Data must be placed on punch cards in a systematic and uniform style. The investigator must be able to tell which columns contain which variables and what the numerical codes mean. Research operations can be conveniently characterized by

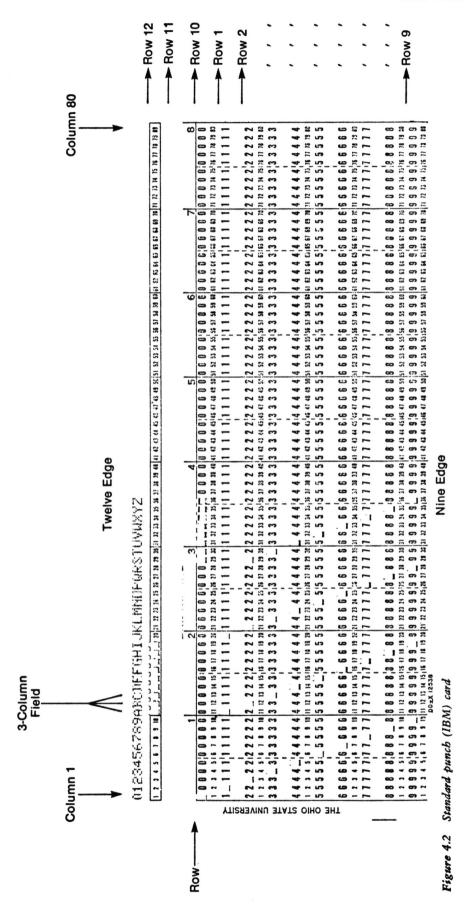

Figure 4.2   Standard punch (IBM) card

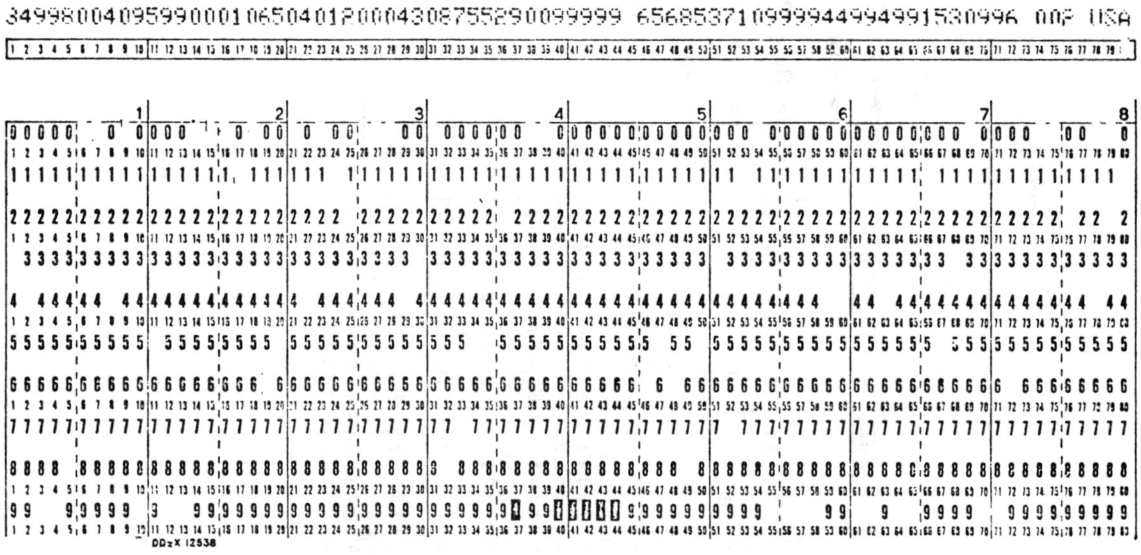

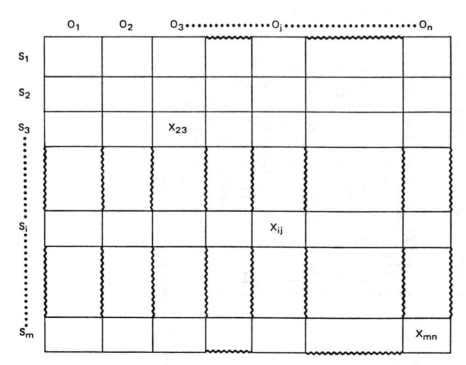

Figure 4.3 *Representation of fields on IBM card*

reference to the data matrix. In the data matrix reproduced in Figure 4.4, we can examine variables, cases, and variable-case combinations. Using a modified notation system from Galtung,[4] we let S = the case, subject, or the unit of analysis (e.g., a nation); let O = the observation, variable, condition, stimulus, or factor in which we are interested (e.g., GNP, defense expenditures, or population); let i represent rows; and let j represent columns. Thus for every S_i and O_j we find ourselves in a cell that we identify as X_{ij} which equals the specific value of the variable O_j for the case S_i.

Figure 4.4 *The data matrix*

The data matrix thus yields three important principles of data collection.

1. The principle of comparability. For every case S we have a value for the variable O. This value, expressed in the data matrix above as X_{23}, X_{ij}, and X_{mn}, means that all cases can be compared with each other with respect to the variable O.
2. The principle of classification. For each cell of R value, the data matrix says there can be one and only one O and one and only one S. Thus, X is exhaustive and mutually exclusive.
3. The principle of completeness. This principle reminds us that we are to have no empty cells in any mxn data matrix (where m and n define the dimensions of the matrix in terms of cases and variables). That is, we are to avoid missing data. This rule is sometimes hard to follow, particularly in cross-national research. It means we should have data on all cases and on all variables. We can reduce the number of empty cells by the process of ***matrix reduction***, where we eliminate cases and/or variables until the number of empty cells is minimized. Or, alternatively, we can try to develop procedures for estimating missing data. For example, a number of statistical techniques—such as "regression estimates"—are sometimes used. The ***expert panel*** is also used to generate estimates for missing data, a method used by Banks and Textor (1963) in the *Cross-Polity Survey* noted in chapter 2.

It is important to understand the characteristics of the data matrix because punch card formats expressed in code manuals typically follow these principles. Each card in a deck of cards represents a *case* (S) and each column or field on each card represents a ***variable*** (O). Thus, the data matrix and the corresponding punch card formats permit comparison between variables on single cases, or more typically, between cases on single variables. Figure 4.5 reveals the printed top line of the IBM cards for the first ten countries (one country per card) of the student raw data deck. These include information on the seventy-two variables in the deck (blanks signifying missing data) for the United States, Canada, Cuba, Haiti, Dominican Republic, Jamaica, Trinidad and Tobago, Mexico, Guatemala, and Honduras.

CODE MANUALS

The code manual guides the transfer of substantive information (e.g., from a questionnaire or a UN statistical source) to punches in cards corresponding to a predetermined coding scheme. It permits the investigator to translate the machine readable punches in cards back into the substantively important information they represent. Code manuals are generally single pages and/or booklets that describe and locate the data found on the punch card. The code manual must be developed

```
34993004035990001065304012000043037552900999999 655553710999941994991590999 6 002 USA
04116005095190001044040000003101125210091524 514349072320022125141021145 020 CAN
00001030 100 3  9 23053250006609930109901413 33333 542000041016031246035 040 CUB
00000 709309039 000 2471611117613510  405020202328201  00 013015011011016 041 HAI
0000105000609 93  200 0831311117616 4500 10802  0333330182000021003011012014 042 DOM
0000103000351930 2012 53  11176199301 2370001010020  6400000000001100001 4 051 JAM
00002011 0 41930 1023073  22277299300 3360000 10040  480000000002011000015 052 TRI
11001050 711933300222332200054002151030614240454943061100000101302101 024 070 MEX
00001060 30303 910100731711166111250 307021202533333051000001004010000012 090 GUA
00000060070303391000 7312111176112250 103010101527230720000011012010000013 091 HON
```

Figure 4.5 ***Data matrix for ten countries***

prior to the actual coding operation because it conveys the coding decision rules—it tells the coders where to place data on the card and what codes to use.

Code manuals should be designed so that all relevant data will be on the card and arrayed in such a way as to give maximum flexibility. By flexibility, we mean that data should not be prematurely collapsed or censored. The data can be placed on the card in original form and reduced at a later point for analysis. For example, if one were to use values of GNP as a variable, these scores might be punched in the form of actual figures (600,000 million; i.e., an interval scale) and later, if necessary or desirable, they may be collapsed (1 = high, 2 = medium, 3 = low; i.e., collapsed from an interval to an ordinal scale).

An example of a code manual for data in *A Cross Polity Survey* is found in Figure 4.6. These data have already been collapsed. The left-hand column (labeled

Inter-University Consortium for Political Research		N = 115

Column Number	N	Code
01–05		Study Number (46135)
06–08		Country Code Number
09–18		Country Name
19–20		1. Areal Grouping
	2	01 Australasia
	5	02 Caribbean
	7	03 Central America
	28	04 Central and South Africa
	5	05 East Africa
	9	06 East Europe
	11	07 Middle East
	5	08 North Africa
	2	09 North America
	5	10 Scandinavia
	10	11 South America
	4	12 South Asia
	9	13 Southeast Asia
	13	14 West Europe
21		2. Land Size
	6	1 Very large (2 million square miles and above)
	26	2 Large (300,000 to 1.0 million square miles)
	36	3 Medium (75,000 to 299,000 square miles)
	47	4 Small (below 75,000 square miles)
22		3. Population Size
	4	1 Very large (100 million and above)
	23	2 Large (17 to 99.9 million)
	34	3 Medium (6 to 16.9 million)
	54	4 Small (under 6 million)
23		4. Population Density
	4	1 Very high (600 per square mile and above)
	13	2 High (300 to 599 per square mile)
	31	3 Medium (100 to 299 per square mile)
	67	4 Low (below 100 per square mile)
24		5. Population Growth Rate
	62	1 High (2 percent or above)
	48	2 Low (less than 2 percent)
	5	3 Unascertained

(continued)

Column Number	N			Code
25		6.		Level of Urbanization
	56		1	High (20 percent or more of population in cities of 20,000 or more and 12.5 percent or more of population in cities of 100,000 or more)
	49		2	Low (Less than 20 percent of population in cities of 20,000 or more and less than 12.5 percent of population in cities of 100,000 or more)
	7		8	Ambiguous
	3		9	Unascertained
26		7.		Agricultural Population as Percent of Total Population
	56		1	High (over 66 percent)
	33		2	Medium (34 to 66 percent)
	17		3	Low (16 to 33 percent)
	7		4	Very low (under 16 percent)
	2		9	Unascertained

Figure 4.6 *A partial representation of the code manual referencing* A Cross-Polity Survey

Column Number) tells which columns on the punch card contain which variables. For example, we know that column 21 contains Land Size and Column 22 is Population Size.

The next column in the code manual (labeled N) tells us the marginal distribution of cases, that is, the N or total number of nations that have been coded in a given category. We see from the marginals for column 21 and 22 respectively that six nations have been coded as having "very large" land areas and four nations have "very large" populations.

The last column in the code manual (labeled Code) describes the codes or punches in the card. A code of 3 (a "three punch") in column 21 means a nation has a "medium" land area and a code of 4 (a "four punch") in column 22 means it has a "small" population.

The first 26 columns of the cards from the *Cross Polity Survey* for the United States and the Upper Volta are reproduced in Figure 4.7. By referencing the code manual in columns 06–08 we would find that country 108 is the United States and 109 is the Upper Volta. In columns 19–20 we know the 09 code for the U.S. means it is located in North America and the 04 for the Upper Volta means it is located in Central and South Africa. In column 21, a 1 code means the U.S. is "very large" in land size and a 3 means the Upper Volta has a "medium" land area. In column 24, we note that a 2 code for the U.S. means it has a "low" population growth rate while the Upper Volta has a "high" population growth rate.

Looking at the code manual, you will notice special codes (7, 8, 9). A code 7 means the variable was unascertainable for the country. A code 8 means the country was ambiguous with respect to how it was to be coded. Code 9 means it was unascertained. These are standard codes and should be used for all cases when there is doubt as to how a variable should be coded. (If a two-column field were used to contain the data, the corresponding codes would be 77, 88, 99.)

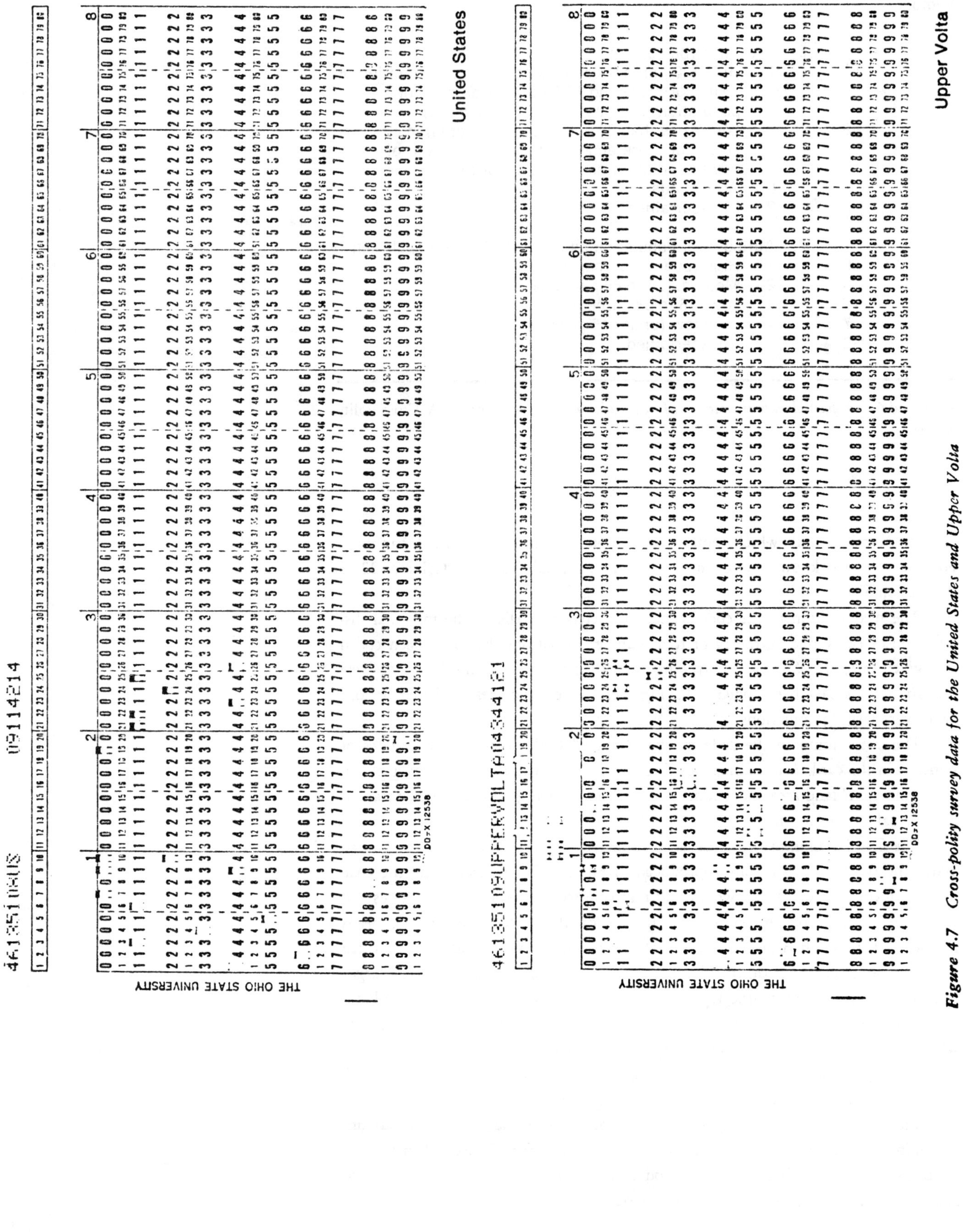

Figure 4.7 *Cross-polity survey data for the United States and Upper Volta*

Similarly, the Survey Research Center's *Manual for Coders* (1967) suggests the following coding conventions. Whenever possible and unless there are overriding reasons for doing otherwise, they should be followed.

Code	*Reference denoted*
1	"yes," "good," "positive," etc.
5	"no," "bad," "negative," etc.
7	"other" (a miscellaneous category for responses or information of low priority and/or not covered by other coding categories).
8	"don't know" (whenever a respondent cannot give an opinion because of ignorance or memory failure).
9	"not ascertained" (whenever a coder cannot categorize information because (a) it is missing, or (b) it appears to fit several categories).
0	"inapplicable" or "none."

In constructing code manuals, care must be taken not to use a special code which also reflects an actual score. For example, there may be a nation that has 77 percent of its labor force in agriculture; therefore a 77 code in the appropriate column could not be used to signify that the data were unascertainable.

Code manuals typically organize the data with a minimum of identification. Usually only case (e.g., a nation or respondent) identification numbers are used to indicate that case to which the data correspond. However, because punch cards are very inexpensive (less than 1/10 of a cent per card), it is possible to reduce the data (i.e., variable information) stored on any one card and to expand the amount of information about the case. For example, you will note in Figure 4.6 that the code manual for the *Cross-Polity Survey* includes an alphabetic representation (i.e., "U.S." and "Upper Volta") to supplement the numeric code (compare columns 06–08 and 09–18). This redundancy reduces the amount of variable information that can be stored on one card, but it greatly facilitates reading the cards and the subsequent printout.

Whatever format you decide to use in constructing your code manual, you should conform to the following general rules.

1. Make your format as flexible as possible. Allow yourself the freedom to add additional studies.

2. Do not collapse or censor your information prematurely.

3. Do not avoid multiple column fields. Punch cards are cheap!

4. Always make a duplicate data deck in case your original is lost or gets damaged by a machine.

5. Always make a copy of your code manual. If your code manual is lost or destroyed, your laboriously prepared data decks are useless.

6. Always produce a listing of your data. The printed list will serve as additional insurance in the event your data deck is lost or destroyed. Further, it will allow you to readily scan your data set for missing data, punching errors, or reproducing errors (which are not uncommon).

7. Do not bend, fold, spindle, or mutilate your data cards.

The appendix provides a good example of an extensive codebook, in this case for the 72-variable Student Data Deck.

UNIT RECORD EQUIPMENT

A student should become familiar with the peripheral computer equipment used for processing data manually. Detailed instruction on the use of such equipment is available at all university computation centers, so we will only briefly introduce the equipment and discuss the function performed by each unit. Operating instructions should be obtained from the installation at which the equipment will be used.

1. Keypunch. A keypunch is the unit used to punch and prepare the IBM card. Its use is like that of a typewriter, and its purpose is to transform alphabetic or numeric data into punches on the appropriate rows and columns of a punch card.

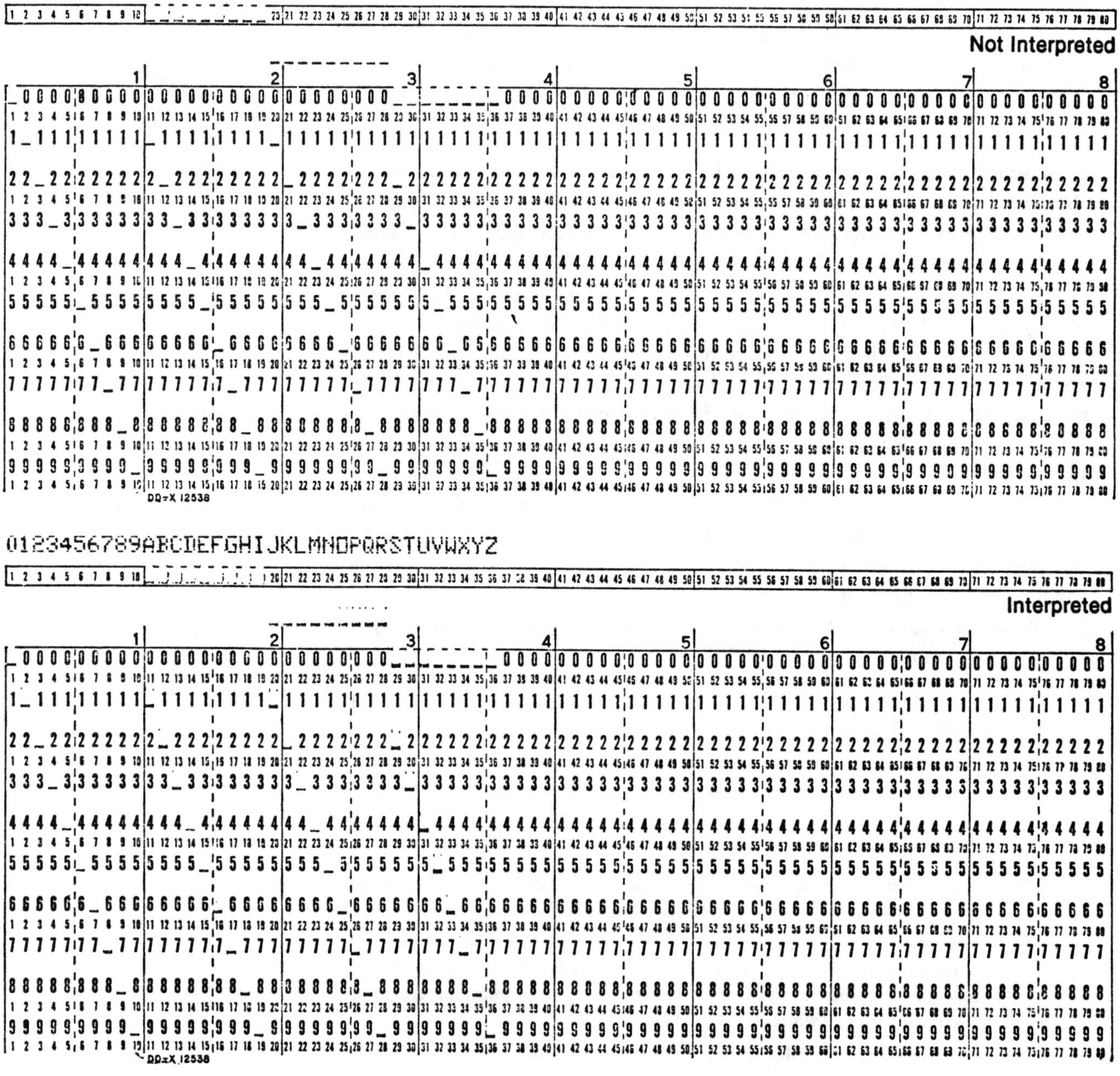

Figure 4.8   Interpreted and uninterpreted IBM cards

2. Interpreter. This unit will print across the top of the card all information stored in each column of the card as in Figure 4.8. This is useful when the IBM cards have been printed by the computer or the reproducer and the information on the card is not represented in print across the top of the card.

3. Lister. This unit will list on a page of paper all information contained on each card within a large data set. The lists of the data are sometimes useful. They allow the researcher to have immediate visual access to his or her data without thumbing through individual IBM cards. They also serve as a neat set of data records.

4. Reproducer. This unit will take a punch card and reproduce an exact copy of that card. Its usefulness is in the preparation of duplicate sets of data without re-punching all the previously prepared data. The machine also has the ability to reformat data, that is, to move information from one column on the original deck to another column on the duplicate deck.

5. Sorter. This unit allows you to sort your data deck by the information stored in each column. For example, if you had codes of 1, 2, 3, and 4 as responses to a question on a survey, all respondents coded 1 will be sorted into one pocket, all respondents coded 2 into another pocket, and so forth. If the sorter has a pocket counter attached to it (called a counter-sorter), frequency counts or histograms can be made as the counter records the number of respondents coded 1 falling into the #1 pocket, and the number of respondents coded 2 falling into the #2 pocket, etc. This machine is also useful in obtaining the marginal distributions and for building contingency tables and other bivariate analysis routines. The counter-sorter is also helpful if one has serialized data (where each respondent or case is numbered) and the cards have gotten out of sequence. By passing them through the counter-sorter, the deck can be reorganized into its original series.

Use of Counter-Sorter for Frequency Distributions

The counter-sorter is an extremely useful machine for ascertaining the frequency distribution of a variable, that is, the number of cases falling into each category (the substantive interpretation of which will be discussed in chapter 5). For example, consider variable 10, "Freedom of the Press," in the Student Raw Data Deck in the appendix of this book. Values for the 87 cases for which we have information range from 0 to 9. The researcher would take his or her data deck to a counter-sorter, set the dial on column 10, and run the cards through the machine. This process would sort the 116 nations into eleven bins or sets: ten representing the values of 0 to 9 respectively, and the eleventh signifying the remaining 29 cases of missing data. Cases for variable 10 would be distributed in the following manner:

Counter-Sorter Bin Number	Number of Cases
0	6
1	9
2	3
3	8
4	7
5	6
6	10
7	10
8	20
9	8
blank	29
Total	116

Use of Counter-Sorter for Contingency Tables

If the investigator were interested in determining how many of the highly urban-ized nations were also economically developed, he or she would want to construct a contingency table. A description of the use of contingency tables in associational analysis will be treated in detail later.[5] Our concern here is with the process of constructing such tables on a counter-sorter.

Assume that 25 nations (cards) have been coded with respect to their values on economic development (coded in column 26) and urbanization (coded in column 25), as in Figure 4.9. The researcher would set the counter-sorter on column 20, and run the cards through the machine. This process would sort the 25 nations into two sets: those that are highly urban (coded 1 in column 25) and those that have a low level of urbanization (coded 2 in column 25). After writing down these results and resetting the counter-sorter to sort on column 26, the analyst would take the group of nations that had been sorted as "highly urban" and re-sort this group alone on column 26. The result would again be two divisions: those that are developed and those that are underdeveloped. By looking at the frequencies on the counter (the number of cards in the #1 pocket and the number of cards in the #2 pocket), the researcher would be able to fill in the cells marked (a) and (b) in the contingency table, as shown in Figure 4.10. Repeating the process for all those

Case number/name	Col. 25	Col. 26
01 Australia	1	1
02 Brazil	1	1
03 Czechoslovakia	1	1
04 Ethiopia	2	2
05 France	1	1
06 Hungary	1	1
07 India	2	2
08 Indonesia	2	2
09 Iraq	2	1
10 Ivory Coast	2	2
11 Japan	1	1
12 Jordan	2	1
13 Mexico	1	1
14 Netherlands	1	1
15 Niger	2	2
16 Norway	1	1
17 Peru	2	1
18 Spain	2	1
19 Thailand	2	2
20 Uganda	2	2
21 USSR	1	1
22 UAR	2	1
23 UK	1	1
24 USA	1	1
25 Yugoslavia	1	2

Code:
Col. 25
    1 = urban
    2 = rural
Col. 26
    1 = developed
    2 = underdeveloped

Figure 4.9 Hypothetical distribution of data

	Developed (1 code in col. 25)	Underdeveloped (2 code in col. 26)	Total
High Urban (1 code in col. 25)	(a) 12	(b) 5	17
Low Urban (2 code in col. 25)	(c) 1	(d) 7	8
Total	13	12	25

Figure 4.10   A contingency table showing the relationship between urbanization and economic development

nations that were coded "less urban" (a 2 punch in column 25), the researcher would then find out which of these nations had a high degree of development or low degree of development and would be able to fill in cells (c) and (d) of the contingency table.

If there are more than 200 observations (nations in this case) to be sorted, it probably will be advisable to use a computer to assist the analysis because the use of a counter-sorter is a time-consuming and not altogether accurate procedure for processing large amounts of data. Attention is also called to the fact that the construction of a simple contingency table is built on the use of nominal or ordinal scales. If you had operationalized economic development by reference to GNP per capita you would have to predetermine a cut-off point in order to dichotomize your interval scale. Then you would find out how many nations had GNP per capita above the value you selected and how many had GNP per capita below that value. (This process is described more fully in Chapter 5.) This would further extend the time required using a counter-sorter in constructing the contingency table. However, many students will not have access to a computer, and those who do not should not shy away from the counter-sorter. A lot of good political science has been published from analyses performed with the aid of the counter-sorter.[6]

In summary, the first three chapters described how one goes about the process of developing a theory, constructing hypotheses, specifying concepts, operationalizing variables, and seeking information about these variables for each case in the sample. This chapter extended the research process further by focusing upon procedures for collecting the information, processing it (transforming it to data), storing it, and retrieving it. Attention now turns in subsequent chapters to using these data for descriptive and analytic purposes.[7]

EXERCISES

1 Consult the following portion of the code book for *French and German Elite Responses*, Deutsch et. al, 1966.

CODE BOOK

Column Number	Germany N	%	France N	%	Code	
3					Q.1.	Respondent's degree of information
					b-2.	Foreign policy
	70	40	19	13	0.	+3 Very high
	68	39	40	27	1.	+2 High
	20	12	46	32	2.	+1 Higher than average
	4	2	21	14	3.	0 Neutral/average
	6	3	13	9	4.	−1 lower than average
	1	1	3	2	5.	−2 Low
	1	1	2	1	6.	−3 Very low
	3	2	2	1	9.	Not ascertained
	173	100%	146	99%		
4					Q.1.	Respondent's degree of information
					b-3.	European integration
	53	31	13	9	0.	+3 Very high
	84	48	27	18	1.	+2 High
	15	9	44	30	2.	+1 Higher than average
	4	2	29	20	3.	0 Neutral/average
	8	5	19	13	4.	−1 Lower than average
	2	1	10	7	5.	−2 Low
	1	1	1	1	6.	−3 Very low
	6	0	3	2	9.	Not ascertained
	173	100%	146	100%		
5					Q.1.	Respondent's degree of information
					b-4.	Arms control
	23	13	11	8	0.	+3 Very high
	37	21	11	8	1.	+2 High
	36	21	10	7	2.	+1 Higher than average
	21	12	19	13	3.	0 Neutral/average
	19	11	23	16	4.	−1 Lower than average
	23	13	23	16	5.	−2 Low
	8	5	40	27	6.	−3 Very low
	6	3	9	6	9.	Not ascertained
	173	99%	146	101%		
6					Q.2.	Respondent's notions about his competence to judge or his ability to make judgments about political processes
					a.	General
	66	38	32	22	0.	+3 Very high
	77	45	58	40	1.	+2 High
	14	8	35	24	2.	+1 Higher than average
	7	4	12	8	3.	0 Neutral/average
	5	3	3	2	4.	−1 Lower than average
	0	0	2	1	5.	−2 Low
	1	1	0	0	6.	−3 Very low
	3	2	4	3	9.	Not ascertained
	173	99%	146	100%		

Column Number	Germany N	%	France N	%	Code
7					Q.2. Respondent's feeling of competence
					b-1. Domestic
	89	51	48	33	0. +3 Very high
	60	35	51	35	1. +2 High
	13	9	30	21	2. +1 Higher than average
	5	3	9	6	3. 0 Neutral/average
	1	1	1	1	4. −1 Lower than average
	1	1	3	2	5. −2 Low
	2	1	2	1	6. −3 Very low
	2	1	2	1	9. Not ascertained
	173	101%	146	100%	
8					Q.2. Respondent's feeling of competence
					b-2. Foreign policy
	83	48	25	17	0. +3 Very high
	65	38	63	43	1. +2 High
	12	7	36	25	2. +1 Higher than average
	6	3	14	10	3. 0 Neutral/average
	3	2	5	3	4. −1 Lower than average
	1	1	2	1	5. −2 Low
	0	0	0	0	6. − Very low
	2	1	1	1	9. Not ascertained
	173	100%	146	100%	

A   What information is stored in column 4?

B   What information is stored in column 8?

C   What does a 4 punch in column 6 signify?

D   What does a 6 punch in column 3 signify?

E   How many German respondents had a "very high" feeling of competence in foreign policy? How many French respondents?

F   What was the total number of German respondents? What was the total number of French respondents?

G   What type of scale is used in this research?

2   How large a field would be required to store the following data on punch cards?

A   GNP stored in millions of U.S. dollars. Range $88,000,000 to $583,900,000,000   _____

B   Central government expenditures per capita. Range $2 to $1497   _____

C   Strategic distance from U.S. mainland. Range to 83.8   _____

D   Defense expenditures as % of
GNP. Range .2 to 16.5   _____

E   Number of nations diplomats
sent to. Range 4 to 100   _____

F   UN voting alignment with U.S.
Range 0 to 100   _____

3   Develop a code manual to guide the coding, storage, and retrieval of the
following data.

VARIABLE

Nation ID No.	Nation	GNP (in millions U.S. $)	Population (thousands)	Defense Expen. (as % GNP)
101	Austria	7,666	7,172	1.6
102	Belgium	13,900	9,290	3.3
111	United Kingdom	84,170	53,817	6.1

4   Using the code manual developed in step 3, code the data on the following code
sheets. Each blank represents one column of an 80-column punch card and
each sheet contains the equivalent of one card. Always use a pencil when coding
to facilitate the correction of coding errors.

Department of Political Science, Polimetrics Laboratory
The Ohio State University
Coding Form for Punching IBM Cards

Study _____   Page No. _____

01	02	03	04	05	06	07	08	09	10	11	12
13	14	15	16	17	18	19	20	21	22	23	24
25	26	27	28	29	30	31	32	33	34	35	36
37	38	39	40	41	42	43	44	45	46	47	48
49	50	51	52	53	54	55	56	57	58	59	60
61	62	63	64	65	66	67	68	69	70	71	72
73	74	75	76	77	78	79	80				

Study _____   Page No. _____

01	02	03	04	05	06	07	08	09	10	11	12
13	14	15	16	17	18	19	20	21	22	23	24
25	26	27	28	29	30	31	32	33	34	35	36
37	38	39	40	41	42	43	44	45	46	47	48
49	50	51	52	53	54	55	56	57	58	59	60
61	62	63	64	65	66	67	68	69	70	71	72
73	74	75	76	77	78	79	80

Study _____   Page No. _____

01	02	03	04	05	06	07	08	09	10	11	12
13	14	15	16	17	18	19	20	21	22	23	24
25	26	27	28	29	30	31	32	33	34	35	36
37	38	39	40	41	42	43	44	45	46	47	48
49	50	51	52	53	54	55	56	57	58	59	60
61	62	63	64	65	66	67	68	69	70	71	72
73	74	75	76	77	78	79	80

5 Sometimes it is necessary to read a card that has not been interpreted. Using the example presented below, answer the following questions.

A What number is punched in column 12?

B How many columns have been punched on the card?

C If columns 78–80 equal the observation identification number, which observation does this represent?

D If this card contains information on the characteristics of a nation and that nation's GNP in millions of U.S. dollars is held in a six-column field starting in column 5, what is the GNP of the nation?

E If one-column fields are used to store data from column 22 to column 30, information on how many variables are contained on this portion of the card?

F If this card contained all variables with three-column fields, how many variables are contained on the card? (Remember that columns 78–80 are the identification numbers.)

6 Consider variable 07, "agricultural workers as a percentage of the total economically active population" in the Student Raw Data Deck in the appendix of this book. Construct a frequency distribution by using the counter-sorter, and place your findings in the appropriate category below.

Value	Number of Cases
0	_____
1	_____
2	_____
3	_____

4	____
5	____
6	____
7	____
8	____
9	____
blank	____

7　Using the counter-sorter, construct a 2 × 2 contingency table from the Student Transformed Data Deck (in the appendix of this book) for variable 1, "total population," and variable 41, "diplomatic representatives sent." Columns 0–4 and 5–9 for each variable should be collapsed and labeled "low" and "high" respectively. Complete the following matrix.

Population

		High	Low
Diplomatic Representatives Sent	High		
	Low		

NOTES

1. All operations on data should be fully reported in your research reports. For an excellent example where research procedures are made visible, see Tanter (1966).

2. These procedures are outlined in detail in Burgess and Peterson (1970). For other guidelines to data quality control, see Rummel (1972, chapter 10) and Janda (1969).

3. For elaboration of these points, see Janda (1969), a very useful handbook devoted entirely to data processing techniques and skills.

4. For elaboration, see Galtung (1967), a book for more advanced students which covers the theory and method of social research, including sections on philosophy of science and statistics.

5. The construction and analysis of contingency tables is treated in detail in chapter 6. The discussion here is intended to provide guidance on the procedures and mechanics of using manual data processing equipment in analysis.

6. For an elaboration of techniques to use in punched card data processing, see Rath (1966).

7. Two student data decks accompany this manual. For a discussion of the distinction between the two, see the appendix.

Chapter Five

DESCRIBING AND DISPLAYING DESCRIPTIVE DATA

Students in the liberal arts do not progress very far before they find themselves face-to-face with statistics and other numerical representations of information. The purpose of the next three chapters is to acquaint you as painlessly as possible with some basic and often used visual displays and statistical concepts and operations. Hence, you will (1) better understand them when their application is encountered in your reading, and (2) be encouraged to use them for describing or testing political phenomena that you generate from your knowledge of world affairs or that are asserted by others.

The word *statistics* is commonly used as a synonym for *numbers* or numerically represented data, such as "crime statistics" or the comparative "statistics" of two opposing football teams or contestants in a beauty contest. However, these notions miss the technical usage of the term statistics which is, as we shall soon see, somewhat different. Moreover, the use of mathematics for purposes of political analysis is not limited to the discipline of statistics, but is also used for modeling political behavior and for simulating political processes. Hence, the primary underlying emphasis in this chapter is on a larger issue—the role of quantification in reducing uncertainty surrounding some empirical domain of interest to the student of international and comparative politics.[1]

As we have stressed throughout, the collection of data is always undertaken in relation to some theoretical interest or to a proposition whose operational definition suggested a data-making technique and implied a measurement routine. After the data have been amassed, the investigator is then faced with the problem of presenting that data in a way that will be informative (that is, in a way that will reduce uncertainty about the proposition or empirical relationship that captured the investigator's interest and attention in the first place). Although a growing number of powerful statistical and mathematical techniques is available for data analysis, you may be surprised to discover how much insight you can obtain with a few, relatively simple quantitative tools.

Given the state of theory and research in international relations, a great deal remains to be learned through relatively simple empirical "mapping" exercises— that is, through the description of empirical trends and the establishment of some rather basic empirical relationships. Description, after all, is a prerequisite to prediction, and international relations still lack an inventory of reliable descriptive statements although, fortunately, this inventory is growing very rapidly.[2] Consider, for example, the following statement that abstracts a study of the patterns of international warfare from 1816–1965:

Patterns in international violence are discovered through the quantitative analysis of international wars which resulted in more than 1,000 battle-connected deaths. Between 1816 and 1965, members of the state system participated in 50 such interstate wars and 43 such colonial and imperial conflicts. Although no secular trends are evident in terms of the frequency, magnitude, severity, and intensity of these wars, the data suggest a twenty-year cycle in the magnitude of systemic war. Over two thirds of all of the wars began in either the spring or the autumn. Major powers have engaged in a disproportionate number of wars and have suffered the most battle-connected deaths. These same powers, however, have won most of their wars. Those on the victorious side have often been the initiators of military hostilities. Enduring military friendships and emnities have been uncommon over the 150-year period (Small and Singer, 1970).

Amazing as it may seem, this abstract references much new information contained in the study that had not been previously known. To what end? As the authors themselves state, "Further use of these basic war data should be helpful in the assault upon the centuries-old problem of the causes of war" (Small and Singer, 1970, p. 145).

Hopefully these basic visual displays and statistical techniques will become powerful tools in the analysis of data that you generate yourself or that you obtain from others. Also, your acquisition of the skills contained in the following pages will be a capital investment, for these elementary displays, concepts, and operations form the foundation for more powerful and sophisticated descriptive and analytical techniques that will increasingly attract your attention. The range of statistical concepts, visual displays, and operations that will be discussed in this and the following chapters is displayed in Figure 5.1.

ONE-VARIABLE DESCRIPTIVE ANALYSIS

Once you have collected and stored your data, you are faced with the problem of describing each variable, and displaying your results so that the reader may quickly understand its basic characteristics. Descriptive analysis, either expressed by a visual display or statistical technique, is used to describe each variable: its frequency distribution, its typical or average value change over time, and the degree of homogeneity among the cases. Associational analysis—the focus of chapters 6 and 7—by contrast serves to provide evidence for or against the propositions under investigation in the study. They are chiefly used to establish the association between two or more variables, either by a visual cross-plot of each case's numerical values or by a statistic that yields a numerical interpretation, such as a correlation coefficient. Figure 5.1 shows the distinction between these two types of analysis.

This chapter focuses on visual displays and statistical techniques relating to the description of one variable, the fifth step in quantitative research. These will serve to provide the four types of information about each variable previously mentioned. The first step in summarizing the raw information contained in the cases for a variable is the construction of a frequency distribution. This visual display, when accompanied by either visual or statistical procedures for determining the average case value and the extent to which the remaining cases approximate the typical case, allows us to gain much insight about the characteristics of the variable, and subsequently about the international system. These three summarizing descriptors may be expressed in two basic ways: (1) visual displays

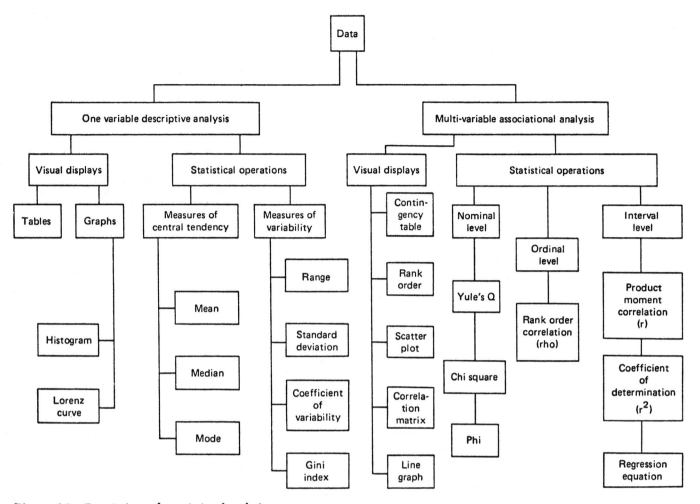

Figure 5.1   *Descriptive and associational analysis*

(graphs and tables); and (2) statistical operations (measures of central tendency, dispersion, and inequality). They are outlined in the left half of Figure 5.1.

VISUAL DISPLAYS

The principal characteristics of each variable may be displayed visually in two ways: by graphical representation or in tabular form. The purpose of each type of display is to give the reader basic information about the variable in a very parsimonious fashion—that is, to reduce uncertainty by conveying as much information as possible in the most efficient and effective way. Information displayed in graphic or tabular form should also avoid introducing distortions.[3] Hence, three general rules should be followed when constructing either graphs or tables.

1.   Data should not distort the impact of the information being considered. The most important information for reducing uncertainty is the order of magnitude of the values you are dealing with. For example, in the metric system there are four basic orders of magnitude: *micro* units (1/1,000,000); *milli* units (1/1,000); *kilo* units (1,000); and *mega* units (1,000,000). Thus, it is important always to show clearly which measurement value units are used as a display. If we know, for example, that

population per square kilometer ranges from over 3,000 in Hong Kong to 1 in South West Africa, we need to express our units in thousands, hundreds, tens, and ones. On the other hand, if we know that deaths per 1000 population range from 31.0 in India to 6.2 in Cyprus, we may decide to drop the decimal and display orders of magnitude only in terms of tens and ones.

2.   The highest and lowest quantitative value (i.e., the range) of an empirical factor should always be displayed. It is often misleading, for example, to imply that the values on a table range between 0 and 100 percent when the true empirical variation is always between 40 and 60 percent.

3.   Always avoid unnecessary censoring of your data; i.e., don't collapse your quantitative measures to the point where you lose information. On the other hand, data displays should not misrepresent the precision or accuracy of the data. The presentation of data that contain measures implying precision that is really not justified by the data is both misleading and inefficient. For example, a measure of defense expenditures as a percent of GNP carried to three decimal places (e.g., 51.230%) is clearly not justified by the quality of the data. Therefore, orders of magnitude—in this case thousandths of a percentage—that do not reduce uncertainty or that are not justified by the quality of the measurements used should not be included in data displays.[4]

GRAPHS AND FREQUENCY DISTRIBUTIONS

Graphs generally display either (1) the relationship between a dependent and independent variable (termed an analytic graph and discussed in chapter 6); or (2) the frequency with which certain values of a variable are distributed. Typical graphs are formed by a right angle intersection of two lines at a point 0 (read "zero"), called the origin. In the frequency distribution, the horizontal line (called *abscissa*) denotes the cases or values of the variable (x); the vertical line (termed *ordinate axis*) refers to the frequencies (f) of the variable. Figure 5.2 displays the basic properties of a frequency distribution.

A good example of the use of a frequency distribution graph appears in Figure 5.3. If we want to show the distribution of wealth in the world in 1968, the graph would look like the following figure. In this case, X = GNP per capita (our operational measure of wealth) and f = the number of nations for each value from the lowest GNP to the highest.

Figure 5.3 clearly shows that wealth is unevenly distributed; that is, many nations (indicated by the high frequency on the left side of the graph) are very poor, and few nations (indicated by the low frequency of high wealth on the right side of the graph) are very rich. It is important to note that most resources in the international system are distributed in the same manner as GNP/capita.

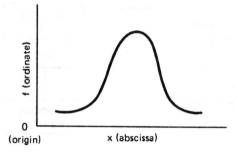

Figure 5.2   Frequency distribution graph

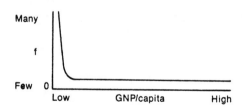

Figure 5.3   The distribution of GNP/capita in 1968

Histogram

Most quantitative data in international politics may be expressed by a bar graph or histogram. For nominal- or ordinal-level data, constructing a histogram is a relatively simple procedure. The number of bars or categories along the horizontal axis simply reflects the number of different values represented in the variable. Figure 5.4 displays the histogram for the bureaucratic character of the world's national regimes.

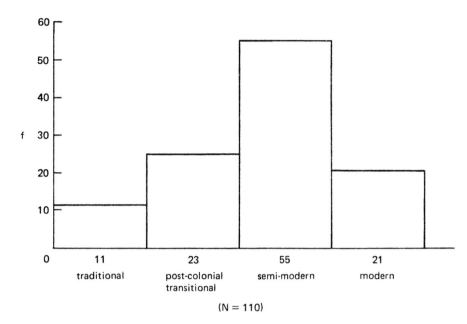

Figure 5.4   *Histogram of bureaucratic character of regimes*

This histogram contains four values or categories of bureaucratic character: traditional, post-colonial transitional, semi-modern, and modern regimes.

Constructing a histogram for interval-level data requires additional steps. Raw data must be grouped so that a manageable number of categories along the horizontal axis can be created. Without collapsing these values, the number of categories would have to be expanded to include every interval value represented among the cases in the sample.

For example, the values for GNP/capita range from $45 to $4313, necessitating far too many categories to be represented in a graph. Therefore, these data must be reduced to an ordinal level. To accomplish this task you first determine the range (in this case, $4313–$45) and the number of bars which you want to incorporate in the histogram (for example, ten). You must then adopt some decision rule for selecting appropriate cutoff points. Common convention suggests that you select cutoff points which reflect equal intervals. For example, if your range is 5000, each interval between the upper and lower limits of each category would be 500.

Figure 5.5 demonstrates the histogram for GNP/capita; the range is 4268 (4313–45) and each of the ten bars has a category range of 426. As you can observe from Figure 5.5, most of the nations have a GNP/capita value of between $45 and $471.

RULES OF GRAPH CONSTRUCTION

When you construct graphs, be careful to follow these basic rules:

1. A good quality of graphing paper should be used. Ten squares to the inch is appropriate for most graphing.
2. The abscissa should be slightly longer than the ordinate, with a ratio of 3 to 2 or 4 to 3 giving the best graph.
3. With large displays, it is usually best to place the X axis (or abscissa) on the wider side of the paper and with the holes at the top on punched paper.

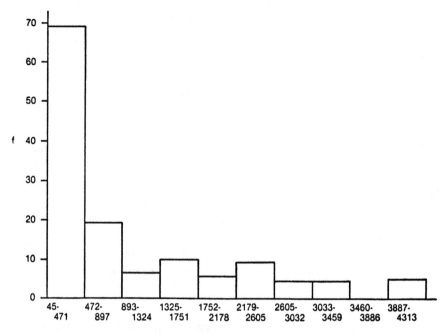

Figure 5.5   Histogram of GNP/capita

4. The graph should always define the range or region of variation that the quantitative information is intended to reduce. One way to do this is to construct a graph with a "squiggle" line on the ordinate axis, as shown in Figure 5.6. If the known empirical variation always lies between 40 percent and 60 percent, the graph might be constructed as shown.[5]

TIME-SERIES OR TREND ANALYSIS

Most descriptive studies are either *cross-sectional*, which measures variables at one moment in time for a set of cases, or *longitudinal*, which examines variables for one or fewer cases across many time periods. In fact, the time periods in the latter instance are more appropriately termed *cases*. The more technical term for this latter type is *time-series analysis*, but we shall continue to use the more popular term, *trend analysis*. We are concerned with examining both long-term trend and short-term changes. The most common trend is any long-term growth or decline in a series of values. Figure 5.6, which describes the changes in the percent in foreign trade of major exporting nations for the twentieth century, is an example of a graph which displays the steady decline of a variable across time.

A second type of trend focuses upon regular fluctuations. Two such types are seasonal variations and cyclical changes. Students of international and comparative politics are more interested in the latter type. For example, the history of war for the last 115 years follows a crude cyclical pattern.

When constructing a time-series graph, the horizontal axis represents *time* (or the cases) and the vertical axis denotes values of the *variable* (see Figure 5.6).

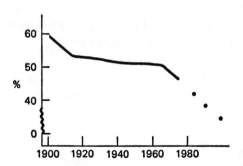

Figure 5.6   Percent in foreign trade of major exporting nations in 20th century

VISUALIZING INEQUALITY

Many people have shown great concern for the unequal distribution of the earth's resources among its nations and people. Some have suggested that the inequities in the distribution of highly valued resources (wealth, land, health, education, political power) have been at the root of revolution both at home and abroad.[6] The argument is often advanced that if the disadvantaged nations acquire the means of comparison so that they can observe each other's unfortunate position, joint action is more likely. This would then lead to a chain of events in which the deprived nations may be able to improve their economic status (probably with the aid of the rich nations) by peaceful means rather than taking these resources by force. The likelihood of this strategy winning acceptance in poor nations is dependent in large measure upon their perception of the trend that describes the gap between rich and poor nations. If this gap is increasing (that is, if the rich are getting richer and the poor getting poorer), disadvantaged nations and people are likely to resort to more violent means to secure what they believe to be their fair share of wealth. Consequently, analysts have the responsibility not only to determine how resources are distributed today, but they must also be able to project future trends.

One particularly useful device for assessing the pattern of inequity for a distribution of values or resources is the Lorenz curve. This curve enables you to observe the fraction of total resources or values held by various proportions of the population. Figure 5.7 represents the Lorenz curve for a hypothetical distribution

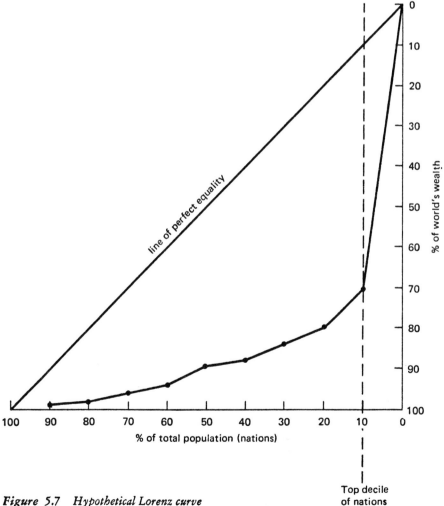

Figure 5.7 Hypothetical Lorenz curve

within the international system. As you can observe, there are a number of conventions for this graph which differ from those adopted for the more typical frequency distributions. The principal difference, of course, is the use of percentages rather than raw data.

The X or horizontal axis represents a proportion of the population; and the Y or vertical axis represents the percentage of the resource. Any point on the Lorenz curve represents that proportion of the population that possesses the corresponding percentage of the value shown on the Y axis. In Figure 5.7, for example, 10 percent of the nations possess 70 percent of the world's wealth, whereas the remaining 90 percent of the nations have only 30 percent of the wealth. If each percentage of the population possessed an equal amount of the value (i.e., 20 percent of the people owned 20 percent of the resources, 30 percent owned 30 percent, etc.), perfect equality would exist. This equality is represented in Figure 5.7 by the line of perfect equality, a 45-degree line.[7]

The area between the diagonal line and the Lorenz curve is known as the area of inequality. The greater this area, the larger the degree of inequality for the distribution. Compare the extreme degrees of inequality represented by the two curves in Figure 5.8. The distribution signified by the line closer to the 45° line marked *high equality* represents a high level of equality; that is, each percentage of the population possesses a relatively equal percentage of the resource. In the other

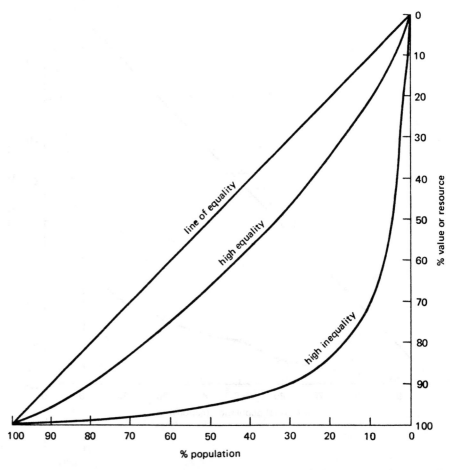

Figure 5.8   High equality and inequality

curve labeled *high inequality*, by contrast, valued resources are distributed very unevenly among the population; i.e., a small segment of the population controls a large portion of the value.

USES OF LORENZ CURVES

It is important to note that Lorenz curves can be used to describe distributions of values among any units—people, regions within nations, or nations themselves. For example, we might find in the future that wealth is very unevenly distributed among nations (using nations as the unit on the horizontal axis) but much more evenly distributed among people within nations (this time using individuals within each nation as the unit on the horizontal axis). We shall first consider the distribution of resources in the international system. Figure 5.9 reveals the distribution of gross national product throughout the globe. As you can observe, the richest 10 percent of nations control 80 percent of the world's wealth (denoted by point A).

The Lorenz curve may also be used to compare distributions within several nations. Figure 5.10 compares the distribution of arable land within four nations: Denmark, Austria, Bolivia, and the United States. Denmark clearly demonstrates a much more equitable distribution of land.

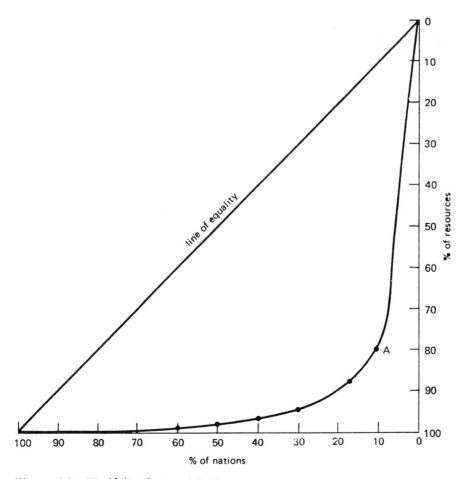

Figure 5.9 World distribution of GNP

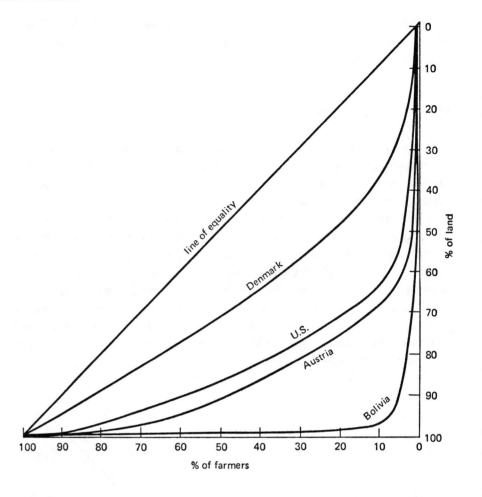

Figure 5.10 Comparison of arable land distribution*

_____

* Adopted from Bruce Russett, *World Handbook of Social and Political Indicators*, Yale University Press (1964).

Changes in distributions across time may also be represented by Lorenz curves. Figure 5.11 compares the world distribution of agricultural workers for the years 1959 and 1975.

Though the Lorenz curve has only recently been used by political scientists, it provides an extremely useful way to assess the level of equality or inequality in the distribution of values in a political system. And the issue of equality has long stood as one of the major normative issues in political philosophy and remains a major issue of concern to citizens and policy-makers alike. The Lorenz curve is a powerful, descriptive tool and is extremely useful for comparative examinations.[8]

CONSTRUCTING A LORENZ CURVE

Calculating a Lorenz curve is a relatively simple procedure requiring six steps. Let us examine the distribution of wealth (measured by total GNP) among the nations of the world. You probably would assume that a small percentage of the population

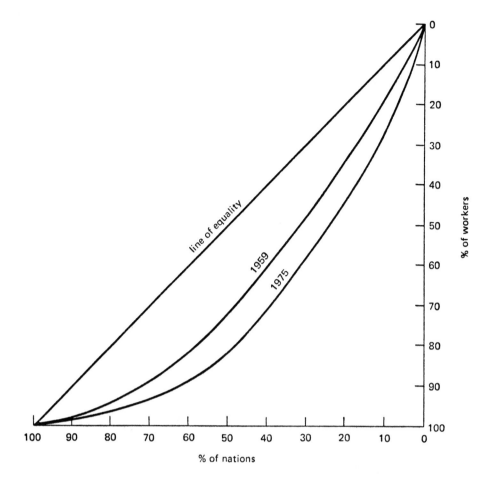

*Figure 5.11   World distribution of agricultural workers for 1959 and 1975**

---

* Adopted from *World Handbook of Social and Political Indicators.*

of nations possesses much of the world's wealth.* Your first step is to rank order these nations according to their level of GNP (from highest to lowest). Figure 5.12 presents these data.

Second, you select a sufficient number of percentage points for representing the population of nations on the X axis. You will obtain an accurate Lorenz curve by selecting points which are multiples of 10 (10 percent of the nations, 20 percent, 30 percent, and so on).

Third, divide your rank ordering into groups representing these same proportions. Since there are 130 nations in the population, you will obtain 10 groups of 13 nations each. The horizontal lines in Figure 5.12 represent these divisions.

Fourth, determine the proportion of the total GNP possessed by each decile, i.e., by each of the 10 groups. This requires you to (a) obtain the sum of GNP

---

* The procedure for calculating the Lorenz curve in this example assumes that your primary interest is the percentage of the nations (say 10 percent) which controls a given level of wealth. If you are more concerned with the percentage of wealth (say 80 percent) controlled by a given percentage of nations, you would reverse the X and Y axis in the following steps.

	Country	Amount of GNP
1.	United States	824,276
2.	Soviet Union	271,950
3.	Japan	124,593
4.	West Germany	116,033
5.	France	109,695
6.	United Kingdom	100,777
7.	China	69,561
8.	Italy	66,543
9.	India	56,950
10.	Canada	53,628
11.	Poland	29,304
12.	Mexico	27,825
13.	Australia	26,496
	Decile Total	1,877,613
14.	Spain	24,528
15.	Brazil	23,925
16.	East Germany	23,161
17.	Sweden	21,222
18.	Netherlands	21,222
19.	Argentina	20,254
20.	Czechoslovakia	18,352
21.	Belgium	17,557
22.	Rumania	16,063
23.	Switzerland	15,936
24.	Pakistan	14,160
25.	South Africa	13,390
26.	Indonesia	12,490
	Decile Total	242,265
27.	Turkey	11,315
28.	Yugoslavia	10,608
29.	Venezuela	10,545
30.	Denmark	10,350
31.	Hungary	10,094
32.	Austria	9,900
33.	Iran	9,052
34.	Finland	8,084
35.	Norway	7,800
36.	Philippines	7,092
37.	Columbia	6,851
38.	Greece	6,650
39.	Bulgaria	6,622
	Decile Total	114,973
40.	United Arab Republic	5,922
41.	South Korea	5,922
42.	New Zealand	5,800
43.	Thailand	5,610
44.	Peru	5,320

	Country	Amount of GNP
45.	Chile	4,800
46.	Portugal	4,416
47.	Israel	4,080
48.	Nigeria	3,955
49.	China (Taiwan)	3,861
50.	Malaysia	3,663
51.	North Korea	3,575
52.	Algeria	3,190
	Decile Total	60,114
53.	Morocco	3,097
54.	Ireland	2,940
55.	Saudi Arabia	2,880
56.	Kuwait	2,832
57.	Cuba	2,666
58.	Iraq	2,600
59.	South Vietnam	2,379
60.	Ceylon	2,322
61.	Burma	1,988
62.	North Vietnam	1,944
63.	Libya	1,938
64.	Ethiopia	1,792
65.	Guatemala	1,696
	Decile Total	31,074
66.	Sudan	1,630
67.	Lebanon	1,624
68.	Congo (Ki.)	1,602
69.	Ghana	1,581
70.	Southern Yemen	1,540
71.	Singapore	1,540
72.	Uruguay	1,508
73.	Kenya	1,456
74.	Afghanistan	1,392
75.	Ecuador	1,386
76.	Syria	1,344
77.	Dominican Republic	1,276
78.	Tunisia	1,166
	Decile Total	19,045
79.	Southern Rhodesia	1,144
80.	Tanzania	1,088
81.	Ivory Coast	1,040
82.	El Salvador	1,008
83.	Uganda	968
84.	Zambia	968
85.	Trinidad and Tobago	957
86.	Jamaica	920
87.	Nepal	920
88.	Albania	880

	Country	Amount of GNP
89.	Cambodia	876
90.	Panama	870
91.	Luxembourg	868
	Decile Total	12,507
92.	Costa Rica	855
93.	Cameroun	826
94.	Nicaragua	777
95.	Honduras	728
96.	Bolivia	720
97.	Malagasy	710
98.	Senegal	680
99.	Jordan	624
100.	Paraguay	575
101.	Mongolia	559
102.	Cyprus	498
103.	Mali	468
104.	Yemen	413
	Decile Total	8,443
105.	Sierra Leone	405
106.	Haiti	378
107.	Guinea	360
108.	Iceland	336
109.	Laos	310
110.	Niger	280
111.	Upper Volta	275
112.	Guyana	272
113.	Rwanda	259
114.	Liberia	252
115.	Congo (Br.)	230
116.	Malawi	230
117.	Chad	228
	Decile Total	3,815
118.	Dahomey	224
119.	Mauritania	216
120.	Mauritius	207
121.	Malta	192
122.	Central African Republic	192
123.	Togo	190
124.	Burundi	185
125.	Muscat and Oman	175
126.	Somalia	174
127.	Gabon	155
128.	Barbados	132
129.	Lesotho	88
130.	Botswana	60
	Decile Total	2,190

Figure 5.12   Total GNP*

* GNP measured in millions of dollars; total GNP = 2,372,000 millions, *Population Reference Bureau, Inc.*

for all nations; (b) obtain the total amount of GNP for each of the 10 groups; and (c) calculate the percentage of the total GNP possessed by each of the 10 groups. These last values are given in column B of Figure 5.13. For example, those nations representing between 41 and 50 percent of the population as shown in column A of Figure 5.13 (nations with rankings 53 to 65 in Figure 5.12) have 1 percent of the world's GNP (column B in Figure 5.13).

Fifth, you add the value of each succeeding decile to the preceding deciles in order to obtain the percentage of GNP residing in various proportions of the population. These values are given in column D of Figure 5.13. For example, according to column D, only 10 percent of the nations (representing the richest ones) control 79 percent of the world's wealth and the richest 20 percent control 89 percent of the wealth (79 percent + 10 percent), whereas the poorest 80 percent of the world's countries possess only 11 percent of its wealth (100 percent — 89 percent).

Sixth, once you have obtained the percentages for the value on the Y axis (column D) you determine each pair of values for x and y axes (columns C and D). These are given in Figure 5.9. You simply connect these points to obtain the Lorenz curve.

TABLES

As political and social scientists increasingly apply techniques of quantitative analysis, they tend to use tabular displays for ordering quantitative information in clear and easy-to-follow visual displays of summary data. Tables, like the preceding graphs, present substantive information—data or the results of analysis—in a condensed form. An example of descriptive data is a table drawn from Alger and Brams' study of diplomatic interaction, presented in Figure 5.14.

This *descriptive table* presents the number of foreign diplomatic missions located in the top ten nations in 1922 and again in 1963–64 with no attempt to analyze the results, for example, in terms of percentages or the ranks of the receiving nations.

Column A Decile of Nations	Column B % of GNP for each Decile of Nations	Column C Cumulative % of Nations	Column D Cumulative* % of GNP
0–10%	79%	10%	79%
11–20%	10%	20%	89%
21–30%	5%	30%	94%
31–40%	3%	40%	97%
41–50%	1%	50%	98%
51–60%	.8%	60%	99%
61–70%	.5%	70%	99%
71–80%	.3%	80%	100%
81–90%	.1%	90%	100%
91–100%	.09%	100%	100%

Figure 5.13 Proportional values for GNP

* Percentages have been rounded to the nearest whole percent.

1922*		Number of Missions		1963–1964		Number of Missions
1.	France	50	1.	United States		107
2.	United Kingdom	50	2.	France		98
3.	United States	48	3.	United Kingdom		96
4.	Italy	44	4.	Germany (Fed. Rep.)		94
5.	Germany	40	5.	Italy		85
6.	Belgium	32	6.	Belgium		75
7.	Netherlands	32	7.	United Arab Republic		73
8.	Spain	31	8.	Japan		70
9.	Brazil	30	9.	Soviet Union		69
10.	Austria/Switzerland	29	10.	India		66
	N = 10			N = 10		

Figure 5.14   Top ten nations ranked according to the number of diplomatic missions in their capitals in 1922 and 1963–1964

---

* Adapted from inside cover map of DeWitt C. Poole, *The Conduct of Foreign Relations Under Modern Democratic Conditions* (New Haven, 1924). The year 1922 is approximate; data were taken from 1923 edition of the *Almanach de Gothe* (Gothe, Germany, 1923). *Patterns of Representation in National Capitals and Inter-Governmental Organizations*, by Chadwick F. Alger and Steven J. Brams, *World Politics* © 1967 by Princeton University Press. Reprinted by permission of Princeton University Press.

Although table formats may be varied slightly, it is important to note the basic features which should be included:

1. Tables usually have only horizontal lines, including a heavy line (or double line when typing) at the top.

2. Tables should always be clearly labeled. The notation "Figure 5.14" tells us that it is the fourteenth figure in chapter 5. The title informs the reader, even without reading the text, that the table contains information about the number of diplomatic missions located in the capitals of the top ten nations. In addition, any footnotes to the table, which should appear immediately below it, provide relevant information regarding the data displayed in the table (e.g., the source of the data or caveats about the data themselves).

3. The table clearly displays the N size, i.e., the total number of cases. In this example, cases are nations. This should always be done so that the reader can evaluate the meaning and value of the distribution.

4. The source of the table (unless the data are original) should always appear immediately after the footnotes.

In sum, the basic rule is that each table should present sufficient information to permit its being read and understood without reference to the text. When the table presents the results of a survey, for example, the question should be included in the text of the table. This facilitates evaluation of the distribution responses. An example of a table from a survey is presented in Figure 5.15 reproduced from Deutsch, et al. (1967, p. 96), *France, Germany and the Western Alliance.*

STATISTICAL OPERATIONS

In the first section of chapter 5, various visual displays revealing descriptive information about the frequency of data points were presented. These exists another set of descriptive procedures—statistical operations such as measures of central

Question: It is often said that a
national deterrent is a prerequisite
of a country's independence.

Do you share this view?	Number of Respondents	Percentage
Yes	61	41
No	76	52
Don't know	4	3
Not Ascertained	6	4
Total	147	100

Figure 5.15 *French views of a national nuclear deterrent**

* Karl Deutsch et al., *France, Germany and the Western Alliance*, copyright © 1967,
Charles Scribner's Sons.

tendency, measures of dispersion, and the Gini Index—which reveal more precise
information about the distribution, particularly its average case value and degree of
homogeneity. Measures of central tendency focus on the former characteristic while
measures of dispersion, including the Gini Index of inequality, describe the later
phenomenon.

Measures of Central Tendency

A measure of central tendency provides a concise description of the typical or
average value of a variable in relation to cases. The measure of central tendency
permits us to (1) describe the average or typical behavior of a group, or (2) compare two or more groups in terms of typical performance. In statistics, three commonly used measures of central tendency are the mean, the median, and the mode.

The Mean

The mean is most familiar and is typically used with interval data and symmetrical
distributions. It is a simple arithmetic average and is computed as follows:

$$\text{Mean} = \overline{X} = \frac{\text{sum of scores}}{\text{number of scores}} = \frac{\Sigma X}{N}.$$

where:

Sigma or Σ = sum or add up everything that follows
X = a score or measure
N = total number of scores or measures
"X-bar" or $\overline{X}$ = the mean

In other words, the formula for computing the mean ($\overline{X} = \frac{\Sigma X}{N}$) asks you to
add up all the individual scores and then divide by the total number of scores:

$$\overline{X} = \frac{X_1 + X_2 + X_3 + \ldots + X_N}{N}.$$

Figure 5.16 gives the distribution that reflects the items of domestic mail per
capita for 13 nations. The mean for the data in Figure 5.16 is computed as follows:

1. First we sum the 13 scores:
   $X_1 + \ldots + X_{13} = 1087$ or $(350 + \ldots 1 = 1087)$.

Thus the sum of the scores (ΣX) equals 1087.

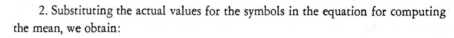

Country (N = 13)	Items per capita
1. USA	350
2. UK	190
3. France	166
4. West Germany	152
5. East Germany	83
6. Spain	62
7. Taiwan	33
8. Mexico	18
9. Hong Kong	14
10. Egypt	8
11. India	8
12. Indonesia	2
13. Togo	1

Figure 5.16   Distribution of domestic mail per capita

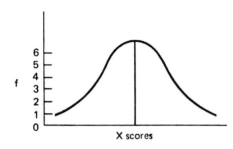

Figure 5.17   Example of a normal distribution

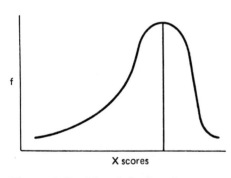

Figure 5.18   Negatively skewed distribution

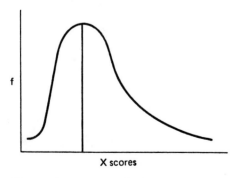

Figure 5.19   Positively skewed distribution

2. Substituting the actual values for the symbols in the equation for computing the mean, we obtain:

$$\overline{X} = \frac{1087}{13} = 83.6;$$

3. thus:

$$\overline{X} = 83.6.$$

Thus, the average of pieces of domestic mail per capita for each of the 13 nations is 83.6.

Computing the mean is like finding the center of gravity. If a distribution were suspended by the mean, it would hang level or balanced as shown in the bell-shaped curve or normal distribution displayed in Figure 5.17.

If the distribution of scores include disproportionate numbers of very high or very low scores, then the mean will shift toward those extremes, giving a skewed curve or skewed distribution. Unlike the symmetrical shape of the normal curve in Figure 5.17, the skewed distribution is asymmetrical.

If a distribution is such that scores cluster at the right end of the curve (as in Figure 5.18), the curve is said to *negatively skewed* because the mean is to the right of the center of the range of scores. If scores cluster to the left (as in Figure 5.19), the curve is said to be *positively skewed* because the mean is to the left of the center of the range of scores.

The Median

When extreme scores are included in a distribution (giving a skewed curve), this tends to pull the mean scores away from the centrally located scores and toward the extreme score. Thus, if the analyst wants to eliminate the effects of extreme scores, he or she may rely on another measure of central tendency, the median (the middle score or midpoint). The median is less affected by the existence of extreme scores and appropriate to use whenever skewed or asymmetrical distributions are encountered. Using the median in this case, even though the data are expressed at the ordinal level, probably is more consistent with one's intuitive view of the typical case.

This measure is most often used, however, when the data are in ordinal form. The median score, thus, is simply the middle ranking score in a distribution with an odd number of cases. For example, the middle ranking score or median in Figure 5.16 is 33, the value represented by Taiwan, the seventh or middle-ranked nation.[9] This median value of 33 is considerably lower than the mean of 83.6. Given the skewness of the distribution for items of domestic mail per capita, we are probably better advised to use the median in this case if our purpose is to give the reader the least distorted view of the average case of this distribution.

The Mode

The third measure of central tendency is the mode, which is simply the one value or score that occurs with the most frequency. Consider the range of the following 21 scores: 1, 7, 2, 8, 3, 9, 7, 5, 4, 8, 3, 4, 5, 6, 6, 6, 9, 7, 5, 6, 10. The modal score is 6 (note that the mean is approximately 6 and that the median is also 6). On returning to Figure 5.16, we see that the modal score for items of domestic mail per capita is 8.

The mode is most useful when there are a large number of cases in a distribution or when an average is meaningless—for example, when you want a measure of the most characteristic value. Thus, the mode is particularly appropriate when your data are in nominal form. Also, extreme scores have absolutely no influence on a modal score. Thus, if you are comparing different channels of interaction (diplomatic messages, telephone, face-to-face meetings, the use of third party intermediaries, etc.) a mean value would probably not be as useful as a modal value. One is looking for the mode of communication, i.e., the most characteristic form of channel of communication.

The concept of modality is also useful for describing the shape of distributions. Figure 5.20 shows the following distribution on a histogram: 5, 5, 6, 6, 6, 6, 6, 7, 7, 8, 9, 9, 9, 9, 10. We can observe more than one peak on the graph in this distribution. These peaks display scores of high frequency or modes. Thus, a normal curve, with only one peak (in the center) is unimodal. The curve in Figure 5.20 displays a bimodal distribution in the two peaks of the graph. If a distribution has more than two peaks, it is multi-modal.

It should be obvious from this discussion that the frequency distribution (histogram) and measures of central tendency (mean, median, and mode) may be used simultaneously to characterize typical values or cases. Figure 5.17 represents

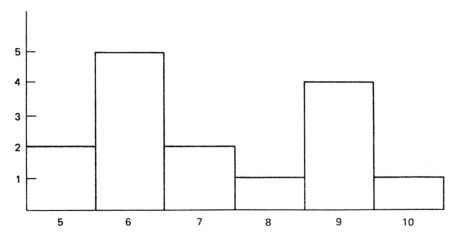

Figure 5.20 Typical bimodal histogram

a normal distribution (bell-shaped curve) where the mode, median, and mean will all be represented by the same value; hence bell-shaped curves are called *normal* distributions or a *normal curve*. In contrast, skewed distributions result in different values for the three measures of central tendency, as Figure 5.21 suggests.

Measures of Variability

In the previous section we concerned ourselves with certain measures (the mean, median, and mode) which refer to the location of the center of a distribution. Keeping in mind the discussion of these descriptive statistics, consider the following samples of political stability scores for a number of different countries.

Sample 1: 41, 54, 60, 42, 53, 60, 55, 40, 41, 54; Where $\overline{X} = 50$

Sample 2: 160, 10, 200, 8, 2, 100, 20, 10, 44, 6; Where $\overline{X} = 50$

Sample 3: 80, 82, 86, 89, 81, 20, 18, 15, 19, 10; Where $\overline{X} = 50$

Note that in all three samples the mean ($\overline{X}$) equals 50. In other words, even though we can see from looking at the individual political stability scores for each nation that considerable differences exist among the three hypothetical samples, using the mean ($\overline{X}$) as the measure of central tendency makes them all appear the same. What we need, therefore, is a measure that will describe in summary form the rich variation that we can easily observe in each distribution. If the variation is small we have confidence that specific case values are close to the mean, but if the amount of variation is large, we need additional information in order to determine the probability that a single case will occupy a certain position within the distribution. Figure 5.22 illustrates this point.

Each distribution has a value of 10 for the mean, median, and mode. However, in the diagram on the left of Figure 5.22, most cases cluster around the mean, whereas the cases are much more dispersed in the right diagram.

Range. Descriptive statistics used to summarize the variation in a distribution of scores are called *measures of variability* or *measures of dispersion*. Three im-

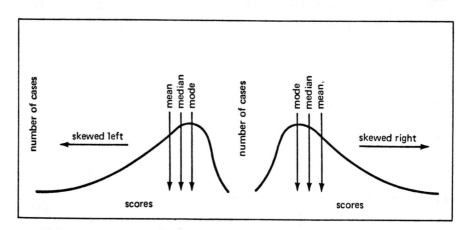

*Figure 5.21 Skewed distributions**

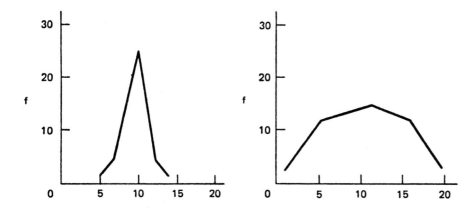

Figure 5.22   Comparison of amounts of variation

portant indices of variability are the range, standard deviation, and coefficient of variability. The range, the simplest of the three measures to compute, is the difference between the highest and lowest value in a distribution. For example, if you go back to the data on items of mail per capita in Figure 5.16, you will find that the range is very wide (range = 349, i.e., the largest score—350 for the USA —minus the smallest score—1 for Togo).

The range is a useful statistic because it gives us additional information about the way our data are distributed. Let's say, for example, that we are comparing international geographic regions with respect to the distribution of national wealth within regions (Figure 5.23). Again we find that the measures of per capita national income for all nations in Region A have the same mean, median, and mode as the measures of per capita national income for the nations in Region B. In other words, with respect to measures of mean, median, and mode, Region A is equivalent to Region B. But a closer inspection of the data may reveal that Region A has considerably more rich and more poor nations than Region B. Thus, if we were to graph the distribution of data for both regions, we might find distributions such as those shown in Figure 5. 23.

It is obvious from Figure 5.23 that even though Regions A and B have levels of per capita national income that are equal when measured by the mean ($250), the median ($250), or the mode ($250), they are quite different regions with respect to the distribution of wealth. Because of the broader range of cases in

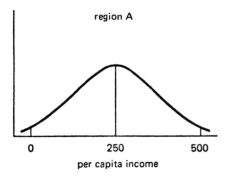

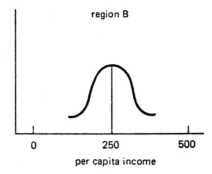

Figure 5.23   Per capita income

Region A, it is clear that Region B is much more homogeneous with respect to the distribution of wealth among the nations in the region than is Region A.

Standard Deviation. Another common and perhaps the most important measure of variability is the standard deviation, i.e., the difference between the unit score X (e.g., the GNP of a given nation) and the average score $\overline{X}$ (e.g., the mean GNP of all the nations). When the cases comprising a group (a sample or population) are not very different from one another, their standard deviation is very small. Highly variable or diverse groups, by contrast, will have high standard deviations. Thus, in Figure 5.23, we would expect Region B to have a lower standard deviation with respect to wealth than would Region A. The standard deviation is the most versatile and stable of the measures of variability. Although the range is easier to calculate and understand, it does not have many applications; whereas standard deviation is used as the foundation in many other statistical analyses.[10] Hence, it is essential to take the time necessary to understand both intuitively and operationally the concept of the standard deviation.

Computing the Standard Deviation. The conventional symbol for standard deviation is SD when working with a sample of cases, and the lower-case Greek letter sigma "σ" when using a population, i.e., the totality of cases. The standard deviation is computed by the following formula:

$$SD = \sigma = \sqrt{\frac{\Sigma d^2}{N}}$$

where:

SD and σ = symbol for standard deviation
Σ = add or sum
d = each unit score minus the mean ($X - \overline{X}$)
$\sqrt{}$ = square root
N = total number of observations

Consider, for example, the number of diplomats assigned to the missions of 10 countries in country Z. This information is given in Figure 5.24.

The mean value for this sample is 10; that is, each nation with diplomatic representation in country Z has, on the average, 10 diplomats assigned to its diplomatic mission. However, there is considerable variation in the sample, with a range of 13

Country	Score (X)
A	15
B	14
C	12
D	12
E	11
F	10
G	9
H	8
I	7
J	2

Figure 5.24 *Number of diplomats assigned to mission in country Z*

X	$\overline{X}$ (mean)	$d = (X - \overline{X})$	d^2
15	10	5	25
14	10	4	16
12	10	2	4
12	10	2	4
11	10	1	1
10	10	0	0
9	10	−1	1
8	10	−2	4
7	10	−3	9
2	10	−8	64
			$\Sigma d^2 = 128$

Figure 5.25   Standard deviation worksheet

in the distribution.[11] Once the mean is determined, it is relatively simple to compute the standard deviation, as Figure 5.25 attests.

Assuming that country Z has only a total of 10 accredited diplomatic missions with an average of 10 representatives, we are working with the entire population; therefore, we shall use the symbol "σ".

$$\sigma = \sqrt{\frac{\Sigma d^2}{N}} = \sqrt{\frac{128}{10}} = \sqrt{12.8} = 3.58$$

This standard deviation value suggests that any nation whose size of diplomatic staff is within 3.58 of the mean value of 10 is considered to be within one standard deviation (denoted $\pm 1\ \sigma$). In this case, countries C, D, E, F, G, H, and I are within a range for 2 σ of 10 $\pm$ 3.58 (6.42 ←——→ 13.58). Similarly, we know that the staff sizes of countries A and B fall within two standard deviations (2 $\times$ 3.58 = 7.16 or 10 $\pm$ 7.16 or 2.84 ←——→ 17.16). Country J, however is within three standard deviations from the mean. Finally, we know that three standard deviations are required to represent the total empirical variation in the distribution.

In summary the steps for calculating a standard deviation are as follows:

1. Sum the scores and compute the mean ($\overline{X}$) by dividing the sum of the scores by N.
2. Subtract the mean ($\overline{X}$) from each score (X) to obtain deviations (d) from the mean.
3. Square each deviation from the mean (d^2). Note that the deviations are squared in order to remove the negative signs.
4. Sum the squares of the deviations (Σd^2).
5. Divide the sum of the squares by the total number of scores ($\Sigma d^2/N$).
6. Extract the square root of result from step 5.
7. Thus, we can define the standard deviation as the square root of the average of the squared deviations from the mean.

Coefficient of Variability. The standard deviation allows one to acquire a sense for the degree of homogeneity among the cases in a population or sample. If, however, the researcher wishes to compare the homogeneity among several samples, the standard deviation may be slightly misleading because of different mean values. As the mean increases, the likelihood that the standard deviation will also increase is greater. Consequently, the *coefficient of variability*, which controls for differences in the respective mean values, is a better measure of variability for the comparison of different samples. The coefficient of variability (V) is obtained by dividing the standard deviation by the mean. Thus, in the preceding example, $V = \frac{3.58}{10}$ or .358.

The value of this statistic ought to be apparent in the following example. Let us assume that we have some theoretical or policy interest in knowing more about the proportion of the population in various countries that are involved in the military. For example, it has been argued that the size of defensive armies is dependent on the length of frontiers and the population density of a nation. Other variables, such as the absolute size of a nation's population and GNP per capita are strong determinants of the size of offensive armies (Robinson, 1967). Moreover, if we assume that during the 19th century between the Napoleonic Wars and the turn of the century, armies have been generally offensive, we have a testable proposition that can easily be explored simply by the use of means, standard deviation, and coefficients of variability.

The data in Figure 5.26, extracted from Pryor (1968), provide two cross-sectional views—one in 1858 and one in 1958—of military personnel as a percentage of total population. These data show clearly that the proportion of the population in military service increased over the 100-year period (note the mean scores in rows 1 and 5). Thus, if the offensiveness of an army is a function of the number of military personnel as a percentage of population, then armies of this century appear to be more offensive. This result is particularly startling when you consider that today's army is more capital intensive than the army of yesteryear. Moreover, scores in the V column for rows 1 and 5 indicate greater numerical spread among nations in 1958 (.55) than in 1858 (.40); that is, nations 100 years ago tended to be more similar with respect to the allocation of human resources to the military establishment than they are today.

Moreover, we can see from the data in rows 2 and 3 that the Warsaw Pact nations have a higher ratio of military personnel than do the NATO nations (compare the means of 140 and 183 men per 10,000 population respectively). And the variation among nations within each alliance differs slightly (V = .52 for NATO and V = .42 for Warsaw Pact nations).

Figure 5.26 provides a wealth of information obtained from simply comparing the average values and amount of variation in a single variable—percentage of the civilian population in the military. Two different comparative samples may be studied: (1) one over time (all nations for 1858 and 1958 respectively), and (2)

Rows	Date	Data	Sample size	Mean	SD	V
1	1858	All nations	18	103 men per 10k pop.	41 men per 10k pop.	.40
2	1958	NATO nations	15	140 men per 10k pop.	73 men per 10k pop.	.52
3	1958	Warsaw Pact nations	8	183 men per 10k pop.	77 men per 10k pop.	.42
4	1958	Non-pact nations	6	143 men per 10k pop.	102 men per 10k pop.	.71
5	1958	All nations	29	152 men per 10k pop.	83 men per 10k pop.	.55

Figure 5.26   Military personnel

* From Frederic L. Pryor, *Public Expenditures in Communist and Capitalist Nations*, George Allen & Unwin Ltd.

different groups for the same period (all nations, Warsaw Pact, NATO, and non-pact nations for 1958). For each sample you can compare the average number of military personnel as a percentage of the civilian population as well as the degree of homogeneity or variation within each group.

Gini Index

In the preceding pages we have described the more typical statistical measures of central tendency and dispersion. Another important descriptive statistic, the Gini index, is less widely used than those described above. The Gini index allows you to measure precisely the level of inequality represented graphically by the Lorenz curve. The values of the Gini index range from 0 to 1.0, with the higher value representing a greater degree of inequality. That is, a value of "0" reveals that a resource is distributed evenly among the population, whereas an index of approximately 1.0 denotes that the resource is controlled by the smallest possible percentage of the population.

The principal utility of the Gini index is that it allows you to compare the distribution of several resources with greater precision than the Lorenz curve. For example, Figure 5.27 reveals the curves for literacy, hospital beds, radios, and GNP respectively (Russett, 1965, p. 119). Although it is possible visually to distinguish whether literacy or GNP is more equally distributed, a difficulty arises when comparing radios and GNP because their respective Lorenz curves cross. The Gini index allows you to demonstrate that GNP is slightly more equally distributed

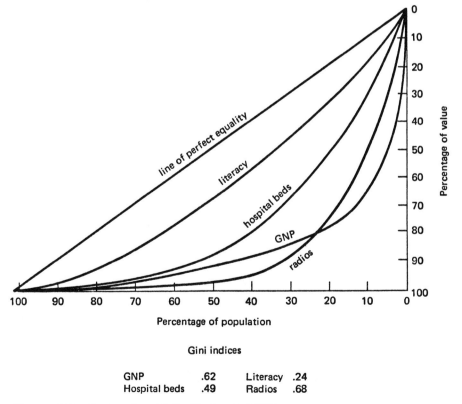

Gini indices

| GNP | .62 | Literacy | .24 |
| Hospital beds | .49 | Radios | .68 |

Figure 5.27   Projected world distributions in 1975

* Russett, 1965, p. 119.

(.62) than radios (.68)—remembering that the higher the Gini index value, the greater the level of inequality.

Computation of the Gini Index.   The Gini index is defined formally as the area of inequality (as shown in Figure 5.28) divided by the maximum are of inequality

$$\left(\text{Gini index} = \frac{\text{area of inequality}}{\text{maximum area of inequality}}\right).$$

Thus, it is necessary to (a) determine both the maximum and actual areas of inequality, and (b) divide the value of the actual area by the maximum area. It is the product of this operation that represents the Gini index. Before computing either area it is helpful to change the percentage values for both the X and Y axes to decimals. These new values are given in Figure 5.28. The denominator of the equation, the maximum area of inequality is, of course, a constant which is equal to the area of the triangle with sides of the X and Y axis values respectively. Computing from the formula for the area of a triangle

$\left(\dfrac{ab}{2}\right.$ where a and b = the value of the X and Y axes respectively) we obtain $\dfrac{lxw}{2}$ or .5.

Thus, the Gini index is equal to the area of inequality for the specific Lorenz curve divided by .5. Determining the actual value for the numerator involves a series of relatively easy steps. First, you obtain the area under the Lorenz curve by dividing it into a series of triangles and rectangles (see Figure 5.28), obtaining the area of

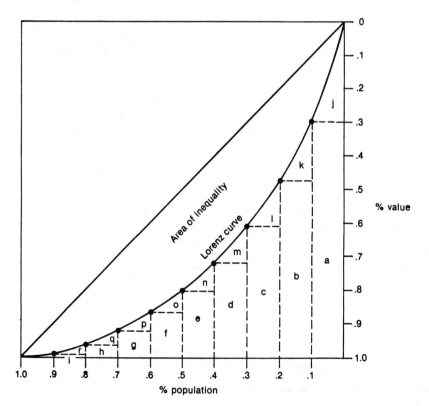

Figure 5.28   Hypothetical Lorenz curve

each, and summing these. Second, subtract this area from the area of the right triangle (.5); this process yields the area of inequality. This value becomes the numerator in the formula for the Gini index. This index, in turn, is computed by dividing the numerator by the maximum area of inequality. For example, if the area under the curve is .3, the area of inequality is .2 (.5 — .3). The Gini index in this case is .2/.5 or .4 (see Figure 5.29).

Let's work out a problem step-by-step for the hypothetical Lorenz curve in Figure 5.28. In this example, the rectangles are labeled a through i, and the triangles are labeled j through s.

Remember, the higher the Gini index, the greater the level of inequality. Consequently, an index of .36 reveals a moderately low level of inequality.[12]

		Triangles				*Rectangles*	
ID	l	w	area (½ lxw)	ID	l	w	area (lxw)
j	.3	.1	.02	a	.7	.1	.07
k	.15	.1	.01	b	.55	.1	.06
l	.15	.1	.01	c	.4	.1	.04
m	.1	.1	.01	d	.3	.1	.03
n	.1	.1	.01	e	.2	.1	.02
o	.05	.1	0	f	.15	.1	.02
p	.05	.1	0	g	.1	.1	.01
q	.05	.1	0	h	.05	.1	.01
r	.03	.1	0	i	.02	.1	0
s	.02	.1	0			Total =	.26
		Total =	.06				

area of triangles = .06
area of rectangles = .26
area under the Lorenz curve = .32
area of inequality = .5 — .32 = .18
$$\text{Gini Index} = \frac{\text{area of inequality}}{.5}$$
$$= \frac{.18}{.5}$$
$$= .36$$

Figure 5.29   Worksheet for Gini index

Applications of the Gini Index.   The Gini index is probably the most underutilized descriptive statistic, yet its potential uses are many. It allows comparisons (1) across nations for a given moment in time, (2) across several moments in time for a given nation or the international system as a whole, and (3) across variables or indicators for a given moment. And finally, as Benson (1969) has suggested, it provides a mechanism for making hypothetical comparisons of the likely outcomes of alternative policy decisions.

TRANSFORMATIONS OF DATA

Before moving to analysis of the association among variables, it is important that we briefly focus on a typical problem encountered by researchers which relates to the nature of the distribution of data. Many of the associational statistics require that the scores approximate a normal distribution (mean = median = mode).

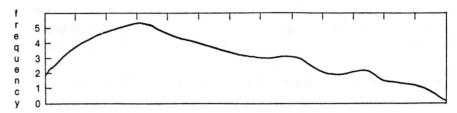

Figure 5.30   Population in cities over 20,000 as percent of total population

In cross-national research, however, we seldom find our data normally distributed. One close approximation to normally distributed data is found in Figure 5.30, displaying the frequency distribution of the percent total population in cities over 20,000. Although this distribution may not appear to be normally distributed, a standard test of normality reveals that it is a fairly close approximation to a normal distribution.[13] Much more frequently, we encounter data that are highly skewed, such as national income, displayed in Figure 5.31.

This positively skewed distribution reflects the great inequalities in the distribution of nation's income among nations, with many nations having little wealth; and a few nations having much of the wealth (e.g., the USSR around $250 billion and the USA around $500 billion). A good example of a negatively skewed dis-

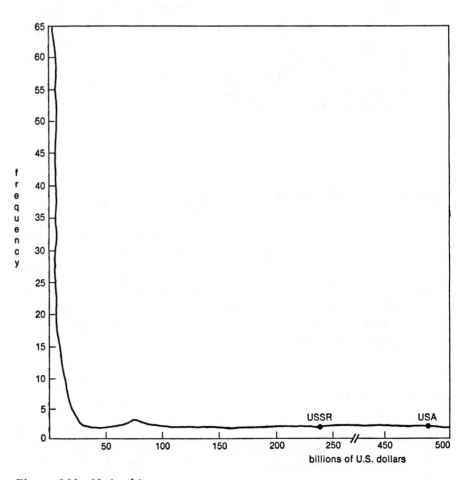

Figure 5.31   National income

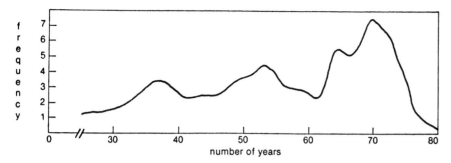

Figure 5.32 *Female life expectancy at age zero*

tribution is a cross-national measure of the distribution of health, displayed in Figure 5.32.

In this figure, we can see that the value of health measured by female life expectancy is more widely shared than are the wealth values displayed in Figure 5.31. While many nations remain health deprived, a fairly large number of nations have high levels of life expectancy (thus we see one of the reasons for the so-called population explosion—the extension of mortality).

As long as we do not want to use higher order inferential statistics for purposes of analysis, deviations from the normal distribution are no problem. However, if we want to use higher order statistics, then we may want to normalize our distributions in order to increase our ability to give substantive interpretations to the statistics we obtain (e.g., a correlation coefficient). More technically, the validity of many statistical measurements requires our data to be normally distributed. Therefore, let's briefly examine the issue of normalizing distributions of data so that you'll have a feeling for what is being done in much of the international politics literature that you'll encounter.

A distribution can often be normalized by applying a mathematical transformation. For example, many cross-national data can be normalized by looking at the distributions as logarithms of the raw scores. A log transformation merely sketches out the distribution of raw scores by arranging or transforming the scores such that, for example, differences between magnitudes of 1, 10, 100, 1,000 and 1,000,000 appear as intervals of equal distance. If a logarithmic transformation is used to normalize a distribution, then we describe the distribution of the variable as being log normal.

In Figure 5.33, we have displayed a logarithmic transformation of national income. Compare the shape of the distribution in this figure with the raw data distribution in Figure 5.31.

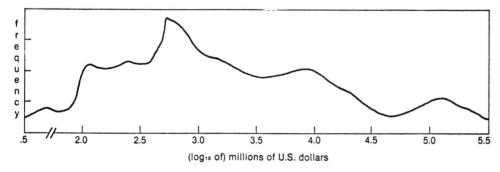

Figure 5.33 *Log_{10} transformation of national income*

Although the transformed distribution of national income in Figure 5.33 is nearly log normal, it retains a slight positive skew (slightly more scores to the left). Nevertheless, it approximates a normal distribution and is visibly closer to normality than the curve obtained from the untransformed data in Figure 5.31.

Although we shall not expect you to engage in the process of transforming data into normal distributions, it is important to remember that (a) many statistical tests assume that data are normally distributed, (b) most cross-national data are *not* normally distributed, (c) procedures do exist for normalizing distributions, and (d) interpretations of statistical results are altered ("change" becomes "proportional change"). Another common way for dealing with data that are not normally distributed in the case of ratio or interval measures like we have just reviewed is to collapse the data into ordinal scales. Statistics appropriate to ordinal scales do not require data to be normally distributed, and we shall emphasize these kinds of statistics in the following two chapters.

SUMMARY

This chapter has focused on the usefulness of describing and displaying the data for each variable in your research design. Procedures have been presented for three kinds of descriptive displays: a variable's frequency distribution, its typical value or central tendency, and its degree of homogeneity or variation. Both the visual and statistical routines used in the descriptive displays allow the reader to quickly discover the basic characteristics of each variable. This information is not only useful when employing the variable in data analysis, but allows the reader to describe how values and resources are distributed throughout the international system. This type of mapping exercise is important because we must be able to describe the system and patterns of behavior which occur within it before we can attempt in a systematic and cumulative way to understand the causes of behavior.

EXERCISES

1 Refer to the following table.

A What information is contained in the table and what conclusions might be drawn from it? That is, what changes took place between 1958 and 1968? What changes did not take place? How do you account for it?

B What information is lacking which might contribute to better visualizing the change, or lack of it, between 1958 and 1968?

Number of Common IGO Memberships by Dyads

1958–1968

1958			1968		
1	France/United Kingdom	76	1	France/West Germany	91
2	Belgium/France	75	2.5	France/Netherlands	88
3.5	France/Netherlands	70	2.5	France/Italy	88
3.5	France/Italy	70	4	Belgium/Netherlands	87
5	France/West Germany	64	5	Belgium/France	85
6	Belgium/Netherlands	63	6.5	Netherlands/West Germany	84
7	Belgium/United Kingdom	61	6.5	Belgium/West Germany	84
8	Belgium/Italy	60	8	France/United Kingdom	83
9.5	Italy/Netherlands	59	9.5	Italy/West Germany	82
9.5	Belgium/West Germany	59	9.5	Italy/Netherlands	82

2 The histogram on the next page seems to suggest that wars tend to begin relatively more often at certain times of the year than at others. What times? Would this same conclusion necessarily be reached if twelve categories (divisions of the year) were used instead of four? Could a different division of the year (for example, February–April, May–July, etc.) create a frequency diagram suggesting other conclusions?

3   The following shows two rank orders, with the interval data included, of GNP/capita. The left ranking presents the data in raw form and the right ranking in transformed form. You are to construct a histogram of ten categories each. What comparisons can you make about the raw and transformed distributions of GNP/capita?

f

GNP/capita—raw

f

GNP/capita—transformed

Raw Data				*Transformed Data*			
1 KUW	3300.000	59 GHA	225.999	1 KUW	1.876	59 GHA	1.534
2 USA	3083.000	60 HON	216.000	2 USA	1.868	60 HON	1.528
3 CAN	2100.000	61 IRN	216.000	3 CAN	1.823	61 IRN	1.528
4 SWD	2046.000	62 KON	203.999	4 SWD	1.820	62 KON	1.520
5 SWZ	2002.000	63 GAB	199.999	5 SWZ	1.817	63 GAB	1.517
6 NEW	1747.000	64 SEN	199.999	6 NEW	1.801	64 SEN	1.517
7 AUL	1732.999	65 ECU	199.000	7 AUL	1.800	65 ECU	1.516
8 ICE	1719.000	66 JOR	199.000	8 ICE	1.799	66 JOR	1.516
9 DEN	1675.000	67 BRA	196.000	9 DEN	1.796	67 BRA	1.514
10 FRN	1658.000	68 IVO	196.000	10 FRN	1.794	68 IVO	1.514
11 GMW	1634.999	69 PAR	192.999	11 GMW	1.793	69 PAR	1.512
12 LUX	1615.000	70 ALG	185.000	12 LUX	1.791	70 ALG	1.506
13 UNK	1564.000	71 TUN	185.000	13 UNK	1.787	71 TUN	1.506
14 NOR	1536.999	72 SAU	175.000	14 NOR	1.785	72 SAU	1.498
15 BEL	1496.000	73 MOR	173.000	15 BEL	1.782	73 MOR	1.496
16 FIN	1277.999	74 LBR	170.000	16 FIN	1.763	74 LBR	1.493
17 USR	1226.000	75 CHT	168.999	17 USR	1.757	75 CHT	1.493
18 NTH	1205.000	76 BOL	153.999	18 NTH	1.755	76 BOL	1.479
19 CZE	1201.000	77 CON	150.000	19 CZE	1.755	77 CON	1.475
20 GME	1138.000	78 SYR	148.000	20 GME	1.748	78 SYR	1.473
21 ISR	1111.000	79 CEY	142.000	21 ISR	1.745	79 CEY	1.467
22 AUS	1068.999	80 PHI	142.000	22 AUS	1.740	80 PHI	1.467
23 ITA	894.000	81 UAR	138.999	23 ITA	1.718	81 UAR	1.464
24 HUN	833.000	82 MAU	135.000	24 HUN	1.709	82 MAU	1.460
25 IRE	797.000	83 CAM	127.000	25 IRE	1.703	83 CAM	1.450
26 POL	730.000	84 KOS	114.000	26 POL	1.692	84 KOS	1.434
27 VEN	728.000	85 VTS	114.000	27 VEN	1.692	85 VTS	1.434
28 ALB	704.000	86 TAI	105.999	28 ALB	1.687	86 TAI	1.423
29 TRI	630.000	87 SIE	100.000	29 TRI	1.673	87 SIE	1.414
30 JAP	626.000	88 SUD	100.000	30 JAP	1.672	88 SUD	1.414
31 CYP	619.999	89 CHN	94.999	31 CYP	1.671	89 CHN	1.406
32 ARG	614.000	90 VTN	94.999	32 ARG	1.670	90 VTN	1.406
33 BUL	567.999	91 NIG	92.999	33 BUL	1.660	91 NIG	1.403
34 RUM	554.999	92 CAO	92.000	34 RUM	1.657	92 CAO	1.401
35 GRC	517.000	93 CEN	90.000	35 GRC	1.647	93 CEN	1.398
36 SAF	492.000	94 MAG	90.000	36 SAF	1.641	94 MAG	1.398
37 CHL	482.999	95 YEM	90.000	37 CHL	1.638	95 YEM	1.398
38 SPN	482.000	96 LAO	87.000	38 SPN	1.638	96 LAO	1.393
39 URU	478.000	97 IND	86.000	39 URU	1.637	97 IND	1.391
40 MON	458.999	98 PAK	81.000	40 MON	1.632	98 PAK	1.381
41 PAN	447.999	99 AFG	79.999	41 PAN	1.628	99 AFG	1.380
42 JAM	429.000	100 COP	79.999	42 JAM	1.622	100 COP	1.380
43 MEX	401.999	101 HAI	79.999	43 MEX	1.614	101 HAI	1.380
44 COS	384.999	102 INS	79.999	44 COS	1.608	102 INS	1.380
45 LEB	383.000	103 NIR	75.000	45 LEB	1.607	103 NIR	1.369
46 YUG	380.000	104 TOG	75.000	46 YUG	1.606	104 TOG	1.369
47 LBY	358.999	105 UGA	74.000	47 LBY	1.598	105 UGA	1.367
48 CUB	349.999	106 BUR	72.000	48 CUB	1.595	106 BUR	1.363
49 POR	321.000	107 DAH	70.000	49 POR	1.583	107 DAH	1.358
50 MAL	295.000	108 MLI	65.000	50 MAL	1.572	108 MLI	1.346
51 COL	292.000	109 GUI	59.999	51 COL	1.570	109 GUI	1.333
52 GUA	284.000	110 NEP	59.000	52 GUA	1.566	110 NEP	1.331
53 NIC	282.000	111 CHA	55.000	53 NIC	1.565	111 CHA	1.319
54 ELS	275.000	112 ETH	48.000	54 ELS	1.562	112 ETH	1.297
55 DOM	268.999	113 SOM	44.999	55 DOM	1.559	113 SOM	1.286
56 PER	262.000	114 UPP	44.999	56 PER	1.555	114 UPP	1.286
57 TUR	233.000	115 BUI	40.000	57 TUR	1.539	115 BUI	1.266
58 IRQ	227.999	116 RWA	40.000	58 IRQ	1.536	116 RWA	1.266

4   The two Lorenz curves on the next page show a change in the distribution of GNP among the top ten nations between 1950 and 1975. What is that change? How do you account for it? What further information is necessary to complete

an analysis of the distribution for the entire international system? Which decile showed the largest growth, vis-a-vis the others?

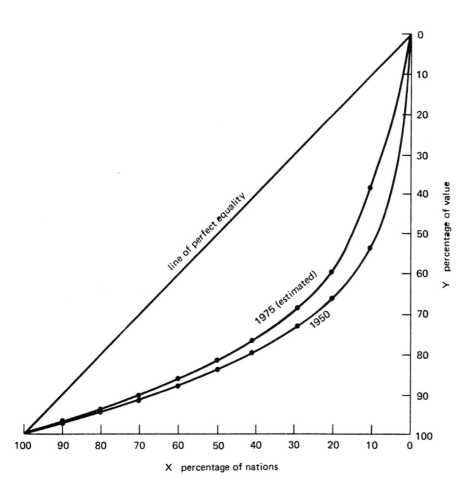

5 Construct a Lorenz curve from the proportional values for coal production in the world for 1971. Complete the two columns on the right first.

Decile of Nations	% of CP for each Decile	Cumulative % of Nations	Cumulative % of CP
0–10%	78%	_____	_____
11–20%	15%	_____	_____
21–30%	5%	_____	_____
31–40%	1%	_____	_____
41–50%	.4%	_____	_____
51–60%	.1%	_____	_____
61–70%	.08%	_____	_____
71–80%	.04%	_____	_____
81–90%	.01%	_____	_____
91–100%	.001%	_____	_____

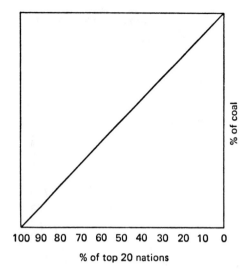

6 Construct a Lorenz curve for the projected distribution of energy consumption for 1975. The sample is the 20 largest consuming nations.

A Decile of Nations	B % of Energy Consumption for each Decile of Nations	C Cumulative % of Nations	D Cumulative % of Energy Consumption
0–10%	52%		
11–20%	16%		
21–30%	8%		
31–40%	6%		
41–50%	4%		
51–60%	3%		
61–70%	3%		
71–80%	2%		
81–90%	2%		
91–100%	2%		

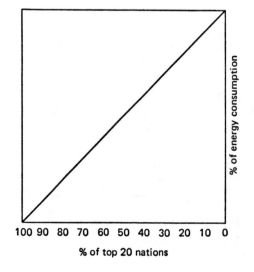

7 Using the data for the Lorenz curve in problem 6 for the projected
distribution of energy consumption, determine the Gini index.

8 The military expenditures as percentage of GNP for ten Middle East-North
African countries are as follows:

Iraq	7.8
Israel	12.0
Kuwait	1.7
Lebanon	3.3
Saudi Arabia	9.1
Syria	11.9
Algeria	3.2
Libya	3.6
Tunisia	.8
United Arab Republic	7.4

Calculate the following statistics for military expenditures as a percentage
of GNP.

A Measures of central tendency

  a. mean = _____

  b. median = _____

  c. mode = _____

B Measures of dispersion

  d. range = _____

  e. standard deviation = _____

9 Given the following four steps of data, assess the differences among groups.
In particular, attempt to analyze the degree to which "bloc voting" is
involved. What trends do you see? What particular information here interests
you? Do you find it unusual or predictable? Why?

Index of Agreement with U.S. in U.N. Voting on Selected Issues

	N	Mean	Median	Mode	Range	Standard Deviation	Coefficient of Variability
South America	10	70.4	68.5	68	20	5.9	.08
Southeast Asia	7	49.2	43	—	46	19.8	.4
Western Europe	7	92.4	95	95	14	4.9	.05
Eastern Europe	6	.3	0	0	1	.5	1.6

NOTES

1. For an interesting and easy to read introduction to the use of numbers in social analysis, see Zeisel's *Say It With Figures* (1968). An enlightening and often humorous introduction to the use of graphic displays of descriptive data is Huff's *How To Lie With Statistics* (1954). For a basic introduction to statistics, see Downie and Heath (1965). For an introduction to basic statistics in a political science context, see Palumbo (1969) or Garson (1971).

2. See Jones and Singer (1972) for an inventory of major quantitative works in international relations.

3. On the issue of distortions, see Huff (1954).

4. For elaboration of these points, see Huff (1954) and Zeisel (1968).

5. For a more elaborate discussion of the construction of graphic displays, see Bennett (1970).

6. Russett (1965, pp. 106–124) and Alker (1965, pp. 29–53) show excellent overviews of trends in the inequalities of valued resources in the world. The ideas expressed in this discussion owe their origin to these two sources.

7. This is not to imply that perfect equality is always a desired goal. It is simply a base against which to judge the actual empirical distributions.

8. Although the Lorenz curve provides a graphical representation of inequality, it is sometimes difficult to compare the distributions of a number of resources. Consequently, a statistic has been developed, termed the Gini index, which provides an accurate *comparative* measure. Because the Gini index represents a statistical rather than visual display, it is discussed later in this chapter.

9. Note that the median may not always be associated with an actual case (as will the mean). The mode, however, must have a corresponding case. In the particular example the mean (83.6) falls between East Germany (83) and West Germany (152).

10. The usefulness and versatility of the standard deviation will be discussed in chapter 7.

11. Note also that the modal score is 12 and that the median is 10.5 (derived by summing the two middle scores in a distribution with even numbers and dividing by two). In this case, the median, mean, and mode are fairly close. Thus, this distribution is approximately normal.

12. For a general discussion of the Lorenz curve and its applications, see Lyons (1970).

13. A chi square (x^2) goodness of fit test = 5.39; measures of skewness and kurtosis = .69 and −.15 respectively.

Chapter Six

DISPLAYING ASSOCIATIONAL DATA

In the preceding chapter we emphasized that the collection and processing of data are not enough; the analyst has the responsibility of describing and displaying findings with clarity sufficient to allow the reader to grasp quickly and easily the importance of the results that were obtained. Thus, it is very important for reports of quantitative research to include the basic statistical data that will allow the reader independently to assess the central tendencies—the mean, median, and mode —of the empirical distributions that have been discovered. In addition, because so many statistical operations rely on assumptions about the variability found in an empirical distribution, the analyst should give the reader a clear sense of the range and standard deviation of the empirical distributions with which he or she is working. Once these basic descriptive operations have been performed, it is possible to move from descriptive to associational analysis, that is, from describing data distributions to the analysis of data in the light of relationships between two or more variables that have been hypothesized. This stage, covered in chapters 6 and 7, completes the six steps in quantitative research.

ASSOCIATIONAL DISPLAYS

Associational operations involve the search for a relationship between two or more variables. The search for two-variable associations is called *bivariate analysis.* For example, the positive correlational proposition asserting that the more a nation is developed economically, the more it will be involved in the international system represents a problem of bivariate analysis. In this example, the analyst will be required to examine the association between two variables and their corresponding indicators—level of economic development and level of involvement.

An example of multivariate analysis can be seen in an expanded version of the example just mentioned. Consider the following proposition: larger and more developed nations are more involved in the international system. In this example, the analyst faces a problem of multivariate analysis because he or she will have to examine three variables—the simultaneous effect of two independent variables (the indicators of size and level of economic development) and one dependent variable (an indicator of involvement). These associational tasks can be performed by using procedures that show whether an association between two or more variables actually exists. These include *visual displays* which represent the data points for two or more variables, and *statistics techniques* which yield a numerical value that will permit the analyst to make a quantitative judgment about the degree of association between the variables.

The various kinds of visual displays and statistical techniques with associational applications are displayed in Figure 6.1. The former procedure is the subject of this chapter while chapter 7 focuses on the latter.

VISUAL DISPLAYS

In chapter 5 we discussed visual methods (histograms and Lorenz curves) for describing each individual variable. Similiar kinds of representations may also be applied to the task of assessing the degree of association among several variables. These have the same purpose as visual descriptive displays: to facilitate the reader's ability to comprehend more easily some pattern, in this case the relationship between two or more variables. Stated another way, the visual representation should allow the reader to determine whether the presence (absence) of X is associated with the presence (absence) of Y, or whether an increase in the value of one variable is associated with an increase in the other. We shall consider three basic associational displays: (1) contingency tables, which are used primarily for nominal data and, to a lesser extent for ordinal categories; (2) comparative crisscross or rank orders, designed for ranked information, and (3) scatter plots or cross-plots, which contain interval-level data.

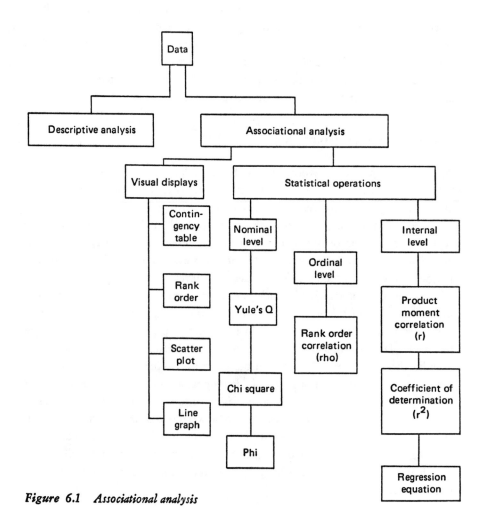

Figure 6.1 Associational analysis

Contingency Tables

The first basic method for the visual presentation of the association between two variables is the contingency table, which serves to display the joint occurrence of variables X and Y.[1] Consider the consequential proposition, "If X, then Y." That is, is the presence or absence of X associated with the presence or absence of Y? If the empirical study of this observation involved 100 observations or cases, and if the proposition were found to be empirically true with no exceptions, then the contingency table displaying the joint occurrence (or joint frequencies) of X and Y might appear as shown in Figure 6.2 where:

$$X, Y = \text{presence of X and Y}$$

$$\overline{X}, \overline{Y} \text{ (read X bar, Y bar)} = \text{absence of X and Y}$$

Because this contingency table clearly shows that among the 100 observations of Y, all are jointly associated with the presence or absence of X, the proposition, "If X, then Y" is deemed to be true or verified.

Conventional alpha representations are given in Figure 6.2 where: X and Y are the independent and dependent variables; $a + b$, $c + d$, $a + c$, and $b + d$ are the marginal frequencies or marginal distributions; a, b, c, and d are the conditional frequencies; and N is equal to the total number of cases ($N = a + b + c + d$). Convention dictates that in constructing the contingency table, the dependent variable (Y) of a proposition is presented in the rows and the independent variable (X) is presented in the columns.

The contingency table is particularly well suited to nominal or ordinal scales, although it may also be used to examine joint distributions that are based on higher levels of measurement so long as their distributions are collapsed into discrete class intervals or ordinal level groupings. For example, let us assume a theory suggests an association between the level of satisfaction among a nation's population and the degree of political stability within that nation's borders. Degree of satisfaction and level of political stability are each represented by two qualitative categories (frustration/satisfaction and stable/unstable), respectively. If you assume that the association suggested by the theory is positive (i.e., that satisfaction leads to stability), the independent variable—satisfaction—is represented by X; and the dependent variable—stability—is represented by Y, as shown in Figure 6.3.

Referring back to the definitions of the basic elements of a contingency table displayed in Figure 6.2, we can make the following inferences from the sample display of data in Figure 6.3.

1. The title tells us the proposition—the relationship between level of satisfaction and the degree of political stability.

2. The arrangement of the variables reveals that the level of satisfaction is the independent variable and that the political stability is the dependent variable.

3. The N cell tells us that there were 62 total observations or cases.

4. Each cell entry (a,b,c,d) reveals the frequency of joint occurrences of values of X and Y. For example, the 20 in cell A tells us that 20 cases where satisfaction was observed also included joint observations of stability—a finding consistent with the proposition; while cell C tells us that 6 observations of satisfaction included observations of instability—a finding inconsistent with the proposition.

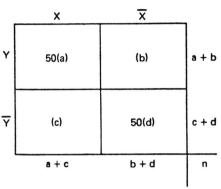

Figure 6.2   If X, then Y

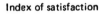
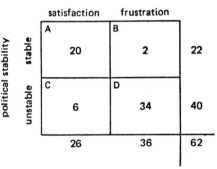

Figure 6.3   Association between level of satisfaction and degree of political stability

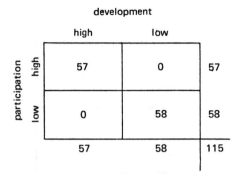

Figure 6.4 Perfect positive association

5. The marginals at the bottom tell us that of the 62 cases, 26 (or fewer than half) were cases manifesting satisfaction while 36 cases were observed as manifesting frustration. The row marginals tell us that of the 62 cases, approximately one-third (i.e., 22) involved stable political regimes.

6. We can note fairly easily from each of the cell entries that the level of satisfaction is associated positively with the degree of political stability. Of the 26 nations that manifested a condition of satisfaction, most of them (20) represented stable political regimes. Conversely, almost all of the 36 nations which exhibited frustration were unstable political systems (34 nations). Without employing any statistical routines, therefore, you are able to make some judgments about this particular proposition. And the data suggest that the proposition is supported by the evidence.

In short, as the above verbage clearly points out, a contingency table provides a very efficient way to present a wealth of information from empirical investigations of bivariate relationships.

In order to discuss the various kinds of joint frequencies which may occur for a given set of variables, assume that we are interested in testing the following multivariate proposition:

> The more economically developed and larger a nation, the more it will be active in the international system (Rummel, 1969, p. 234).

Using the "number of nations with whom a nation has diplomatic representation" to operationalize *participation*, "GNP per capita" to operationalize *development*, and "population" to operationalize *size*, we can use hypothetical or "dummy data" to construct the following contingency tables. Figures 6.4 and 6.5 show perfect association or high positive dependence between "development" and "participation" and between "size" and "participation" in the international system respectively.[2]

In contrast to the strong dependent associations displayed, Figure 6.6 depicts highly independent associations among the same variables where the dummy data entries for each of the joint occurrences of X and Y are distributed more or less evenly among all the cells. In other words, the data in Figure 6.6 do not suggest that occurrences of high (or low) levels of economic development are in any obvious way related to observations of high (or low) participation.

However, using actual data, contingency tables seldom reflect perfect association or perfect dependence as the empirical world of international politics is not that precise. The actual relations between the variables stated in the proposition appear in Figures 6.7 and 6.8.

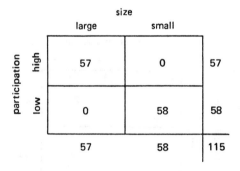

Figure 6.5 Perfect positive association

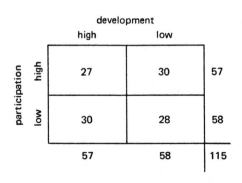

Figure 6.6 Low association

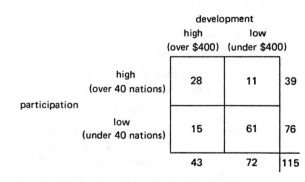

Figure 6.7 Relationship between development and participation

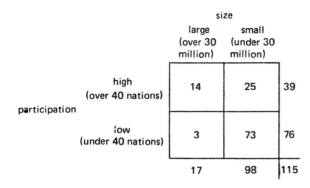

Figure 6.8   Relationship between size and participation

From the joint frequencies displayed in each contingency table, you ought to be able to make some judgments concerning the associations between size and development on the one hand, and participation on the other. The most general warranted observation, for example, is that both size and development appear to influence the amount of a nation's participation in the international system. In chapter 7 you will be acquainted with more precise and reliable methods to measure these associations; in the meantime, it is important to remember that the visual associational presentation yields useful and interpretable information.

Multivariate Tables and Control Variables

Note that the preceding figures involved two bivariate contingency tables to examine the multivariate proposition that larger (X_1) and more economically developed (X_2) nations will participate (Y_1) more in the international system. We can also construct a single multivariate contingency table to examine the same proposition. Multivariate contingency tables require us to nest the independent variables in relation to the dependent variable—as shown in Figure 6.9.

The data in Figure 6.9 reproduce the same data originally displayed in Figures 6.7 and 6.8. In the former figure, however, we are able to display the joint frequencies among three variables in contrast to the two-variable relationships displayed earlier.

dependent variable / independent variables (X_1, X_2)	high economic development (X_1)		low economic development (X_1)	
	large (x_2)	small (x_2)	large (x_2)	small (x_2)
high participation (Y)				
low participation (Y)				

Figure 6.9   Multivariate contingency table

dependent variables \ independent variables	X_1		Y_1	
	X_2	X_2	X_2	X_2
Y_1 — Y_2				
Y_1 — Y_2				
Y_1 — Y_1				
Y_1 — Y_2				

Figure 6.10   Multivariate contingency table with two independent and two dependent variables

It should be noted that a multivariate contingency table may be used to display relationships between two or more independent variables with one or more dependent variables—or vice versa. Consider, for example, the following proposition:

Larger (x_1) and more economically developed (x_2) nations tend to belong to alliances (y_1) and tend to have more wars (y_2).

This multivariate proposition, which includes two independent variables (x_1, x_2) and two dependent variables (y_1, y_2), can be displayed as shown in Figure 6.10.

Note that two dichotomized independent and two dichotomized dependent variables displayed in the same figure yields 16 cells—probably too large a number for an easily interpreted visual display.

It should also be noted that the order in which you nest your variables enables you to impose the desired controls on your empirical observations. In other words, if you want to control for the level of economic development and look at the effects of size, then you should nest your size variable within your level of economic development variable, as in Figure 6.9. On the other hand, if you want to control for size and then examine the effects of development on participation, then you should reverse the order of the nesting that is found in Figure 6.9, as shown in Figure 6.11.

dependent variables \ independent variables	large		small	
	high development	low development	high development	low development
high participation				
low participation				

Figure 6.11   The effect of economic development on participation controlling for size

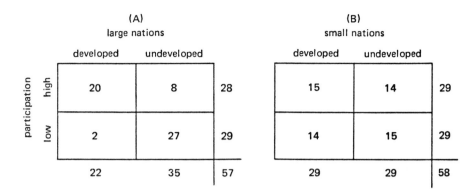

Figure 6.12 Dummy data showing relationship between development and participation controlling for size

It should be emphasized that the moderating effects of control variables can be substantial. For example, we might find that the level of economic development is strongly related to international participation among large nations but is not at all associated with participation among small nations—as suggested by the data in Figure 6.12.

In Figure 6.12(A), the relationship is quite pronounced—showing a strong dependence (or high association) between levels of development and participation among large nations only. Figure 6.12(B) shows strong independence (or little association) among levels of development and participation among small nations only. If we had failed to control for levels of size and simply looked at level of economic development in relation to participation, the interesting relationship that was found would have been largely washed out—as noted in Figure 6.13.

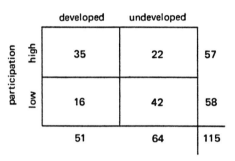

Figure 6.13 Association between development and participation development

Criss-Cross Diagrams and Rank Orders

In the preceding section, we used contingency tables to show the association between two nominal variables. Other kinds of visual analytic displays exist for data points measured by ordinal or interval scales. For example, we often use measures that allow us to rank cases along a continuum from higher to lower or from more to less. Recalling from chapter 3, these kinds of measures are called ordinal scales— which permit us to rank order observations. Even though we do not know the distance (or the intervals) between each case, we do know enough from ordinal level measures to rank cases along a continuum that represent increasing or decreasing quantities of a characteristic or attribute of interest. When you have data that permit you to rank order your cases, you can use a visual analytic display—called the *criss-cross diagram*—to help make some judgments about the strength and direction of the association between the ranks of the two variables being measured.

For example, Figure 6.14 presents the rank orders of a group of European nations for two variables—total number of diplomats sent abroad by a nation, and the total value of the exports of each nation. Your purpose is to determine if a nation that ranks high on one list will rank high on the other list and conversely, if a nation ranking low on one variable is accompanied by a low ranking on the other.

As Figure 6.14 shows, one can acquire a better sense of the association by drawing lines connecting a nation's position on each ranked list, thus creating a

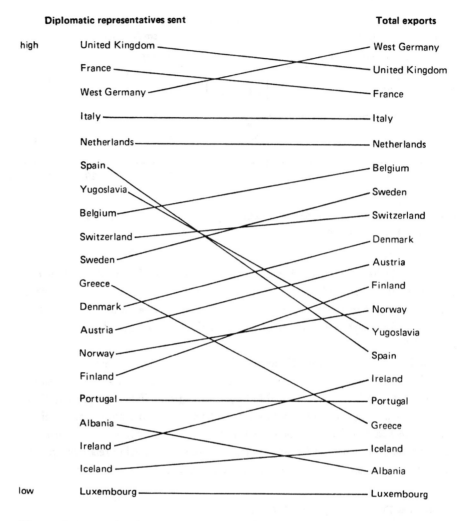

Figure 6.14 *Rank orders for western and southern Europe*

criss-cross diagram. This procedure allows you to step back and quickly examine all pairs simultaneously. Most nations, according to Figure 6.14, occupy a relatively similar rank on each variable (i.e., nearly all lines approach a horizontal position). There are a few exceptions (Spain, Greece, and Yugoslavia), but such a small number of exceptional cases in a sample of 20 nations does not detract too much from the typical horizontal pattern.[3]

On the other hand, if most of the lines do not approximate a horizontal pattern (i.e., most nations do not occupy relatively similar rank positions), two possible general conclusions may be drawn. First, if you can discern no recognizable pattern to the lines, the association between the two variables is probably small. Second, if the lines appear to follow an extreme criss-cross path (from the top of one rank to the bottom of the second and vice versa) a strong association probably exists between the two variables but it will be a negative one. That is, nations exhibiting high ranking scores on one variable will have low ranking scores on the second one.

Figure 6.15, which displays the rank comparisons of a group of European nations for the two variables *Percentage of Communist Vote* and *Military Expenditures as a Percentage of GNP*, is an example of the first conclusion. Eyeballing the ranks reveals no discernible pattern of correspondence. It does appear

% Communist vote   Military expenditures as % of GNP

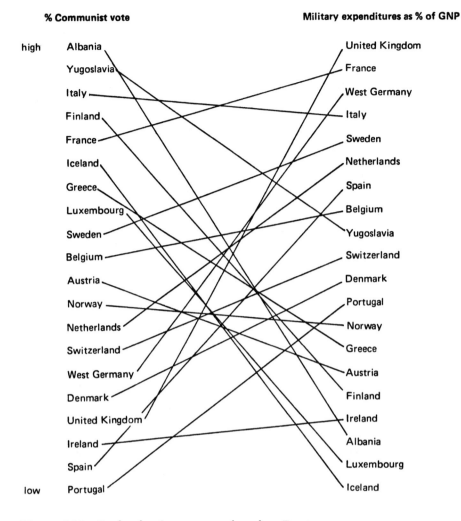

Figure 6.15 *Rank orders for western and southern Europe*

that more lines approach a somewhat vertical rather than horizontal path, which should be interpreted as a negative tendency. But this tendency appears only to be slight. Thus, you might conclude that the association between communist vote and military expenditures is a very weak one and in a slightly inverse direction.[4]

An example of the second general conclusion that may be drawn from a criss-cross diagram—that a strong negative association exists—occurs in Figure 6.16, which shows the association between *Freedom of the Press* and *Percentage of Communist Vote* for a group of European and Southeast Asian nations. As can be observed, extreme cases in each rank are connected with those at the opposite end of the other rank. This clearly discernible extreme criss-cross pattern strongly suggests negative association between these two variables.[5] In chapter 7 we will discuss more precise and reliable ways for measuring the degree of association between two rank ordered lists of cases.

Scatter Plots

Another type of joint frequency distribution is a scatter plot (sometimes called a scatter diagram or cross-plot). This type of visual display is used for bivariate

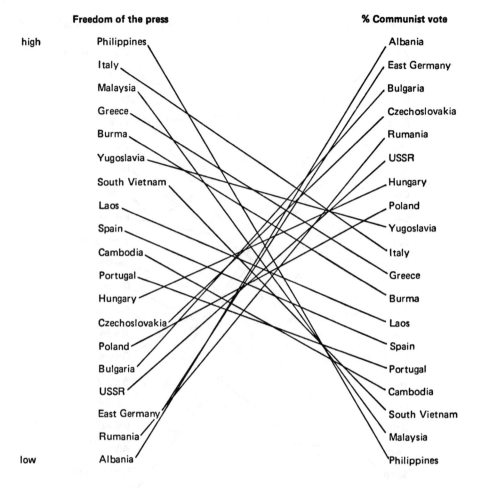

Figure 6.16 *Rank orders for southern/eastern Europe and Southeast Asia*

associations whose variables are measured at the ordinal or interval level. For example, consider once again the association between the level of want satisfaction and the degree of political stability. This time, each variable is measured on a 10-point scale (0 and 9 representing the extreme low and high values respectively for want satisfaction and stability). The two scores for each nation are given in Figure 6.17. It should be emphasized that it makes little difference whether these scores represent ordinal or interval level measurement.

Nation	Want Satisfaction	Stability
A	6	7
B	3	2
C	5	4
D	7	6
E	8	9
F	2	1
G	9	8
H	7	8
I	5	5
J	4	3

Figure 6.17 *Scores of want satisfaction and political stability*

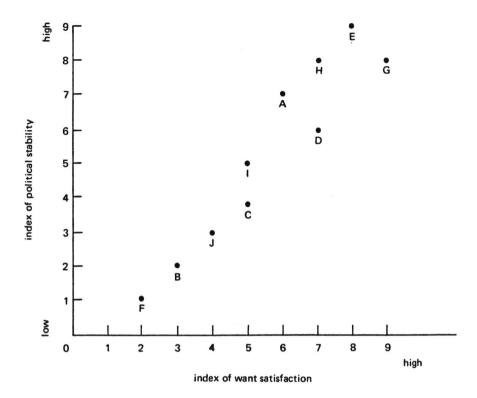

Figure 6.18 *Scatter plot of want satisfaction and political stability*

The scatter plot for these data is given in Figure 6.18. As can be observed, the data—expressed as points on two interval indices—suggest a positive association between the two variables in the figure. In fact, the relationship appears to be linear; in this case, the dependent variable (political stability) generally increases one unit as the independent variable (want satisfaction) increases by one unit.

A number of conventions used in Figure 6.18 should be noted. First, the independent and dependent variables are typically plotted along the horizontal (abscissa) and vertical (ordinate) axes, respectively. Second, the discrete points on each axis are equidistant. And third, low values appear closer to the intercept of the two axes (called the origin or zero point) than the high values. That is, we usually assign numbers up and across from the origin.

Figure 6.19 demonstrates a clearly definable positive association between two variables, *the freedom of press existent in a nation* and *the extent of agreement with the United States in votes within the United Nations*. You can observe that the greater a nation's press freedom index (moves from left to right along the X axis), the more likely it is to support the United States in UN roll call votes (its score on the Y axis moves upward).

In Figure 6.18 (as well as Figure 6.19), both variables were represented simply as positive values (0 to +n); that is, there were no negative levels of satisfaction or political stability. Consequently, the two axis were only extended from the origin in a positive direction (upward and to the right). It is also possible, however, to use both positive and negative values in a scatter plot—termed a rectangular coordinate graph. In this case, each axis extends both directions from the origin, as shown in Figure 6.20.

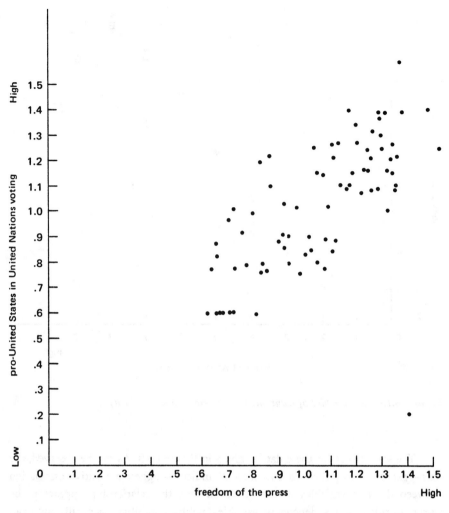

Figure 6.19 *Scatter plot of freedom of the press and pro-U.S. voting*

For example, consider again the relationship between want satisfaction and political stability. If a certain point on the continuum of values for each variable represented the point at which a qualitative change occurred (e.g., from a stable regime to an unstable one), that value would be assigned to the origin. In the proposition described in Figure 6.18, the origin would separate stable/unstable

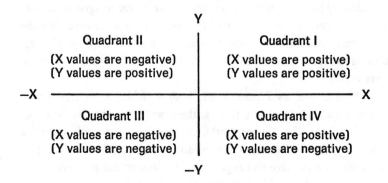

Figure 6.20 *Structural features of a rectangular coordinate graph*

regimes on the vertical or Y axis, and satisfied/frustrated regimes on the horizontal or X axis, thereby creating four kinds of nations as shown in Figure 6.21.

If the proposition "satisfaction leads to stability" accurately reflects the empirical world, we would expect to find that joint values for nations in our sample should fall in either the northeast or southwest quadrants. Using this technique allows the analyst to examine more easily clusters of nations which do not follow the typical pattern in order to assess the reason(s) for their deviant behavior.

The usefulness of the four-quadrant scatter plot can be seen in Figure 6.22, which shows the association between the amount of U.S. foreign aid that a nation receives and the extent to which the nation is supportive of the United States' position when voting within the United Nations. In this case, the data were transformed to approximate a normal distribution (see chapter 5) and the transformed mean values were placed at the origin. Those nations which received more than the average amount of aid appear to the right of the origin, and those receiving less than the mean are represented to the origin's left. Similarly, nations whose support of the United States was above the mean are plotted above the origin, and the remaining nations below this point. An alternative strategy might have been adopted for this latter variable. Instead of using the origin to represent $\overline{X}$, it would have been as appropriate to allow the origin to equal the number "one" for the ratio of pro-U.S. votes/anti-U.S. votes. If a nation voted with the United States more often than against it, the value of this dependent variable would be greater than one. Conversely, a nation which habitually voted against the United States would possess a value of less than one. In Figure 6.22, each positive and negative interval represents one standard deviation from the mean.

There are a number of observations that can be made about the procedures used in Figure 6.22. First of all, the raw data rather than the transformed scores could have been used for plotting the association between the two variables. In this case, the transformed scores were used so that nations would cluster together better. Second, the mean score is only one value among several that might have otherwise been used to denote the qualitative distinction between pro- and anti-U.S. voting behavior. Third, using a standard deviation for each variable allows the use of a standardized one-unit interval for each of the two scales, and thus standardizes the impact of the visual representation of the association.

Examine Figure 6.22 closely and you will discover a great deal of information about the association between "U.S. foreign aid received" and "support for the U.S. in United Nations voting." You should immediately see a pattern of southwest to northeast, suggesting a positive association. An examination of the northwest quadrant, moreover, indicates that there are no strong supporters of the U.S. (high

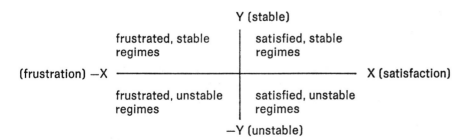

Figure 6.21   *Four possible nation types*

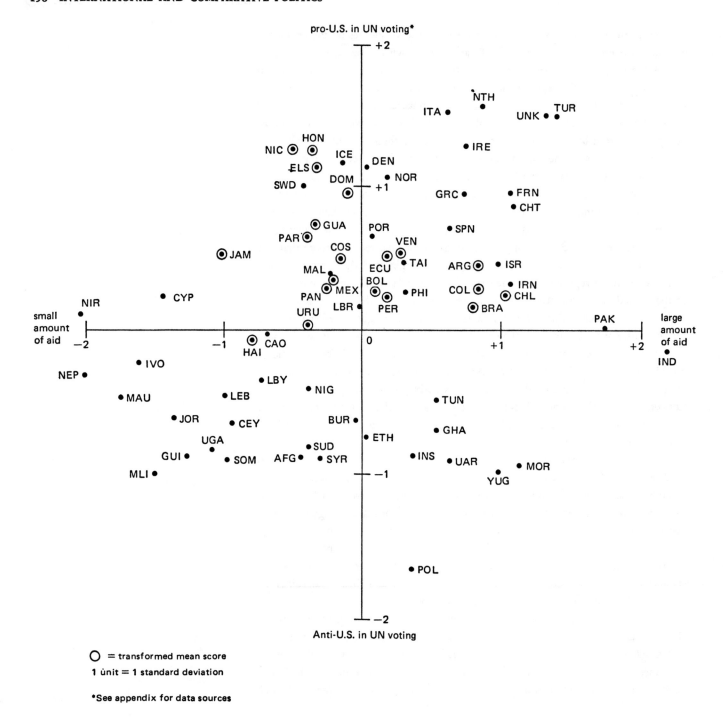

Figure 6.22 *Scatter plot: Index of agreement with U.S. in UN voting and amount of U.S. foreign aid received*

positive Y values) who receive only a small amount of U.S. aid (high negative X values). There does exist a cluster of nations around the mean on the X axis (average amount of aid received) who are very pro-American in United Nations voting (high positive Y values). These countries appear to be typically Central American and northern Latin American nations (Nicaragua, Honduras, Dominican Republic, Venezuela, Guatemala, and Mexico, for example).

Moreover, if you can recognize the southwest to northeast flow in Figure 6.22, a number of countries should immediately catch your eye as deviant cases—that is, they do not follow this typical pattern. Poland, Yugoslavia, Morocco, and India represent nations, for example, whose level of aid received suggests that they ought to be demonstrating a stronger support for the United States in the UN. The analyst, thus, is alerted to the need to search for explanations behind this apparent deviant behavior. By focusing upon these unusual cases, it may be possible to discover additional factors that should be included in the structure of a theory.[6]

Another eye-catching feature of Figure 6.22 is the unusual pattern exhibited by the Latin American group of nations (designated by the circles in the scatter plot). Whereas the general pattern for all nations appears to be a slightly positive one (the cases move up as they move right) the opposite situation exists for the Latin American subgroup—the cases move *down* as they move right.

This observation provides a graphic illustration of the importance of control variables, for different patterns of association may be revealed as different subsets of cases are examined.

Scatter Lines

Another type of visual analytic display, the scatter line graph, is derived from the scatter plot. If a pattern among the data points is readily discernible, one can simply draw a line which best captures the relationship among the scatter plot. Figures 6.23 and 6.24 show two different relationships uncovered by drawing a free hand line that passes through the center of the scatter. In both instances, the line serves to focus attention on the typical pattern that emerges from the scatter plot.

Figure 6.23 displays the relationship between GNP per capita (X) and defense expenditures per capita (Y). This scatter line shows that the greater the wealth, the larger the amount of money spent for defense. Thus, we have a linear relationship between the two variables—wealth and level of expenditures on defense.

Similarly, Figure 6.24 displays a relationship between wealth and internal violence that has been discovered. Here, X = GNP per capita, and Y = level of internal violence. Figure 6.24 seems to indicate that very poor countries have little internal violence. However, as wealth increases, so does violence, until a certain threshold point—denoted X' (read "X prime")—when increasing wealth tends to be related to decreasing internal violence. Such a relationship is called a *curvilinear* relationship.

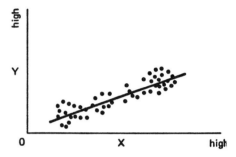

Figure 6.23   Relationship between GNP/population and defense expenditures per capita

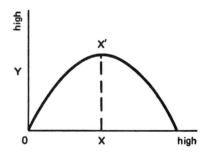

Figure 6.24   Relationship between wealth and domestic violence

SUMMARY

In this chapter we have emphasized different visual methods for displaying associational data—contingency tables, comparative rank ordered criss-cross diagrams, and scatter plots; we have discussed bivariate and multivariate analysis; and we examined briefly the concept of control variables in multivariate analysis. You should now be aware of the kinds of information that can be extracted from an associational visual display. In the following chapter, we will examine more precise and reliable techniques for assessing the relationships among variables in both bivariate and multivariate analysis.

EXERCISES

1 What conclusions can be drawn concerning the association between these two variables?

Percentage of Communist Vote

Freedom of Press		High	Low	
	High	4	41	45
	Low	11	21	32
		15	62	77

2 What conclusions can be drawn concerning the association between these two variables? Does this second matrix alter your interpretation of the first? Explain why or why not.

Status of Communist Party

Freedom of Press		in power	not in power	
	High	0	50	50
	Low	12	25	37
		12	75	87

3 Consult the rank ordering in the appendix.

A Calculate all entries for the following 2 × 2 table from the rank ordering. Remember that you need to determine a cutoff point between high and low categories. In this case, use the median.

Military Expenditures / Percentage of GNP

Total Exports		High	Low	
	High			
	Low			

B   Given the matrix in exercise 3A, attempt to construct an hypothesis you think
has been confirmed by the data.

C   Identify the following from your hypothesis:

Independent variable:
Dependent variable:
Intervening variable (if any):

4   Given the ranks on the "mass participation/turmoil" variable and the
"strategic distance from power centers: United States/USSR" variable,
interpret visually. Is there a relationship? If so, is it strong or weak? Positive
or negative? How do you explain it?

Mass participation/turmoil	Strategic distance from centers: United States/USSR
— France	— Czechoslovakia
— Argentina	— USSR
— Italy	— Finland
— Chile	— Turkey
— Ceylon	— Poland
— Poland	— Yugoslavia
— Cuba	— Italy
— Turkey	— Netherlands
— United States	— Burma
— Ecuador	— France
— El Salvador	— Ceylon
— Yugoslavia	— Phillipines
— Finland	— Malagasy
— Burma	— Argentina
— Czechoslavakia	— Chile
— Malagasy	— Ecuador
— USSR	— El Salvador
— Netherlands	— Cuba
— Phillipines	— United States

5   The following scatter plot represents positions of actors on North–South and
     East–West issues.[7] What information can you obtain from this plot?
     Sketch in the estimated scatter line. Identify deviant cases and describe the
     reason for this deviance (in a statistical, not substantive, sense).

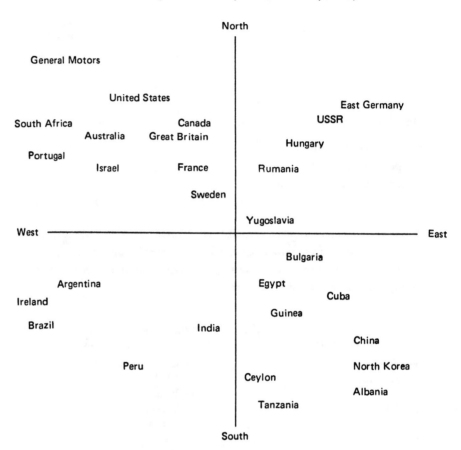

*Estimated positions of selected actors on North-South and East-West issues**

* R. F. Hopkins and R. W. Mansbach, *Structure and Process in International Politics*,
Harper and Row, 1973, p. 117.

6   Construct a scatterplot from the following data and estimate the regression
     line. Assess the direction and strength of the relationship, if any, between per
     capita GNP and the percentage of agricultural workers. Now, attempt to
     explain your findings, that is, explain why such a relationship either does or does
     not exist. Can you account for any extreme results—individual nations
     which appear to deviate from the typical pattern?

	GNP per capita	Percentage of agricultural workers
USA	4303	6
Dominican Republic	295	57
Guatemala	305	64
Costa Rica	454	48
Ecuador	259	52
Paraguay	229	51
United Kingdom	1862	4
Luxembourg	2277	11
Portugal	529	40
Austria	1544	20
Albania	928	58
Cyprus	704	39
Finland	1709	32
Iceland	2383	35
Mauritania	155	89
Upper Volta	50	87
Togo	120	79
Cen. African Rep.	136	90
Uganda	91	89
Ethiopia	63	88
Algeria	260	60
Iran	297	57
Syria	248	50
Saudi Arabia	478	72
China	129	63
Mongolia	569	59
Japan	1404	27
Ceylon	149	54
Laos	72	81
Phillipines	203	59

Percentage of agricultural workers

GNP per capita

NOTES

1. See Alker (1965) for a discussion of contingency table analysis.

2. Note that although the data were originally interval measures, they have been collapsed into nominal or qualitative categories of "high" and "low."

3. This conclusion is verified by a statistic, the Spearman rho (covered in chapter 7), which yields a value of +.84. A perfect positive association is denoted by a rho value of +1.00.

4. Again, Spearman's rho yields a value of −.20, which can be interpreted as a weak negative association between the two variables.

5. This interpretation is supported by a Spearman's rho of −.78 where a perfect negative association is −1.00.

6. See Lazarsfeld and Rosenburg (1955, pp. 167–170) and Tufte (1969) for a discussion of the usefulness of deviant case analysis.

7. See Hopkins and Mansbach (1973, pp. 117, 280) for excellent examples of the use of the four-quadrant approach.

Chapter Seven

STATISTICAL OPERATIONS FOR ASSOCIATIONAL ANALYSIS

In chapter Six we examined various types of visual displays that facilitate the exploration of analytical associations and that help the analyst communicate findings to readers in an efficient and effective manner. Visual displays, however, are useful primarily as a means for approximating or estimating relationships. Consequently, it is necessary to employ statistical tests in order to determine the precise nature of the association. Hence, this chapter will emphasize the more useful measures of association; that is, the emphasis will be on procedures for making precise and reliable estimates of the common variation between X and Y.

There are two principal elements of concern with respect to the examination of common variation—degree and form.[1] The *degree* of the association refers to the amount of covariation between the two variables. If they are highly related, we would find that they vary together and, hence, would have a high degree of association. If the variables are only slightly related, however, they would display only minimal common variation and, hence, a low degree of association. Tests of association—often termed *correlation coefficients*—permit the analyst to measure the degree that the relationship actually covaries.

The second element of covariation, the *form* of the association, answers the question of the direction of a relationship. When nominal level measures are used, the form suggests which values of one variable are associated with which values of the second variable. For either ordinal or interval data, the form reveals whether the variables move up and down together (a direct or positive relationship), as displayed in Figure 7.1.

NOMINAL LEVEL TESTS

In the previous chapter we described viewing the cell frequencies of contingency tables in order to estimate whether the presence of X is associated with the presence of Y. Three statistical tests will now be introduced that will allow you to obtain more precise and reliable estimates of associations displayed in contingency tables. These are the Yules Q, chi square, and phi.

Yules Q

This statistic has severe limitations, but it does provide two useful and easily computed measures. Q tells us the approximate degree of association between two variables, yielding a statistic that ranges from +1.0 (perfect positive association) to −1.0 (perfect negative association), where 0.00 refers to no association or

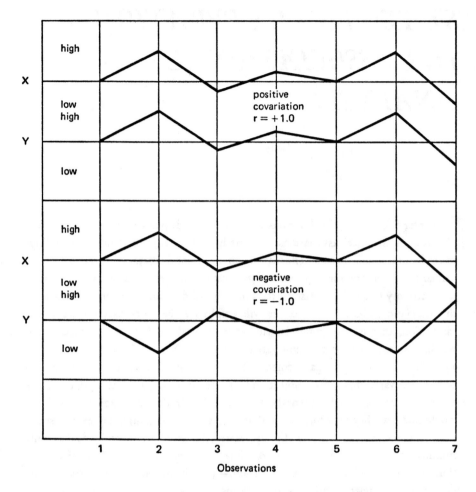

Figure 7.1   Strong positive and negative covariation between X and Y

perfect independence. Q also tells us the direction of the association. That is, a +.75 denotes a positive correlation and a —.75 denotes a negative correlation.

Yules Q is simply a measure of the difference between the cross-products of a 2 × 2 table divided by their sum. In other words, Q is computed entirely from the observed or conditional frequencies and is not concerned with the marginal frequencies (see Figure 6.2 again). Hence, Q is a margin-free statistic—one of its basic limitations.[2] On the other hand, Q can be used to compute associations among variables expressed in percentages, i.e., where the entries in the cells of a 2 × 2 table are percentages and not raw numerical data. At the same time, Q can be used only with 2 × 2 tables, i.e., where both variables are dichotomized, and when no cell entries equal zero.

Given the conventional labels for the four cells in a 2 × 2 table, the formula for Q is as follows:

$$Q = \frac{ad - bc}{ad + bc} \text{ where:}$$

		x_1	x_2
y	y_1	a	b
	y_2	c	d

Using the distributions in Figures 7.2 and 7.3 (discussed in the previous chapter), you can compute the values for Q as follows:

$$Q = \frac{axd - bxc}{axd + bxc} \qquad\qquad Q = \frac{axd - bxc}{axd + bxc}$$

$$Q = \frac{28 \times 61 - 11 \times 15}{28 \times 61 + 11 \times 15} \qquad\qquad Q = \frac{14 \times 73 - 25 \times 3}{14 \times 73 + 25 \times 3}$$

$$Q = \frac{1708 - 165}{1708 + 165} = \frac{1543}{1873} \qquad\qquad Q = \frac{1022 - 75}{1022 + 75} = \frac{947}{1097}$$

$$Q = .82 \qquad\qquad\qquad Q = .86$$

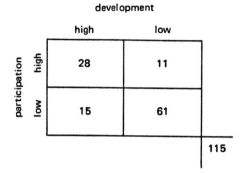

Figure 7.2 *Relationship between economic development and international participation*

Q = .82

Hence, we conclude from these two tests that a fairly high and positive association exists between the two independent variables "size" and "level of development," and the dependent variable "international participation." Q allows the interpretation that large, more economically developed nations are more involved in the international system.

Although we have already suggested that Yules Q has limitations that affect its precision, one is particularly important. When the value for any one cell is zero (hence, the product of the diagonal is equal to zero), the Q test will always yield a perfect ±1.0 association. Similarly, if two non-diagonal cells contain zeros, the Q test yields no association (.0). Consequently, another statistical test may be more appropriate for uncovering an association otherwise hidden by the existence of a zero in one or more cells in a contingency table.

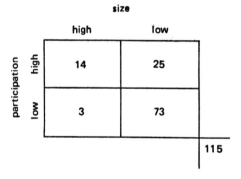

Figure 7.3 *Relationship between size and international participation*

Q = .86

Chi Square Test (X^2)

One of the most widely used statistical tests is the chi square. Chi square is used principally to determine the probability that the difference between an observed frequency and an expected frequency is likely to have occurred simply by chance. The *observed frequencies* are the numerical values obtained from empirical observations (for example, the number of alliance commitments, the number of battle deaths, the number of treaties signed in a given period, or the number of IGO's to which a nation belongs); the *expected frequency* is a numerical value for the same events obtained, not from observations, but derived from previous experience, from some theoretical prediction, or from probability theory. Chi square is then applied to determine whether an observed frequency deviates significantly from an expected frequency. The formula for chi square is as follows:

$$X^2 = \sum \frac{(0-E)^2}{E}$$

where

X^2 = symbol for chi square

0 = observed frequency or value

E = expected frequency or value

To illustrate how the chi square test is computed and what it tells us, return to the example from Figure 7.2 where we examined the relationship between in-

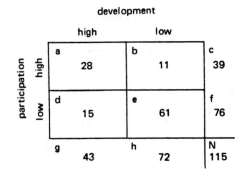

ternational participation and economic development, finding a strong positive relationship denoted by a Yules Q value of .86. Reproducing Figure 7.2, we obtain the following distribution:

where:

a,b,c,d = cell frequencies (conditionals)
e,f,g,h = marginals
N = total number of observations

The numerical values in each of the four cells represent the *observed* frequencies. Next, we obtain the *expected* frequencies. This can be done in a number of ways. If you have a theory that allowed you to derive a proposition about the relationship between wealth and participation, you could use this as a method for estimating the expected frequencies. For example, the theory may tell you that no relationship exists between wealth and participation, so you might enter 28.75 (i.e., 115 divided by 4) in each cell as the expected frequency. These values would give you a Yules Q of 0.00 showing no relationship—which is what your theory suggests.[3] Or you may be comparing two historical periods—one in the 19th century and one in the 20th. You might then use the observed values in the 19th century as the expected values for the 20th century. In short, the expected frequencies can be obtained from previous research or from theory.

The most typical procedure for estimating the expected value involves the assumption of independence among the variables. If you develop a *null proposition* that wealth and participation are not related, then the following procedures (Figures 7.4 and 7.5) can be used to generate expected frequencies.

Figure 7.4 Worksheet for chi square: Method 1[4]

A method for computing chi square for 2 × 2 tables involves squaring the difference between the sum of the cross-products and multiplying this value by N, the total number of observations. This result is then divided by the value obtained from summing the results achieved from multiplying each of the cross-products. The formula for method 1 is:

$$X^2 = \frac{N(ad-bc)^2}{(a+c)\ (b+d)\ (a+b)\ (c+d)}$$

Referring again to the values in Figure 7.2, we obtain the following substitutions:

$$X^2 = \frac{115[(28\times61)-(11\times15)]^2}{(28+15)\ (11+61)\ (28+11)\ (15+61)}$$

$$X^2 = \frac{115\ (1708-165)^2}{(43)\ (72)\ (39)\ (76)}$$

$$X^2 = \frac{115\ (1543)^2}{9,176,544}$$

$$X^2 = \frac{(115)\ (2,380,849)}{9,176,544}$$

$$X^2 = \frac{273,797,635}{9,176,544}$$

$$X^2 = 29.84$$

First, identify the conditionals as a, b, c, and d; the marginals as e, f, g, and h; and the total number of observations as N, giving us:

Second, recall the original formula where

$$X^2 = \sum \frac{(0-E)^2}{E};$$

hence, in order to obtain the expected frequencies, use the following computational procedure:

Figure 7.5 Worksheet for chi square: Method 2[5]

Step 1: Substitute the observed values from Figure 7.2 for a through h, including N.

Observed frequencies	Marginals
a = 28	e = 39
b = 11	f = 76
c = 15	g = 43
d = 61	h = 72
	N = 115

Step 2: Take the cross-products of the marginals and divide by N, giving you E.

g $\times$ c = x divided by 115 = Ea
43 $\times$ 39 = 1677 divided by 115 = 14.58

h $\times$ e = x divided by 115 = Eb
72 $\times$ 39 = 2808 divided by 115 = 24.41

g $\times$ f = x divided by 115 = Ec
43 $\times$ 76 = 3268 divided by 115 = 28.41

h $\times$ f = x divided by 115 = Ed
72 $\times$ 76 = 5472 divided by 115 = 47.58

Step 3: Substitute your results in the following table and perform the necessary computations:

Cell	0	E(expected)	O—E	$(O-E)^2$	$(O-E)^2/E$
a	28	ge/N=14.58	13.42	180.09	12.35
b	11	he/N=24.41	−13.42	179.82	7.36
c	15	gf/N=28.41	−13.42	179.82	6.32
d	61	hf/N=47.58	13.42	180.09	3.78

Step 4: Compute the chi square, recalling that:

$$X^2 = \sum \frac{(0-E)^2}{E},$$

then for this example,

$$X^2 = \sum 12.35 + 7.36 + 6.32 + 3.78$$

$$X^2 = 29.81$$

The decision rule for interpreting the X^2 value. Having obtained a X^2 value of 29.84, what are we to make of it? What does this value tell us about the null proposition that wealth and participation are not related? In order to assess the value of X^2, it is necessary to understand the concept of *degrees of freedom*, usually denoted *df*.

The concept of degrees of freedom is used in nearly all statistics. The problem is to establish the number of degrees of freedom in any given empirical situation. Although the computation of *df* varies from statistic to statistic, for the X^2 and the contingency table *df* can be computed by the following formula:

$$df = (R-1)(C-1)$$

where:

df = symbol denoting degrees of freedom

R = number of rows in a contingency table

C = number of columns in a contingency table

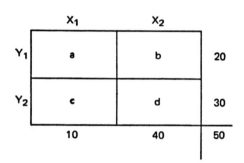

Figure 7.6   2 x 2 table

Thus, for a 2 × 2 contingency table, the *df* always equals 1. In a 3 × 3 contingency table, *df* = 4; in a 3 × 2 contingency table, *df* = 2; etc.

The concept of *df* refers to the freedom you have to alter the entries in the cells in a contingency table. Consider, for example, the 2 × 2 table in Figure 7.6. Assume you have 50 observations with marginal distributions.

Note that once you have made a single entry in cells a, b, c, or d, all other entries are predetermined. It is in this sense that a 2 × 2 contingency table yields only 1 *df*, and it is for this reason that we noted earlier that Yules Q is a margin-free statistic. Unlike Q, the value of X^2 depends on the marginal frequencies as well as the cell entries. In a 2 × 2 table, once one cell and the marginals are fixed, consequently, all the other cells are fixed; hence, one *df*. Recall that we said above that a 3 × 2 contingency table yields 2 *df*. Consider the marginal distribution shown in Figure 7.7.

Note that you are now free to make *two* free entries in any two cells a through f. However, also note that once we have made two entries, all other entries are predetermined. Hence, a 3 × 2 contingency table is said to yield 2 *df*.

Degrees of freedom is an important concept because it provides entry to the table that allows us to decide whether the X^2 value we have computed is statistically significant—that is, whether the relationship that has been found could have occurred by chance. Recall that our test of the relationship between wealth and participation yielded a X^2 value of 29.84. Recall also that our null proposition stated there was no relationship between wealth and participation. Finally, recall that our test was performed on a 2 × 2 table, giving us *df* = 1.

Now we can go to the table of values for X^2 in order to determine whether 29.84 is significant or not. If our X^2 value is sufficiently large, we can reject the null proposition that no relation exists between wealth and participation. That is, a

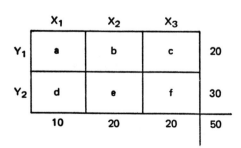

Figure 7.7   3 x 2 table

sufficiently high X^2 value will allow you to assume that the differences found between observed and expected frequencies were not likely to have occurred by change. Given this information, we can now enter Figure 7.8 at $df = 1$. Moving horizontally across to the .05 and .01 columns, we find that our X^2 value of 29.84 far exceeds the minimum necessary to reject the null proposition. Note that the minimum $X^2 = 3.84$ at the .05 level. Clearly, our value of 29.84 is sufficient to reject the null proposition. Hence, we accept the proposition that wealth and participation are related. Moreover, $p = .01$ tells us that there is less than one chance in a hundred that our finding has occurred by chance or random variation.

We will return later in this chapter to a further discussion of tests of significance. For the moment, it is sufficient to say we have found a strong relationship in which we can have considerable confidence.

Phi Test (ϕ)

Another measure of association useful for 2×2 tables is the phi coefficient. This measure is derived from the chi square value. More precisely, phi is the square root of X^2 divided by N or symbolically,

$$\text{phi} = \sqrt{\frac{X^2}{N}}.$$

The interesting property of the phi is that, unlike the chi square, its value is directly interpretable as a measure of association. The values of phi range from —1 to +1, indicating a perfect negative covariation and perfect positive covariation respectively.[6]

df	$p = .05$	$p = .01$
1	3.84	6.64
2	5.99	9.21
3	7.82	11.34
4	9.49	13.28
5	11.07	15.09
6	12.59	16.81
7	14.07	18.48
8	15.51	20.09
9	16.92	21.67
10	18.31	23.21
12	21.03	26.22
14	23.68	29.14
16	26.30	32.00
18	28.87	34.80
20	31.41	37.57

*Figure 7.8   Values of X^2 for significance at the .05 and .01 levels**

* Fisher and Yates: *Statistical Tables for Biological, Agricultural and Medical Research,* published by Oliver and Boyd, Edinburgh, and by permission of the authors and publishers.

Another formula for ϕ in a 2×2 table is as follows:

$$\phi = \frac{ad-bc}{\sqrt{(a+b)\ (c+d)\ (a+c)\ (b+c)}}$$

when

a = 28	b = 11
c = 15	d = 61

$$= \frac{(28\times 61) - (11\times 15)}{\sqrt{(28+11)\ (15+61)\ (28+61)\ (11+61)}} =$$

$$\frac{1708 - 165}{\sqrt{39\times 76\times 89\times 26}} = \frac{1543}{\sqrt{6,858,696}} = \frac{1543}{2619} = .59$$

Again using the data in Figure 7.2, we obtain the following measure association between wealth and participation:

$$X^2 = 29.84$$

$$\phi^2 = \frac{X^2}{N}$$

$$\phi^2 = 29.84/115$$

$$\phi^2 = .26 \text{ (take square root of each side of equation to get } \phi)$$

$$\phi = \sqrt{.26}$$

$$\phi = +.51$$

Note that if you calculate phi by using the chi square value rather than the basic formula given above for phi, you must examine your data to determine the sign or direction of the relationship. Since high variables of the independent variable in Figure 7.2 are associated with high values in the dependent variable and also low values with low variables, the direction of the relationship is positive.

Summary of Nominal Tests

We have examined three measures of association for nominal scales: Yules Q, chi-square, and phi. Each has specific uses and limitations, and it is important to recognize these before selecting the most appropriate one for your nominal data. The Yules Q is a good measure if (1) you are interested in an *approximate* degree of association as well as its *direction*; (2) your data are arranged in a 2×2 contingency table (that is, the variables are dichotomous); and (3) you do not have any cells with zero entries.

Chi-square is an appropriate statistic if you are working with observations drawn from a random sample and you want to compute the probability that the relationships observed in the sample are likely to also exist in the population. If you are working with the entire population rather than a sample, chi-square probably is not as relevant. In short, chi-square is most useful when you are interested in whether observed relationships are significantly different from chance. Chi-square is also useful when your contingency table exceeds the 2×2 dimensions that are severe limitations for both Yules Q and phi.

The phi, although it may be derived from the chi square, is directly interpretable as a measure of association. That is, it reveals the degree of the relationship as well as the form or direction. It is a more accurate measure than Yules Q, but is more difficult to compute. Therefore, your decision between Yules Q and phi will probably rest upon whether you wish to sacrifice a certain amount of accuracy (usually a slight difference) for computational speed.

ORDINAL LEVEL TESTS

A popular statistic designed for ordinal level data such as the criss-cross displays in chapter 6 is a rank order correlation. This measure is used to determine the degree to which two sets of scores are related to each other. A rank order correlation is particularly appropriate when you have ordinal data—that is, when you are able to rank order cases (nations, people, etc.) on a scale from higher to lower, more or less, richer or poorer, etc., and where you want to know the extent to which rankings on one scale (say, a measure of wealth) is related to rankings on another scale (for example, a measure of participation). A typical measure of rank order correlation is Spearman's rho, denoted by a lower case Greek rho ρ). The formula for rho is as follows:

$$\text{rho} = \rho = 1 - \frac{6\Sigma d^2}{N(N^2-1)} \text{ or } 1 - \frac{6\Sigma d^2}{N^3-N}$$

where:

ρ = symbol denoting the statistic

d = the difference between a pair of ranks

N = the total number of pairs

The rho yields the same numerical value as Yules Q, ranging from -1.0 (perfect negative association) to $+1.0$ (perfect positive association) with the .0 value indicating the absence of any association. However, rho has a major advantage over Q because values of rho are unique. Hence, the analyst can establish precise probabilities to their occurrence for a specified number of ranks. This point, however, will require us to give some attention to the issue of significance tests—touched on earlier in our discussion of chi square.

Consider the association between a nation's level of wealth and its degree of participation in the international system. Assume a sample of 10 nations (labelled A through J). The following worksheet presents the raw data and rank for each nation on each variable. The difference in ranks for each nation is also computed. These values are then placed in the formula for rho and the Spearman rank order correlation coefficient is computed.

As the worksheet shows, three columns are required for each of the two variables. The left column identifies the nation; the center column reveals its raw score on the wealth and participation indices respectively; and the right column gives each nation's rank (1 = highest and 10 = lowest). The formula for rho requires the sum of the squared differences in rank. Consequently, the two columns on the right side of the worksheet reveal the difference in ranks for each nation as well as its square. Plugging these values into the formula and computing it, a rho value of $+.88$ is obtained. Thus it can be concluded that a high positive association exists between a nation's wealth and its participation in the international system.

Nation	Wealth (X) Score	Rank	Nation	International Participation (Y) Score	Rank	d (Rank Y–Rank X)	d²
A	20	1	A	28	2	1	1.0
B	19	2	B	31	1	−1	1.0
C	16	3	C	17	6	3	9.0
D	15	4.5*	D	23	3	−1.5	2.25
E	15	4.5*	E	19	5	.5	.25
F	14	6	F	21	4	−2	4.0
G	13	7	G	14	7	0	0.0
H	11	8	H	10	8	0	0.0
I	9	9	I	3	10	1	1.0
J	3	10	J	5	9	−1	1.0

N = 10
N² = 100

$\Sigma d^2 = 19.5$

$$\rho = 1 - \frac{6\,\Sigma d^2}{N(N^2-1)} = 1 - \frac{6(19.5)}{10(100-1)} = 1 - \frac{117.0}{990} = 1 - .118 = +.88$$

(or)

$$\rho = 1 - \frac{6\,\Sigma d^2}{N^3 - N} = 1 - \frac{6(19.5)}{10^3 - 10} = \left[\frac{117}{1000-10} = \frac{117}{990} = .118 \right]$$

$$= 1 - .118 = +.88$$

Figure 7.9 *Worksheet for rho*

* Note that when ranks are tied (nations D and E) you assign the average of the sum of the tied ranks. Thus, the ranks for D and E are added (4+5=9) and divided by 2, giving 4.5.

THE SIGNIFICANCE TEST

You will recall that the principal difference between the nominal level statistic Yules Q and the ordinal statistic rho is that the values of the latter are unique and thus permit the analyst to establish exact probabilities to their occurrence. For example, if we assume that our ten nations were randomly selected from the population of all nations, we are able to establish whether the value of the rank order correlation we obtained is statistically significant or whether it might have occurred by chance.

It is important to note that when we ask if a correlation is significant, we are asking a purely statistical—not a substantive—question. A correlation may be statistically significant but this only means that the observed relationship is *probably* not a function of chance. Moreover, a statistically significant relationship may be substantively trivial.

In addition, it is important to emphasize the *probably*, for assessments of statistical significance are always probability statements. When it is written that a statistical finding is "significant at the .01 level" or that a correlation "is significant at the .05 level," the author is merely saying that 99 times out of a hundred (for the .01 level) or 95 times out of a hundred (for the .05 level) the relationship obtained is not likely to be attributable to chance. Or, put another way, the author is saying that the probability is only 1 in a hundred (for the .01 level) or 5 in a hundred (for the .05 level) that the relationship could have occurred by some random or chance variation in the values of the variables being examined.

In Figure 7.10, the values for rho are displayed for both the .01 and .05 significance levels. The table is read by entering the N column (the first column) and

N	p — .05	p — .01
5	1.000	—
6	.886	.929
7	.786	.881
8	.738	.833
9	.683	.815
10	.648	.794
12	.591	.777
14	.544	.715
16	.506	.665
18	.475	.625
20	.450	.591
22	.428	.562
24	.409	.537
26	.392	.515
28	.377	.496
30	.364	.478

Figure 7.10 *Values of rho significant at the .05 and .01 levels of significance**

* Table from Underwood (1954).

then moving horizontally to the p — .05 column. If the observed correlation (i.e., the rho value that you actually obtained) is equal to or greater than the value displayed in the column, then the probability is .95 that the correlation did not occur by chance—that the observed correlation is, in fact, statistically significant.

If you return to your worksheet example where you found a .88 rank order correlation between wealth and participation for 10 nations, you can consult Figure 7.10 to see whether the correlation is likely to be statistically significant. If we enter the table at "10" in the N column and move across to the .05 and .01 columns, we find that our correlation of .88 is significant at both the .01 and .05 levels because it exceeds the minimum necessary for .05 (.64) and .01 (.79). Thus, there is less than one chance in a hundred that our finding of a relationship between wealth and participation occurred by chance.

Interval Level Measures of Association

The most commonly-used measure of association for interval level data is the product moment correlation coefficient.

When a high correlation exists between variables (either positive or negative), it is then possible to predict the variation in the value of one variable by knowing the variation of the other (the one with which it is associated). For example, if we know that international integration increases as transactions among nations increase, then we can assume increased integration from our observations of increased transactions. Or, if the correlation between exports and number of diplomats sent is $+.85$, we know that a strong positive association exists between diplomatic participation and expenditures in international trade (Alger and Brams, 1967).

However, the discovery of a strong correlation does not allow us to say that change in the value of one variable *causes* the observed corresponding change in the value of another. A high correlation between two variables tells us only that an association—or covariation—exists. Causality may or may not be involved. In any case, it cannot be inferred simply from the correlation. X does not necessarily cause Y; X simply covaries with Y.

Positive correlations occur when an increase (decrease) in one variable corresponds to an increase (decrease) in another. Negative conditions occur when an increase (decrease) in one variable corresponds to a decrease (increase) in another. The most common numerical measure of correlation is the product moment correlation coefficient, which is commonly symbolized by small letter (r). The r measures the degree to which the relationship between the two variables can be represented by a straight line. The value of r ranges from +1.00 to −1.00, where +1.00 and −1.00 represent perfect linear relationships.

Examine the scatter plots in Figure 7.11. Scatter plot A represents no discernible relationship among the cloud of data points. Scatter plot B, by contrast, approaches a perfect positive correlation (+1.00); and scatter plot C approaches a perfect negative correlation (−1.00), for in C as the value of X increases the value of Y decreases (i.e., a negative correlation).

A correlation of +1.00 is as high (strong) as a correlation of −1.00. This is because the size of the correlation coefficient indicates the strength or closeness of the relationship. The plus (+) or minus (−) merely represents the direction of the relationship. A positive sign indicates a direct relationship and a negative sign indicates an inverse relationship. Therefore, an r equal to −.65 is a stronger correlation than an r equal to +.60.

A *correlation coefficient* is not a percentage nor does it represent a scale of equal (interval) measurements. It is simply a measure of association. Thus an r equal to +.60 cannot be read as two variables "correlating 60 percent of the time." Nor can you say that an r equal to +.60 is twice as large as an r equal to +.30. The comparison of the relative strengths of correlation coefficients is done through the derivation of a coefficient of determination.

The *coefficient of determination* is equal to the square of the correlation coefficient (r^2). The coefficient of determination indicates the percentage of variance in one variable accounted for by variance in the other. A correlation of +.60 has a coefficient of determination of .36 (i.e., $.60^2$). Therefore, the discovery of a correlation of .60 makes it possible to say that 36 percent of the variance in one variable can be explained by variance in the other. Because a correlation does not establish a causal relationship, you can reverse the statement and say that 36 percent of the variance in the second variable can be explained by variance in the first.

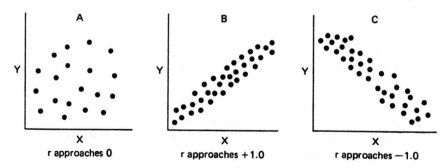

Figure 7.11 Sample scatter plots

Computation of r

Although the computational formula for r requires us to perform several mathematical steps, the formula is fairly simple to compute.

$$r_{xy} = \frac{\Sigma xy - n(\bar{x}\bar{y})}{\sqrt{[x^2 - n(\bar{x})^2]\,[\Sigma y - n(\bar{y})^2]}}$$

where:

r = correlation coefficient

x and y = individual variable values

Σ = summation sign

n = number of cases

$\bar{x}$ and $\bar{y}$ = mean value

In order to compute the correlation coefficient for a set of variables, consider the association between the number of diplomats sent and received by each nation. Let x = the number of diplomats sent, and y = the number received. The following worksheet (Figure 7.12) displays the data for a sample of ten nations and the procedures for determining the value of r.

Interpretation of r

In the case below, there exists a high positive relationship between variables X and Y. But again, remember that it is not possible to say that X causes Y. Indeed,

Given the following observations, the following calculations would be made:

X	Y	XY	X²	Y²
10	13	130	100	169
14	16	224	196	256
18	22	396	324	484
15	20	300	225	400
19	21	399	361	441
20	23	460	400	529
31	34	1054	961	1156
16	19	304	256	361
11	14	154	121	196
12	13	156	144	169
$\Sigma x = 166$	$\Sigma y = 195$	$\Sigma(XY) = 3577$	$\Sigma X^2 = 3088$	$\Sigma Y^2 = 4161$
$\bar{x} = 16.6$	$\bar{y} = 19.5$			

$$r_{xy} = \frac{\Sigma xy - n(\bar{x}\bar{y})}{\sqrt{[\Sigma x^2 - n(\bar{x})^2]\,[\Sigma y^2 - n(\bar{y})^2]}}$$

$$r_{xy} = \frac{3577 - 10(16.6 \times 19.5)}{\sqrt{(3088 - 10(16.6)^2)\,(4161 - 10(19.5)^2)}}$$

$$r_{xy} = \frac{3577 - 3237}{\sqrt{(3088 - 2756)\,(4161 - 3803)}}$$

$$r_{xy} = \frac{340}{\sqrt{(332)\,(358)}} = \frac{340}{\sqrt{118,856}} = \frac{340.0}{344.0} = .986$$

Figure 7.12   Worksheet for calculating the correlation coefficient

Y may cause X or some other variable—Z—may be causing both X and Y, giving us what is termed in this latter instance, a *spurious* correlation.

The r value of .99 obviously suggests a very strong association between the two variables. If we square r ($.986^2 = .97$), we can say that 97 percent of the variance in Y is accounted for by the variance in X. But what about other less readily interpretable values of r? How can you assign verbal meaning to the degree of association from the numerical r value? One set of decision rules has been provided by Franzblau (1971, p. 81) in response to the following question:

When may we call a correlation coefficient "high or low"? Since these coefficients vary all the way from −1.00 to +1.00, the reader may wish to know how to designate the degree of association implied.

Answer: While there are no sharp lines of demarcation, the following characterizations may prove helpful. It should be borne in mind that they apply equally whether the correlation coefficient is negative or positive.

- Reliable coefficients of correlation ranging from zero to about .20 may be regarded as indicating *no or negligible* correlation.

- Reliable coefficients of correlation ranging from about .20 to .40 may be regarded as indicating a *low* degree of correlation.

- Reliable coefficients of correlation ranging from about .40 to .60 may be regarded as indicating a *moderate* degree of correlation.

- Reliable coefficients of correlation ranging from about .60 to .80 may be regarded as indicating a *marked* degree of correlation.

- Reliable coefficients of correlation ranging from about .80 to 1.00 may be regarded as indicating *high* correlation.

It should be emphasized, however, that these verbal descriptors for the numerical values obtained from correlation analysis are only guidelines. How analysts finally decide to interpret the value of a correlation will ultimately depend on the theory with which they are working, the empirical domain they are observing, and the purpose for which they are doing the research. For example, higher correlations may be desired if the product of the research may be used to shape policies that will have the effect of depriving some people and indulging others.

Caveats about Correlation Coefficients

Caveats regarding high correlations should be made clear. Three points can be made. First, the discovery of a high correlation may be the artifact of the particular location of observations in the cross-plot. For example, consider the problem of *outliers.* If, for instance, the relationship to be explored was that between wealth and total diplomats sent, the position of the United States, given its overwhelming wealth compared to other nations, would have great influence on the correlation (Figure 7.13).

The "line of best fit" would be that line which ran from the origin of the graph to the United States. Such a line would not pass through the vast majority of points on the graph. This problem can be partially corrected by the transformation of data (discussed in chapter 5). Transformation has the effect of reducing the impact of outliers on the correlation coefficient.

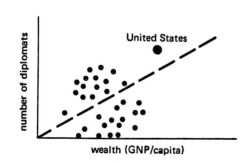

Figure 7.13 Sample scatter plot

Second, we must fight the temptation to be "seduced" by correlation coefficients. A correlation of ± .70, while high for most studies in political science, accounts for only 49 percent of the variance—leaving 51 percent unexplained variance.

Third, the correlation itself may be the result of non-normal distributions. For example, consider the three scatter plots in Figure 7.14 extracted from Tufte (1969, pp. 647–48). These three plots clearly reveal widely different relationships between X and Y. The plot on the left shows no relationship if you discount the extreme outlier in the upper right corner of the graph. The middle plot suggests a moderately strong linear relationship between X and Y. The right plot shows a rather distinct *curvilinear* relationship between X and Y, suggesting that as X increases, so does Y, but at a faster rate. And yet in all three cases r = .65. This example clearly indicates the use of a correlation coefficient should be accompanied by visual displays of the data, such as by a scatter plot, to supplement the statistical procedures in order to guard against misinterpretation.

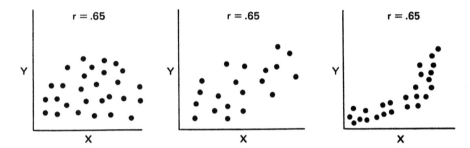

Figure 7.14   Scatter plot = .65

REGRESSION ANALYSIS

While the scatter plot gives you a visual representation of a relationship expressed in a correlation, a more precise method of determining the form is the regression equation. If you assume that a linear relationship exists (i.e., as the value of the independent variable increases, the dependent variable will increase at a constant rate), you may use a regression equation to construct a straight line through the scatter plot which best captures the relationship between the independent and dependent variables.

Let's consider for a moment the concept of linearity. *Linear* is a common term used to describe straight-line relationships between variables or to describe an underlying model of a statistical routine (for example, a *linear* regression model). A linear relationship or model can, therefore, be stated as an equation describing a straight line:

$$Y = aX$$

where the value of Y (the dependent variable) is linearly related to the value of X (the independent variable). The relationship itself is expressed by the constant (called a parameter) *alpha* or a. Hence, if a = 2, then we know that for every unit increase in X, we will obtain a two-unit increase in Y.

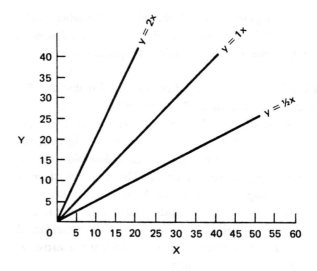

Figure 7.15   Linear relationship (Y = aX)

A non-linear relationship or model always is expressed in an equation with higher order terms. For example, the equation

$$Y = aX^2$$

expresses a nonlinear relationship because the fit between X and Y will not yield a straight line. For an example of this, compare Figure 7.15 with Figure 7.16.

Now, let's turn to the discussion of the linear regression model. Recall that the correlation model simply describes in quantitative terms the degree of covariation in the relationship between two variables, x and y. Regression analysis, by contrast, tells us a great deal more. First, regression analysis allows us to predict the value of y given some value of x. The predicted value of y is usually written $\hat{y}$ (read "y hat"), and the error in the prediction is called a *residual*. Second, regression analysis tells

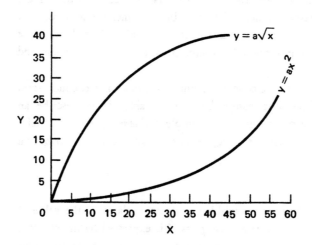

Figure 7.16   Nonlinear relationship (Y = aX²;
Y = a√x)

the analyst how much the correlation deviates from a straight-line relationship. This statistic is called *the standard error of the estimate* and measures the over-all accuracy of the regression line. Third, regression analysis tells the analyst how much change in y, the dependent variable, can be expected from a change in x, the independent variable. The amount of change is illustrated by the slope of the regression line and is represented by the value of the *beta coefficient*.

For example, Figure 7.17 reproduces the data points from Figure 6.19 showing the cross-plot of freedom of the press scores and scores from the index of agreement with the United States in UN voting. As was noted earlier, as a nation's freedom of the press increases, its support of America's voting position in the international organization also increases. The straight line drawn in Figure 7.17 represents the average or typical relationship between the two variables for each value of X, the independent variable along the horizontal axis. That is, for each value of X, the corresponding value of Y on the regression line signifies the value of the latter typically associated with the former. Thus, we say that the regression line best captures, describes, or summarizes the scatter plot. In this case, the upward direction of the line from left to right indicates a positive relationship. The steeper the slope, the greater the effect of the independent variable upon the dependent variable.

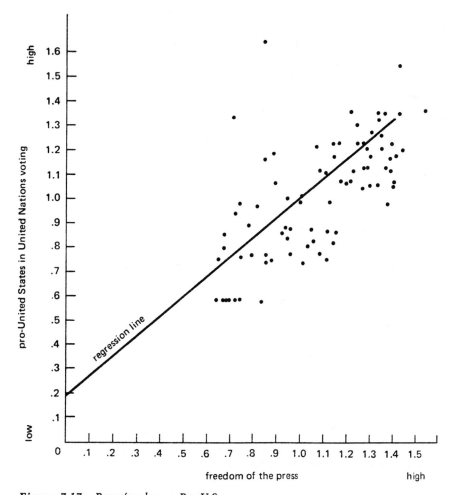

Figure 7.17 *Press freedom → Pro U.S.*

The equation for the regression line is the same as the straight line formula noted previously. That is,

$$Y = a + bX,$$

where:

Y = dependent variable

X = independent variable

a = Y-intercept (the point when the line crosses the Y axis)

b = slope of the line (also called the regression or beta coefficient)

In other words, a and b are the two points which constitute the straight line. These two points are called parameters.

Computing the Regression Line

As indicated, the location and slope of the regression line are the primary analytical problems to solve in regression analysis.

The most common method for drawing the regression is called the *least squares solution*—hence, the term *least squares regression*. The least squares solution simply tries to draw a straight line through the scatter plot such that the distance of the line from each of the actual data points is minimized. The solution is called least squares because, as shown in Figure 7.18, the distance between the regression line and the data point will sometimes be positive and sometimes negative. Thus, the distances are squared in order to remove the plus and minus signs.

The least squares solution requires the computation of both *beta* and the *a-intercept*. The formula for beta and a are as follows:

$$b = \frac{\Sigma\, xy - N\bar{x}\bar{y}}{\Sigma(x-x)^2} = \frac{\Sigma xy - N\bar{x}\bar{y}}{\Sigma x^2 - [(\Sigma x)^2/N]}$$

$$a = \bar{y} - bx$$

Thus, in order to compute a, we need first to compute beta. First, we have to compute the mean values for x and y (denoted $\bar{x}$, $\bar{y}$ in the formula). Second, we have to compute xy for each case so we can sum them (denoted Σxy in the formula). Third, we have to compute the x^2 and y^2. These steps are shown in the worksheet in Figure 7.19.

Now, to compute the *a intercept*, recall that:

$$a = \bar{y} - b\bar{x}$$

$$a = 4.37 - .97(3.75)$$

$$a = 4.37 - 3.63$$

$$a = .73, \text{ i.e., the regression line will cross the y axis at .73}$$

Now it is possible to plot the regression line. The regression line in Figure 7.18 was plotted free-hand. Now that we know the intercept is .73, we can locate that point on the y axis. Next, from the beta computation, we know that y increases .97 units for every 1.0 unit increase in x. Thus, beginning at .73 on the y axis and moving to the right 1 unit on the x axis and then up .97 units on the y axis, we can

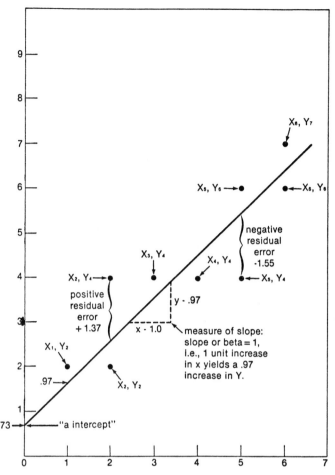

Figure 7.18 Least squares solution

Case	X	Y	XY	X^2	Y^2
1	1	2	2	1	4
2	2	2	4	4	4
3	3	4	12	9	16
4	3	4	12	9	16
5	4	4	16	16	16
6	5	6	30	25	36
7	6	6	36	36	36
8	6	7	42	36	49
N = 8	$\Sigma x = 30$	$\Sigma y = 35$	$\Sigma xy = 154$	$\Sigma x^2 = 136$	$\Sigma y^2 = 177$
	$\bar{x} = 3.75$	$\bar{y} = 4.37$			

$$b = \frac{\Sigma xy - N\bar{x}\bar{y}}{\Sigma x^2 - [(\Sigma x)^2/N]}$$

$$b = 154 - 8(3.75 \times 4.37) = 8(16.38)$$

$$b = \frac{154 - 131.1}{136 - (30)^2/8} = \frac{22.9}{136 - 900/8}$$

$$b = \frac{22.9}{136 - 112.5} = \frac{22.9}{23.5} = .974$$

b = .974, i.e., for every unit increase in the value of x, there will be a .97 increase in the value of y.

Figure 7.19 Regression worksheet

locate a second point. Now, having established two points, we can draw a straight line. In other words, .73y exists with zero value for x, but y increases .97 for every additional unit increase in x—shown as follows:

x	y		
0	.73	=	0.73
1	.73 + .97	=	1.70
2	.73 + 1.94	=	2.67
3	.73 + 2.91	=	3.64
10	.73 + 9.70	=	10.43

Now, consider another example. Assume you have a sample of seventeen Latin American nations (Caribbean nations excluded), and you are interested in the relationship between the amount of U.S. foreign aid received (X or the independent variable) and the index of agreement with the U.S. in UN voting (Y or the dependent variable). The scatter plot for this relationship is given in Figure 7.20. As you can observe, it is difficult to determine the exact nature of the relationship form.

Following the same procedure from Figure 7.19, we can set up our worksheet as follows in Figure 7.21.

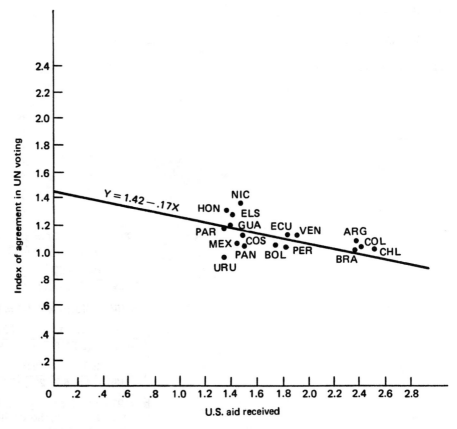

Figure 7.20 *Regression line of U.S. aid received and index of agreement with U.S. in UN voting (Latin America)*

		(U.S. Foreign Aid)	(Pro-U.S.)			
		X	Y	XY	X^2	Y^2
1	Bolivia	1.59	1.09	1.73	2.53	1.19
2	Brazil	2.14	1.06	2.27	4.58	1.12
3	Colombia	2.16	1.08	2.33	4.67	1.17
4	Ecuador	1.68	1.16	1.95	2.83	1.35
5	Peru	1.66	1.08	1.79	2.76	1.17
6	Venezuela	1.75	1.16	2.03	3.06	1.35
7	Argentina	2.17	1.13	2.45	4.71	1.28
8	Chile	2.31	1.08	2.49	5.34	1.17
9	Paraguay	1.21	1.18	1.43	1.46	1.39
10	Uruguay	1.20	1.01	1.21	1.44	1.02
11	Costa Rica	1.35	1.14	1.54	1.82	1.30
12	El Salvador	1.28	1.30	1.66	1.64	1.69
13	Guatemala	1.26	1.20	1.51	1.59	1.44
14	Honduras	1.23	1.33	1.64	1.51	1.77
15	Mexico	1.32	1.10	1.45	1.74	1.21
16	Nicaragua	1.33	1.33	1.77	1.77	1.77
17	Panama	1.34	1.09	1.46	1.80	1.19
N = 17		$\Sigma x = 26.98$	$\Sigma y = 19.52$	$\Sigma xy = 30.71$	$\Sigma x^2 = 45.24$	$\Sigma y^2 = 22.58$
		$\bar{x} = 1.59$	$\bar{y} = 1.15$			

$$b = \frac{\Sigma xy - N\bar{x}\bar{y}}{\Sigma x^2 - [(\Sigma x)^2/N]}$$

$$b = 30.71 - 17(1.59 \times 1.15) = 17(1.83)$$

$$b = \frac{30.71 - 31.11}{45.24 - (26.98)^2/17} = \frac{-.40}{45.24 - 42.82}$$

$$b = \frac{-.40}{2.42} = -.17$$

Figure 7.21   Regression worksheet

Recall that

$$a = \bar{y} - b\bar{x}; \text{ hence}$$

$$a = 1.15 - (-.17)\ 1.59 = 1.15 + .27$$

$$a = 1.42$$

Now that we know the value of a, we can locate that point on the y axis. After putting a point at 1.42 on the y axis, we can increase x by one unit. We know from the computation of beta that the slope is —.17. Hence, as we increase x by 1 unit, we need to decrease y by .17 of a unit (because of the negative sign). Thus, in Figure 7.20, note that the plot of the regression line moves downward and to the right—indicating a negative relationship between foreign aid received and favorable voting choices in the UN General Assembly. The regression equation is thus expressed as $Y = -.17x + 1.42$.

COMPUTING THE STANDARD ERROR OF THE ESTIMATE

Next, we want to compute the confidence level we should have in the predictions that we are able to obtain from the regression. Recall from Figure 7.20 that some of the data points fall right on the regression line; hence the predicted value of y and its actual value are the same: $y = \hat{y}$. However, note that some values of y fall above or below the regression line. That is, if we use the regression line to predict the value of y from the value of x, we will have some error—for not all cases fall exactly on the line. The standard error of the estimate is used to measure just how much error there is around the regression line. Specifically, it reveals the range above and below the regression line necessary to include 67 percent of the cases. Hence, the standard error tells us how much error there is between the observed values of y (i.e., y) and the predicted value of y (i.e., $\hat{y}$).

More technically, the standard error (written s) is equal to the root of the sum of the squared differences between the observed minus the expected values of y divided by N—2. The formula expressing this computation is as follows:

$$s = \sqrt{\frac{\Sigma(y - \hat{y})^2}{N - 2}}$$

which is equal to the following, more easily computed formula:

$$s = \sqrt{\frac{\Sigma y^2 - [(\Sigma xy)^2 / \Sigma x^2]}{N - 2}}$$

If we go back to our sample regression noted in Figure 7.19 and substitute the appropriate values in the equation, we obtain the following:

$$s = \sqrt{\frac{177 - 23.716/136}{8 - 2}}$$

$$s = \sqrt{\frac{177 - 174.38}{6}}$$

$$s = \sqrt{\frac{2.62}{6}}$$

$$s = \pm .66$$

This reveals that any value of y that is predicted from x will be within $\pm$ .66 of the expected value (that is, within $\pm$ .66 of the regression line) 67 percent of the time, and also within 2 times $\pm$ .66 or $\pm$ 1.32 of the expected value 95 percent of the time. Hence, in this particular instance we would have considerable confidence in our predictions of y from x.

Figure 7.22 shows the area within one standard error of estimate of the regression line. The light area represents an error of $\pm$ .66 for the regression equation of $Y = .73 + .97X$.

SUMMARY

In this chapter you have learned a variety of statistical operations for analyzing relationships and associations between two variables. Tests for all three levels of measurement have been included. We have, however, only begun to scratch the surface for all the procedures which you may utilize for determining associations among variables. Appropriate tests, including some presented in this chapter, exist for relationships among more than two variables. However, the repertoire in this chapter should allow you to evaluate some rather complex theories about nations and their behavior in the international arena.

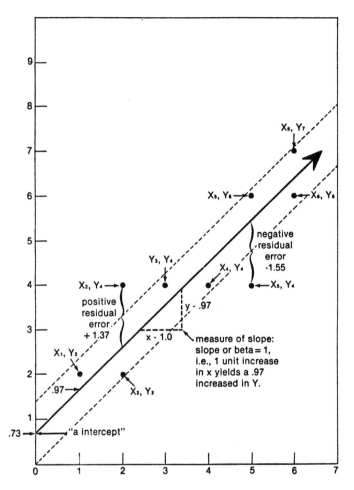

Figure 7.22   One standard error of estimate

EXERCISES

1 Calculate Yules Q for the following matrix. Does this measure help in assessing the existence, the direction, or magnitude of a relationship?

$$Q = \underline{\hspace{2cm}}$$

Percentage of Communist Vote

Freedom of Press		High	Low	
	High	4	41	45
	Low	11	21	32
		15	62	77

2 What correlation coefficient is most appropriate for the following matrix? Why? Calculate it.

Status of Communist Party

Freedom of Press		In power	Not in power	
	High	0	50	50
	Low	12	25	37
		12	75	87

3 Calculate chi square for the two preceding matrices. How "significant" (in the statistical sense) are the results? Do you have now still another opinion as to the relationship between freedom of the press and percentage of Communist vote?

matrix a   *matrix b*

$x^2 = \underline{\hspace{2cm}}$ $x^2 = \underline{\hspace{2cm}}$

4 Calculate Spearman's rho for the following ranks. Does this confirm your visual interpretation? Under what circumstances might Spearman's rho be an inaccurate measure of correlation? rho = \underline{\hspace{2cm}}

Mass participation/turmoil

— France
— Argentina
— Italy
— Chile
— Ceylon
— Poland
— Cuba
— Turkey
— United States
— Ecuador
— El Salvador
— Yugoslavia
— Finland
— Burma
— Czechoslavakia
— Malagasy
— USSR
— Netherlands
— Phillipines

Strategic distance from centers: United States/USSR

— Czechoslovakia
— USSR
— Finland
— Turkey
— Poland
— Yugoslavia
— Italy
— Netherlands
— Burma
— France
— Ceylon
— Phillipines
— Malagasy
— Argentina
— Chile
— Ecuador
— El Salvador
— Cuba
— United States

5 For the following data compute:

A regression equation _____

B r = _____

C r² = _____

D standard error of estimate = _____

Interpret these results in terms of the strength and direction of the relationship (if any). Explain why these two variables should or should not be correlated. Compute Spearman rho and compare the values.

rho = _____.

	Births per thousand	Deaths per thousand
Dominican Republic	51.0	10.0
Honduras	47.5	13.1
Mexico	45.5	14.5
Malaya	44.4	11.3
Taiwan	42.8	8.0
Chile	35.5	12.5
Poland	27.4	9.0
USSR	25.3	7.5
Czechoslavakia	18.5	9.7
Denmark	16.8	9.1

6 Sketch the following regression line.

$y = 1 + 2x$

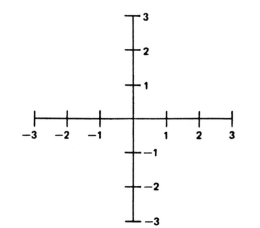

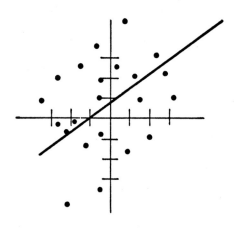

7 If $r = .70$, the coefficient of determination = _____. Interpret this result.

8 Given the following regression line and a standard error of estimate of 1, how many cases fall within this estimate? _____

9 In the regression equation $y = 4.2 + 2x$, the equation crosses the y axis at _____. For every one unit change in x, y changes _____ units.

10 If all cases fell precisely on the regression line in question 9, the standard error of estimate would equal _____.

NOTES

1. See Jones (1971, pp. 110–133) for an insightful description of two-variable relationships. The discussion of degree and form is extracted from this section in Jones. Alker (1965, pp. 54–65) provides another excellent discussion of measures of association. For an example of the application of contingency tables in research, see the Feierabends' (1966) cross-national analysis of internal violence from 1948–1962.

2. See Alker (1965) for a discussion of marginal free distribution.

3. Recall $Q = \dfrac{ad - bc}{ad + bc} = \dfrac{(28.75)^2 - (28.75)^2}{(28.75)^2 + (28.75)^2} = \dfrac{826.5 - 826.5}{826.5 + 826.5} = \dfrac{0}{1653} = 0.00.$

4. Method 1 is much simpler than Method 2 but it's applicable only on 2 × 2 tables. If you have contingency tables with more than 2 rows or 2 columns, use Method 2.

5. The difference between the X^2 value of Method 1 and Method 2 is from rounding error.

6. It is important to note that phi is equal to the product moment correlation coefficient (to be discussed later) for a 2 × 2 table.

In the introduction to this laboratory text a number of reasons for such a handbook were suggested. We wanted to provide the student of comparative and international politics with a resource which was closely linked to the literature, the techniques, and the substantive issues in the study of cross-national phenomena. We have sought to present our ideas in such a fashion so that you can better understand the findings of quantitative research, whether you confront them later in your chosen professional career or as an interested layperson.

We have brought to this basic goal a clearly defined value position; that is, advances in both the social and physical sciences have created a vast reservoir of information about people and their environment, including the international milieu. Moreover, technological innovation has enabled humans to develop supporting systems to store and retrieve this overwhelming body of information, and to reduce it to a level which yields comprehensive knowledge to serve whatever ends desired. As tomorrow's generation of citizens, it is imperative that you utilize this information in such a manner so as to increase the likelihood that you—as citizen spectators—will be able to make intelligent decisions about which public positions to support, and—as gladiators—will pursue policies which maximize desired outcomes. Thus, we have sought to provide the tools for the systematic utilization of these large bodies of information to help you make analytical judgments or assessments about the nature of the real world. This alludes to both assertions about the manner in which values, structures, and resources are distributed within the international arena, as well as about the antecedents of these conditions. This capacity requires a knowledge of analytical problems, propositions, concepts, methodology, measurement, evidence, theory, and a rather extensive accompanying set of abilities. This text is designed to achieve educational objectives associated with the acquisition of such knowledge.

We have attempted to meet these objectives in the context of an active learning environment. Thus, ample opportunity has been provided for you to test the knowledge and skills required for quantitative research. At the end of each chapter we have included a series of exercises which allow you to determine the extent to which you have mastered the materials. In addition, the appendix contains a data scheme and deck designed to help you apply the techniques and skills of quantitative analysis to a large number of research problems associated with the comparative study of foreign policy. By applying the techniques of descriptive and associational analysis (chapters 5, 6, and 7), you should sharpen your analytical skills and increase your ability to design, execute, and present findings from your own empirical research on other topics and issues in comparative and international politics.

LABORATORY ANALYSIS DECK

This appendix is designed to help you apply the techniques and skills covered in the previous chapters—techniques for generating, coding, analyzing, and displaying data, and interpreting the findings suggested by these data. Whereas earlier chapters emphasized the design and execution of research, this section provides the raw materials of research in the context of a framework for approaching the comparative study of foreign policy. By applying the techniques you have already acquired, you should sharpen your analytical skills and increase your ability to design, execute, and present findings from your own empirical research on topics and issues of interest in comparative and international politics.[1] (Exercises are found at the end of the appendix.)

A CLASSIFICATION SCHEME FOR CROSS-NATIONAL INDICATORS

If you are going to search for factors that influence the foreign behavior of a nation —or at least try to determine certain sets of conditions that are somehow associated with an observed pattern of behavior, you need a framework that will allow you to identify the nations and the conditions or factors relating to that behavior. Hence, in the following pages a framework is presented that distinguishes among various types of nations and factors that condition behavior—thereby facilitating the investigation of foreign behavior for any subset of nations (e.g., the "Latin American" group or "small powers") as well as for the entire universe of nations.[2]

Consider first the classification of our cases—the nations. Several scholars (Sawyer, 1967; Rosenau, 1966; Rummel, 1968) have suggested that nations be classified according to three dichotomized attributes: (1) the size of a nation (large and small); (2) its level of economic development (developed and underdeveloped); and (3) its political accountability (open and closed societies). If these three national attributes are combined, eight nation types (or "genotypes") emerge, as shown in Figure A.1.

Large				Small			
Developed		Underdeveloped		Developed		Underdeveloped	
Open	Closed	Open	Closed	Open	Closed	Open	Closed

Figure A.1   Nation genotypes

Now, rather than a strategy of research which examines *all* nations, you are now able to select a sample of countries which fall into any one of the categories displayed in Figure A.1. For example, you may decide to use only one attribute—such as size—in order to examine the behavior of nations within either the large or the small group. Alternatively, you may use all three genotypes to create a subset of nations—such as the large-developed-closed group of nations—for the purpose of analyzing behavior moderated by these factors. Consequently, examine Figure A.2 in order to discover the genotypic category into which each nation falls based on indicators from the year 1963. The operational indicators used to determine each genotype are total population (size), GNP/capita (economic development), and freedom of the press (political accountability). In order to divide nations into dichotomized categories, the mean score for each indicator was calculated. Those nations whose value was greater than the mean were placed in the high category; the remaining countries fell into the low group.

Be sure to note that the data set provided in this appendix contains several alternative variables for measuring and identifying genotypic nation groups. This allows you to create a different typology of nations by utilizing other indicators of the genotype.

Similarly, you may wish to use the indicators for size, economic development, and political accountability as independent variables in a proposition rather than as moderating or genotypic variables. For example, the proposition, "As the size of a nation increases, the amount of hostile activity in which it engages will also increase" uses the size variable as an independent variable rather than as a variable for typing or subsetting the universe of nations.

This framework is elaborated further by noting that behavior may be influenced by characteristics of the nation itself (structural factors) or by characteristics of the nation's environment (contextual factors), as discussed in chapter 3. These contextual and structural factors can be divided into more detailed factors assumed by many to be important conditions affecting the foreign behavior of nations. Therefore, borrowing from the conceptual work of Deutsch and Edinger (1959) and Rosenau (1966), we have clustered the contextual and structural sources of foreign behavior into the following three "source variable" categories: governmental factors and societal factors (structural variables) and external factors (contextual variables) which are included in the analysis deck containing 72 variables.

In the context of the framework suggested here, 35 of these 72 variables may be considered independent variables; that is, they represent attributes of nations—their size, level of economic development, degree of political accountability, governmental and societal factors (such as civil-military relations, literacy, and population growth) and external variables (geographic position vis-a-vis the major powers, nations attributes in comparison to one's neighbors, and access to the seas). The remaining 37 variables represent foreign policy output measures and may typically be utilized as dependent variables. This list of variables is displayed in Figure A.3. For example, the proposition, "The greater the percentage of communist vote, the smaller the amount of foreign aid received from the United States" makes use of variables 18 and 45, respectively.

In addition to this basic data set of 72 variables, each divided into 10 ordered categories, the specific rank orders for 63 variables in this set are included.* These

---

* Nine of the 72 variables were coded ordinal originally. Consequently these have been excluded in these rank orderings.

Large

Developed		Underdeveloped	
Open	Closed	Open	Closed
France—229	Poland—290	Brazil—140	Red China—710
W. Germany—225	U.S.S.R.—365	India—750	Indonesia—850
Italy—325		S. Korea—732	Pakistan—770
Japan—740		Mexico—070	Spain—230
U.K.—200		Nigeria—475	U.A.R.—651
U.S.—002		Philippines—840	
		Thailand—800	
		Turkey—640	
N = 6	N = 2	N = 8	N = 5

Small

Developed		Underdeveloped	
Open	Closed	Open	Closed
Argentina—160	Albania—339	Bolivia—145	Afghanistan—700
Australia—900	Bulgaria—355	China (T)—713	Algeria—615
Austria—305	Czechoslovakia—	Colombia—100	Burma—775
Belgium—211	315	Costa Rica—094	Cambodia—811
Canada—020	E. Germany—265	Dom. Rep.—042	Cameroun—471
Cyprus—352	Hungary—310	Ecuador—130	Ceylon—780
Denmark—390	Rumania—360	El Salv.—092	Chad—483
Finland—375		Greece—350	Congo (Ki)—490
Ireland—205		Guatemala—090	Cuba—040
Israel—666		Honduras—091	Ethiopia—530
Netherlands—210		Jamaica—051	Ghana—452
New Zealand—920		Lebanon—660	Haiti—041
Norway—385		Malaysia—820	Iran—630
Sweden—380		Morocco—600	Iraq—645
Switzerland—225		Panama—095	Jordan—663
Venezuela—101		Peru—135	N. Korea—731
		S. Africa—360	Laos—812
		Uganda—500	Nepal—790
		Uruguay—165	Portugal—235
			Senegal—433
			S. Vietnam—817
			Syria—652
			Tunisia—616
			Upper Volta—439
			Yugoslavia—345

Iceland—395**		Burundi—516**	Mauritania—435
Kuwait—690		Central African	Mongolia—712
Luxembourg—212		Republic—482	Nicaragua—093
Trinidad and		Chile—155	Niger—436
Tobago—052		Congo (BR)—484	N. Vietnam—816
		Dahomey—434	Paraguay—150
		Gabon—481	Rwanda—517
		Guinea—438	Saudi Arabia—670
		Ivory Coast—437	Sierra Leone—451
		Liberia—450	Somalia—520
		Libya—620	Sudan—625
		Malagasy—580	Togo—461
		Mali—432	Yemen—678
N = 16	N = 6	N = 19	N = 25

Figure A.2   *1963 genotypic nation clusters by means**

* Cut-off point = mean
  Mean of pop. = 26,737
  Mean of Dev. = 527.9310
  Mean of open-closed = 438.3678
** Missing data for the political accountability variable.

Figure A.3   Variable list

Column-Variable Number	Variable Name	Variable Type
1	Total Population	Genotype: Size
2	Total Land Area	
3	Total GNP	
4	KWH of electrical production	
5	GNP per capita	Genotype: Economic Development
6	Energy production per capita	
7	Agr. workers as percent of total economically active population	
8	KWH per capita	
9	Current electoral system	Genotype: Political Accountability
10	Freedom of the press	
11	Competitiveness: head of government's election	
12	Legal status of the Communist Party	Source Variable: Governmental
13	Political participation by military	
14	Character of bureaucracy	
15	Current status of legislature	
16	Government stability	
17	Central government revenue as percent of GNP	
18	Percent Communist vote	
19	Newspapers per 1000 population	Source Variable: Societal
20	Percent population in cities over 20,000	
21	People per hospital bed	
22	Rate of population increase	
23	Westernization	
24	Mass participation/turmoil	
25	Palace revolution/revolt	
26	Strategic distance from power centers: composite	Source Variable: External
27	Strategic distance from power centers: United States/USSR	
28	Strategic distance from power centers: United States/China	
29	Strategic distance: China	
30	Strategic distance: USSR	
31	Strategic distance: United States (mainland)	
32	Geopolitical scores: GNP	
33	Geopolitical scores: Population	
34	Geopolitical scores: GNP/capita	
35	Aqua access	
36	Administrative personnel per diplomat	Output Variable: Political
37	Contributions to UN assistance and relief programs	
38	Political alignment-UN voting	
39	Alliance commitments to United States/USSR	
40	Index of agreement with United States in UN voting	
41	Diplomatic representatives sent	
42	Number of nations diplomats sent to	
43	Number of diplomats received	

(continued)

Column-Variable Number	Variable Name	Variable Type
44	Number of nations diplomats received from	
45	United States foreign aid expenditures (cumulative 1948–63)	
46	Total inter-regional membership in IGO's	
47	Total intra-regional membership in IGO's	
48	Total IGO memberships	
49	Shared IGO memberships	
50	Total socio-economic IGO's	
51	Diplomatic linkage: Contiguous nations	
52	Foreign conflict index	
53	Percent trade to two largest buyers	Output Variable: Economic
54	Total foreign trade as percent GNP	
55	Total imports	
56	Total exports	
57	Military capability	Output Variable: Military
58	Military expenditures	
59	Military expenditures as percent of GNP	
60	Military expenditures as percent of Central Government	
61	Volume of total events	Output Variable: WEIS Events
62	Scope of total events	
63	Balance of total events	
64	Volume of diplomatic exchange	
65	Scope of diplomatic exchange	
66	Balance of diplomatic exchange	
67	Volume of non-military conflict	
68	Scope of non-military conflict	
69	Balance of non-military conflict	
70	Volume of cooperation	
71	Scope of cooperation	
72	Balance of cooperation	

rankings will allow you to utilize the Spearman's rho, the rank order correlation coefficient discussed in chapter 6, as a measure of association. Figure A.4, describing each nation's geographic location (in one of nineteen suggested regions), is also inserted to allow you to use an alternative classification scheme to the type suggested in Figure A.2.

VARIABLE DEFINITIONS AND SOURCES

The data set outlined in Figure A.3 is derived from a data matrix with row and column dimensions of 116×217. The number 116 represents those national political units that were members of the United Nations in 1963 or that were excluded from membership because of their divided status (such as Germany or North and South Vietnam). The number 217 represents the current number of variables in the data set. For this appendix a smaller data matrix of 116×72 has been extracted in order to allow all the information for each nation to be placed on one standard IBM punch card. The complete data set may then be punched on 116 cards, each of which represents one nation in our sample.

Western Europe
Austria
Belgium
West Germany
France
Luxembourg
Netherlands
Switzerland
Great Britain
Ireland

Scandinavia
Norway
Sweden
Finland
Denmark
Iceland

Southern Europe
Albania
Greece
Italy
Portugal
Spain
Yugoslavia

Eastern Europe
Bulgaria
Czechoslovakia
East Germany
Hungary
Poland
Rumania
USSR

East Asia Mainland
Red China
Mongolia
North Korea
South Korea
Japan
China (Taiwan)

Middle South Asia
Afghanistan
Ceylon
India
Iran
Pakistan
Nepal

Southeast Asia
Burma
Cambodia
Indonesia
Laos
Malaysia
Philippines
Thailand
North Vietnam
South Vietnam

Southwest Asia
(Middle East)
Cyprus
Iraq
Israel
Jordan
Kuwait
Lebanon
Saudi Arabia
Syria
Turkey
Yemen

North America
Canada
United States

Tropical Latin America
Bolivia
Brazil
Colombia
Ecuador
Peru
Venezuela

Temperate Latin America
Argentina
Chile
Paraguay
Uruguay

Central America
Costa Rica
El Salvador
Guatemala
Honduras
Mexico
Nicaragua
Panama

Caribbean
Cuba
Dominican Republic
Haiti
Jamaica
Trinidad and Tobago

West Africa
Dahomey
Ghana
Guinea
Ivory Coast
Liberia
Mali
Mauritania
Niger
Nigeria
Senegal
Sierra Leone
Togo
Upper Volta

East Africa
Burundi
Ethiopia
Madagascar
Rwanda
Somalia
Uganda

North Africa
Algeria
Libya
Morocco
Sudan
Tunisia
United Arab Republic

Middle Africa
Cameroon
Central African Republic
Chad
Congo (Brazzaville)
Congo (Democratic Repub.)
Gabon

South Africa
Union of South Africa

Oceania
Australia
New Zealand

Figure A.4 Sovereign nations—1963

The 80 columns of the IBM card are divided in the following manner. The one-field code values assigned to the 72 variables are given in the first 72 columns. Three alphabetic and three numeric codes providing a unique alphanumeric identification for each country are given in columns 74–76 and 78–80, respectively. For example, the card representing the data for the United States contains the letters USA in columns 74–76 and the numbers 002 in columns 78–80. Columns 73 and 77 remain blank to facilitate visual identification and easy selection of a particular nation for observation.

VARIABLE CODING SCHEME

All the variables in the analysis deck are presented as ordinal measures. That is, each variable has been divided into categories and assigned a number in such a fashion that each number stands in a definite and consistent relationship to every other number. Its quantity is greater than or less than that represented by the remaining numbers. For example, variable 15 represents the Current Status of the Legislature's Effectiveness. This variable is divided into four categories, numbered in the following order:

0 = fully effective
3 = partially effective
6 = largely ineffective
9 = wholly ineffective

As you can observe from the category names, it is impossible to determine the exact distance between each category—as you could with an indicator that measured, for example, the number of times per year the legislature overrules the executive's veto. You only know that if a nation has been assigned the code value 3, the effectiveness of its legislature is greater than that of a nation which has been assigned the value 6, but less than that nation which is given the value 0.

In their original format, only 9 of the 72 variables selected for the data set were ordinal in nature, while the remaining 63 were comprised of interval-level data. Consequently, these interval-level measures have been reduced to ordinal data for this manual. This was done for two reasons. First, since earlier chapters do not give high priority to statistical techniques requiring interval data (such as regression analysis), ordinal measures will suffice for practicing techniques covered earlier. Once mastered, you will be able to move easily to more sophisticated analytical applications that do require higher order measurements.

The second reason is convenience. In order to maintain a manageable number of cards in the student's analysis deck—no more than one card per country—it is necessary to fit all 72 variables on one card allocating one column per variable. Moreover, because interval measures often require more than one column to express the value of the datum, ordinal measures are used to facilitate the use of the counter-sorter for those who do not have access to a computer. The coding procedures for these 63 variables are described below.

RAW AND TRANSFORMED DATA SETS

The basic data set has been produced in two versions. In the first version the raw scores were utilized when creating the ordinal categories. The following steps were employed: (1) the interval-level variables (63 in number) to be included in the analysis deck were retrieved from the larger CAPE data files noted earlier; (2) the range of each variable was computed; (3) each range was divided into ten equal intervals (called "deciles");[3] (4) ordinal values from 0 to 9 were assigned to each decile with 0 denoting the lowest decile and 9 denoting the highest; and (5) the appropriate ordinal category substitutions for the raw values on every variable were placed in the proper column of each country's card. The category values for the remaining nine original ordinal variables were simply transferred in the same form to new decks.

The second version of the data set contains the same 72 variables but their scores have been transformed to reflect a more normal distribution. This permits you to meet most of the assumptions required of interval data and, consequently, allows their use in more sophisticated statistical routines.

The following steps were employed to transform the raw interval data into normalized, transformed, ordinal measures: (a) the distribution for each variable was normalized; hence, for each variable the mean = the median = the mode, and (b) the procedure outlined in the preceding steps 3 through 5 was implemented a second time for the standardized scores.*

DATA ANALYSIS

Below is a listing of various aids that appear at the end of this appendix. They should prove useful in applying the various data analysis routines that you have learned in this manual.

1. Codebook—contains the column number and n size for each variable, the n size for each category of a variable, and the category ranges;
2. Country Identification (Figure A.5)—alphabetic and numeric codes with full country name;
3. Variable Definitions—with citations;
4. Data Printout (Figure A.6)—the 116 × 72 data matrix for both data sets to allow you to keypunch the values;
5. Rank Orders (Figure A.7)—each nation's ranking on the 63 interval variables to allow the application of Spearman's rank order correlation as a measure of association.

---

* Variables 11, 18, 20, 31, 38, 52, 53, and 63 do not appear in this second version as transformed values; rather they remain in the raw form. The raw distributions of variables 20, 31, 53, and 63 already approximate a normal curve, and there exists no transformation routines for the remaining four variables.

CODEBOOK
STUDENT DATA DECK

N = 116

Variable 1 — Total Population (thousands) — Column 01, N = 116

N	Code	Range
102	0	−37,582.37 — 37,952.57
10	1	37,952.57 — 113,487.50
0	2	113,487.50 — 189,022.44
2	3	189,022.44 — 264,557.38
0	4	264,557.38 — 340,092.31
0	5	340,092.31 — 415,627.25
1	6	415,627.25 — 491,162.19
0	7	491,162.19 — 566,697.13
0	8	566,697.13 — 642,232.06
1	9	642,232.06 — 717,767.00

Variable 2 — Total Land Area (square kilometers) — Column 02, N = 116

N	Code	Range
99	0	−1,286,755 — 1,291,934
11	1	1,291,934 — 3,870,623
0	2	3,870,623 — 6,449,312
2	3	6,449,312 — 9,028,001
3	4	9,028,001 — 11,606,690
0	5	11,606,690 — 14,185,379
0	6	14,185,379 — 16,764,061
0	7	16,764,061 — 19,342,736
0	8	19,342,736 — 21,921,424
1	9	21,921,424 — 24,500,112

Variable 3 — Total GNP (millions of U.S. dollars) — Column 03, N = 116

N	Code	Range
106	0	−32,346.06 — 32,521.94
8	1	32,521.94 — 97,389.94
0	2	97,389.94 — 162,257.94
0	3	162,257.94 — 227,125.94
1	4	227,125.94 — 291,993.94
0	5	291,993.94 — 356,861.94
0	6	356,861.94 — 421,729.94
0	7	421,729.94 — 486,597.94
0	8	486,597.94 — 551,465.94
1	9	551,465.94 — 616,333.94

Variable 4 — KWH of Electrical Production (millions) — Column 04, N = 109

N	Code	Range
101	0	−56,179.25 — 56,199.25
6	1	56,199.25 — 168,577.75
0	2	168,577.75 — 280,956.25
1	3	280,956.25 — 393,334.75
0	4	393,334.75 — 505,713.25
0	5	505,713.25 — 618,091.75
0	6	618,091.75 — 730,470.25
0	7	730,470.25 — 842,848.75
0	8	842,848.75 — 955,227.25
1	9	955,227.25 — 1,067,605.00

Variable 5 — GNP per Capita (U.S. dollars) — Column 05, N = 116

N	Code	Range
57	0	−141.11 — 221.11
27	1	221.11 — 583.33
10	2	583.33 — 945.55
7	3	945.55 — 1,307.78
6	4	1,307.78 — 1,670.00
5	5	1,670.00 — 2,032.22
2	6	2,032.22 — 2,394.44
0	7	2,394.44 — 2,756.67
1	8	2,756.67 — 3,118.89
1	9	3,118.89 — 3,481.11

Variable 6 — Energy Production per Capita (metric tons) — Column 06, N = 93

N	Code	Range
90	0	−18.38 — 18.38
2	1	18.38 — 55.15
0	2	55.15 — 91.91
0	3	91.91 — 128.68
0	4	128.68 — 165.44
0	5	165.44 — 202.20
0	6	202.20 — 238.97
0	7	238.97 — 275.73
0	8	275.73 — 312.50
1	9	312.50 — 349.26

Variable 7 — Agricultural Workers as Percent of Total Economically Active Population — Column 07, N = 116

N	Code	Range
6	0	−1.11 — 9.11
15	1	9.11 — 19.33
6	2	19.33 — 29.56
10	3	29.56 — 39.78
8	4	39.78 — 50.00
26	5	50.00 — 60.22
10	6	60.22 — 70.44
12	7	70.44 — 80.67
18	8	80.67 — 90.89
5	9	90.89 — 101.11

Variable 8 — KWH per Capita — Column 08, N = 109

N	Code	Range
75	0	−596.78 — 598.78
17	1	598.78 — 1,794.33
8	2	1,794.33 — 2,989.89
4	3	2,989.89 — 4,185.44
2	4	4,185.44 — 5,381.00
2	5	5,381.00 — 6,576.55
0	6	6,576.55 — 7,772.11
0	7	7,772.11 — 8,967.66
0	8	8,967.66 — 10,163.22
1	9	10,163.22 — 11,358.77

* This codebook serves two data sets: raw values and transformed values. The category ranges for the raw deck are presented here. The same procedure (dividing the range into ten equal categories) was used for the transformed deck. Variable definitions follow the codebook.

(continued)

Column Number	N	Variable Number	Code*
09	81	9.	Current Electoral System
	43	0	Competitive
	8	5	Partially Competitive
	30	9	Non-Competitive
10	87	10.	Freedom of the Press
	6	0	12.50 — 85.50
	9	1	85.50 — 158.50
	3	2	158.50 — 231.50
	8	3	231.50 — 304.50
	7	4	304.50 — 377.50
	6	5	377.50 — 450.50
	10	6	450.50 — 523.50
	10	7	523.50 — 596.50
	20	8	596.50 — 669.50
	8	9	669.50 — 742.50
11	116	11.	Competitiveness: Head of Government's Election
	58	0	−4.94 — 4.94
	7	1	4.94 — 14.82
	3	2	14.82 — 24.69
	2	3	24.69 — 34.57
	3	4	34.57 — 44.45
	15	5	44.45 — 54.33
	16	6	54.33 — 64.21
	10	7	64.21 — 74.08
	1	8	74.08 — 83.96
	1	9	83.96 — 93.84
12	116	12.	Legal Status of the Communist Party
	59	1	No Known Legal Restriction
	14	0	In Power
	40	8	Formally Proscribed
	3	9	Informally Proscribed
13	107	13.	Political Participation by Military
	21	0	Interventive
	31	5	Supportive
	55	9	Neutral
14	109	14.	Character of Bureaucracy
	21	0	Modern
	55	3	Semi-Modern
	24	6	Post-Colonial Transitional
	9	9	Traditional
15	99	15.	Current Status of Legislature
	28	0	Fully Effective
	23	3	Partially Effective
15 (cont.)	99	15.	Current Status of Legislature
	20	6	Largely Ineffective
	28	9	Wholly Ineffective
16	83	16.	Government Stability
	22	0	Government generally stable since World War I or major inter-war constitutional change.
	28	3	Government generally stable since World War II or major post-war constitutional change.
	11	6	Government moderately stable since World War II or major post-war constitutional change.
	22	9	Government unstable since World War II or major post-war constitutional change.
17	115	17.	Central Government Revenue as Percent of GNP
	10	0	1.11 — 9.69
	47	1	9.69 — 18.28
	32	2	18.28 — 26.87
	8	3	26.87 — 35.46
	3	4	35.46 — 44.05
	8	5	44.05 — 52.64
	1	6	52.64 — 61.23
	3	7	61.23 — 69.82
	2	8	69.82 — 78.41
	1	9	78.41 — 86.99
18	104	18.	Percent Communist Vote
	82	0	−5.56 — 5.56
	6	1	5.56 — 16.67
	3	2	16.67 — 27.78
	0	3	27.78 — 38.89
	0	4	38.89 — 50.00
	0	5	50.00 — 61.11
	0	6	61.11 — 72.22
	0	7	72.22 — 83.33
	0	8	83.33 — 94.44
	13	9	94.44 — 105.56
19	107	19.	Newspapers per 1,000 Population
	47	0	−27.72 — 27.72
	19	1	27.72 — 83.17
	11	2	83.17 — 138.61
	7	3	138.61 — 194.06

(continued)

Column Number	N	Variable Number	Code*		
			Newspapers per 1,000 Population		
19 (cont.) 107		19.			
	4	4	194.06 —		249.50
	5	5	249.50 —		304.94
	6	6	304.94 —		360.39
	3	7	360.39 —		415.83
	3	8	415.83 —		471.28
	2	9	471.28 —		526.72
			Percent Population in Cities over 20,000		
20	61	20.			
	3	0	2.94 —		11.06
	13	1	11.06 —		19.17
	5	2	19.17 —		27.28
	14	3	27.28 —		35.39
	10	4	35.39 —		43.50
	8	5	43.50 —		51.61
	0	6	51.61 —		59.72
	4	7	59.72 —		67.83
	2	8	67.83 —		75.94
	2	9	75.94 —		84.06
			People per Hospital Bed		
21	100	21.			
	62	0	-376.11 —		516.11
	23	1	516.11 —		1,408.33
	9	2	1,408.33 —		2,300.56
	1	3	2,300.56 —		3,192.78
	3	4	3,192.78 —		4,085.00
	0	5	4,085.00 —		4,977.22
	0	6	4,977.22 —		5,869.44
	0	7	5,869.44 —		6,761.66
	0	8	6,761.66 —		7,653.88
	2	9	7,653.88 —		8,546.11
			Rate of Population Increase		
22	112	22.			
	1	0	-0.44 —		.04
	3	1	.04 —		.52
	13	2	.52 —		.99
	11	3	.99 —		1.47
	18	4	1.47 —		1.95
	18	5	1.95 —		2.43
	17	6	2.43 —		2.91
	22	7	2.91 —		3.38
	8	8	3.38 —		3.86
	1	9	3.86 —		4.34
			Westernization		
23	111	23.			
	26	0	Historically Western Nation		
	7	1	Significantly Westernized (No Colonial Relationship)		
	28	3	Significantly Westernized (Colonial Relationship)		

Column Number	N	Variable Number	Code*		
			Westernization		
23 (cont.) 111		23.			
	8	5	Partially Westernized (No Colonial Relationship)		
	40	7	Partially Westernized (Colonial Relationship)		
	2	8	Non-Westernized (No Colonial Relationship; little or no visible Westernization)		
			Mass Participation/Turmoil		
24	82	24.			
	30	0	-4.33 —		4.33
	28	1	4.33 —		13.00
	17	2	13.00 —		21.67
	2	3	21.67 —		30.33
	1	4	30.33 —		39.00
	1	5	39.00 —		47.67
	2	6	47.67 —		56.33
	0	7	56.33 —		65.00
	0	8	65.00 —		73.67
	1	9	73.67 —		82.33
			Palace Revolution/Revolt		
25	82	25.			
	25	0	-2.06 —		2.06
	14	1	2.06 —		6.17
	12	2	6.17 —		10.28
	7	3	10.28 —		14.39
	10	4	14.39 —		18.50
	3	5	18.50 —		22.61
	5	6	22.61 —		26.72
	2	7	26.72 —		30.83
	2	8	30.83 —		34.94
	2	9	34.94 —		39.06
			Strategic Distance from Power Centers: Composite		
26	116	26.			
	61	0	-17.14 —		17.14
	25	1	17.14 —		51.42
	19	2	51.42 —		85.69
	4	3	85.69 —		119.97
	1	4	119.97 —		154.25
	1	5	154.25 —		188.53
	1	6	188.53 —		222.81
	3	7	222.81 —		257.08
	0	8	257.08 —		291.36
	1	9	291.36 —		325.64
			Strategic Distance from Power Centers: U.S./USSR		
27	116	27.			
	4	0	-0.06 —		0.06
	10	1	0.06 —		0.17
	5	2	0.17 —		0.28

(continued)

Column Number	N	Variable Number	Code*	
27 (cont.) 116		27.	Strategic Distance from Power Centers: U.S./USSR	
	5	3	0.28 —	0.39
	1	4	0.39 —	0.50
	7	5	0.50 —	0.61
	23	6	0.61 —	0.72
	21	7	0.72 —	0.83
	19	8	0.83 —	0.94
	21	9	0.94 —	1.06
28	116	28.	Strategic Distance from Power Centers: United States/China	
	4	0	−0.06 —	0.06
	12	1	0.06 —	0.17
	7	2	0.17 —	0.28
	2	3	0.28 —	0.39
	19	4	0.39 —	0.50
	27	5	0.50 —	0.61
	15	6	0.61 —	0.72
	8	7	0.72 —	0.83
	7	8	0.83 —	0.94
	15	9	0.94 —	1.06
29	116	29.	Strategic Distance: China	
	18	0	−5.59 —	5.59
	8	1	5.59 —	16.78
	21	2	16.78 —	27.97
	25	3	27.97 —	39.16
	15	4	39.16 —	50.35
	8	5	50.35 —	61.54
	2	6	61.54 —	72.73
	12	7	72.73 —	83.92
	3	8	83.92 —	95.11
	4	9	95.11 —	106.29
30	116	30.	Strategic Distance: USSR	
	27	0	−4.14 —	4.14
	23	1	4.14 —	12.42
	15	2	12.42 —	20.69
	14	3	20.69 —	28.97
	13	4	28.97 —	37.25
	2	5	37.25 —	45.53
	9	6	45.53 —	53.81
	6	7	53.81 —	62.08
	4	8	62.08 —	70.36
	3	9	70.36 —	78.64
31	116	31.	Strategic Distance: United States (Mainland)	
	4	0	−4.66 —	4.66
	11	1	4.66 —	13.97
	6	2	13.97 —	23.28
	12	3	23.28 —	32.59
	23	4	32.59 —	41.90

Column Number	N	Variable Number	Code*	
31 (cont.) 116		31.	Strategic Distance United States (Mainland)	
	20	5	41.90 —	51.21
	16	6	51.21 —	60.52
	16	7	60.52 —	69.83
	6	8	69.83 —	79.14
	2	9	79.14 —	88.46
32	116	32.	Geopolitical Scores: GNP	
	33	0	−0.05 —	0.06
	31	1	0.06 —	0.17
	10	2	0.17 —	0.28
	16	3	0.28 —	0.39
	2	4	0.39 —	0.50
	5	5	0.50 —	0.61
	3	6	0.61 —	0.72
	2	7	0.72 —	0.83
	1	8	0.83 —	0.94
	13	9	0.94 —	1.06
33	116	33.	Geopolitical Scores: Population	
	26	0	−0.05 —	0.06
	37	1	0.06 —	0.17
	13	2	0.17 —	0.28
	11	3	0.28 —	0.39
	8	4	0.39 —	0.50
	3	5	0.50 —	0.61
	2	6	0.61 —	0.72
	2	7	0.72 —	0.83
	1	8	0.83 —	0.94
	13	9	0.94 —	1.06
34	116	34.	Geopolitical Scores: GNP/Capita	
	4	0	0.09 —	0.38
	20	1	0.38 —	0.66
	33	2	0.66 —	0.95
	38	3	0.95 —	1.24
	8	4	1.24 —	1.52
	5	5	1.52 —	1.81
	4	6	1.81 —	2.09
	1	7	2.09 —	2.38
	1	8	2.38 —	2.66
	2	9	2.66 —	2.95
35	116	35.	Aqua Access	
	17	0	Island Nation	
	80	5	Direct access to the sea or a large body of water with an outlet to the sea	
	19	9	Landlocked	

(continued)

Column Number	N	Variable Number	Code*	
			Administrative Personnel per Diplomat	
36	71	36.		
	48	0	−382.50 —	414.50
	16	1	414.50 —	1,211.50
	3	2	1,211.50 —	2,008.50
	1	3	2,008.50 —	2,805.50
	1	4	2,805.50 —	3,602.50
	1	5	3,602.50 —	4,399.50
	0	6	4,399.50 —	5,196.50
	0	7	5,196.50 —	5,993.50
	0	8	5,993.50 —	6,790.50
	1	9	6,790.50 —	7,587.50
			Contributions to UN Assistance and Relief Programs (U.S. million dollars)	
37	50	37.		
	43	0	−4.21 —	4.41
	5	1	4.41 —	13.02
	1	2	13.02 —	21.63
	0	3	21.63 —	30.24
	0	4	30.24 —	38.85
	0	5	38.85 —	47.46
	0	6	47.46 —	56.07
	0	7	56.07 —	64.68
	0	8	64.68 —	73.29
	1	9	73.29 —	81.91
			Political Alignment— UN Voting	
38	108	38.		
	9	0	−1.11 —	−0.89
	15	1	−0.89 —	−0.67
	13	2	−0.67 —	−0.44
	14	3	−0.44 —	−0.22
	10	4	−0.22 —	0.00
	15	5	0.00 —	0.22
	12	6	0.22 —	0.44
	11	7	0.44 —	0.67
	0	8	0.67 —	0.89
	9	9	0.89 —	1.11
			Alliance Commitments to United States or USSR	
39	116	39.		
	43	0	Alliance with U.S.	
	59	3	No Military Commitments	
	2	6	Neutrality Commitment with USSR	
	12	9	Alliance with USSR	
			Index of Agreement with United States in UN Voting	
40	108	40.		
	9	0	−0.06 —	0.06
	0	1	0.06 —	0.17
	11	2	0.17 —	0.28

Column Number	N	Variable Number	Code*	
			Index of Agreement with United States in UN Voting	
40 (cont.)	108	40.		
	11	3	0.28 —	0.39
	14	4	0.39 —	0.50
	11	5	0.50 —	0.61
	14	6	0.61 —	0.72
	13	7	0.72 —	0.83
	16	8	0.83 —	0.94
	9	9	0.94 —	1.06
			Diplomatic Representatives Sent	
41	116	41.		
	76	0	−148.22 —	160.22
	32	1	160.22 —	468.67
	4	2	468.67 —	777.11
	0	3	777.11 —	1,085.56
	2	4	1,085.56 —	1,394.00
	1	5	1,394.00 —	1,702.44
	0	6	1,702.44 —	2,010.89
	0	7	2,010.89 —	2,319.33
	0	8	2,319.33 —	2,627.78
	1	9	2,627.78 —	2,936.22
			Number of Nations' Diplomats Sent to	
42	116	42.		
	13	0	−3.44 —	7.44
	28	1	7.44 —	18.33
	27	2	18.33 —	29.22
	10	3	29.22 —	40.11
	14	4	40.11 —	51.00
	10	5	51.00 —	61.89
	8	6	61.89 —	72.78
	1	7	72.78 —	83.67
	2	8	83.67 —	94.56
	3	9	94.56 —	105.44
43	101	43.	**Number of Diplomats Received**	
	28	0	−54.50 —	100.50
	46	1	100.50 —	255.50
	15	2	255.50 —	410.50
	6	3	410.50 —	565.50
	1	4	565.50 —	720.50
	3	5	720.50 —	875.50
	0	6	875.50 —	1,030.50
	0	7	1,030.50 —	1,185.50
	1	8	1,185.50 —	1,340.50
	1	9	1,340.50 —	1,495.50
			Number of Nations' Diplomats Received from	
44	101	44.		
	7	0	−0.67 —	10.67
	22	1	10.67 —	22.00
	17	2	22.00 —	33.33

(continued)

Column Number	N	Variable Number	Code*	
			Number of Nations' Diplomats Received from	
44 (cont.)	101	44.		
	26	3	33.33 —	44.67
	13	4	44.67 —	56.00
	7	5	56.00 —	67.33
	4	6	67.33 —	78.67
	1	7	78.67 —	90.00
	3	8	90.00 —	101.33
	1	9	101.33 —	112.67
			United States Foreign Aid Expenditures (Cumulative 1948–63) (U.S. million dollars)	
45	72	45.		
	50	0	−83.72 —	84.52
	18	1	84.52 —	252.77
	2	2	252.77 —	421.01
	0	3	421.01 —	589.26
	1	4	589.26 —	757.50
	0	5	757.50 —	925.74
	0	6	925.74 —	1,093.99
	0	7	1,093.99 —	1,262.23
	0	8	1,262.23 —	1,430.48
	1	9	1,430.48 —	1,598.72
			Total Inter-Regional Membership in IGO'S	
46	116	46.		
	6	0	−2.89 —	2.89
	38	1	2.89 —	8.67
	24	2	8.67 —	14.44
	13	3	14.44 —	20.22
	16	4	20.22 —	26.00
	9	5	26.00 —	31.78
	7	6	31.78 —	37.56
	1	7	37.56 —	43.33
	1	8	43.33 —	49.11
	1	9	49.11 —	54.89
			Total Intra-Regional Membership in IGO'S	
47	116	47.		
	26	0	−1.94 —	1.94
	33	1	1.94 —	5.83
	19	2	5.83 —	9.72
	10	3	9.72 —	13.61
	13	4	13.61 —	17.50
	8	5	17.50 —	21.39
	3	6	21.39 —	25.28
	1	7	25.28 —	29.17
	2	8	29.17 —	33.06
	1	9	33.06 —	36.94
			Total IGO Memberships	
48	116	48.		
	17	0	−1.50 —	7.50
	32	1	7.50 —	16.50

Column Number	N	Variable Number	Code*	
48 (cont.)	116	48.	**Total IGO Memberships**	
	25	2	16.50 —	25.50
	20	3	25.50 —	34.50
	11	4	34.50 —	43.50
	4	5	43.50 —	52.50
	1	6	52.50 —	61.50
	4	7	61.50 —	70.50
	1	8	70.50 —	79.50
	1	9	79.50 —	88.50
49	116	49.	**Shared IGO Memberships**	
	5	0	6.50 —	17.50
	2	1	17.50 —	28.50
	4	2	28.50 —	39.50
	0	3	39.50 —	50.50
	4	4	50.50 —	61.50
	1	5	61.50 —	72.50
	11	6	72.50 —	83.50
	19	7	83.50 —	94.50
	52	8	94.50 —	105.50
	18	9	105.50 —	116.50
50	116	50.	**Total Socioeconomic IGO'S**	
	17	0	−2.39 —	6.39
	33	1	6.39 —	15.17
	18	2	15.17 —	23.94
	24	3	23.94 —	32.72
	12	4	32.72 —	41.50
	6	5	41.50 —	50.28
	0	6	50.28 —	59.06
	3	7	59.06 —	67.83
	2	8	67.83 —	76.61
	1	9	76.61 —	85.39
			Diplomatic Linkages: Contiguous Nations	
51	103	51.		
	18	0	−0.28 —	0.28
	23	1	0.28 —	0.85
	24	2	0.85 —	1.42
	18	3	1.42 —	1.98
	10	4	1.98 —	2.55
	6	5	2.55 —	3.12
	2	6	3.12 —	3.68
	0	7	3.68 —	4.25
	1	8	4.25 —	4.82
	1	9	4.82 —	5.38
52	104	52.	**Foreign Conflicts Index**	
	77	0	−2.72 —	2.72
	20	1	2.72 —	8.17
	1	2	8.17 —	13.61
	1	3	13.61 —	19.06

(continued)

Column Number	N	Variable Number	Code*		Column Number	N	Variable Number	Code*	
52 (cont.)	104	52.	**Foreign Conflicts Index**		56 (cont.)	111	56.	**Total Exports** (U.S. million dollars)	
	1	4	19.06 —	24.50		2	3	6,446.90 —	9,025.38
	1	5	24.50 —	29.94		0	4	9,025.38 —	11,603.86
	0	6	29.94 —	35.39		1	5	11,603.86 —	14,182.33
	1	7	35.39 —	40.83		1	6	14,182.33 —	16,760.80
	0	8	40.83 —	46.28		0	7	16,760.80 —	19,339.28
	2	9	46.28 —	51.72		0	8	19,339.28 —	21,917.75
						1	9	21,917.75 —	24,496.23
53	105	53.	**Percent Trade to Two Largest Buyers**		57	93	57.	**Military Capability**	
	1	0	9.72 —	18.28		90	0	−15,925.78 —	15,925.78
	8	1	18.28 —	26.83		1	1	15,925.78 —	47,777.34
	24	2	26.83 —	35.39		0	2	47,777.34 —	79,628.88
	14	3	35.39 —	43.94		0	3	79,628.88 —	111,480.44
	19	4	43.94 —	52.50		0	4	111,480.44 —	143,332.00
	9	5	52.50 —	61.06		0	5	143,332.00 —	175,183.56
	12	6	61.06 —	69.61		1	6	175,183.56 —	207,035.13
	7	7	69.61 —	78.17		0	7	207,035.13 —	238,886.69
	8	8	78.17 —	86.72		0	8	238,886.69 —	270,738.25
	3	9	86.72 —	95.28		1	9	270,738.25 —	302,589.81
54	76	54.	**Total Foreign Trade as Percentage of GNP**		58	116	58.	**Military Expenditures** (U.S. million dollars)	
	2	0	0.44 —	17.56		110	0	−2,851.28 —	2,851.28
	19	1	17.56 —	34.67		4	1	2,851.28 —	8,553.83
	29	2	34.67 —	51.78		0	2	8,553.83 —	14,256.39
	13	3	51.78 —	68.89		0	3	14,256.39 —	19,958.94
	8	4	68.89 —	86.00		0	4	19,958.94 —	25,661.50
	2	5	86.00 —	103.11		0	5	25,661.50 —	31,364.05
	1	6	103.11 —	120.22		1	6	31,364.05 —	37,066.61
	0	7	120.22 —	137.33		0	7	37,066.61 —	42,769.16
	1	8	137.33 —	154.44		0	8	42,769.16 —	48,471.71
	1	9	154.44 —	171.56		1	9	48,471.71 —	54,174.27
55	111	55.	**Total Imports** (U.S. million dollars)		59	116	59.	**Military Expenditures as Percent of GNP**	
	81	0	−928.87 —	974.27		13	0	−0.93 —	0.93
	18	1	974.27 —	2,877.42		44	1	0.93 —	2.78
	2	2	2,877.42 —	4,780.56		29	2	2.78 —	4.64
	3	3	4,780.56 —	6,683.70		10	3	4.64 —	6.49
	3	4	6,683.70 —	8,586.85		11	4	6.49 —	8.35
	1	5	8,586.85 —	10,489.99		2	5	8.35 —	10.21
	0	6	10,489.99 —	12,393.14		3	6	10.21 —	12.06
	2	7	12,393.14 —	14,296.28		0	7	12.06 —	13.92
	0	8	14,296.28 —	16,199.42		3	8	13.92 —	15.77
	1	9	16,199.42 —	18,102.57		1	9	15.77 —	17.63
56	111	56.	**Total Exports** (U.S. million dollars)		60	116	60.	**Military Expenditures as Percent of Central Government Expenditures**	
	89	0	−1,288.52 —	1,289.96		16	0	−6.36 —	6.36
	12	1	1,289.96 —	3,868.43		60	1	6.36 —	19.07
	5	2	3,868.43 —	6,446.90						

(continued)

Column Number	N	Variable Number	Code*		Column Number	N	Variable Number	Code*	
			Military Expenditures as Percent of Central Government Expenditures		64 (cont.)	116	64.	Volume of Diplomatic Exchanges	
60 (cont.)	116	60.				1	4	357.78 —	460.00
						0	5	460.00 —	562.22
	22	2	19.07 —	31.78		0	6	562.22 —	664.44
	6	3	31.78 —	44.49		0	7	664.44 —	766.67
	6	4	44.49 —	57.20		0	8	766.67 —	868.89
	2	5	57.20 —	69.91		1	9	868.89 —	971.11
	2	6	69.91 —	82.62					
	1	7	82.62 —	95.33	65	116	65.	Scope of Diplomatic Exchange	
	0	8	95.33 —	108.04		8	0	−0.56 —	0.56
	1	9	108.04 —	120.76		52	1	0.56 —	1.67
						34	2	1.67 —	2.78
61	116	61.	Volume of Total Events			10	3	2.78 —	3.89
	99	0	−223.22 —	225.22		7	4	3.89 —	5.00
	10	1	225.22 —	673.67		2	5	5.00 —	6.11
	4	2	673.67 —	1,122.11		2	6	6.11 —	7.22
	1	3	1,122.11 —	1,570.56		0	7	7.22 —	8.33
	1	4	1,570.56 —	2,019.00		0	8	8.33 —	9.44
	0	5	2,019.00 —	2,467.44		1	9	9.44 —	10.56
	0	6	2,467.44 —	2,915.89					
	0	7	2,915.89 —	3,364.33	66	112	66.	Balance of Diplomatic Exchange	
	0	8	3,364.33 —	3,812.78		12	0	−0.61 —	0.61
	1	9	3,812.78 —	4,261.22		73	1	0.61 —	1.83
						19	2	1.83 —	3.06
62	116	62.	Scope of Total Events			6	3	3.06 —	4.28
	42	0	−0.64 —	2.64		0	4	4.28 —	5.50
	47	1	2.64 —	5.92		0	5	5.50 —	6.72
	8	2	5.92 —	9.19		0	6	6.72 —	7.94
	11	3	9.19 —	12.47		1	7	7.94 —	9.17
	1	4	12.47 —	15.75		0	8	9.17 —	10.39
	2	5	15.75 —	19.03		1	9	10.39 —	11.61
	3	6	19.03 —	22.31					
	0	7	22.31 —	25.58	67	116	67.	Volume of Nonmilitary Conflict	
	0	8	25.58 —	28.86		93	0	−8.72 —	8.72
	2	9	28.86 —	32.14		14	1	8.72 —	26.17
						4	2	26.17 —	43.61
63	116	63.	Balance of Total Events			1	3	43.61 —	61.06
	2	0	0.32 —	0.38		1	4	61.06 —	78.50
	3	1	0.38 —	0.43		1	5	78.50 —	95.94
	6	2	0.43 —	0.48		0	6	95.94 —	113.39
	22	3	0.48 —	0.54		1	7	113.39 —	130.83
	23	4	0.54 —	0.59		0	8	130.83 —	148.28
	33	5	0.59 —	0.64		1	9	148.28 —	165.72
	11	6	0.64 —	0.70					
	11	7	0.70 —	0.75	68	116	68.	Scope of Nonmilitary Conflict	
	4	8	0.75 —	0.80		35	0	−0.42 —	0.42
	1	9	0.80 —	0.86		29	1	0.42 —	1.25
						23	2	1.25 —	2.08
64	116	64.	Volume of Diplomatic Exchanges			11	3	2.08 —	2.91
	102	0	−51.11 —	51.11		8	4	2.91 —	3.74
	10	1	51.11 —	153.33		4	5	3.74 —	4.57
	2	2	153.33 —	255.56		3	6	4.57 —	5.40
	0	3	255.56 —	357.78		1	7	5.40 —	6.23

(continued)

Column Number	N	Variable Number	Code*			Column Number	N	Variable Number	Code*		
68 (cont.)	116	68.	Scope of Nonmilitary Conflict			71	116	71.	Scope of Cooperation		
	1	8	6.23 —	7.06			10	0	—0.51 —	0.51	
	1	9	7.06 —	7.90			49	1	0.51 —	1.53	
							35	2	1.53 —	2.54	
							8	3	2.54 —	3.56	
							7	4	3.56 —	4.58	
69	98	69.	Balance of Nonmilitary Conflict				3	5	4.58 —	5.60	
	41	0	—0.41 —	0.41			3	6	5.60 —	6.62	
	22	1	0.41 —	1.22			0	7	6.62 —	7.63	
	20	2	1.22 —	2.04			0	8	7.63 —	8.65	
	3	3	2.04 —	2.85			1	9	8.65 —	9.67	
	4	4	2.85 —	3.66							
	1	5	3.66 —	4.48		72	116	72.	Balance of Cooperation		
	2	6	4.48 —	5.29			10	0	—0.06 —	0.06	
	1	7	5.29 —	6.11			0	1	0.06 —	0.17	
	1	8	6.11 —	6.92			1	2	0.17 —	0.28	
	3	9	6.92 —	7.74			5	3	0.28 —	0.39	
							15	4	0.39 —	0.50	
							50	5	0.50 —	0.61	
70	116	70.	Volume of Cooperation				22	6	0.61 —	0.72	
	102	0	—45.28 —	45.28			6	7	0.72 —	0.83	
	10	1	45.28 —	135.83			4	8	0.83 —	0.94	
	2	2	135.83 —	226.39			3	9	0.94 —	1.06	
	1	3	226.39 —	316.94							
	0	4	316.94 —	407.50		73			Blank		
	0	5	407.50 —	498.06							
	0	6	498.06 —	588.61		74–76			Country Numeric Code (See Figure A.5 for the identification key)		
	0	7	588.61 —	679.17							
	0	8	679.17 —	769.72		77			Blank		
	1	9	769.72 —	860.28							
						78–80			Country Alphabetic Code (See Figure A.5 for the identification key)		

END OF CODEBOOK

Number	Name	Country	Number	Name	Country
002	USA	United States	438	GUI	Guinea
020	CAN	Canada	439	UPP	Upper Volta
040	CUB	Cuba	450	LBR	Liberia
041	HAI	Haiti	451	SIE	Sierra Leone
042	DOM	Dominican Republic	452	GHA	Ghana
051	JAM	Jamaica	461	TOG	Togo
052	TRI	Trinidad and Tobago	471	CAO	Cameroun
070	MEX	Mexico	475	NIG	Nigeria
090	GUA	Guatemala	481	GAB	Gabon
091	HON	Honduras	482	CEN	Cen. African Rep.
092	ELS	El Salvador	483	CHA	Chad
093	NIC	Nicaragua	484	CON	Congo (Br.)
094	COS	Costa Rica	490	COP	Congo (Ki.)
095	PAN	Panama	500	UGA	Uganda
100	COL	Colombia	516	BUI	Burundi
101	VEN	Venezuela	517	RWA	Rwanda
130	ECU	Ecuador	520	SOM	Somalia
135	PER	Peru	530	ETH	Ethiopia
140	BRA	Brazil	560	SAF	South Africa
145	BOL	Bolivia	580	MAG	Malagasy
150	PAR	Paraguay	600	MOR	Morocco
155	CHL	Chile	615	ALG	Algeria
160	ARG	Argentina	616	TUN	Tunisia
165	URU	Uruguay	620	LBY	Libya
200	UNK	United Kingdom	625	SUD	Sudan
205	IRE	Ireland	630	IRN	Iran
210	NTH	Netherlands	640	TUR	Turkey
211	BEL	Belgium	645	IRQ	Iraq
212	LUX	Luxembourg	651	UAR	United Arab Rep.
220	FRN	France	652	SYR	Syria
225	SWZ	Switzerland	660	LEB	Lebanon
230	SPN	Spain	663	JOR	Jordan
235	POR	Portugal	666	ISR	Israel
255	GMW	West Germany	670	SAU	Saudi Arabia
265	GME	East Germany	678	YEM	Yemen
290	POL	Poland	690	KUW	Kuwait
305	AUS	Austria	700	AFG	Afghanistan
310	HUN	Hungary	710	CHN	Red China
315	CZE	Czechoslovakia	712	MON	Mongolia
325	ITA	Italy	713	CHT	China (Taiwan)
339	ALB	Albania	731	KON	North Korea
345	YUG	Yugoslavia	732	KOS	South Korea
350	GRC	Greece	740	JAP	Japan
352	CYP	Cyprus	750	IND	India
355	BUL	Bulgaria	770	PAK	Pakistan
360	RUM	Rumania	775	BUR	Burma
365	USR	USSR/Russia	780	CEY	Ceylon
375	FIN	Finland	790	NEP	Nepal
380	SWD	Sweden	800	TAI	Thailand
385	NOR	Norway	811	CAM	Cambodia
390	DEN	Denmark	812	LAO	Laos
395	ICE	Iceland	816	VTN	North Vietnam
432	MLI	Mali	817	VTS	South Vietnam
433	SEN	Senegal	820	MAL	Malaysia
434	DAH	Dahomey	840	PHI	Philippines
435	MAU	Mauritania	850	INS	Indonesia
436	NIR	Niger	900	AUL	Australia
437	IVO	Ivory Coast	920	NEW	New Zealand

Figure A.5   Country identification key

VARIABLE DEFINITIONS AND CITATIONS

Variable 1:   Total Population

Variable Definition: "The total population of a country is conventionally described as *de facto* or *de jure*. A true *de facto* or present-in-area concept implies that all persons physically present in the country—residents and nonresidents alike—have been counted in the local area where they were found at the time of the census. The *de jure* count, in contrast, comprises all persons who usually reside in the area, irrespective of where they might happen to be at the time of the census. Simple as these concepts appear, strict conformity to either of them is rarely found. . . . In an effort to provide better information for constructing world and regional population aggregates from the results of censuses taken around 1950, the Population Commission of the United Nations recommended a *modified de facto* tabulation of the total population in addition to any other total used for national purposes. This same concept was included in the *Principles and Recommendations for National Population Censuses* designed to provide guidance for the taking of the 1960 cycle of censuses. In the 1960 recommendations, the new total was called *international conventional total*, and it was defined as 'the total number of persons present in the country at the time of the census, *excluding* foreign military, naval and diplomatic personnel and their families located in the country but including military, naval and diplomatic personnel of the country and their families located abroad, and merchant seamen resident in the country but at sea at the time of the census.' . . . Since the computed total was called for in addition to any other total used for national purposes, there is no expectation that it would necessarily have been used in the detailed census tabulations. Therefore, beginning with the *1963 Demographic Yearbook*, the assumption that all census results refer to the modified *de facto* population was abandoned, and the modification has been described only where it is known to have been made (pp. 7–8). 'Unless otherwise noted, population figures are present-in-area estimates for the present territory.' " (p. 96) (*de facto*)

The data are in thousands of persons. The year of the data is 1963.

Citation: *Demographic Yearbook 1966*. 185th Issue, Statistical Office of the United Nations, Department of Economic and Social Affairs, New York, 1967.

Variable 2:   Total Land Area

Variable Definition: "Unless otherwise specified, all of these figures are assumed to represent total area, that is, they comprise the land area and inland waters, excluding only polar regions and some uninhabited islands. Inland waters are assumed to consist of major rivers and lakes. . . . In this yearbook, *area is given in square kilometers*, the conversion from square miles (if required) having been accomplished by equating 1 square mile to 2.589998 square kilometers." (p. 17)

Citation: *Demographic Yearbook 1963*. Statistical Office of the United Nations, Department of Economic and Social Affairs, New York, 1964.

Variable 3:   Total GNP

Variable Definition: GNP in millions of U.S. dollars. No definition given in source. For a definition of GNP refer to variable 54.

The data are for the year 1963.

Citation: "Estimates of GNP, 1963." Agency for International Development, Report Control #137, (01), Statistics and Reports Division, February 19, 1965.

Variable 4: KWH of Electrical Production

Variable Definition: KWH of electrical production for 1963. ". . . All the figures on capacity and production represent combined totals for electrical utilities and industrial establishments having generating facilities for providing all or part of their own requirements." (p. 1)

The data are in millions of KWH.

Citation: *World Power Data, 1964*. Bureau of Power, Federal Power Commission, Washington, May 1966.

Variable 5: GNP per Capita

Variable Definition: GNP per capita. No definition given in source. The data are in U.S. dollars per capita. The year of data is 1963.

Citation: *Statistics and Reports Division*. Agency for International Development, February 19, 1965.

Variable 6: Energy Production per Capita

Variable Definition: A nation's total energy production divided by its total population, calculated by the CAPE staff. Non-1963 population data were collected to correspond with the two cases of non-1963 Energy production data. The unit of measure is million metric tons of coal equivalents.

Citation: *World Energy Supplies 1962–1965*. Department of Economic and Social Affairs, Statistical Office of the United Nations, New York, 1967.

Variable 7: Agricultural Workers as Percentage of Total Economically Active Population

Variable Definition: "Agricultural population for the purpose of this may be defined as all persons actively engaged in agriculture, forestry, hunting and fishing for a livelihood, that is to say, persons actively engaged in agriculture, forestry, hunting and fishing and their non-working dependents. . . . In general, the *economically active population* is defined as all persons engaged in an economic activity, whether employers, own-account workers, salaried employees, or unpaid workers assisting in the operation of a family farm or business. Similarly the population economically active in agriculture includes all economically active persons engaged principally in agriculture, forestry, hunting and fishing. . . . This general definition differs somewhat from country to country. In some countries, for example, the estimates are based on data relating to all persons reporting an occupation, whether or not they were actually working at the time of the census or survey; in others, on data regarding persons actually employed during a specific short period, unemployed persons seeking work being excluded. Some countries report information on economic activity for persons of all ages, others only for persons of specified ages, e.g., 14 years of age and over." (p. 647)

The data are expressed as a percentage and are for the year 1965.

Citation: *Production Yearbook 1966*. Vol. 20, Food and Agriculture Organizations of the United Nations, Rome, 1967.

Variable 8: KWH per Capita

Variable Definition: KWH per capita for 1963. The data were calculated within the source. ". . . All the figures on capacity and production represent combined totals for electrical utilities and industrial establishments having generating facilities for providing all or part of their own requirements." (p. 1)

Citation: *World Power Data, 1964.* Bureau of Power, Federal Power Commission, Washington, May 1966.

Variable 9: Current Electoral System

Variable Definition: 0 = Competitive (no party ban, or ban on extremist or extra-constitutional parties only).

5 = Partially competitive (one party with 85 percent or more of legislative seats).

9 = Non-competitive (single-list voting or no elected opposition).

Citation: *A Cross-Polity Survey.* Arthur S. Banks and Robert B. Textor, The M.I.T. Press, Massachusetts Institute of Technology, Cambridge, Massachusetts, 1963.

Variable 10: Freedom of the Press

Variable Definition: Freedom of the press scores (100 IPICA index + 4). The PICA index is based on 23 indices of freedom of the press. The strength of the indices were judged by both native and non-native judges in response to a questionnaire. The scores were averaged separately for the native and non-native judges. Where there were disagreements of more than 6 percent between the averages, only the non-native averages were used. Where there was less than a 6 percent disagreement, the average of the two was used for the PICA index.

Citation: *PICA: Measuring World Press Freedom.* Lowenstein, Freedom of Information Center, University of Missouri, 1966.

Variable 11: Competitiveness: Head of Government's Election

Variable Definition: Competitiveness is defined as (1-%) of vote cast for the head of government in the last election before December 31, 1963. If the national political system is parliamentary, competitiveness is defined as 1-% vote cast for the head of government's party, regardless of coalition rule. If the head of government is appointed by the head of state or some other official, competitiveness is defined as (1-%) vote cast for the appointing official. If the head of government was not elected or appointed by an elected official, competitiveness is defined as 0%. If the head of government was elected by a special body which had no responsibility to vote according to the wishes of the people (however assessed), then competitiveness is defined as (1-%) of vote cast for the head of government in that body. If the vote for a party in a parliamentary system is not available, then competitiveness is defined as (1-%) of the seats controlled by the head of government's party.

Citation: *Review of Elections, 1961–62 and 1963–64.* Institute of Electoral Research, London, 1964 and 1967, and other sources.

Variable 12: Legal Status of the Communist Party

Variable Definition: "Legal status gives only minimal facts regarding the legal position of communist parties. On the one hand, parties in power in their governments are rated. On the other hand, where communist parties have been proscribed —whether by law, administrative decree, or constitutional provision—this fact is noted and the date of proscription is given. Where no entry appears and where a party is shown, in the membership column to be in existence, the reader may assume that its activities are in some degree legal, though not necessarily in all respects." (p. 3) Four categories are utilized for these 1963 data:

> 0 = In power
>
> 1 = No known legal restriction
>
> 8 = Formally proscribed
>
> 9 = Informally proscribed

Citation: *World Strength of the Communist Party Organization*. 16th Annual Report, Bureau of Intelligence and Research, United States of America, Department of State, January 1964.

Variable 13:   Political Participation by Military

Variable Definition: 0 = Interventive (presently exercises or has recently exercised direct power).

5 = Supportive (performs para-political role in support of traditionalist, authoritarian, totalitarian, or modernizing regime).

9 = Neutral (apolitical, or of minor political importance).

"The present raw characteristic asks . . . whether a nation's military establishment performs in a politically 'interventive,' 'supportive,' or 'neutral' manner. It does not attempt to distinguish between 'oppressive' and 'constructive' intervention or support. In the case of both 5 and 9, the military is presumed to be under civilian control. But in 5, as contrasted with 9, the military is used by the regime as a means of consolidating, enlarging, or defending political power." (p. 114)

Citation: *A Cross-Polity Survey*. Banks and Textor.

Variable 14:   Character of Bureaucracy

Variable Definition: 0 = Modern (generally effective and responsible civil service or equivalent, performing in a functionally specific, non-ascriptive social context).

3 = Semi-modern (largely "rationalized" bureaucratic structure of limited efficiency because of shortage of skilled personnel, inadequacy of recruitment or performance criteria, excessive intrusion by non-administrative organs, or partially non-congruent social institutions).

6 = Post-colonial transitional (largely rationalized ex-colonial bureaucratic structure in process of personnel "nationalization" and adaptation to the servicing or restructuring of autochthonous social institutions).

9 = Traditional (largely non-rationalized bureaucratic structure performing in the context of an ascriptive or "deferential" stratification system).

"... our typology for this characteristic is less than adequate. It fails to deal with specific bureaucratic structure or with the calibre of performance of specific functions. The result is a somewhat unproductive characteristic—'unproductive' in the sense that much of its yield was fairly predictable from the beginning." (p. 113)

Citation: *A Cross-Polity Survey*. Banks and Textor.

Variable 15: Current Status of Legislature

Variable Definition: 0 = Fully effective (performs normal legislative function as reasonably "co-equal" branch of national government).

3 = Partially effective (tendency toward domination by executive, or otherwise partially limited in effective exercise of legislative function).

6 = Largely ineffective (virtually complete domination by executive or by one-party or dominant party organization).

9 = Wholly ineffective (restricted to consultative or "rubber-stamp" legislative function).

"This characteristic is largely self-explanatory. ... the developed West is virtually the exclusive locale of 0, while 3 tends to occur in Latin America, and 6 in the African states. All of the Communist states fall in 9." (p. 110)

Citation: *A Cross-Polity Survey*. Banks and Textor.

Variable 16: Government Stability

Variable Definition: 0 = Government generally stable since World War I or major inter-war constitutional change.

3 = Government generally stable since World War II or major post-war constitutional change.

6 = Government moderately stable since World War II or major post-war constitutional change.

9 = Government unstable since World War II or major post-war constitutional change.

"... Instability is ... present when a constitution is suspended or when an elected president is forcibly ousted from office. And yet major changes of this sort may have a purgative effect and be followed by periods of relative stability. Even more difficult to access is the significance of frequent cabinet changes under a parliamentary system. The coder must rely primarily on his own judgment in determining the point at which cabinet changes become so frequent as to justify coding a particular polity as 'unstable.' ... We have regarded differentiation between 3 and 6 as unascertainable ... when the major constitutional change in question occurred after 1 January 1959. This entails, of course, the disadvantage that most of the twenty-odd states (primarily African) that achieved independence after this date are excluded. The disadvantage is somewhat mitigated, however, in that those newly independent polities evidencing obvious instability since independence are coded under 9." (p. 84)

Citation: *A Cross-Policy Survey*. Banks and Textor.

Variable 17:   Central Government Revenue as Percentage of GNP

Variable Definition: The revenue of the central government in 1963 expressed as a percentage of that nation's GNP for that year. Exceptions to the data year 1963 are noted in the appropriate CAPE Code Book at the Behavioral Sciences Laboratory (The Ohio State University).

Citation: Central Government Revenue: *The Europa Yearbook*, Volumes I & II. Europa Publications Limited, London, 1962–1966.
GNP: "Estimates of GNP, 1963." Agency for International Development Report Control #137, (01), Statistics and Reports Division, February 19, 1965.

Variable 18:   Percent Communist Vote

Variable Definition: The vote of the communist party (or parties), in name or political leaning, in the last national election, legislative or executive, before Dec. 31, 1963, expressed as a percentage of the total votes cast. If the communist party is outlawed but elections were held, then percent communist vote is defined as 0%. If no elections were held since 1957 under the regime present in 1963, regardless of the legal status of the communist party, the percent communist vote is undefined. Year of data varies between 1957 and 1964.

Citation: *World Strength of Communist Party Organizations*. Sixteenth Annual Report, Bureau of Intelligence and Research, Department of State, January, 1964.
Review of Elections, 1961–62 and 1963–64. Institute of Electoral Research, London, 1964 and 1967.

Variable 19:   Newspapers per 1000 Population

Variable Definition: Table 33 of the source presents data on the number, total circulation and circulation per 1,000 inhabitants, concerning general interest daily newspapers, for the years 1952, and 1960 to 1963, for 152 countries and territories.

For the purposes of the tables, a "general interest newspaper" is any periodical publication intended for the general public which is devoted primarily to recording current events connected with public affairs, international questions, politics, etc. A newspaper thus defined, issued 4 or more days per week is considered to be a "daily newspaper"; those appearing 3 days per week or less frequently are considered as non-daily newspapers. In principal, specialized newspapers (published either daily or non-daily) are excluded from statistics on newspapers of general interest.

The year of data varies between 1952 and 1963.

Citation: Published in 1966, by the United Nations Educational, Scientific and Cultural Organization, Place de Fontenoy, Paris — 7°.
Printed by Imprimene Joseph Flock,
Mayenne (France).

Variable 20:   Percent Population in Cities Over 20,000

Variable Definition: The percentage of the national population living in cities of 20,000 or greater. Data are taken from the latest census available for each nation the year of which is indicated in the code book.

The CAPE figure are equal to the sum of the three categories, cities over 100,000, cities between 50,000 and 99,999, and cities between 20,000 and 49,999, taken from the source.

Citation: *Compendium of Social Statistics: 1963.* United Nations, New York, 1963.

Variable 21: People per Hospital Bed

Variable Definition: The reader is cautioned that these are simple indicators of availability and not of quality: the number of inhabitants per hospital bed or physician does not show how well equipped the hospitals are, nor how competent the physicians and other medical persons are.

There is, as yet, no universally accepted definition of the term "hospital bed"; therefore any decision concerning the composition of the denominator in the construction of the ratio population/hospital bed is somewhat arbitrary. It was decided to include beds in the following categories of establishments: general hospitals, specialized hospitals and medical centers (e.g., dispensaries and infirmaries possessing some beds for the diagnosis treatment or observation of patients). Thus, excluded from these data are beds in establishments such as leprosaria, preventoria, children's homes, nursing homes, establishments for the blind and deaf-mutes, mental deficients, epileptics, the form, aged, and incurables, etc. (p. 123–124)

The data are for various years between 1956 and 1960.

Citation: This Compendium is issued as a joint undertaking of the United Nations, the International Labor Office, the Food and Agriculture Organization of the United Nations, the United Nations Education, Scientific and Cultural Organization and the World Health Organization. New York, 1963.

Variable 22: Rate of Population Increase

Variable Definition: "The average annual percent rate of change in population size between 1958 and 1966 has been computed from data in the table, using the following formula:

$$r = \left(\sqrt[t]{\frac{P_1}{P_0}} - 1 \right) \times 100$$

where

    P_0 is the population in 1958,

    P_1 is the population in 1966,

    t is 8 (years between 1958 and 1966),

    r is the annual percent rate of change."

Citation: *Demographic Yearbook 1966.* 18th Issue, Statistical Office of the United Nations, Department of Economic and Social Affairs, New York, 1967.

Variable 23: Westernization

Variable Definition:
- 0 = Historically Western nation
- 1 = Significantly Westernized (no colonial relationship)
- 3 = Significantly Westernized (colonial relationship)
- 5 = Partially Westernized (no colonial relationship)
- 7 = Partially Westernized (colonial relationship)
- 8 = Non-Westernized (no colonial relationship; little or no visible Westernization).

"For this characteristic, the demarcation of the 'historic West' on the European continent is based on the limits of the Ottoman Empire, with the exception that Greece is considered Western. Czechoslovakia, Hungary, and Poland are thus regarded as historically Western; Rumania, Bulgaria, and Yugoslavia are not.

Australia, Canada, New Zealand, and the United States are included in (1); the former Latin America colonies of Spain and Portugal are included in (3) or (5)." (p. 76)

Citation: *A Cross-Polity Survey.* Banks and Textor.

Variable 24:   Mass Participation/Turmoil

Variable Definition: Mass participation-Turmoil (MP-T) is defined as the sum of the frequencies of the political instability events from 1948–1962 as coded in the preceding quoted source, which were found by the Feierabends to load higher than .50 on the Mass Participation-Turmoil factor.

These variables were:

— micro strikes

— general strikes

— micro demonstrations

— macro demonstrations

— macro riots

— severe macro riots

— mass arrests of insignificant persons

— terrorism and sabotage

Citation: "Aggressive Behaviors within Polities, 1948–1962:   A Cross-National Study." Ivo and Rosalind Feierabend, *Journal of Conflict Resolution*, Vol. X, No. 3, September 1966.

Variable 25:   Palace Revolution/Revolt

Variable Definition: Palace Revolution-Revolt (PR-R) is defined as the sum of the frequencies of the political instability events from 1948–1962 as coded in the Feierabend *Cross-National Data Bank of Political Instability Events*, which were found by Ivo and Rosalind Feierabend to load higher than .50 on the Palace Revolution-Revolt factor.

These variables were:

— repressive action against specific groups

— arrests of significant persons

— martial law

— coups d'etat

— revolts

Citation: See the citation for Variable 24.

Variable 26:   Strategic Distance From Power Centers: Composite

Variable Definition: Strategic distance from power centers:

$$composite = \frac{U.S. \times USSR \times CHINA}{1000}$$

where

U.S. = strategic distance: USA mainland (Variable 31)
USSR = strategic distance: USSR (Variable 30)
CHINA = strategic distance: China (Variable 29)

Straight-line distance from nearest borders of 1963 CAPE countries, measured in centimeters on a 32 inch globe. Natural Scale is 1: 15,840,000 or 250 miles per inch. Refer to notes on "Measuring the Distance Between Nations" in CAPE variable files for complete measuring methods.

Citation: Gustan Brueckmann (designer, editor, cartographer). 32 inch Library Globe by Replogue Globes, Inc., Chicago, Illinois.

Variable 27: Strategic Distance From Power Centers: United States/USSR

Variable Definition: Strategic distance from power centers:

$$U.S./USSR = \frac{U.S.}{U.S. + USSR}$$

where

U.S. = strategic distance: USA mainland (Variable 31)
USSR = strategic distance: USSR (Variable 30)

Citation: See citation for Variable 26.

Variable 28: Strategic Distance From Power Centers: United States/ China

Variable Definition: Strategic distance from power centers:

$$U.S./CHINA = \frac{U.S.}{U.S. + CHINA}$$

where

U.S. = strategic distance: USA mainland (Variable 31)
CHINA = strategic distance: China (Variable 29)

Citation: See citation for Variable 26.

Variable 29: Strategic Distance: China

Variable Definition: The straight-line distance to China.

Citation: See citation for Variable 26.

Variable 30: Strategic Distance: USSR

Variable Definition: The straight-line distance to USSR.

Citation: See citation for Variable 26.

Variable 31: Strategic Distance: United States (Mainland)

Variable Definition: The straight-line distance to U.S. mainland.

Citation: See citation for Variable 26.

Variable 32:   Geopolitical Scores: GNP

Variable Definition: A nation's total GNP divided by the sum of the same nation's GNP plus the total of the GNP's of its bordering nations. GNP scores for non-CAPE countries were collected from the *U.N. Statistical Yearbook, 1966*, wherever available.

Variable 33:   Geopolitical Scores: Population

Variable Definition: A nation's total population divided by the sum of the same nation's population and the total population of its bordering nations. Population data for non-CAPE nations were collected from the population source.

Variable 34:   Geopolitical Scores: GNP/Capita

Variable Definition: A nation's GNP per capita divided by the sum of the same nation's GNP per capita plus the total of the GNP per capita's of the bordering nations. GNP per capita scores for non-CAPE countries were collected from the *U.N. Statistical Yearbook, 1966*, wherever available.

Variable 35:   Aqua Access

Variable Definition: 0 = Island nation

5 = Direct access to the sea or a large body of water with an outlet to the sea

9 = Landlocked

Included as island nations are those separated from major continents though sharing the island with another country (e.g., Haiti and Dominican Republic). Landlocked countries with navigable rivers are *not* included in the Code 9 category. The data are taken from a 1964 atlas and therefore can be considered 1964 data.

Citation: *Rand McNally Cosmopolitan World Atlas*. Rand McNally & Company, Chicago, New York, San Francisco, 1964.

Variable 36:   Administrative Personnel per Diplomat

Variable Definition: Administrative personnel per diplomat is defined as the total number of executive, administrative, and managerial personnel divided by the number of diplomatic representatives sent. There is a discrepancy in the year of data for the entire variable because the year of data for the administrative personnel variable varies between 1956 and 1967, and the diplomatic data are averaged over 1963 and 1964.

Citation: Total executive, administrative and managerial personnel: *1968 Yearbook of Labour Statistics*. International Labour Office, Geneva, 1968.
Diplomatic representatives sent: "Patterns of Representation in National Capitals and Intergovernmental Organizations." Chadwick Alger and Steven T. Brams, *World Politics*. Volume XIX, Number 4, July 1967, pp. 646–663. Year: 1967, Table No. II, p. 651.

Variable 37:   Contributions to United Nations Assistance and Relief Programs

Variable Definition: Includes both contributions to voluntary funds (UNICEF, UNEPTA, etc.), and assessed contributions to UNTA *in 1960*.

Data are in millions of U.S. dollars.

Citation: *Statistical Yearbook, 1961.* Statistical Office of the United Nations, New York, 1961.

Variable 38: Political Alignment: United Nations Voting

Variable Definition: Political Alignment in UN Voting:

$$\frac{f(A) - f(B)}{N}$$

where

A = votes with USSR

B = votes with U.S.

f = frequency

N = total number of votes nation participated in.

The 39 votes from which the index is calculated are those listed in the CAPE UN Voting Alignment Code Manual. These are the votes relevant to the East-West Issue on the UN as described by Bruce Russett in *International Regions and the International System.* All the voting took place between October and December, 1963.

Citation: UN Voting Alignment Code Manual (CAPE).

Variable 39: Alliance Commitments to United States/USSR

Variable Definition: All countries not mentioned in either source as being involved in treaties with either the U.S. or with the USSR were coded by a CAPE panel as "no military commitments." The year of data is the year of the treaty. If the treaty was no longer in effect in 1963 as determined by the CAPE panel, a new code was assigned. The year of data for all CAPE panel decisions is 1963. Four categories were utilized:

0 = Alliance with U.S.

3 = No military commitments

6 = Neutrality commitment with USSR

9 = Alliance with USSR

Citation: (1) Jan F. Triska and Robert M. Slusser, *The Theory, Law, and Policy of Soviet Treaties.* Stanford: Stanford University Press, Hoover Institution, 1962.
(2) *Treaties in Force.* U.S. Department of State, 1962.
(3) CAPE Panel.

Variable 40: Index of Agreement With United States in UN Voting

Variable Definition: Index of Agreement with U.S. in UN voting:

$$(IA) = \frac{f + \frac{1}{2}g}{t}$$

where

f = number of votes with the U.S.

g = number of abstentions

t = total number of votes cast

This is the Rice-Beyle technique as described in Arend Lijphart's article "The Analysis of Bloc Voting in the General Assembly" in the December, 1963 issue of the *APSR* (Vol. LVII, No. 4, pp. 909–910). The votes from which the index is calculated are those listed in the CAPE UN Voting Alignment Code Manual. These are the votes relevant to the East-West Issue in the UN as described by Bruce Russett in *International Regions and the International System*. All voting took place between October and December, 1963.

Citation: UN Voting Alignment Code Manual (CAPE).

Variable 41:   Diplomatic Representatives Sent

Variable Definition: Total diplomats that a nation sent abroad in the two year period 1963–64. ". . . the sending totals for each nation given in Table II were derived by summing across all the receiving lists the number of each nation's diplomats that were reported by the host nations as stationed in their capitals." (Alger and Brams, 649) "In our compilation, honorary representatives and non-professional support staff were excluded from the diplomatic totals. Furthermore, only representatives who were physically present in a foreign nation were counted; we did not include those serving *in absentia* as representatives to one or more nations—a practice frequently employed by smaller nations, which station representatives only in major and neighboring capitals but gain accreditation for these representatives in many other capitals. Foreign-aid and military-aid personnel were excluded from the figures in order to preserve the comparability of the data across all nations. All specialists (including military) listed as attaches to an embassy or legation were counted in the totals, however, as were consuls residing in national capitals." (Alger and Brams, 648–649)

Citation: Chadwick Alger and Steven T. Brams, "Patterns of Representation in National Capitals and Intergovernmental Organizations." *World Politics*, Volume XIX, Number 4, July 1967, pp. 646–663.

Variable 42:   Number of Nations Diplomats Sent to

Variable Definition: "The number of nations a nation sent any diplomats to in the two year period 1963–64." See the note for Variable 41.

Citation: Chadwick Alger and Steven J. Brams, "Patterns of Representation in National Capitals and Intergovernmental Organizations." *World Politics*, Vol. XIX, Number 4, July 1967, pp. 646–663.

Variable 43:   Number of Diplomats Received

Variable Definition: Total number of the diplomats received in national capitals in the two year period 1963–64. Lists of diplomats received were official publications of the host governments. See the note for Variable 41.

Citation: Chadwick Alger and Steven J. Brams, "Patterns of Representation in National Capitals and Intergovernmental Organizations." *World Politics*, Vol. XIX, No. 4, July 1967, pp. 646–663.

Variable 44:   Number of Nations Diplomats Received From

Variable Definition: The number of nations that sent any diplomats to a receiving nation in the two year period 1963–64. Lists of diplomats received were official publications of the host governments. The number of nations data were computed in the source. See the note for Variable 41.

Citation: Chadwick Alger and Steven J. Brams, "Patterns of Representation in National Capitals and Intergovernmental Organizations." *World Politics*, Vol. XIX, No. 4, July 1967, pp. 646–663.

Variable 45: United States Foreign Aid Expenditures (Cumulative 1948–63)

Variable Definition: The cumulative aid (including developmental loans, supporting assistance, and other) received from the U.S. from 1948–63.

Development loans. "This category covers loans, both for projects and commodity programs, designed to stimulate economic development; also includes Alliance for Progress loans for Latin America."

Supporting assistance. "Funds used to meet urgent political or military requirements. This category can provide economic aid to a country engaged in a major defense effort." (p. II)

Data are in millions of U.S. dollars.

Citation: Operations Report, Agency for International Development, FY 1964, W-129, Washington, D.C.

Variable 46: Total Inter-Regional Membership in IGO'S

Variable Definition: Inter-regional IGO's are organizations in which one or more member states come from more than one geographic region as defined by the *Yearbook*. The year of data is 1964.

Citation: *Yearbook of International Organizations*, 1964–65. Union of International Associations, Brussels, 1965.

Variable 47: Total Intra-Regional Membership in IGO'S

Variable Definition: Intra-regional IGO's refer to those organizations in which all members come from the same geographic region, as defined by the *Yearbook*. If an organization contains one "super power" and the rest of the members are from one region different from that of the super power, then the organization is still considered to be intra-regional. The year of data is 1964.

Citation: *Yearbook of International Organizations*, 1964–65. Union of International Associations, Brussels, 1965.

Variable 48: Total IGO Memberships

Variable Definition: Inter-governmental organizations are those organizations designated as such in the *Yearbook of International Organizations*. All intergovernmental organizations are listed under the chapters the "European Community" and "Other IGO's." The year of data is 1964.

Citation: *Yearbook of International Organizations*, 1964–65. Union of International Associations, Brussels, 1965.

Variable 49: Number of Nations With Shared IGO Membership

Variable Definition: Shared memberships of 118 nations in 161 IGO's in 1963.

Citation: Chadwick Alger and Steven T. Brams, "Patterns of Representation in

National Capitals and Intergovernmental Organizations." *World Politics*, Volume XIX, Number 4, July 1967, pp. 646–663.

Variable 50:   Total Socioeconomic IGO'S

Variable Definition: An IGO is classified "socioeconomic" according to the title of the organization and on the aims and activities of the organization as defined by the *Yearbook*. The year of data is 1964.

Citation: *Yearbook of International Organizations*, 1964–65. Union of International Associations, Brussels, 1965.

Variable 51:   Diplomatic Linkage: Contiguous Nations

Variable Definition: The diplomatic linkage for contiguous nations index is defined as the ratio of the average number of diplomats sent to neighbors divided by the average number of diplomats sent to all countries.

Citation: Diplomatic data: "Patterns of Representation in National Capitals and Intergovernmental Organizations," Chadwick Alger and Steven T. Brams, *World Politics*, Vol. XIX, No. 4, July 1967, pp. 646–663.

Bordering Nations: *Rand McNally Cosmopolitan World Atlas*, Rand McNally & Company, Chicago, New York, San Francisco, 1964.

Variable 52:   Foreign Conflict Index

Variable Definition: Total number of threats, accusations, and protests for Rummel's 1963 conflict variables.

Citation: Rudolph Rummel, *1963 Attribute Space Data*, Dimensionality of Nations Project (unpublished).

Variable 53:   Percent Trade to Two Largest Buyers

Variable Definition: The total value of trade (exports only) to the two largest buyers expressed as a percentage of the nation's total amount of exports. The percentage was calculated from the data in the *Yearbook* and is for the year 1963 except for Gambia, which is for 1962.

Citation: *Yearbook of International Trade Statistics*, 1962, 1965, and 1966. The United Nations, New York.

Variable 54:   Total Foreign Trade as Percentage of GNP

Variable Definition: Total foreign trade as a percent of GNP is the sum of two tables listed in the source, "Imports of goods and services" and "Exports of goods and services," within the chart called "Expenditure on Gross National Product at Market Prices." The tables employ as far as possible ". . . the concepts and classifications that are defined in detail in the United Nations report *A System of National Accounts and Supporting Tables*, Studies in Methods, Series F, No. 2, Rev. 2. The figures are based on estimates of gross national product and its components which appear for most countries in the standard table Expenditure on gross national product of this Yearbook." (p. 789) The yearbook defines gross national product at market prices as ". . . the market of the product, before deduction of provisions for the consumption of fixed capital, attributable to the factors of production supplied by normal residents of the given country. It is identically equal to the sum of consumption expenditure and gross domestic capital formation, private and public, and the net export of goods and services plus the net factor incomes received from abroad." (p. xiii) Concerning the exports and imports of goods and services the yearbook defines these as "the value of the goods and services sold to the rest of the world and the value of corresponding purchases, respectively. These goods and services comprise merchandise and transportation, insurance and other non-factor services. The value of gifts in kind and other exports and imports financed by means of international transfers in included but the value of military equipment transferred between governments is excluded." (p. xx)

The percentage figures for imports and exports were calculated within the source and summed to get the CAPE variable. The year of data is 1963 for all but three cases. One datum is from the 1966 source.

Citation: *Yearbook of National Account Statistics, 1967*. Statistical Office of the United Nations, Department of Economic and Social Affairs, New York, 1968.

Variable 55: Total Imports

Variable Definition: A nation's total imports for 1963. Non-1963 data years are noted in the data and in Code Book *Economic 2*.

Data are expressed in millions of U.S. dollars.

Citation: *The Europa Yearbook, Volumes I and II*. Europa Publications, Limited, London, 1960, 1964, 1965, 1966, 1968, 1969.

Variable 56: Total Exports

Variable Definition: A nation's total exports for 1963. Non-1963 data years are noted in the data and in Code Book *Economic 2*.

Data are expressed in millions of U.S. dollars.

Citation: *The Europa Yearbook, Volumes I and II*. Europa Publications, Limited, London, 1960, 1964, 1965, 1966, 1968, 1969.

Variable 57: Military Capability

Variable Definition: The product of a nation's total population and its total energy production in units of coal equivalents is the measure of military capability developed in Quincy Wright's *The Study of International Relations*, p. 599. The exact unit of measure is "trillion man-tons of coal equivalents."

Citation: The citation for population is given in Variable 1. *Total Energy Production*: *World Energy Supplies 1962, 1965*. Department of Economic and Social Affairs, Statistical Office of the United Nations, New York, 1967.
Year: 1967.
Table No.: 2; pp. 14–33.

Variable 58: Military Expenditures

Variable Definition: The "total military expenditures of national defense agencies, as well as the military component of mixed civilian-military activities such as atomic energy. Excluded are expenditures for civilian space activities and civil defense. Except for the Warsaw Pact countries (for which rough purchasing power equivalents are used) defense expenditures in national currencies are generally converted into dollars at official exchange rates. . . ." (p. 2) Defense expenditures include "total military expenditures of national defense agencies, plus certain types of para-military forces, retirement pensions of career military and appropriate civilian personnel, expenditures for foreign military assistance covering grants of end-items, stockpiling of military equipment and supplies, and the military component of mixed civilian-military activities such as atomic energy and research and development. Excluded are expenditures on civilian space programs, civil defense, stockpiling of industrial raw materials or semi-finished products." (Sprecher, p. iii)

The data are for 1964. The unit of measure is millions of U.S. dollars.

Citation: "World-Wide Defense Expenditures and Selected Economic Data, 1964." William M. Sprecher, Research Report 66-1, January, 1966.

Variable 59: Military Expenditure as Percent of GNP

Variable Definition: The expenditures a nation devoted to defense in 1964 expressed as a percentage of its gross national product in 1964. This variable was generated by calculating Sprecher's defense expenditure data (Variable 58) as a percentage of his GNP data (not included in this data set).

Citation: See citation for Variable 58 for military expenditures. Sprecher GNP: "World-Wide Defense Expenditures and Selected Economic Data, 1964," William Sprecher, Research Report 66-1, January 1966.
Year: 1966.
Table No.: 1; pp. 7–13.

Variable 60: Military Expenditures as Percent of Central Government Expenditures

Variable Definition: The expenditure a nation devoted to defense in 1964 (Variable 58) expressed as a percentage of the total expenditure of the central government in 1963.

Citation: See citation for Variable 58.

Central Government Expenditures: *The Europa Yearbook, Volumes I and II.* Europa Publications Limited, London, 1962–1966.

Variable 61: Volume of Total Events

Variable Definition: Volume = total number of events initiated by a country.

Citation: Charles A. McClelland, "The World Event/Interaction Survey: A Research Project on Theory and Measurement of International Interaction and Transaction." University of Southern California, 1967.

Variable 62: Scope of Total Events

Variable Definition: Scope = number of events sent divided by the number of nations the events were sent to.

Citation: See citation for Variable 61.

Variable 63: Balance of Total Events

Variable Definition: Balance = A/A + B where:

$$A = \text{Total events initiated by a country}$$
$$B = \text{Total events received by a country}$$

Citation: See citation for Variable 61.

Variable 64:   Volume of Diplomatic Exchange

Variable Definition: Volume = total number of diplomatic exchange events initiated by a country. The WEIS combevent categories that have been aggregated into the category "diplomatic exchange" are: Yield, Comment, Consult, Approve, Promise, Grant, Reward, Agree, Request, Propose, Reject, Deny, Warn, and Reduce relationship.

Citation: The source for the event totals is WEIS. The category "diplomatic exchange" was generated by Robert Young via factor analysis for a paper presented to the Conference on International Forecasting at San Ysidro, California, Dec. 14–17, 1970, entitled, "An Event-Based Nation Taxonomy," p. 13.

Variable 65:   Scope of Diplomatic Exchange

Variable Definition: Scope = number of diplomatic exchange events initiated divided by the number of countries sent to. See definition for Variable 64.

Citation: See citation for Variable 64.

Variable 66:   Balance of Diplomatic Exchange

Variable Definition: Balance = $A/A + B$ where:

> A = number of diplomatic exchange events initiated
>
> B = number of diplomatic exchange events received

See definition for Variable 64.

Citation: See citation for Variable 64.

Variable 67:   Volume of Non-Military Conflict

Variable Definition: Volume = total number of non-military conflict events initiated by a country. The WEIS combevent categories that have been aggregated into the category "non-military conflict" are: Accuse, Protest, Demand, Threaten, Demonstrate, Expel, and Seize.

Citation: See citation for Variable 64.

Variable 68:   Scope of Non-Military Conflict

Variable Definition: Scope = total number of non-military conflict events initiated by a country divided by the total number of nations these events were sent to. See definition for Variable 67.

Citation: See citation for Variable 64.

Variable 69:   Balance of Non-Military Conflict

Variable Definition: Balance = $A/A + B$ where:

> A = total number of non-military conflict events initiated
> B = total number of non-military conflict events received

See definition for Variable 67.

Citation: See citation for Variable 64.

Variable 70:   Volume of Cooperation

Variable Definition: Volume = total number of cooperative events initiated by a country. The combevents included under the rubric of cooperation are: Approve, Promise, Agree, Request, Propose, Yield, Grant, Reward, Comment, and Consult.

Citation: Charles A. McClelland and Gary D. Hoggard, "Conflict Patterns in the Interactions Among Nations." In James N. Rosenau (ed.) *International Politics and Foreign Policy*, 2nd edition (1969). The Free Press, New York, p. 714.

Variable 71:   Scope of Cooperation

Variable Definition: Scope = total number of cooperative events initiated by a country divided by the number of nations these events are sent to. See definition for Variable 70.

Variable 72:   Balance of Cooperation

Variable Definition: Balance = A/A + B where:

$$A = \text{total number of cooperative events initiated}$$
$$B = \text{total number of cooperative events received}$$

See definition for Variable 70.

Citation: See citation for Variable 70.

```
34998004095990001065040120004308755290099999 65685371099994499491530996 002 USA
04116005096190001044040000003101125210091524 51484907232002212514102145 020 CAN
00001030 100 3  9 23053260006609930109901413 33383 54200004101603124603 040 CUB
00000 709308039 000 247161117613510  405020202328201  00 013015011011016 041 HAI
00001050060893  200 0831311176164500 10802  033383018200002100301012014 042 DOM
000010300851930 2012 53  11176199301 2370001010020  64000000000011000014 051 JAM
000020110 41930 1028073  22277299300 3360000 10040  48000000002011000015 052 TRI
11001050 711933300222832200054002151030614240454948061100001013022101 024 070 MEX
00001060 80803 9101007317111661112501 2070212025383305100001004010000012 090 GUA
0000060070803391000 73121117611225010 108010101527230720000110120100000013 091 HON
00001050098180369101108313111761333511 10802120153732042000011013011 000019 092 ELS
000010505 180366 0111731211176133350 10802010153733063000011005011000015 093 NIC
00001040008589336102109302111771333501 20702020153833072000000004012000016 094 COS
00001040007680339102307315111771113501 30603130142732074000000001301302 017 095 PAN
00001040 8419336101507326111771112510306031312438320610000110160110 026 100 COL
000021210879 339201508338121771216500207031303438320520000110150110101026 101 VEN
00000050080853391 110731332188211250 2070213024393406200001101702200 0026 130 ECU
00001040 96803 9101 0732632288211350030603130243833042000002201302102 025 135 PER
13000040075803391013073112227623515403061535144494204111002201402101 014 140 BRA
0000006008419336600 033285328830019  30602  013272208200001001601100015 145 BOL
00000 505 18039 100106317732984002901 20701010246250410010 022005010000013 150 PAR
00001021 0 71933611240532273299322450030614141243832041000011016021012026 155 CHL
010020100678033900350435973299432551 0207151  1444843021000011014012022025 160 ARG
000010100851930310610 33219339950035004503130232736021000011007012011 016 165 URU
1011400030851900020970202007431399401200959882968981302750132233241231245 200 UNK
0000203108619000204401010  064313002001 13801011322825084000011108021011 027 205 IRE
0003001097190002055030000084313112500009172416878850353200022005012022016 210 NTH
00004 0208619000205302010074313113500009163610 68797403432 021017022022026 211 BEL
00004 150 619000218030300007531400390 0090100 36494310 9  011004000000000 212 LUX
101140120721 03322530309407431332351110849581899993211530132135241131255 220 FRN
00005013097190000073040000853140049001 0 3 1625 55585402321001300501100016 225 SWZ
000010319308539010340204307431313150023715251635855021100022015031147 025 230 SPN
000010409308539010110202216442312250 2070413053494512200004601502302 2026 235 POR
10114012086890031065010 000085304333521 0 285816779720127601331341511311 155 255 GMW
00003012900053938923000110853041135   9 0111 11020215 110041125021131025 265 GME
000020419100539359330302309520411251 09901523041393503 11002101602115 025 290 POL
00002031930053910 593 3101209520400290 9901413 31293404 10001001601103901 5 315 HUN
00003012910053935952020020952040039009901524 41293304 11003113301116 2016 305 CZE
000030220861900033044010100853040029901681535 5458530321100110040110000 14 310 AUS
10112021086190003222402031085314332510009284717679740214200210150210230 25 325 ITA
0000205090005393191107502085315114510 9900101 11161105 0000110150211320 24 339 ALB
00001051950053931911031100952041115007321525152384302 1000340150210110 25 345 YUG
00001050076893361240201008620521350010814131534842031000021013021031 025 350 GRC
000  3  731930 1 21033000862169930010 3360011011161  5300 011023022101 024 352 CYP
000010519100539379320210109620511451 9901413 31292406 0000410150120220 16 355 BUL
000010509000539379310210109620401251 9901313 41393204 10002101502101102 5 360 RUM
39433031910053903944041000990026265 19904656 41283292 43666346446178236 5 365 USR
00003032098190002263020100952040025002970413 42393403210001101302100002 5 375 FIN
00006014095190002094020000952035445011381624044484302221003201702202 018 380 SWD
000040190951900020730200009520300350010804130544853024100021005012042015 385 NOR
000050110871900020650200008530311350010815130545856033110021006019011 018 390 DEN
000050330 619000218404000063312993001 1080100022272  250000000040110000 15 395 ICE
00000 809 01966 100 157  1644341119 7320112012161104 00 02100801301 016 432 MLI
000000705201566 2001157  2545445265 5340213 12282109 00001100701100015 433 SEN
00000 809 01966 100  67  2654350035 53401  12161008 00 011005012000015 434 DAH
000 0 8 9 01966 10  447  1544340025 534000012171108 00 02100701 000019 435 MAU
00000 90  01966 1 0 277  1653250019 53501  012171009 00 011001000000000 436 NIR
000000809 08966 200  77  2545452155 43501 02226210530000100040000022000 437 IVO
```

Figure A.6a   Printout: Raw data deck

(continued)

```
000000809 015393200 167  2545441215  6330112012161102 0000011013021131024 438 GUI
00000 805101966 10   57  2644351219  53401   12111106 00 022008012000017 439 UPP
000000709 015360200 14510244545114500336020201181205 000010007013000018 450 LBR
00000 800 61963 200 ·137  25454433250 5340101 11181109300 00000902202 029 451 SIE
0000105095115393201 16703254445545500633141402128210320000110140211122025 452 GHA
00000 70  0106  100 167  2644450125  6370001 02020005200 0110110000000000 461 TOG
00000080 151963 100  57  2654361125  43501010131811072000022003000000000 471 CAO
10000070 571963 000 257  16543577350 5340214031292104 00001103501201 016 475 NIG
000000809 11966 300 047  2654461145  4350000 12181006 0000100070000000000 481 GAB
000000809 01966 200 157  2653360039  4350000 12181107 00001100201 000000 482 CEN
00000 905101966 100  47  1753250019  4350001 12161006200 01100301 01 000 483 CHA
000000605 11966 300 047  2654461035  5340101 12171004 00002100200000000000 484 CON
01000060 401 6 9100 057  2663362225  4350012 1118100240000000013021021025 490 COP
000000800661963 100 167  2663371139  63300010121610 4 00001100601201201 6 500 UGA
000 009 5 21966  0   57  3664470129  73200   010400    00010040110100015 516 BUI
00000090  21966 00   77  2664470119  43500   010501 8   00010010210000024 517 RWA
00000 805 31 66 200  87  1772270125  7320101001020118 00 02100401101 015 520 SOM
00000080 1085996000 345001862273415 6330212001040214100001200201100000015 530 ETH
00001021 6585000101305 644465557748610138120121181 033110022016023118037 560 SAF
000000800 01963 100 087  3663499930  3360001 12181 06 000011003012000017 580 MAG
00000050 608933320021671416442455350 732031414138321420000320030110220015 600 MOR
010000509008566 5001053 07431433350 7320224 211711 830000210150210220023 615 ALG
000005094089363100103712075314222575 53402 031282206200000000050110100145 616 TUN
01001150  019333400 0870107531500750 5340112021161203 00002205000000000000 620 LBY
01000070  0806 92 0 167241762261125 063302130212811012000011015011011015 625 SUD
01000050 30859 9200 167240981060115003061313130282302200002201301100015 630 IRN
000010700768033 101 16124097105011510009152124348430200003201502102202525 640 TUR
00001050  3080  92 09177240971061105 07320213 201811124000043015022011026 645 IRO
00000050 208039350 106314086215460500732263614138322200004126513135441355 651 UAR
00000050 20803 9500 1771609720611150 732021302017111113000062135031242035 652 SYR
00001050 69853391 1 063240862162225  53404250402820113000021015011014016 660 LEB
00000 30 4085999300 177110862160115006330213010080203300 084154021131025 663 JOR
0000301107719003303708 0008621631951023716141402830123000064394131261136 666 ISR
010 007  0959 07 0 148000871162305 5340213 10171112 00005101302104002525 670 SAU
000 0 8  010  0   44  1772272425  73201   1000030    013013011011014 678 YEM
000 990  01   40050    0871163095006330101 100400 46000010017017000018 690 KUW
00000080 3015990100 945000990070009 6630212010070204 000011004011000015 700 AFG
94100 60 000     490 24 010990051415   9 13   1000029 10 142245141993145 710 CHN
010 1 5 9 005393892 075  0990050029  99001 4 100002  00 03101702101 025 712 MON
0000040960853931019471010790269930000201412121181 0420000570140110260144 713 CHT
00000 619000539359   65  0990050015   3 01   1000021    041033022021026 731 KON
00000050 55803 9001 265  08900556251  0 0201021181005100000240340310440355 732 KOS
10112021085193031088031200980049930301082636 60384 021420011135141031155 740 JAP
6110006006619303110 25362099007333550534163596148444535 11102413415115316565 750 INO
10000070 5080  9100  57150990071125104051424441383411000002202314114214555 770 PAK
00000060 50806 9500 1571307902700255 0633021201016130110000410000110000155 775 BUR
000000500671933921100632417812999301 6330213030272 03300001000401101 0135 780 CEY
00000090 408 9990 0 948  08901800291 534010000101040 00000100201000000135 790 NEP
00000070 60809961 0 175150790283425002071223031272112200001101503102103555 800 TAI
00000 7093015996200 2670107803811350 7320112 20181013200 032037021169025 811 CAM
00000 80 471 999100 267010790280029  5340111 2017120 00 046025021012025 812 LAO
00000 709 00539339   77  0790270035   3 01   1000001 00 095265141479144 816 VTN
0000008094085 9620 177  0790384335   3 02111201811121000085154031020034 817 VTS
00001 5007589303105   70116813821650 336011202017111 411 011023031011044 820 MAL
0000005008589303100 17301078027993000306021202117155 0710000110260320440466 840 PHI
11000060 4015 661 0 157191681376810 0633142403028201255 0000089024161020165 850 INS
0300501208619000206705000267257993010000913135 50393 02111002201602202502655 900 AUL
00005013085190003077055 0006555779930101080102 40282 062000010018013015 017 920 NEW
```

Figure A.6a   Printout: Raw data deck

```
8899960807599000408513054000550997579009999  7775657109999789944995852996 002 USA
5867861807619000308404030000430454567007666  7455590758856561255753435 65 020 CAN
44345136 100 3  9 733436720077099505199055  56444  545561474016564767555 040 CUB
32122 639208039 003 647584117817820  404342334644401  13 247015243233136 041 HAI
3323414505089 3  405 3734541178188701 10644  556444018535035600334323533 3 042 DUM
212352360651930 4062 43  41178199505 2352122332111  67350113000132000133 051 JAM
212367160 41930 4068263  62278299505 3342111 32111  494521120021330000134 052 TRI
67565546 5119333107266365000660362553305556546765680625654250133532 3 353 070 MEX
34334154 70803 920503635841177145555 206433344854550543502240041310001 31 090 GUA
34224054060803393040 634441178166553 1073232437434507524023501213200013? 091 HON
32234245961803692061463454117817755 1 10743334373434504635122501313 00013 9 092 ELS
242241455 180366 061463454117817755 0 107432244743450662402350051330001 34 093 NIC
2323534607589336307129334511781775 52 205433343843450762401130041360001 36 094 COS
2323513506680339307326356511781546 52 30544454474344077340112013238 25 247 095 PAN
56454535 641933630653636751178166556030545446575550634643350163454 7 346 100 COL
464567260779 33950653737851178165854320555445575554056555445015345233346 101 VEN
452343440608533 93 614635562178256452 205444455756560642523360172560002 46 130 ECU
46454446 76803 9305 4636762288255555130555545575555045463456013355 44 345 135 PER
785644460558033 9306336354622782783584304676667666504367455601444333 443 140 BRA
3623345507419336805 433687228932339  30544  54633450852422220162450002 45 145 BUL
35124 445 18039 20413534882289422493 20533334474247043 03 246005132000132 150 PAR
464555260 7193363174243648229936665423055555757545404356343601636543435 6 155 CHL
5756651605780339107523389822994767 5 220567  66754550225545450143454343 45 160 ARG
34345316075193032 08  33639329954365304044555446434702335123400733633 336 165 URU
6478860807519000509712061353433996057007899889889833059867662337847527 75 200 UNK
3334652707619000508401 0  35353334404 137332265544470875623450182542 3 248 205 IRE
53567517087190005085130102644235655560076856668985870388455600534655533 5 210 NTH
42568 070761900040831205136443345554400767 77 79878603778 556017456445446 211 BEL
10248 180 61900051930200036443411593 0082111 586565  9   23400400000000 0 212 LUX
657785170621 0334283130962644337665561068989799989521388576661357846537 75 220 FRN
43568418097190001093040303644344369 35 3 5766 776576027773547005335000335 225 SWZ
6556543693085390207432085353533367355223667666766566023664546015464668454 230 SPN
44455336920853903061220644535436645 4 205554457667671255625780153670454 56 235 POR
657786180768900330851 0322744247765 66 0 78887788584014996767134784552775 255 GMW
5467761890005393897300054274424565 5   9 5352 23101415 67466512555455344 5 265 GME
6566663791005393797313065094404454 5 299066655655657 03 67565401645467 444 290 POL
445575279200539 7973 1055094404335 94 9906554 65464604 664444016444459445 310 HUN
54567617910053937982120340944043469429906666 64464504 674665133445584435 315 CZE
435675280661900035084120402744244449911665666 776565036673434004332000333 305 AUS
65677427066190003427412073274424774555007787868885860248846560154544354 45 325 ITA
2233654590005393496126534274425546 5  9903322 33121305 242335015353555343 339 ALB
55565546940053933961231422744245635437326666765355502 564568015555333555 345 YUG
4444644605689336417422042275425656531106555467665650335524560135654534 55 350 GRC
111 6 3  631930 3 712230027542699502 3343132233222  5724 245023363232353 352 CYP
444565464910053938972221231854156565 9905655 54454606 563565015436454436 355 BUL
545565469000539389711213309540434 45 9906554 64464504 56455401555433354 5 360 RUM
89887637900053909841313209900286 75 69908787 64454492 888987464894994885 365 USR
4546742807819000529312040094404225540296565 4 655656035562434013353000354 375 FIN
455685180851900050940200117441388654613657664676465026773666017446 44 348 380 SWD
3546851909519000409312030094403225545106554456765650286634550052363642 35 385 NOR
435584170771900040851202027442355554510657555776567037672545006349 23 339 390 DEN
041384380 6190041941400034344299502 1072111545333  282400000413300013 4 395 ICE
36111 729 01966 401 547  5435544539 7323343235222304 12 24600823823 136 432 MLI
342240645201566 403 657  5436648785 5334444 46343409 340234007234000235 433 SEN
34101 629 01966 401  57  5445653355 53321  25222208 02 145005136000134 434 DAH
260 3 7 9 01966 30  737  4435543455 5331100126232308 03 15400713 000139 435 MAU
36102 91  01966 3 0 767  4545453349 53411  025232109 03 135001000000000 436 NIR
352241749 08966 502  67  6435656675 43332  24532320563502340040002550 00 437 IVO
```

Figure A.6b *Printout: Transformed data deck*

(continued)

```
351210749 01539350    657  5436645635   6323344225222402 1401450134535553343 438 GUI
45100 715001966 40     57  5445554629    53322   36203306 12 246008237000237 439 UPP
241231659 015360502 5354263366565651233434335241414os 240123007337000338 450 LBR
33122 730 61963 403 637   64366477552 5333122 34232309724 12300915625 149 451 SIE
443341449491153934os 55735644565887520632555665434330354513440145555554545 452 GHA
23012 62  0106   203 457  6445654545   6351111  15111105503 1450110000000000 461 TOG
45242265 151963 402  47   5545565545   4343232326233207524125600030000000000 471 CAO
66442363 471963 203 647   554455599654 5335455454454304 46432503534623 346 475 NIG
150146649 11966 603 237   6445666565   4341100 35242006 1411430070000000000 481 GAB
250021729 01966 500 447   5545563359   4341111 25232207 03013400213 000000 482 CEN
36101 825101966 200  37   4544453429   4331111 25222206503 12400313 23 000 483 CHA
251134545 11966 601 237   6545665365   5332221 36233204 1411550020000000000 484 CON
57342255 301 6 9402 247   5555567755   4342144 34242002835222301345443344S 490 COP
442312740461963 303 457   5554575559   63200223352232 4 251224006136235136 500 UGA
320 008 5 21966 30   47   6555674549   73211   140100     0114004345232345 516 BUI
32000081  21966 20   67   6555674549   43401   251213 8   0114001252000243 517 RWA
35000 715 31 66 401  67   4654474445   7323232304000218 13 15600423323 235 520 SOM
56220072 0085996202 735014754477845   63244445040105143241346002343000334 530 ETH
56566627 5585000306325 867445779895501365332 53343 036674557016468538357 560 SAF
452221630 01963 403 377   6555699950   3352122 35242 06 240235003237000237 580 MAG
55343344 508933340424575645354488553 732445576445451454524660033434543J4 600 MOR
573446449008566 7051343   35444477654 7324465 442323 87564444015452434442 615 ALG
3423414493089363405143744364434774S 53344  65445440663402230052JJ2J2233 616 TUN
26225745  019333703 3773336443543853 533434334J222403 3532560050000000000 620 LBY
57322063  0806 95 3 557663654466555 063244444543434015350345015132232134 625 SUD
56444644  30859 9504 5576609720624454330555547523435024465556013343000344 630 IRN
664544550668033 306 451660953053535640076662866545502 554567015443554444 640 TUR
45344745  2080   95 494676618631655IS 1732545440242312746447701545523J446 645 IRQ
66453445 108039370 1453463654358815347327777664444 265645752265674876664 651 UAR
44233044 20803 9704 5675728532645252 7324444440222311635048613557476455S 652 SYR
31235245 59853394 6 253663754366645  53345663603540117441356015335336235 660 LEB
34124 34 3085999605 4675337533645351063243442301414036J3 397154554652445 663 JOR
32347317067190035077L6 303754367495512356755760454012655158739467577J665 666 ISR
473 375    0959 08 2 638002763367705  5335444 40131312 464475013454361444 670 SAU
441 2 7    010   1    73  4654477745   73133  2000050     247013232333233 678 YEM
123 990    01    70251   2763367395206323222 301112 494333333017339000339 690 KUW
55322272 2015990202 945220990071209  662433342203150 242225004133000134 700 AFG
98762 54 000    794 63 330990056825    9.65  2000049  56 776245774995664 710 CHN
262 5 4 9 005393997 165 0990050049   99032  200005  24 36401724323 244 712 MON
533534469408539320698610316814699504320666643743242 044453478014343437333 713 CHT
54364 579000539379    55 0990051235    3 43  2000041     475033445443446 731 KON
54442444  45803 9106 755  17812588455  0 543164324300524444570344734664G4 732 KOS
75786527075193033098121601872149950741067777  72555 0228856251355754S3575 740 JAP
97662454056193032L4 753850890177765865336777973545643 676657134683775674 750 IND
76552263  4080  9303  47470990075545624045565864454611156454602368456467J 770 PAK
56331353  40806 9703 6474506904722S5 063243545422250143534650003430003J4 775 BUR
4333314305719339515035366466359995Os 6324344352333 036451223004232J3 232 780 CEY
44201080 308 9991 1 948  07903811495 533222101300060  230125002132000132 790 NEP
65432163  40809964 5 5655716815877453220554645543343124462445015564443554 800 TAI
44223 6392015996503 6570335725855653 7323243 42232213524 3660375646894SS 811 CAM
34112 62 371 999204 757130690581159  5333242 4223240 00 268025364235355 812 LAO
54332 639 00539369    67 0590573355    3 43  2000011  24 598265683889673 816 VTN
5433217393085 9650  467  2581587765   3 4342652243412334259815457343256J 817 VTS
45445 4506589303308    73345735865755 335324345222341 867 445023573233563 820 MAL
65453245075A930330G 5630325724799504230554435Su333 07446243502657S366566 840 PHI
76542453 3015 663 4 647594563578930 0632666552344012 46569902469544268S 850 INS
486686180761900050870403164546799506500765S4 72555 024674546016566447456 900 AUL
354585180651900060970 030844687995054106423J 62454 06656243401834743 337 920 NEW
```

Figure A.6b Printout: Transformed data deck

Figure A.7 *Rank orderings—63 interval variables**   Variables 1–22

N\V	1	2	3	4	5	6	7	8	10	11	17	18	19	20	21	22
USA	4	4	1	1	2	7	114	4	7.5	38.5	69.5	74.5	14	13.5	86	82
CAN	27	2	10	6	3	8	111.5	2	5	21	80.5	43	22	21.5	95	68
CUB	58	81	50	46	48	72	80.5	41	78	95	1		39.5	28	50.5	54
HAI	74	107	98	95	100.5		28.5	91	69	95	115	74.5	87.5		15	68
DOM	79	99	72	73	55	81.5	56.5	61	40	95	45	74.5	61.5		46.5	4
JAM	100	112	76	62	42	68	84	44	25	38.5	55	74.5	45	42		63.5
TRI	110	115	82	64	29	5	96.5	34		44	66	74.5	41	3	63.5	27.5
MEX	14	13	16	24	43	29	67.5	46	36	56	112.5	38	36	42	12	8
GUA	75	85	66	76	52	74.5	42.5	78	13	95	103	74.5	59.5	59.5	48	21.5
HON	96	82	91	93	60	86	40.5	80	31	95	87.5	74.5	67	61		12
ELS	87	109	78	77	54	66	51.5	63	22	55	100	74.5	54.5	57.5	43.5	8
NIC	102	74	92	81	53	74.5	51.5	55		54		74.5	50.5	55.5	35.5	17
COS	104	98	88	67	44	60	72.5	42	9	40	91	39	37	49.5	65	1
PAN	106	93	87	78	41	77.5	76.5	48	33	18.5	75	74.5	38	31.5	59	17
COL	32	24	36	37	51	31	76.5	47	24	46	87.5	74.5	52.5	15	50.5	17
VEN	53	30	32	33	27	2	90.5	31	14	10	38	74.5	42	13.5	56	4
ECU	68	56	70	71	65.5	56	67.5	64	26	95	92		52.5	49.5	39	12
PER	43	18	48	40	56	38	74.5	43	6	16	72	74.5	57		41.5	37.5
BRA	8	5	17	13	67.5	53	72.5	40	38	36	93.5	74.5	50.5	39.5	55	27.5
BOL	78	25	81	66	76	50	40.5	58	19	45	7	34	63.5		41.5	86
PAR	97	45	97	91	69		69	76.5		57	95.5	74.5	75	55.5	45	38.5
CHL	52	32	41	35	37	33	93	33		6	90	20	31	17	57.5	54
ARG	25	8	21	26	32	28	99	37	45	7.5	112.5	74.5	29	11.5	71.5	77
URU	88	69	62	53	39	59	101	36	12	30	104.5	27	13			86
UNK	11	62	4	3	13	13	116	9	20.5	37	37	42	2	5	88	104
IRE	86	95	52	47	25	32	87.5	27	20.5	23	39	44	21	25.5	100	111
NTH	39	103	19	21	18	26	11.5	19	3	7.5	33	31	16.5	10	81	86
BEL	49	104	20	23	15		114	16	15.5	20	51	28	15	34.5	77	108
LUX	115	116	86	52	12		107.5	3		15	32	22	3	36	95	94
FRN	13	38	5	7	10	25	99	17	30	50	50	16	19	31.5	81	90
SWZ	64	101	22	20	5	39	109.5	6	1.5	3	111	33	8	37.5	98.5	68
SPN	15	40	18	19	38	37	82.5	29	62	95	95.5	74.5	26	20	54	98
POR	50	91	47	39	49	54	79	38	67	95	93.5	74.5	46.5	53.5	69	104
GMW	9	60	3	5	11	15	107.5	14	18	26	71	34.5	12	11.5	92	
GME	30	86	12	9	20	10	96.5	10	83.5	95	3	6	33	28	95	112
POL	16	52	11	12	26	12	78	26	75	61	12.5	12	29	34.5	73.5	90
AUS	60	92	29	22	22	23	95	13	27	27	26	29	20	23	90	109
HUN	47	90	26	30	24	21	89	28	68	64.5	15	11	25	28		110
CZE	36	77	14	17	19	9	102	15	74	73	8	8	18	44.5	90	104
ITA	12	53	8	8	23	42	94	23	28	14	56	14	34	18.5	81	104
ALB	99	105	64	80	28	36	55	59	87	95	63.5	2.5	54.5	52	62	27.5
YUG	26	59	30	25	46	30	65.5	32	53	60	87.5	13	44	46.5	61	90
GRC	51	76	39	45	35	52	65.5	45	37	22	49	18	35	24	66.5	104
CYP	112	114	94		31		80.5		29	47	80.5		32	57.5	63.5	94
BUL	54	84	37	34	33	24	51.5	30	76	95	4	7	29	44.5	66.5	98
RUM	28	65	23	29	34	20	51.5	35	83.5	71.5	5	9	24	46.5	75.5	104
USR	3	1	2	2	17	14	85.5	18	79	68	19	10	23	25.5	75.5	82
FIN	71	48	33	28	16	46	87.5	12	7.5	2	30	15	9	39.5	86	98
SWD	56	42	15	10	4	35	105.5	5	4	34	29	24	1	18.5	98.5	104
NOR	76	50	34	11	14	22	99	1	1.5	32	46	30	7	31.5	86	98
DEN	69	100	28	32	9	49	103	22	11	9	53	36	11	16	81	98
ICE	116	87	99	61	8	41	82.5	7		18.5	57	17	4	21.5	90	71
MLI	72	22	100	99	108		6.5	103.5		95	60	74.5	101		24.5	57.5
SEN	81	67	80	84	63.5	90.5	32.5	76.5	70	95	52	74.5	87.5		19.5	50.5

(continued)

N = country identification alpha code (see Figure 5).
V = variable identification number (see Figure 3).
* Blank spaces signify missing data.

Variables 1–22 (*Continued*)

N \ V	1	2	3	4	5	6	7	8	10	11	17	18	19	20	21	22
DAH	95	80	108	104	107		20.5	102		95	61	74.5	101			38.5
MAU	109	26	114		82		10			95	77.5	74.5			4	77
NIR	83	20	101	105.5	103.5		1	106		95	85		105.5		9.5	17
IVO	77	51	79	88	67.5	74.5	16	82		63	27	74.5	91.5			27.5
GUI	80	61	105	89	109	90.5	17.5	82		67	35	74.5	105.5		19.5	34.5
UPP	70	55	104	103	114		14.5	108	80	95	68	74.5				50.5
LBR	107	83	106	85	74	81.5	25.5	52		66	44	74.5	93.5		27	77
SIE	93	94	102	96	87.5		10	87		24.5	47	74.5	84		19.5	90
GHA	57	64	59	72	59	81.5	58.5	74	52	52	48	74.5	59.5		22.5	38.5
TOG	101	97	110	100	103.5		28.5	97.5		62	99	74.5	81		37.5	38.5
CAO	65	41	93	57	92	63	20.5	51	73	35	65	74.5	96.5			57.5
NIG	10	29	43	59	91	55	25.5	93.5	49	4	107	74.5	78.5		11	63.5
GAB	113	58	115	98	63.5	18	20.5	71		58	21	74.5	78.5		71.5	82
CEN	105	36	111	102	94	81.5	6.5	97.5		95	36	74.5	105.5		34	57.5
CHA	82	19	107	107	111		4.5	103.5	77	69.5	97.5	74.5	105.5			82
CON	111	47	109	97	77	48	42.5	79		53	24	74.5	101		60	77
COP	35	11	65	49	100.5	64	38	54	57	95	59	74.5	96.5		69	57.5
UGA	59	63	85	65	105	69	10	70	46	17	87.5	74.5	84		31	47
BUI	84	106	113		115.5	90.5	2.5			51	83.5	74.5				63.5
RWA	85	108	112	108.5	115.5	90.5	2.5	106		49	107	74.5				21.5
SOM	92	35	116	108.5	113		10	106		48	54	74.5	101			8
ETH	24	23	71	87	112	86	13	101	81	95	107	74.5	96.5		6	73.5
SAF	31	21	24	18	36	19	90.5	21	42	29	83.5	74.5	48.5	31.5	69	50.5
MAG	62	37	84	90	94	81.5	20.5	91		64.5	67	74.5	81		46.5	4
MOR	38	44	53	56	73	58	63.5	67	43	95	58	74.5	71	42	32.5	43
ALG	42	10	55	58	70.5	17	47	68	85	69.5	10	74.5	65.5	49.5	50.5	63.5
TUN	73	78	73	79	70.5	77.5	47	72	61	71.5	63.5	32	63.5	49.5	43.5	90
LBY	103	14	90	82	47	3	47	57		95	18	74.5	86		53	2
SUD	37	9	63	83	87.5	90.5	30.5	95		95	41.5		89.5		26	34.5
IRN	23	15	35	51	61	11	56.5	65	63	95	34	74.5	72		24.5	34.5
TUR	18	31	31	42	57	47	34.5	62	34.5	13	73	74.5	56		37.5	43
IRQ	55	43	60	55	58	6	70.5	53	66	95	41.5		75	2	30	21.5
UAR	20	27	42	38	81	45	61	56	72	95	14	74.5		53.5	40	47
SYR	66	70	74	70	78	86	70.5	66	71	95	9	74.5	68.5		28	27.5
LEB	94	113	77	63	45	65	61	49	39	1	62		43		57.5	43
JOR	98	89	95	92	65.5		85.5	75	59	95	23	74.5	61.5		35.5	17
ISR	91	110	49	44	21	57	105.5	24	32	12	25	25	27	7	73.5	6
SAU	61	12	68		72	4	34.5			95	6		96.5		16.5	73.5
YEM	67	68	96		94		10			95	110				5	77
KUW	114	111	67		1	1	114			95	17	74.5	93.5	9	81	
AFG	34	34	69	86	100.5	70	14.5	99	65	95	102	74.5	91.5		1.5	71
CHN	1	3	6	14	89.5		44	82	82	95	16	2.5	68.5		13.5	82
MON	108	16	89		40		51.5			95	2	5	39.5		81	27.5
CHT	40	102	54	36	75	40	74.5	39	48	95	97.5	74.5	46.5	1	3	12
KON	41	79	51	27	62		36.5	25	86	95	11	2.5				32
KOS	21	88	46	50	84.5	44	58.5	69	50	31	109	74.5	48.5	37.5	7.5	34.5
JAP	7	46	7	4	30	34	92	20	17	42	82	26	5	4	81	94
IND	2	7	9	15	97	51	36.5	73	44	24.5	104.5	21	73		9.5	50.5
PAK	6	28	25	43	98	62	32.5	85.5	54	59	79	74.5	89.5			60
BUR	22	84	57	68.5	106	61	45	91	51	95	12.5	23	81		16.5	63.5
CEY	46	96	61	75	79.5	74.5	63.5	84	41	11	28	19	58	59.5	50.5	43
NEP	48	75	83	105.5	110	90.5	4.5	109	60	95	114		101		1.5	71
TAI	19	39	45	60	86	81.5	30.5	88	47	95	69.5		65.5		22.5	27.5
CAM	63	71	75	94	83		25.5	93.5	64	95	43	74.5	84		13.5	43
LAO	90	66	103	101	96		23	100	58	5	101	37	75		7.5	47
VTN	29	73	58	74	89.5		25.5	89		95	22	2.5				12
VTS	33	72	56	68.5	84.5	71	17.5	85.5	56	95	31	74.5			32.5	21.5
MAL	45	49	44	48	50		61	50	34.5	41	77.5	74.5	16.5			

(continued)

Variables 24–41

N	24	25	26	27	28	29	30	31	32	33	34	36	37	38	40	41
PHI	17	54	40	41	79.5	67	51.5	60	10	43	74	74.5	70		29	12
INS	5	17	27	54	100.5	43	39	96	55	95	76		77		19.5	54
AUL	44	6	13	16	7	16	109.5	11	15.5	28	40	40	10	6	95	63.5
NEW	89	57	38	31	6	27	104	8	23	33	20	41	6	8	95	
USA	29	38	105.5	115	115	38	51	115	14	16	11	5	1	108	1	1
CAN	58	75.5	105.5	115	115	62	75	115	80.5	73	73	6	3	102.5	6.5	13
CUB	22	8.5	77	113	113	21	22	113	6.5	6.5	44.5	21	37.5	4	105	32
HAI	27.5	7	46	108.5	111	14.5	15	111	42	19	107			52	59	85.5
DOM	49.5	30.5	42	108.5	108.5	14.5	18	108	17	25	13	67		89	18.5	68
JAM			53	112	112	17	18	112	6.5	6.5	44.5	20		76	33.5	101
TRI			17	99	99.5	8	13	101	6.5	6.5	44.5	25		58	52	105.5
MEX	8.5	33.5	105.5	115	115	27	28	115	100.5	53	111	17	21	70	40	37
GUA	27.5	6	47	108.5	108.5	20	21	110	7	75	61	27		83.5	27	77
HON	49.5	36	39	108.5	108.5	19	20	109	55	48	71	55		97.5	11.5	96.5
ELS	41	27.5	37	106	106	18	18	106	35	38	34	69.5		93.5	13.5	75
NIC	41	33.5	40	108.5	108.5	16	14	107	36.5	37	35	71		97.5	11.5	72
COS	66	38	35	104	103.5	12	11	105	31	35	35	60		75	35	73
PAN	34.5	14	31	104	103.5	11	10	103	70	88	24	61		67	43.5	58
COL	8.5	10.5	33	104	103.5	10	9	104	56	59	69	9	45.5	62.5	47	53
VEN	6	3.5	32	102	103.5	9	12	102	47	76	5	41	23.5	77	31.5	50
ECU	34.5	27.5	10	101	101	7	7	100	66	57	76	66		78	31.5	59.5
PER	12.5	10.5	9	100	99.5	6	6	99	67	74	51	29	37.5	64	47	51
BRA	25.5	44.5	18	98	98	13	16	98	33	20	98	3	15	59.5	50.5	20
BOL	22	3.5	6	97	97	5	5	93	107	102	106			67	43.5	68
PAR	41	5	3.5	94	94.5	4	4	77.5	110	108.5	92	56		80	29.5	87
CHL	10	41.5	3.5	96	96	1	2	88	50	50	19	36	31	62.5	47	40
ARG	4	1.5	2	95	94.5	3	3	75	27	49	9		31	73	37	19
URU	22	54.5		93	93	2	1	58.5	89	103.5	28.5	47.5	45.5	55	56	57
UNK	11	66	6	56	84.5	53.5	74	94	13	13	16	15	2	102.5	6.5	2
IRE				67.5	90.5	45	69	95	100.5	91.5	91	34		99	10	89.5
NTH	72.5	75.5		39	74	60	86.5	84	64	55	68	28	8	106	3	16
BEL	30.5	66	6	42	77	56	81.5	87	77	83.5	52	31	19.5	102.5	6.5	24
LUX	78	75.5	65.5	42	71.5	57	77	80	114	114.5	38	50		107	2	107
FRN	1	15.5	71.5	44.5	79	59	78	90.5	38	45	25	16	7	91	18.5	4
SWZ	58	75.5	69	39	69.5	61	84.5	77.5	88	99	14	51	13.5			29
SPN	5	30.5	58	61	82.5	47	70	92	57	33	97	24	31	83.5	27	18
POR	22	41.5	54	75	89	40	63	90.5	53.5	46	74.5	35		79	29.5	49
GMW	58	60.5	82	31	68	64	91	81.5	29	36	28.5	7	5.5			5
GME	34.5	44.5	85	23	66.5	65.5	95	76	63	58	55					45
POL	17.5	27.5	105.5	7.5	52	75	110.5	72	78	65	90		26.5	4	105	14
AUS	41	75.5	84	25	61	67	94	70	92	93	74.5	1	37.5	86	23.5	39
HUN	34.5	33.5	105.5	7.5	49.5	71	110.5	67	100.5	99	60	38		8.5	100.5	26
CZE	58	41.5	105.5	7.5	55	72	110.5	71	93	94.5	33	39.5	31	4	105	10
ITA	7	54.5	79	36	64	65.5	88.5	73	39	32	82	19	12	102.5	6.5	8
ALB	66	38	75.5	31	47	69	88.5	60	68	88	17			4	105	81.5
YUG	45	60.5	86	20.5	52	70	97	66	73	54	99	30	23.5	12.5	97	23
GRC	45	60.5	83	23	43	76.5	93	56	51.5	62	32	52	37.5	91	18.5	31
CYP	78	75.5	71.5	31	34.5	86.5	86.5	40	6.5	6.5	44.5	65		61	49	96.5
BUL	70	50.5	90	16	40.5	79	102	58.5	59	72	21			4	105	28
RUM	66	47.5	105.5	7.5	40.5	83	110.5	63	95.5	86	77			8.5	100.5	15
USR	66	60.5	105.5	7.5	6	11	110.5	96.5	19	47	7		5.5	4	105	3
FIN	49.5	75.5	105.5	7.5	52	82	110.5	81.5	105.5	107	67	42	45	81.5	27	48
SWD	78	66	88	20.5	58	76.5	100	86	21	23	20	32	4	86	23.5	30
NOR	66	75.5	105.5	7.5	58	80	110.5	89	105.5	110.5	37	37	13.5	88	21	41
DEN	70	75.5	81	36	69.5	63	90	85	74	82	36	46	11	91	18.5	34
ICE	78	75.5	62	78	92	52	67	96.5	6.5	6.5	44.5	58		96	13.5	105.5
MDI			36	82.5	80.5	36	48	68	80.5	62	100			15.5	94	83
SEN			25	90.5	90.5	24	33	69	24	41	6			43.5	66.5	74
DAH			24	80	71.5	33	38	47	97	101	53			45	65	103.5

(continued)

Variables 24–41 (Continued)

N\V	24	25	26	27	28	29	30	31	32	33	34	36	37	38	40	41
MAU			38	86	87	34	49	79	95.5	91.5	63			37	73	112.5
NIR			41	63.5	61	48	58	50	98	96	95			47	54.5	111
IVO			19	87	80.5	28	30	53	48	56	12			48.5	63	93.5
GUI			23	88	87	26	31	64	71	51	105			22.5	87	80
UPP			28	82.5	77	32	40	52	82	52	110			33.5	76.5	98.5
LBR	49.5	60.5	12	92	92.5	23	26	55	61	69	18	68	31	59.5	50.5	84
SIE			14	89	87	22	27	61	28	34	64	62		40.5	70	95
GHA	58	27.5	22	85	77	30	36	49	20	27	10	63	45.5	27	82	33
TOG			20.5	82.5	74	31	37	48	85	69	84			30	33.5	109
CAO			29	72	58	42	44	33	72	79.5	72			53	58	92
NIG			34	75	64	41	47	45	16	15	23	39.5		40.5	70	46
GAB			15	78	61	35	29	29	58	83.5	15			50	61	114
CEN			30	67.5	47	46	45.5	30	94	99	59			51	60	109
CHA			43	60	49.5	58	59	43	100.5	94.5	108			48.5	62	109
CON			16	75	55	37	34	28	75.5	97	22			42	68	102
COP			27	70	45	49	41	26	45.5	43	62			57	53	98.5
UGA			26	63.5	39	53.5	42	16	65	62	58			22.5	85	116
BUI			11	70	43	43	32	10	87	69	87.5			11	97	112.5
RWA			13	70	43	44	35	12	91	79.5	93			56	54.5	115
SOM			44	52	26	85	56.5	11	90	85	87.5			20	89.5	93.5
ETH	78	66	45	27	32.5	73.5	61	23	41	24	94			26	83	70.5
SAF	2	20.5	7	82.5	55	29	23	13	15	22	3	22	45.4	26	15.5	38
MAG			8	66	36.5	50	25	2	6.5	6.5	44.5			65	43.5	103.5
MOR	25.5	23.5	50	73	84.5	39	60	83	23	21	56	53		17	92	52
ALG			56	57.5	74	51	68	74	34	40	30	44		15.5	94	59.5
TUN		41.5	57	50	66.5	55	71	65	43	42	81			35	75	61
LBY	58	54.5	59	44.5	47	68	72	57	86	106	4	57		46	64	76
SUD	17.5	17.5	55	47.5	36.5	78	66	31	61	61	66		45.5	25	84	62
IRN	14.5	20.5	105.5	7.5	19	98	110.5	37	108	90	96	43	23.5	71	40	27
TUR	22	20.5	105.5	7.5	28	92	110.5	51	104	71	102	10	19.5	102.5	6.5	11
IRQ	17.5	17.5	89	16	25	93	101	34.5	69	16.5	113		37.5	12.5	97	47
UAR	49.5	23.5	61	39	38	81	73	42	25	18	114	49	16.5	18	91	7
SYR	30.5	8.5	87	18.5	28	90	96	39	83	66.5	112	64		19	89.5	54
LEB	14.5	15.5	69	31	32.5	88	84.5	38	51.5	44	86			37	73	63.5
JOR	38	47.5	69	31	31	89	83	34.5	84	77	101	69.5	45.5	31	78.5	68
ISR	58	75.5	63	36	34.5	86.5	76	36	36.5	88	1	23	37.5	72	37	21
SAU	78	75.5	75.5	31	24	94	81.5	32	44	39	115			33.5	76.5	42.5
YEM			48	47.5	28	84	62	19	45.5	28	89			10	99	88
KUW			73	31	23	91	79.5	27	40	103.5	2	59	45.5	28	78.5	81.5
AFG	70	60.5	105.5	7.5	6	111	110.5	24	114	110.5	116			22.5	87	66
CHN	58	50.5	105.5	7.5	6	111	110.5	54	53.5	26	109					12
MON			105.5	7.5	6	111	110.5	44	116	116	78			4	105	91
CHT	78	54.5	91	47.5	12.5	105	65	25	6.5	6.5	44.5	45	23.5	81.5	23.5	25
KON			105.5	7.5	6	111	103.5	46	111	112	104					55
KOS			92	23	14.5	103	92	41	22	17	85	13				42.5
JAP	17.5	75.5	93	18.5	18	101	99	62	6.5	6.5	44.5	4	18	86	23.5	6
IND	3	33.5	105.5	16	6	111	98	18	32	31	27	2	9	37	73	9
PAK	45	12	105.5	7.5	6	111	103.5	21.5	75.5	79.5	79.5	11	26.5	54	57	36
BUR	49.5	25	105.5	42	6	111	64	15	109	108.5	70		45.5	29	80.5	65
CEY	12.5	20.5	49	47.5	21	95	52	1	6.5	6.5	44.5	18		32	80.5	78
NEP			105.5	26	6	111	79.5	7	112	113	83	14		43.5	66.5	100
TAI	34.5	13	94	52	12.5	104	54	6	30	29	79.5	47.5	31	73.5	37	35
CAM	78	54.5	64	59	16.5	99	45.5	4	62	64	26	54		14	94	85.5
LAO	72.5	47.5	65.5	52	6	111	53	5	114	114.5	65			39	70	89.5
VTN			105.5	54.5	6	111	55	14	103	105	54					70.5
VTS			80	57.5	14.5	102	50	8	26	30	31					56
MAL	58	47.5	51	63.5	20	97	39	3	49	79.5	8	26		69	40	79

(continued)

Variables 42–57

N \ V	42	43	44	45	46	47	48	49	50	51	52	53	54	55	56	57
PHI	78	54.5	78	54.5	16.5	100	56.5	21.5	6.5	6.5	44.5	33	31	67	43.5	44
INS	34.5	1.5	52	63.5	22	96	43	17	18	14	103		45.5	22.5	87	17
AUL	58	66	20.5	78	30	73.5	24	9	6.5	6.5	44.5	8	10	102.5	6.5	22
NEW	58	75.5	5	90.5	64	25	8	20	6.5	6.5	44.5	12	16.5	93	15.5	63.5
USA	1	1	1		8	13.5	7	37	9	36	3	98	76	1	1	1
CAN	21.5	13	20		12	66.5	21.5	22.5	21	1	33	18	47.5	8	6	11
CUB	38	43	41		46.5	37.5	41	54	40		4	56.5	45.5	36	39	68.5
HAI	61.5	85	66	59	68	33	54.5	47.5	53.5	99	12			101	99	
DOM	64			40	46.5	33	36	42.5	36	99	8.5	7.5	42.5	74	65	87
JAM	114	91.5	86.5	63	91.5	97.5	104	107	102			29.5	10	66	63	77
TRI	110	95	97		91.5	97.5	104	103	102			41.5	2	55	50	49
MEX	29.5	22.5	27.5	45.5	30	13.5	14	15	14.5	2	79.5	21	71.5	26	30	13
GUA	67.5	72	61.5	49	68	8.5	28.5	64.5	30.5	26	79.5	33.5	59	72	68	77
HON	88	82	76.5	50	91.5	10.5	45.5	74.5	50	23	79.5	16.5	38	92	82	87
ELS	72	73	60	48	81	13.5	41	72	45	41	79.5	43	28.5	76	67	71.5
NIC	74.5	89.5	74.5	56	75.5	10.5	36	86.5	36	30.5	79.5	29.5	23.5	86	75	87
COS	67.5	79.5	64	42	81	8.5	36	68	36	30.5	79.5	12	30.5	81	77	77
PAN	48	53	32	43	75.5	19.5	45.5	83	45	50	46.5	13	9	73	94	87
COL	44.5	56	41	15	50.5	25	32	22.5	33	46	79.5	25	66	51	46	29
VEN	40.5	51	52	28	46.5	27	28.5	22.5	30.5	60	46.5	38.5	27	38	60	12
ECU	52.5	67	52	31	50.5	19.5	28.5	6.5	27	16.5	79.5	23	54	82	70	56
PER	44.5	42	41	32	55.5	19.5	32	37	30.5	30.5	33	52.5	42.5	50	44	38
BRA	15.5	11	15.5	16	25	25	16.5	6.5	17	41	46.5	52.5	68.5	24	20	17
BOL	52.5			34	75.5	29.5	58	83	57.5	46	46.5	10.5	38	91	81	57
PAR	77	76.5	73	53	68	28	49.5	93	50	9	79.5	56.5	66	104	97	
CHL	29.5	38	29	10	50.5	19.5	28.5	54	27	55.5	79.5	46	61.5	44	40	39
ARG	15.5			14	33.5	19.5	19	42.5	19.5	36	79.5	86	71.5	31	71	23
URU	42.5	41	33.5	55	60	29.5	45.5	78.5	45	4	79.5	74.5	66	71	66	67
UNK	3	2	3	4	1	6.5	2	1	2	80.5	6	105	49.5	2	3	5
IRE	82.5	86	78.5	17	46.5	50.5	51.5	54	50	7	79.5	9	11.5	37	41	52
NTH	6	27	20	13	4	2	3	22.5	3	5	79.5	62	4	9	9	34
BEL	7	10	6		5	3	4	3.5	4	11.5	46.5	62	13	10	10	
LUX	101	98	97		41	5	12.5	15	13	30.5			1			
FRN	2	4	2	7	2	1	1	2	1	36	7	98	64	4	4	9
SWZ	9	22.5	12		14.5	13.5	8.5	22.5	7	14	79.5	94.5	19	12	15	45
SPN	17	16	13.5	20	6	33	10	22.5	9	10	70.5	91	69.5	20	35	22
POR	32	49.5	52	35	16.5	33	16.5	3.5	17	7	15.5	94.5	45.5	43	47	50
GMW	4	3	4	9	8	4	6	15	6	55.5	79.5	104	51	3	2	4
GME	82.5	45	80		105	86	106	109	106.5	52.5	8.5	38.5		15	13	14
POL	21.5	24	33.5	26	21.5	59	32	6.5	30.5	7	33	59.5		19	18	7
AUS	24	12	11		16.5	19.5	11	30.5	11	26	46.5	59.5	28.5	23	22	36
HUN	35.5	39.5	52		36	59	45.5	10	45	19	46.5	52.5		25	25	32
CZE	19.5	20.5	17.5		33.5	66.5	54.5	10	45	23	79.5	46		16	14	15
ITA	5	6	5	21	3	6.5	5	15	5	11.5	79.5	91	59	5	8	16
ALB	84.5	84	82		85.5	86	98	98.5	98	77.5	33	31.5		96	93	58
YUG	19.5	19	15.5	11	19	50.5	23.5	30.5	23	36	46.5	82.5		29	33	26
GRC	32	30	38	18	14.5	36	16.5	30.5	17	41	46.5	68	63	39	58	46
CYP	105	70.5	78.5	67	81	86	94	97	92.5			35.5	14	79	92	
BUL	26.5	39.5	30.5		38	66.5	51.5	15	52	19	33	28		32	32	35
RUM	39	36	52		30	66.5	41	65	40	41	79.5	41.5		30	31	18
USR	11	5	9		30	77	45.5	22.5	45	55.5	1	86		6	5	2
FIN	25	46	46.5		21.5	50.5	25.5	10	25	14	79.5	70	38	27	26	54
SWD	13	25	20	44	27.5	19.5	16.5	42.5	14.5	23	33	91	32.5	11	11	42
NOR	35.5	49.5	46.5	33	18	25	12.5	30.5	12	21	79.5	78.5	8	21	27	44
DEN	18	33	30.5	37	12	19.5	8.5	37	9	3	79.5	64.5	17.5	17	17	55
ICE	101	97	97	41	60	50.5	61	85	61.5			74.5	5	87	76	87
MLI	77	69	66	68	91.5	55.5	87	91	88	77.5	79.5	56.5		103	109	

(continued)

Variables 42–57 (Continued)

N	42	43	44	45	46	47	48	49	50	51	52	53	54	55	56	57
SEN	64	55	38		75.5	40.5	66	60	65.5	65	79.5	2		75	74	87
DAH	101				105	45	87	93	88	88.5	79.5	6		105	108	
MAU	110	100	100.5	70	97.5	40.5	79	80.5	78.5	73.5	79.5	4		106	107	
NIR	101			71	97.5	45	82	72	82.5	93	79.5	3		111	104	
IVO	90.5			69	71.5	45	66	100	65.5	83.5	79.5	31.5	21	69	61	77
GUI	80	58	57	65	105	55.5	94	93	95	65	79.5	82.5		97	95	87
UPP	96				91.5	40.5	73.5	110	74.5	77.5	79.5	23		102	110	
LBR	64	74	63	38	97.5	66.5	98	54	98	50	70.5	35.5		89	84	87
SIE	101	91.5	84		91.5	66.5	94	68	95	69.5	79.5	1	16	94	88	
GHA	35.5	31	17.5	23	50.5	66.5	63	60	63.5	77.5	33	70	38	56	57	71.5
TOG	110	94	92		113	55.5	101	106	102	93	79.5	33.5	42.5	109	106	
CAO	96	81	82	57	97.5	37.5	73.5	68	74.5	83.5	79.5	14.5	38	88	73	62
NIG	55.5	37	22	51.5	41	66.5	54.5	15	53.5	73.5	79.5	40		47	42	28
GAB	114	101	100.5		85.5	55.5	82	64.5	82.5	99	79.5	26.5		99	87	63
CEN	105	99	97		105	45	87	68	88	83.5	79.5	16.5		110	103	87
CHA	107	96	94		105	45	87	90	88	88.5	79.5	19.5	47.5	107	102	
CON	98	83	92		91.5	40.5	73.5	72	74.5	88.5		49		98	96	71.5
COP	105	58	59		91.5	66.5	94	60	95	99	33	86	7	70	56	53
UGA	116	87.5	86.5	64	81	50.5	73.5	96	74.5	88.5		52.5		93	69	64.5
BUI	110				113	77	108.5	104	111.5	99						87
RWA	110				111	59	101	101	102	80.5		5				87
SOM	96	78	82	61	115.5	66.5	108.5	108	111.5	83.5	15.5	10.5		100	101	
ETH	58.5	63	57	36	115.5	66.5	108.5	105	111.5	41	15.5	49	70	85	78	68.5
SAF	74.5	75	76.5		55.5	86	69	60	68		33	66.5	26	22	21	19
MAG	114	89.5	89.5		85.5	50.5	79	60	78.5		79.5	19.5		80	83	77
MOR	47	32	23	5	25	77	39	30.5	40	46	15.5	44	42.5	54	49	48
ALG	61.5	17.5	24.5		63.5	77	73.5	78.5	78.5	73.5		7.5	17.5	41	38	24
TUN	50			24	38	77	54.5	30.5	57.5	52.5	46.5	23	32.5	67	72	77
LBY	80	64	70	58	63.8	86	79	95	82.5	60	79.5	62		64	51	41
SUD	52.5	60	43.5	51.5	55.5	66.5	66	50.5	68	65	79.5	100	35	63	62	77
IRN	42.5	29	38	8	43.5	97.5	63	54	63.5	26	79.5	94.5	54	49	29	10
TUR	23	15	86.5	3	27.5	33	21.5	50.5	23	30.5	46.5	86		40	52	33
IRQ	52.5	28	35.5		63.5	110.5	87	60	88	69.5	10.5	78.5	11.5	59	34	21
UAR	10	7	7	19	21.5	77	36	42.5	36	55.5		89	34	33	43	31
SYR	58.5	48	46.5	47	63.5	110.5	87	88.5	88	69.5	10.5	98	23.5	65	64	87
LEB	35.5	14	13.5	62	33.5	110.5	58	37	57.5	99	23	102	15	53	90	71.5
JOR	67.5	54	43.5	66	81	110.5	101	60	102	60	33	72	20	77	105	
ISR	13	35	24.5	12	25	110.5	49.5	30.5	45	99	15.5	94.5	22	42	55	64.5
SAU	58.5	65.5	52		75.5	110.5	98	86.5	98	73.5	23	86		61	23	20
YEM	84.5				105.5	110.5	113.5	114	116	36	79.5					
KUW	88	93	86.5		85.5	110.5	104	102	105	88.5		56.5	3	58	100	40
AFG	72	70.5	66	54	105	97.5	108.5	83	106.5	46	79.5	49		84	89	59
CHN	40.5				105	110.5	113.5	114	115	60	2			28	24	
MON	93				105	110.5	113.5	114	111.5	46				83	86	
CHT	28	68	70	6	68	86	82	47.5	78.5		46.5	46	52	57	54	37
KON	77				105	110.5	113.5	114	111.5	60	23					
KOS	58.5	76.5	92	25	60	86	73.5	47.5	71	99	79.5	37	73	48	80	30
JAP	8	9	8		10	97.5	23.5	22.5	23		79.5	80.5	74	7	7	6
IND	13	8	10	1	8	86	20	42.5	19.5	14	5	70		14	19	3
PAK	32	20.5	26	2	21.5	77	36	30.5	36	19	15.5	102	75	34	48	27
BUR	72	34	57	39	75.5	97.5	94	98.5	92.5	30.5	79.5	102	59	68	59	43
CEY	67.5	58	52	60	43.5	97.5	63	76	61.5		79.5	66.5	25	60	53	66
NEP	93	87.5	97	72	113	86	113.5	111	111.5	16.5	46.5			95	98	87
TAI	49	26	46.5	29	41	77	58	74.5	57.5	69.5	23	77	54	46	45	61
CAM	88	62	70		68	97.5	87	68	82.5	88.5	23	64.5	49.5	90	79	
LAO	93	65.5	89.5		71.5	97.5	91	80.5	88	50	33			108	111	
VTN	80				105	110.5	113.5	114	111.5	93	23			78	91	
VTS	70	52	74.5	22	55.5	97.5	73.5	47.5	71	65	23	74.5	61.5	62	85	60
MAL	86	61	70	45.5	55.5	97.5	73.5	88.5	71	65	23		6	18	16	

(continued)

N \ V	58	59	60	61	62	63	64	65	66	67	68	69	70	71	72
PHI	55.5	47	61.5	30	55.5	77	68	77	68	46.5	14.5	56.5	45	36	47
INS	26.5	17.5	27.5	27	38	97.5	60	42.5	57.5	99	23	80.5	52	37	8
AUL	46	44	35.5		12	97.5	25.5	15	27	46.5	74.5	56.5	13	12	25
NEW	90.5	79.5	50		33.5	97.5	54.5	37	57.5	46.5	26.5	30.5	35	28	51
USA	1	10	7	1	2	76.5	1	1	28	3	20	62	1	1	28
CAN	9	41.5	26	17	23	34	13	11	37	52.5	42	40	13	11	44
CUB	39.5	14.5	85	25	30	25	21.5	21	55	8.5	16	7	22.5	22	44
HAI	91	65	13	86.5	74	40	88	64.5	74	73.5	67.5	40	94	93.5	20
BOM	65	36	43.5	85	93	103.5	53	72.5	90	62	67.5	19.5	58.5	75	97.5
JAM	99	110	110	110.5	108.5	115	95.5	96.5	97	98.5	99	81	94	93.5	99.5
TRI	108.5	114	114	105.5	111	111	104.5	96.5	74	98.5	99	81	103	93.5	79
MEX	45	109	67	66	59.5	86.5	53	39	86	73.5	67.5		51.5	33	87
GUA	82	104.5	83.5	92	94.5	82	104.5	96.5	104	98.5	99	81	103	93.5	106
HON	96	93	73	78	50	109	104.5	96.5	102	98.5	99	81	103	93.5	104
ELS	86.5	101.5	68	75	28.5	97	104.5	96.5		98.5	99	81	103	93.5	2
NIC	92	86.5	54	100	81.5	50.5	95.5	96.5	74	98.5	99	81	94	93.5	79
COS	108.5	112	111	92	86.5	82	95.5	96.5	19	98.5	99	81	94	93.5	20
PAN	114	115	115	86.5	64	92.5	82.5	76	4.5	62	33.5		85	61.5	11.5
COL	59	93	75	64	62	25	63.5	60.5	32.5	43	10		62.5	55.5	20
VEN	42	69	79	70.5	70	50.5	60	64.5	40.5	73.5	67.5	40	62.5	55.5	20
ECU	71.5	78.5	48	75	28.5	6	82.5	46	19	98.5	99	81	79.5	39.5	20
PER	49	47.5	32	49	39	86.5	63.5	46	32.5	43	44.5		67	52	55.5
BRA	18	41.5	33	47	59.5	76.5	41.5	55	83	52.5	67.5		42	61.5	92
BOL	91	101.5	113	73	64	25	88	64.5	40.5	98.5	99	81	85	61.5	44
PAR	79.5	52.5	29.5	103	107	29.5	104.5	96.5	102	98.5	99	81	103	103.5	104
CHL	57	81	42	53	47	19.5	48.5	26	31	43	67.5	32	47	27.5	20
ARG	33	73.5	59	60	69	64	48.5	57.5	27	34.5	49.5	35	58.5	50	44
URU	74.5	93	89	83	84	14	72	96.5	19	52.5	67.5		71.5	93.5	24
UNK	3	21	21	5	15	86.5	3	8	52.5	8.5	29	56	3	8	50.5
IRE	60.5	69	69.5	78	43	3.5	82.5	46	54	73.5	67.5		79.5	39.5	8
NTH	16	33	39	51	77	29.5	57	68	19	24.5	33.5	19.5	62.5	73	34.5
BEL	20	50	43.5	40	41.5	8.5	33	31	12	43	44.5	19.5	39	39.5	31
LUX	86.5	89.5	97.5	103	114	64	112.5	112.5	108.5	98.5	99	81	111.5	111.5	111.5
FRN	5	22.5	24.5	9	17	57.5	4	6	49.5	14.5	26	51	4	6	55.5
SWZ	26	60.5	14	63	80	50.5	72	82.5	40.5	98.5	99	81	71.5	78	44
SPN	19	58.5	28	32	36	50.5	29.5	22	57	14.5	13	5	32	29.5	65
POR	35	16	4	45.5	49	40	72	24	8	98.5	41	19.5	32	29.5	28
GMW	6	28	18	8	11	64	6	4	47.5	22.5	27.5	57	5	5	50.5
GME	10	17.5	75.5	15	20	40	25.5	32	52.5	16.5	19	40	25	34.5	37.5
POL	12	38.5	86	24	34	22	29.5	41	66.5	12.5	9		27.5	45	67.5
AUS	44	86.5	100	61	75	64	67.5	84	99	82	99	81	67	80	92
HUN	38	69	103	43	48	25	43.5	65	60	27.5	24.5	2.5	42	61.5	55.5
CZE	13	25.5	75.5	12	14	97	34.5	59	29	19.5	5	25.5	34.5	66	32.5
ITA	8	45	45	47	53	34	31	50	64	34.5	39	14	29.5	49	50.5
ALB	67.5	78.5	71	56.5	54	29.5	48.5	40	74	19.5	21.5	19.5	47	39.5	87
YUG	22	25.5	8	20	38	50.5	18	37	36	52.5	67.5	46	18	32	37.5
GRC	41	43	46.5	35	35	92.5	21.5	28	40.5	34.5	21.5	52	25	25.5	59.5
CYP	90	69	57	65	22	92.5	57	29	87.5	73.5	67.5	54.5	55	23.5	87
BUL	27	19.5	75.5	52	71	34	43.5	79.5	11	43	33.5	32	44	79	14
RUM	21	38.5	97.5	22.5	37	45	20	35.5	45	52.5	67.5	40	20	48	62
USR	2	7	16	2	3	68	2	2	47.5	2	2	34	2	2	55.5
FIN	50	86.5	84.5	78	56	86.5	60	35.5	82	98.5	99	81	58.5	31	79
SWD	15	29.5	35	38	40	16	45.5	53	13	43	44.5		47	61.5	6.5
NOR	36	47.5	54	75	83	50.5	82.5	96.5	19	52.5	16	30	85	93.5	44
DEN	32	58.5	52	56.5	78	19.5	53	72.5	1	62	67.5		55	76.5	4
ICE	116	116	116	108	114	70.5	95.5	86.5	74	98.5	99	81	94	93.5	79
MLI	86.5	55	49	92	86.5	3.5	82.5	76	4.5	73.5	67.5		94	93.5	20
SEN	82	96.5	88	88	88	14	77	79.5	60	98.5	99	81	75.5	76.5	62

(continued)

N \ V	58	59	60	61	62	63	64	65	66	67	68	69	70	71	72
DAH	102	64	60	105.5	105	50.5	95.5	96.5	19	98.5	99	81	103	93.5	79
MAU	108.5	38.5	87	88	102	8.5	104.5	96.5		98.5	99	81	103	93.5	2
NIR	99	78.5	54	113.5	104	112	112.5	112.5	108.5	98.5	99	81	111.5	111.5	111.5
IVO	82	91	102	95.5	99	76.5	112.5	112.5	108.5	62	33.5	19.5	111.5	111.5	111.5
GUI	99	69	79	70.5	67	103.5	45.5	46	84.5	22.5	27.5	45	51.5	57	89
UPP	91	55	36	113.5	114	5	88	96.5	9.5	98.5	99	81	85	93.5	11.5
LBR	108.5	97.5	107	92	100	11.5	67.5	96.5	6.5	98.5	99	81	71.5	93.5	6.5
SIE	108.5	107	108	108	76	1	95.5	46	21	62	33.5		94	39.5	2
GHA	64	69	83.5	50	52	64	19	33.5	44	19.5	33.5	25.5	21	44	59.5
TOG	104	75.5	58	113.5	68	114	112.5	112.5	108.5	98.5	99	81	111.5	111.5	111.5
CAO	74.5	34	29.5	116	114	100	112.5	112.5	108.5	98.5	99	81	111.5	111.5	111.5
NIG	62	97.5	61	19	10	57.5	72	64.5	19	73.5	67.5		71.5	61.5	20
GAB	108.5	75.5	104.5	108	110	14	112.5	112.5	108.5	98.5	99	81	111.5	111.5	111.5
CEN	108.5	83	94.5	103	79	109	104.5	96.5		98.5	99	81	111.5	111.5	111.5
CHA	108.5	97.5	91.5	98	102	92.5	104.5	96.5		73.5	67.5		111.5	111.5	111.5
CON	99	50	62.5	101	108.5	109	112.5	112.5	108.5	98.5	99	81	111.5	111.5	111.5
COP	79.5	104.5	104.5	48	61	92.5	41.5	51	63	34.5	49.5	40	39	39.5	50.5
UGA	94.5	97.5	93	80	96	19.5	95.5	96.5	19	62	67.5	19.5	94	93.5	20
BUI	114	112	96	98	102	76.5	60	64.5	40.5	73.5	67.5	60.5	58.5	61.5	44
RWA	114	112	91.5	110.5	89.5	113	82.5	46	97	98.5	99	81	79.5	39.5	99.5
SOM	102.5	38.5	46.5	83	89.5	70.5	88	96.5	74	73.5	67.5		85	93.5	44
ETH	70	73.5	27	56.5	85	106.5	53	72.5	81	98.5	99	81	51.5	70.5	79
SAF	24	45	19	42	51	19.5	34.5	25	3	16.5	53	4	47	20	11.5
MAG	86.5	83	82	113.5	114	100	88	96.5	9.5	98.5	99	81	85	93.5	11.5
MOR	47.5	29.5	22.5	69	81.5	86.5	67.5	69.5	84.5	43	33.5	32	67	68	79
ALG	58	52.5	99	34	45	34	39.5	46	95	34.5	49.5	25.5	42	53.5	101.5
TUN	94.5	107	106	67	91	57.5	77	79.5	74	73.5	67.5	60.5	79.5	73	92
LBY	74.5	45	24.5	92	94.5	57.5	112.5	112.5	108.5	98.5	99	81	111.5	111.5	111.5
SUD	66	69	66	62	72.5	29.5	95.5	96.5	97	73.5	67.5	54.5	94	93.5	79
IRN	34	31	37	40	66	86.5	48.5	57.5	80	98.5	99	81	47	61.5	79
TUR	23	24	20	36	33	50.5	39.5	52	74	24.5	33.5	29	37	47	70.5
IRQ	43	15	15	29	32	40	32	42	24	62	67.5	50	32	46	28
UAR	28.5	14.5	65	6	4	40	11	15	62	5	7.5	9	12	17	69
SYR	52	6	31	14	18	57.5	15	18	56	6	11	28	15	21	55.5
LEB	67.5	50	41	45.5	46	34	72	82.5	40.5	52.5	67.5	11	75.5	93.5	32.5
JOR	60.5	3	10	10	7	76.5	27.5	33.5	51	12.5	23	53	27.5	34.5	53.5
ISR	25	5	9	3	1	70.5	9	13	34	7	6	47	9	16	34.5
SAU	37.5	9	56	44	44	92.5	36.5	38	65	52.5	16	63	36	39.5	65
YEM	84	60.5	17	56.5	57.5	103.5	77	79.5	94	52.5	67.5	40	85	93.5	95.5
KUW	71.5	83	109	68	72.5	8.5	63.5	76	2	98.5	99	81	62.5	73	5
AFG	78	97.5	69.5	95.5	105	76.5	95.5	96.5	74	98.5	99	81	94	93.5	79
CHN	4	12	40	4	8	45	6	10	58	1	1	15	6	14	67.5
MON	69	27	90	72	55	11.5	77	56	87.5	73.5	67.5		75.5	53.5	79
CHT	37	8	2	56.5	64	70.5	63.5	60.5	93	34.5	49.5	6	67	68	92
KON	39.5	11	50.5	21	12	97	38	54	26	27.5	38.5	40	39	51	20
KOS	46	32	12	22.5	13	64	36.5	19	68	30	16	11	34.5	18	72
JAP	14	97.5	79	16	16	40	14	12	30	27.5	24.5	49	14	7	37.5
IND	7	35	11	13	19	77.5	8	5	74	10	7.5	14	7	4	79
PAK	30	57	34	26	27	100	12	9	66.5	19.5	12	25.5	11	9	70.5
BUR	51	19.5	72	81	92	116	53	72.5	74	98.5	99	81	51.5	70.5	79
CEY	77	103	112	83	97	82	77	96.5	100	73.6	67.5		75.5	93.5	101.5
NEP	99	107	62.5	89	98	106.5	95.5	106.5	102	98.5	99	81	94	93.5	104
TAI	55	62.5	50.5	31	31	45	23.5	20	49.5	34.5	40	48	22.5	19	65
CAM	63	22.5	22.5	18	9	8.5	27.5	23	46	11	4	2.5	29.5	27.5	44
LAO	74.5	17.5	3	37	24	40	57	29.5	60	62	67.5	19.5	55	23.5	62
VTN	28.5	1	6	7	5	57.5	7	7	89	4	3	1	8	10	95.5
VTS	31	4	5	11	6	64	16	16	92	34.5	49.5	59	16.5	15	97.5
MAL	53.5	62.5	64	40	26	103.5	23.5	17	91	62	67.5	40	19	12	92
PHI	56	89.5	81	30	25	25	17	14	25	52.5	16	11	16.5	13	28
INS	11	2	1	28	21	76.5	10	3	35	27.5	38.5	58	10	3	37.5
AUL	17	55	38	33	41.5	17	25.5	27	14	43	44.5	8	25	25.5	28
NEW	53.5	78.5	101	56.5	57.5	2	67.5	69.5	6.5	43	67.5		67	68	9

EXERCISES

1 Consider this list of eighty-seven nations. You are to place the nations into one of the following eight boxes representing the eight nation genotypes. Use any criteria that you wish to *estimate* each nation's position.

United States	Netherlands	Norway	Israel
Canada	Belgium	Denmark	Afghanistan
Cuba	France	Senegal	Red China
Haiti	Switzerland	Upper Volta	China (Taiwan)
Dominican Republic	Spain	Ghana	North Korea
Jamaica	Portugal	Camoroun	South Korea
Mexico	West Germany	Nigeria	Japan
Guatemala	East Germany	Chad	India
Honduras	Poland	Congo (Ki.)	Pakistan
El Salvador	Austria	Uganda	Burma
Costa Rica	Hungary	Ethiopia	Ceylon
Panama	Czechoslovakia	South Africa	Nepal
Colombia	Italy	Morocco	Thailand
Venezuela	Albania	Algeria	Cambodia
Ecuador	Yugoslavia	Tunisia	Laos
Peru	Greece	Iran	South Vietnam
Brazil	Cyprus	Turkey	Malaysia
Bolivia	Bulgaria	Iraq	Philippines
Argentina	Rumania	United Arab Rep.	Indonesia
Uruguay	USSR/Russia	Syria	Australia
United Kingdom	Finland	Lebanon	New Zealand
Ireland	Sweden	Jordan	

Large-Developed-Open	Small-Developed-Open
Large-Developed-Closed	Small-Developed-Closed
Large-Underdeveloped-Open	Small-Underdeveloped-Open
Large-Underdeveloped-Closed	Small-Underdeveloped-Closed

After this exercise is completed, the class should discuss the various criteria employed by its members. The rationale for each criterion and its implications should be examined. These should be compared to Figure A.2.

2 In this exercise you are to construct a series of propositions by using variables from Figure A.3. In each instance a variable category will be given; you are to supply a variable from this category and use it in a proposition.

Example: Independent Variable — Size
Dependent Variable — Economic Output
Proposition: The greater a nation's total GNP (variable 3), the greater its exports (variable 56).

A Independent Variable — Economic Development
Dependent Variable — Political Output

B Independent Variable — Political Accountability
Dependent Variable — Military Output

C Independent Variable — Societal
Dependent Variable — Political Output

D Independent Variable — Political Output
Dependent Variable — Economic Output

E Independent Variable — Governmental
Dependent Variable — Political Accountability

3 Below is a printout of the first ten cards in the raw data deck. The column number appears at the top. You are to use this printout to answer the following questions.

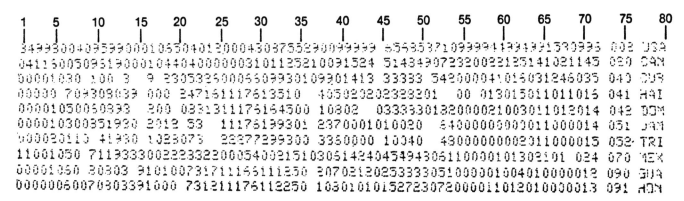

Example 1:   What number appears in column 5 for Canada (CAN)? _____6_____.

Example 2:   What is Mexico's value for variable 8, "KWH per capita"?
0 (column 8).

A   _____ Column 42 for USA.

B   _____ Column 25 for GUA (Guatemala).

C   _____ Numeric code for HAI (Haiti).

D   _____ Cuba's (CUB) value for "Total Exports."

E   _____ Alpha code for country 052.

F   _____ Country 070's value for "Percent Communist Vote."

4   You are to use the codebook on pages 199 to 207 to answer the following questions.

A   List the numbers of the 9 variables which appear only at the ordinal level.

B   One of the ordinal variables, "Political Participation by Military," has three category values. Identify them.

_____

_____

_____

C   A historically Western nation (variable 23) is signified by the value _____.

5   You are to answer the following questions by using the information found in the codebook, pages 199 to 207 in this learning package.

Example: How many cases possess a raw value of 3 for variable 1, "Total Population"? _____2_____.

A   How many cases possess the lowest value for variable 2 "Total Land Area"? _____

B   If a nation possessed a total GNP value of $235,000, it would have a value of _____ in the raw data deck.

C   If a nation was coded as "4" for kilowatt hours of electrical production (variable 4), its KWH ranges from _____ to _____.

D   How many nations possess a competitive electoral system? _____ These are coded by the value _____.

6   The definitions and citations for each variable are given on pages 209 to 226. You are to use this information to answer the questions below.

A   The information for "Political Participation by Military" (variable 13) is extracted from what source? _____

B   Data for "Legal Status of the Communist Party" (variable 12) are taken from what years? _____

C   How is foreign conflict defined?

7   You are to use the rank orderings for the 63 interval variables (pages 231 to 238) to answer the following questions. Use the country code list on page 196.

Example: The United States is ranked _____ on variable 1, "Total Population."

A   Colombia is ranked _____ on variable 4, "KWH of Electrical Production."

B   The nation ranked 38th on variable 10, "Freedom of the Press," is

_____.

C   Two countries, _____ and _____, are tied for the 11th position on variable 20, and thus have a rank order of 11.5.

NOTES

1.   The data constituting the analysis deck were created from a larger data file archived in the Ohio State University's Polimetrics Laboratory. Some indicators were retrieved from the data base of the Comparative Analysis of Policy Environments (CAPE) project under the direction of Philip M. Burgess. Others were obtained from data sets supplied in partially proofed form by the International Relations Archive of the Inter-University Consortium for Political Research (ICPR). The Consortium bears no responsibility for either the analysis or interpretations presented here.

2.   It is important to note that the framework is suggested here only for convenience and in the interests of clarity and continuity with material presented earlier. Given the low level of theoretical development in the field, students should be urged to develop original or synthetic approaches to the study of comparative and international politics and should not become bound to this or any other approach.

3.   The interval size was obtained in three steps. First, the initial interval size was determined by dividing the range by 10 (n). Second, the original interval size was multiplied by n+1 to obtain the final interval size. Third, the lowest interval began with a number that was a multiple of that interval size and whose lowest score fell in the middle of the category. For example, if the range for a variable was 1 to 3, the lowest category would range from 0.89 to 1.11 (so that 1 fell in the middle.)

BIBLIOGRAPHY

Alger, Chadwick F. "Interaction and Negotiation in a Committee of the United Nations General Assembly." *Papers of the Peace Research Society* (International) 5 (1966): 141–59.

Alger, Chadwick F., and Brams, Steven J. "Patterns of Representation in National Capitals and IGO's." *World Politics* 19 (July 1967):646–63.

Alker, Hayward R. "Dimensions of Conflict in the General Assembly." *American Political Science Review* 58 (September 1964):642–57.

Alker, Hayward R., Jr. *Mathematics and Politics.* New York: Macmillan Company, 1965.

Alker, Hayward R., Jr., and Russett, Bruce M. *World Politics in the General Assembly.* New Haven, Connecticut: Yale University Press, 1965.

Almond, Gabriel A., and Verba, Sidney. *The Civic Culture.* Princeton: Princeton University Press, 1963.

Altman, Irwin, and McGrath, Joseph E. *Small Group Research: A Synthesis and Critique of the Field.* New York: Holt, Rinehart and Winston, 1966.

Anderson, Lee F. et al. *Legislative Roll-Call Analysis.* Evanston: Northwestern University Press, 1966.

Azar, Edward. "Analysis of International Events." *Peace Research Reviews* 4 (November 1970):1–113.

Banks, Arthur S. *Cross-Polity Time-Series Data.* Cambridge, Massachusetts: MIT Press, 1971.

Banks, Arthur S., and Gregg, Phillip M. "Grouping Political Systems: Q-Factor Analysis of *A Cross-Polity Survey.*" *American Behavioral Scientist* 9 (November 1965): 3–6.

Banks, Arthur S., and Textor, Robert B. *A Cross-Polity Survey.* Cambridge, Massachusetts: MIT Press, 1963.

Bauer, Raymond A. *Social Indicators.* Cambridge, Massachusetts: MIT Press, 1966.

Bellman, Richard. *Introduction to the Mathematical Theory of Control Processes.* Vol. 1. New York: Academic Press, 1967.

Bennett, A. G. *Graphic Methods of Solving Optical Problems.* London: Hatton Press, 1970.

Benson, Oliver. *Political Science Laboratory.* Columbus, Ohio: Charles E. Merrill Publishers, 1969.

Berelson, Bernard R., Lazarsfeld, Paul F., and McPhee, William N. *Voting.* Chicago: University of Chicago Press, 1954.

Berelson, Bernard, and Steiner, Gary A. *Human Behavior.* New York: Harcourt, Brace, and World, 1964.

Bergson, Abram. "Reliability and Usability of Soviet Statistics: A Summary Appraisal." *The American Statistician* 7 (June–July 1953):19–23.

Beveridge, W. I. B. *The Art of Scientific Investigation.* New York: Vintage Books, 1957.

Bisco, Ralph L. *Data Bases, Computers, and the Social Sciences.* New York: Wiley-Interscience, 1970.

Blau, Peter. "Structural Effects." *American Sociological Review* (April 1960):178–193.

Bloomfield, Lincoln P., and Whaley, Barton. "The Political-Military Exercise: A Progress Report." *Orbis* 8 (Winter 1965):854–70.

Bobrow, Davis, and Schwartz, Judah, eds. *Computers and the Policy-Making Community.* Englewood Cliffs, New Jersey: Prentice-Hall, Inc., 1968.

Boguslaw, Robert. *The New Utopians, A Study of System Design and Social Change.* Englewood Cliffs, New Jersey: Prentice-Hall, 1965.

Borko, Harold, ed. *Computer Applications in the Behavioral Sciences.* Englewood Cliffs, New Jersey: Prentice-Hall, 1962.

Boulding, Kenneth E. *Conflict and Defense: A General Theory.* New York: Harper and Row, 1962.

Bowles, Edmund A., ed. *Computers in Humanistic Research.* Englewood Cliffs: Prentice-Hall, 1967.

Brody, Robert A. "Some Systematic Effects of the Spread of Nuclear Weapons Technology: A Study Through Simulation of a Multi-Nuclear Future." *Journal of Conflict Resolution* 7 (1963):663–753.

Brown, Harrison, and Real, James. "The Community of Fear." In *A World Without War,* edited by Walter Millis. New York: Washington Square Press, 1960.

Burgess, Philip M. *Elite Images and Foreign Policy Outcomes: A Study of Norway.* Columbus, Ohio: The Ohio State University Press, 1967.

Burgess, Philip M. "International Relations Theory: Prospect: 1970–1995." Paper presented at the annual meeting of the American Political Science Association in Los Angeles, September 1970 (mimeo).

Burgess, Philip M., and Moore, David W. "Inter-Nation Alliances: An Inventory and Appraisal of Propositions." In *Political Science Annual, Volume Three*, edited by James A. Robinson. Indianapolis: Bobbs-Merrill Publishing Company, 1972.

Burgess, Philip M., and Munton, Donald. "An Inventory of Archived and Fugitive International Relations Data." In *Theory and Practice of Events Research*, edited by Edward E. Azar and Joseph D. Ben-Dak. New York: Gordon and Breach Science Publishers.

Burgess, Philip M., and Peterson, Lawrence E. "Quality Control Procedures for the Collection and Preliminary Processing of Aggregate Data." Columbus, Ohio: The Ohio State University, Behavioral Sciences Laboratory, BSL Research Report #006, December 1969 (mimeo).

Burgess, Philip M., and Peterson, Lawrence E. "A Single Case/Single Variable Format for Data Base Management." Columbus, Ohio: The Ohio State University, Behavioral Sciences Laboratory, BSL Research Report #005, January 1970 (mimeo).

Burgess, Philip M., Peterson, Lawrence E., and Frantz, Carl D. "Organizing Simulated Environments." *Social Education* 33 (February 1969):185–93.

Burgess, Philip M., and Robinson, James A. "Alliances and the Theory of Collective Action: A Simulation of Coalition Processes." *Midwest Journal of Political Science* 13 (May 1969):194–218.

Campbell, Donald T. "Reforms as Experiments." *American Psychologist* 24 (April 1969):409–29.

Campbell, Donald T., and Stanley, Julian C. *Experimental and Quasi-Experimental Designs for Research*. Chicago: Rand McNally, 1963.

Cattell, R. B. "The Dimensions of Culture Patterns by Factorization of National Characters." *Journal of Abnormal and Social Psychology* 44 (1949):443–69.

Churchman, C. West. *The Systems Approach*. New York: Delacorte Press, 1968.

Cobb, Roger W., and Elder, Charles. *International Community*. New York: Holt, Rinehart and Winston, 1970.

Comparative Analysis of Policy Environments Project (CAPE, 1970). Philip M. Burgess, Director, Columbus, Ohio: The Behavioral Science Laboratory, Ohio State University.

Coplin, William D., ed. *Simulation in the Study of Politics*. Chicago: Markham Publishing Company, 1968.

Coplin, William D. *Introduction to International Politics: A Theoretical Overview*. Chicago: Markham Publishing Co., 1971.

Corson, Walter. "Conflict and Cooperation in East-West Crises: Measurement and Prediction." Paper presented at the Events Data Measurement Conference, Michigan State University, April 1970.

Coser, Lewis. *Functions of Social Conflict*. Glencoe, Illinois: The Free Press, 1956.

Cutler, Neal E. *Emerging Data Sources for Comparative and International Studies*. Beverly Hills: Sage Publishing Co., 1974.

Dahl, Robert A. *A Preface to Democratic Theory*. Chicago: University of Chicago Press, 1956.

Dalkey, Norman C. *Studies in the Quality of Life; Delphi and Decision-Making*. Lexington, Mass.: Lexington Books, 1972.

Dalkey, Norman, and Helmer, Olaf. "An Experimental Application of the Delphi Method to the Use of Experts." *Management Science* 9 (April 1963):458–67.

Davis, James A. et al. "A Technique for Analyzing the Effects of Group Composition." *American Sociological Review* 26 (1961):215–25.

Dawson, Richard E. "Simulation in the Social Sciences." In *Simulation in Social Science: Readings*, edited by Harold Guetzkow. Englewood Cliffs, New Jersey: Prentice-Hall, 1962.

Deutsch, Karl W. *Political Community at the International Level.* Garden City, New York: Doubleday, 1954.

Deutsch, Karl W., and Edinger, Lewis J. *Germany Rejoins the Powers: Mass Opinion, Interest Groups, and Elites in Contemporary German Foreign Policy.* Stanford, California: Stanford University Press, 1959.

Deutsch, Karl W. et al. *Political Community and the North Atlantic Area.* Princeton: Princeton University Press, 1957.

Deutsch, Karl W. et al. *French and German Elite Responses, 1964: Codebook and Data.* New Haven: Yale University, 1966.

Deutsch, Karl W. et al. *France, Germany, and the Western Alliance.* New York: Charles Scribner's Sons, 1967.

Dogan, Mattei, and Rokkan, Stein, eds. *Quantitative Ecological Analysis in the Social Sciences.* Cambridge: MIT Press, 1969.

Dougherty, James E., and Pfaltzgraff, Robert L., Jr. *Contending Theories of International Relations.* Philadelphia: J. B. Lippincott Company, 1971.

Downie, N. M., and Heath, R. W. *Basic Statistical Methods.* New York: Harper and Row, 1965.

Downs, Anthony. *An Economic Theory of Democracy.* New York: Harper and Row, 1957.

Dror, Yehezkel. *Design For Policy Sciences.* New York: American Elsevier Publishing Company, Inc., 1971.

Dubin, Robert. *Theory Building.* New York: The Free Press, 1969.

Duncan, Otis D. "Social Forecasting: The State of the Art." *Public Interest* 17 (1969): 89–118.

East, Maurice, and Gregg, Philip M. "Factors Influencing Cooperation and Conflict in the International System." *International Studies Quarterly* 11 (1967):244–69.

Etzioni, Amitai, and Lehman, Edward W. "Some Dangers in 'Valid' Social Measurement." *The Annals of the American Academy of Political and Social Science* 373 (1967):1–15.

Eulau, Heinz. "Segments of Political Science Most Susceptible to Behavioristic Treatment." In *The Limits of Behaviorism in Political Science,* edited by James C. Charlesworth. Philadelphia: American Academy of Political and Social Science, 1962 (mimeo).

Feierabend, Ivo K., and Rosalind L. "Aggressive Behaviors within Polities, 1948–1962: A Cross-National Study." *Journal of Conflict Resolution* 10 (September 1966): 249–71.

Fisher, R. and Yates, R. *Statistical Tables for Biological, Agricultural, and Medical Research.* Edinburgh and London: Oliver & Boyd, Ltd., 1963.

Fitzgibbon, Russell H. "Measuring Democratic Change in Latin America." *Journal of Politics* 29 (February 1967):129–66.

Forrester, Jay W. *World Dynamics.* Cambridge, Mass.: Wright-Allen Press, 1971.

Franzblau, Abraham N. *Primer of Statistics for Non-Statisticians.* New York: Harcourt Brace Jovanovich, 1971.

Galtung, Johan. "Summit Meetings and International Relations." *Journal of Peace Research* 1 (1964):36–54.

Galtung, Johan. *Theory and Methods of Social Research.* Oslo, Norway: Universitetsforlaget, 1967.

Garson, G. David. *Handbook of Political Science Methods.* Boston: Holbrook, 1971.

Giffin, Sidney F. *The Crisis Game: Simulating International Conflict.* Garden City, New York: Doubleday, 1965.

Goldhamer, Herbert, and Speier, Hans. "Some Observations on Political Gaming." *World Politics* 12 (1959):71–83.

Green, Philip. *Deadly Logic*. Columbus, Ohio: The Ohio State University Press, 1966.

Guetzkow, Harold, ed. *Simulation in Social Science: Readings*. Englewood Cliffs, New Jersey: Prentice-Hall, 1962.

Guetzkow, Harold S. *Inter-Nation Simulation*. Chicago: Science Research Associates, Inc., 1963.

Guetzkow, Harold S. "Isolation and Collaboration: A Partial Theory of Inter-Nation Relations." *Journal of Conflict Resolution* 1 (March 1967):48–68.

Guetzkow, Harold S. et al. *Simulation in International Relations: Developments for Research and Teaching*. Englewood Cliffs, New Jersey: Prentice-Hall, 1972.

Guetzkow, Harold, and Jensen, Lloyd. "Research Activities on Simulated International Processes." *Background* 9 (February 1966):261–74.

Gurr, Ted R. *Politimetrics*. Englewood Cliffs, New Jersey: Prentice-Hall, Inc., 1972.

Haas, Ernst. *Beyond the Nation-State; Functionalism and International Organization*. Stanford: Stanford University Press, 1964.

Haas, E. R., and Whiting, A. S. *Dynamics of International Relations*. New York: McGraw-Hill, 1956.

Haas, Michael. "Comparative Analysis." *Western Political Quarterly* 15 (June 1962): 294–303.

Haas, Michael. "International Relations Theory." In *Approaches to the Study of Political Science*, edited by Michael Haas and Henry S. Kariel. San Francisco: Chandler Publishing Company, 1970.

Helmer, Olaf. *Social Technology*. New York: Basic Books, 1966.

Hergenhahn, Baldwin R. *A Self-Directing Introduction to Psychological Experimentation*. Monterey: Brooks/Cole Publishing Co., 1970.

Hermann, Charles F. "Validation Problems in Games and Simulations with Special Reference to Models of International Politics." *Behavioral Science* 12 (May 1967): 216–31.

Hermann, Charles F. "What is a Foreign Policy Event?" Paper presented at the Events Data Conference, Michigan State University, April 1970.

Hermann, Charles F., and Hermann, Margaret G. "An Attempt to Simulate the Outbreak of World War I." *American Political Science Review* 61 (1967):400–416.

Herz, John. "The Rise and Demise of the Territorial State." *World Politics* 9 (July 1957).

Herz, John H. *International Politics in the Atomic Age*. New York: Columbia University Press, 1962.

Hilgard, Ernest; Atkinson, Richard C.; and Atkinson, Rita I. *Introduction to Psychology*. 5th ed. New York: Harcourt Brace Jovanovich, 1971.

Hitch, Charles J. *Decision-Making for Defense*. Berkeley: The University of California Press, 1965.

Holsti, K. J. "Retreat from Utopia: International Relations Theory, 1945–1970." Paper presented at the 66th annual meeting of the American Political Science Association meeting in Los Angeles, September 1970.

Holsti, K. J. *International Politics: A Framework for Analysis*. 2nd ed. Englewood Cliffs, New Jersey: Prentice-Hall, Inc., 1972.

Holsti, Ole R. "The Belief System and National Images: A Case Study." *Journal of Conflict Resolution* 6 (September 1962):244–52.

Holsti, Ole R. "Content Analysis in Political Research." In *Computers and the Policy-Making Community*, edited by Davis B. Bobrow and Judah L. Schwartz. Englewood Cliffs, New Jersey: Prentice-Hall, 1968.

Holsti, Ole R. *Content Analysis for the Social Sciences and Humanities*. Reading, Mass.: Addison-Wesley, 1969.

Holsti, Ole, and Brody, Richard A. "Measuring Affect and Action in International Reaction Models: Empirical Materials From the 1962 Cuban Crisis." In *International Politics and Foreign Policy*, edited by James N. Rosenau. New York: Free Press, 1969.

Holsti, Ole; Brody, Richard; and North, Robert. "The Management of International Crisis: Affect and Action in Soviet-American Relations." *Journal of Peace Research* (1964):170–90.

Holsti, Ole R.; North, Robert C.; and Brody, Richard A. "Perception and Action in the 1914 Crisis." In *Quantitative International Politics*, edited by J. David Singer. New York: The Free Press, 1968.

Hopkins, R. F. and Mansbach, R. W. *Structure and Process in International Politics.* New York: Harper and Row, 1973.

Hovet, Thomas. *Bloc Politics in the UN.* Cambridge, Massachusetts: Harvard University Press, 1960.

Hovet, Thomas. *Africa in the United Nations.* Evanston, Illinois: Northwestern University Press, 1963.

Hudson, Michael C. "Some Quantitative Indicators for Explaining and Evaluating National Political Performance." Paper presented at the annual meeting of the American Political Science Association in Chicago, September 1967.

Huff, Darrell. *How to Lie with Statistics.* New York: W. W. Norton and Company, 1954.

Huntington, Samuel P. "Patterns of Violence in World Politics." In *Changing Patterns of Military Politics*, edited by S. P. Huntington. New York: Free Press, 1962.

Irish, Marian D., and Prothro, James W. *The Politics of American Democracy.* 5th ed. Englewood Cliffs, New Jersey: Prentice-Hall, 1971.

Janda, Kenneth. "Retrieving Information for a Comparative Study of Political Parties." In *Approaches to the Study of Party Organization*, edited by William J. Crotty. Boston: Allyn and Bacon, 1968.

Janda, Kenneth. *Data Processing: Applications to Political Research.* Evanston, Illinois: Northwestern University Press, 1969.

Jensen, Lloyd. "American Foreign Policy Elites and the Prediction of International Events." *Peace Research Society (International) Papers* 5 (1966):199–209.

Jones, E. Terrence. *Conducting Politics Research.* New York: Harper and Row, 1971.

Jones, Susan D., and Singer, J. David. *Beyond Conjecture in International Politics: Abstracts of Data-Based Research.* Itasca, Ill.: F. E. Peacock, 1972.

Kaplan, Morton A. *System and Process in International Politics.* New York: Wiley, 1957.

Kaplan, Morton A., ed. *New Approaches to International Relations.* New York: St. Martin's Press, 1968.

Kelley, E. W. "Techniques of Studying Coalition Formation." *Midwest Journal of Political Science* 12 (February 1968):62–84.

Kent, George. "Foreign Policy Analysis: Middle East." Paper presented at the 1969 annual meeting of the Peace Research Society (International), Ann Arbor, Michigan, November 11–12, 1969.

Kissinger, Henry A. *The Necessity for Choice; Prospects of American Foreign Policy.* New York: Harper, 1961.

Klingberg, Frank L. "Studies in Measurement of the Relations Among Sovereign States." *Psychometrika* 6 (1941):335–52.

Knorr, Klaus, and Rosenau, James N., eds. *Contending Approaches to International Politics.* Princeton, New Jersey: Princeton University Press, 1969.

Knorr, Klaus, and Verba, Sidney, eds. *The International System.* Princeton: Princeton University Press, 1961.

Kriesberg, Louis. *Social Processes in International Politics*. New York: Wiley, 1968.

Lasswell, Harold D. "The Scientific Study of International Relations." *Yearbook of World Affairs* (1958):1–28.

Lasswell, Harold D. *The Future of Political Science*. New York: Atherton Press, 1963.

Lasswell, Harold D. *A Preview of the Policy Sciences*. New York: American Elsevier Publishing Company, Inc., 1972.

Lazarsfeld, Paul F., and Menzel, Herbert. "On the Relation Between Individual and Collective Properties." In *Complex Organizations*, edited by A. Etzioni. New York: Holt, Rinehart, and Winston, 1961.

Lazarsfeld, Paul F., and Rosenberg, Morris, eds. *The Language of Social Research*. New York: The Free Press, 1955.

Leng, Russell J., and Singer, J. David. "Toward a Multi-Theoretical Typology of International Behavior." Paper presented at the Michigan State University Events Data Conference in East Lansing, April 1970.

Lerner, Daniel, and Lasswell, Harold D. *The Policy Sciences: Recent Developments in Scope and Method*. Stanford, California: Stanford University Press, 1951.

Lijphart, Arend. "The Analysis of Bloc Voting in the General Assembly: A Critique and a Proposal." *American Political Science Review* 52 (December 1963):902–17.

Lindzey, Gardner, and Aronson, Elliot. *The Handbook of Social Psychology*. 5 vols. Reading, Massachusetts: Addison-Wesley Publishing Company, 1969.

Liska, George. *Nations in Alliance*. Baltimore: The Johns Hopkins University Press, 1962.

Luttbeg, Norman R., and Kahn, Melvin A. "Ph.D. Training In Political Science." *Midwest Journal of Political Science* 12 (August 1968):303–29.

Lyden, Fremont J., and Miller, Ernest G. *Planning, Programming, Budgeting; A Systems Approach to Management*. 2nd ed. Chicago: Markham, 1972.

Macridis, Roy C., ed. *Foreign Policy in World Politics*. Englewood Cliffs, New Jersey: Prentice-Hall, 1967.

March, James G., and Simon, Herbert. *Organizations*. New York: John Wiley, 1958.

McClelland, Charles A. "Access to Berlin: The Quantity and Variety of Events, 1948–1963." In *Quantitative International Politics*, edited by J. David Singer. New York: Free Press, 1968a.

McClelland, Charles A. "International Interaction Analysis: Basic Research and Some Practical Uses." Los Angeles: University of Southern California, WEIS Project, November 1968b (mimeo).

McClelland, Charles A. "On the Fourth Wave: Past and Future in the Study of International Systems." Los Angeles: University of Southern California, December 1968c (mimeo).

McClelland, Charles A. *Theory and the International System*. New York: Macmillan, 1966.

McClelland, Charles A. "International Interaction Analysis in the Predictive Mode." Los Angeles: University of Southern California, WEIS Project Technical Report #3, January 1969 (mimeo).

McClelland, Charles A. "Some Effects on Theory from the International Event Analysis Movement." Los Angeles: University of Southern California, WEIS Project, February 1970a.

McClelland, Charles A. "Two Conceptual Issues in the Quantitative Analysis of International Event Data." Paper presented at the Events Data Measurement Conference, Michigan State University, April 1970b.

McClelland, Charles A., and Hoggard, Gary D. "Conflict Patterns in the Interactions Among Nations." In *International Politics and Foreign Policy*, edited by James N. Rosenau. New York: Free Press, 1969.

McGowan, Patrick J., and Shapiro, Howard B. *The Comparative Study of Foreign Policy: A Survey of Scientific Findings.* Beverly Hills: Sage Publications, Inc., 1973.

Meadows, Donella H. et al. *The Limits of Growth; A Report for the Club of Rome's Project on the Predicament of Mankind.* New York: Universe Books, 1972.

Merritt, Richard L., and Puchala, Donald J., eds. *Western European Perspectives on International Affairs: Public Opinion Studies and Evaluations.* New York: Praeger, 1967.

Merritt, Richard L., and Pyszka, Gloria J. *The Student Political Scientist's Handbook.* New York: Harper and Row, 1969.

Merritt, Richard L., and Rokkan, Stein, eds. *Comparing Nations: The Use of Quantitative Data in Cross-National Research.* New Haven: Yale University Press, 1966.

Miles, Edward. "Organizations and Integration in International Systems." *International Studies Quarterly* 12 (1968):196–224.

Milstein, Jeffrey S., and Mitchell, William. "Computer Simulation of International Processes: The Vietnam War and the Pre-World War I Naval Race." *Peace Research Society (International) Papers* 12 (1969).

Montgomery, John D. *The Politics of Foreign Aid.* New York: Praeger, 1962.

Morgenstern, Oskar. *On the Accuracy of Economic Observations.* 2nd ed. Princeton: Princeton University Press, 1963.

Morgenthau, Hans J. *Politics Among Nations.* New York: Alfred A. Knopf, 1962.

Mueller, John. *Approaches to Measurement in International Relations.* New York: Appleton-Century-Crofts, 1969.

North, Robert C., and Choucri, Nazli. "Background Conditions to the Outbreak of the First World War." *Peace Research Society (International) Papers* 9 (1968):125–137.

North, Robert C. et al., eds. *Content Analysis: A Handbook with Application for the Study of International Crises.* Evanston, Illinois: Northwestern University Press, 1963.

Olson, Mancur, Jr. *The Logic of Collective Action.* Cambridge, Massachusetts: Harvard University Press, 1965.

Olson, Mancur, Jr., and Zeckhauser, Richard. "An Economic Theory of Alliances." *Review of Economics and Statistics* 48 (August 1966):266–79.

Paige, Glenn D. "Proposition-Building in the Study of Comparative Administration." Princeton: Princeton University, 1963 (mimeo).

Paige, Glenn D. *The Korean Decision.* New York: The Free Press, 1968.

Palmer, Norman D. "International Studies in the 1970's." Inaugural address before the annual meeting of the International Studies Association in Pittsburgh, April 3, 1970.

Palumbo, Dennis J. *Statistics in Political and Behavioral Science.* New York: Appleton-Century-Crofts, 1969.

Park, Tong-whan. "A Guide to Data Sources in International Relations: Annotated Bibliography with Lists of Variables." Evanston, Illinois: Northwestern University, Department of Political Science, 1968.

Passell, Peter; Roberts, Marc; and Ross, Leonard. Book Review of *The Limits of Growth, World Dynamics,* and *Urban Dynamics. New York Times.* April 2, 1972, pages 1, 10, 12, 13.

Pirro, Ellen B. *International Relations: A Laboratory Manual.* Boston: Little, Brown and Co., 1972.

Platig, E. Raymond. *International Relations Research.* Santa Barbara, California: Carnegie Endowment for International Peace, 1966.

Pool, Ithiel de Sola. *Symbols of Internationalism*. Stanford: Stanford University Press, 1951.

Pool, Ithiel de Sola. *The Prestige Papers: A Survey of Their Editorials*. Stanford: Stanford University Press, 1952a.

Pool, Ithiel de Sola. *Symbols of Democracy*. Stanford: Stanford University Press, 1952b.

Poole, DeWitt C. *The Conduct of Foreign Relations Under Modern Democratic Conditions*. New Haven: Yale University Press, 1924.

Population Reference Bureau, Inc., Washington, D.C.

Pryor, Frederic L. *Public Expenditures in Communist and Capitalist Nations*. Homewood, Illinois: Irwin, 1968.

Pryor, Frederic L. "Macroeconomic Aspects of Defense Expenditures." Swarthmore, Pennsylvania: Swarthmore College, Department of Economics, n.d. (mimeo).

Rapoport, Anatol. "Games Which Simulate Deterrence and Disarmament." *Peace Research Reviews* 1 (August 1967):1–83.

Raser, John R. *Simulation and Society; An Exploration of Scientific Gaming*. Boston: Allyn and Bacon, 1969.

Rath, Gustave J. *Punched Card Data Processing*. Chicago: Science Research Associates, 1966.

Reischauer, Edwin O. *Beyond Vietnam: The United States and Asia*. New York: Random House, 1967.

Riemer, Neal. *The Revival of Democratic Theory*. New York: Appleton-Century-Crofts, 1962.

Riker, William H. *The Theory of Political Coalitions*. New Haven: Yale University Press, 1962.

Rivlin, Alice. *Systematic Thinking for Social Action*. Washington: Brookings Institution, 1971.

Robinson, E. A. G. "The Size of the Nation and the Cost of Administration." In *Economic Consequences of the Size of Nations*, edited by E. A. G. Robinson. New York: St. Martin's Press, 1967.

Robinson, James A., ed. *Political Science Annual, Volume Two*. Indianapolis: Bobbs-Merrill, 1970a.

Robinson, James A. "Participant Observation, Political Internships, and Research." In *Political Science Annual, Volume Two*, edited by James A. Robinson. Indianapolis: Bobbs-Merrill, 1970b.

Robinson, James A. "Crisis Decision-Making: An Inventory and Appraisal of Concepts, Theories, Hypotheses, and Techniques of Analysis." In *Political Science Annual, Volume Two*, edited by James A Robinson. Indianapolis: Bobbs-Merrill, 1970c.

Rokkan, Stein. "The Development of Cross-National Comparative Research: A Review of Current Problems and Possibilities." *Social Science Information* 1:1962.

Rokkan, Stein, ed. *Comparative Research Across Cultures and Nations*. Paris: Mouton, 1968.

Rosecrance, Richard N. *Action and Reaction in World Politics*. Boston: Little, Brown, and Company, 1963.

Rosenau, James N., ed. *International Politics and Foreign Policy*. 1st ed. New York: Free Press, 1961.

Rosenau, James N. "Pre-Theories and Theories of Foreign Policy." In *Approaches to Comparative and International Politics*, edited by R. Barry Farrell. Evanston: Northwestern University Press, 1966.

Rosenau, James N. "Private Preferences and Political Responsibilities: The Relative Potency of Individual and Role Variables in the Behavior of U.S. Senators." In *Quantitative International Politics*, edited by J. David Singer. New York: Free Press, 1968.

Rosenau, James N., ed. *International Politics and Foreign Policy.* 2nd ed. New York: Free Press, 1969.

Rosenau, James N. *Race in International Politics: A Dialogue in Five Parts.* Monograph Series (Vol. 7, No. 2, 1970). Graduate School of International Studies, Denver: University of Denver.

Rossi, Peter H., and Williams, Walter. *Evaluation of Social Programs: Theory, Practice, and Politics.* New York: Seminar Press, 1972.

Rummel, R. J. "The Dimensions of Conflict Behavior within and between Nations." *General Systems Yearbook* 8 (1963):1–50.

Rummel, R. J. "Some Dimensions in the Foreign Behavior of Nations." *Journal of Peace Research* 3 (1966a):201–24.

Rummel, R. J. "The Dimensionality of Nations Project." In *Comparing Nations: The Use of Quantitative Data in Cross-National Research*, edited by Richard L. Merritt and Stein Rokkan. New Haven: Yale University Press, 1966b.

Rummel, R. J. "Understanding Factor Analysis." *Journal of Conflict Resolution* 11 (December 1967):444–80.

Rummel, R. J. "The Relationship Between National Attributes and Foreign Conflict Behavior." In *Quantitative International Politics: Insights and Evidence*, edited by J. David Singer. New York: Free Press, 1968.

Rummel, R. J. "Some Empirical Findings on Nations." *World Politics* 21 (January 1969):226–41.

Rummel, R. J. *Applied Factor Analysis.* Evanston: Northwestern University Press, 1970.

Russett, Bruce M. *Trends in World Politics.* New York: Macmillan, 1965.

Russett, Bruce M. "The Yale Political Data Program: Experience and Prospects." In *Comparing Nations*, edited by Richard L. Merritt and Stein Rokkan. New Haven: Yale University Press, 1966.

Russett, Bruce M. *International Regions and the International System: A Study in Political Ecology.* Chicago: Rand McNally, 1967.

Russett, Bruce M. "Components of an Operational Theory of International Alliance Formation." *Journal of Conflict Resolution* 12 (September 1968):285–301.

Russett, Bruce M. et al. *World Handbook of Political and Social Indicators.* New Haven: Yale University Press, 1964.

Samuelson, Paul A. *Economics.* 9th ed. New York: McGraw-Hill, 1973.

Sawyer, Jack. "Dimensions of Nations: Size, Wealth and Politics." *American Journal of Sociology* 73 (September 1967):145–72.

Schwartz, David. "Problems in Political Gaming." *Orbis* 9 (Fall 1965):677–93.

Scott, Andrew M. *The Revolution in Statecraft.* New York: Random House, 1965.

Scott, Andrew M. *The Functioning of the International Political System.* New York: Macmillan, 1967.

Selvin, Hanan C., and Hagstrom, Warren O. "The Empirical Classification of Formal Groups." *American Sociological Review* 28 (1963):399–411.

Siegel, Sidney. *Nonparametric Statistics for the Behavioral Sciences.* New York: McGraw-Hill, 1956.

Simmel, Georg. *Conflict* (translated by Kurt H. Walff). Glencoe, Illinois: The Free Press, 1955.

Simon, Herbert A. *The Sciences of the Artificial.* Cambridge: MIT Press, 1969.

Simon, Julian. *Basic Research Methods in Social Science.* New York: Random House, 1969.

Singer, J. David. "The Level of Analysis Problem in International Relations." *World Politics* 14 (1961):77–92.

Singer, J. David. "Data-Making in International Relations." *Behavioral Science* 10 (January 1965):68–80.

Singer, J. David, ed. *Quantitative International Politics: Insights and Evidence.* New York: Free Press, 1968.

Singer, J. David, and Hinomoto, Hirohide. "Inspecting for Weapons Production: A Modest Computer Simulation." *Journal of Peace Research* 1 (1965):18–38.

Singer, J. David, and Small, Melvin. "Alliance Aggregation and the Onset of War: 1815–1945." In *Quantitative International Politics*, edited by J. David Singer. New York: Free Press, 1968.

Small, Melvin, and Singer, J. David. "Patterns in International Warfare, 1816–1965." *The Annals of the American Academy of Political and Social Science* 391 (September 1970):145–55.

Snyder, Richard C. "Experimental Techniques and Political Analysis: Some Reflections in the Context of Concern over Behavioral Approaches." In *The Limits of Behavioralism in Political Science*, edited by James C. Charlesworth. Philadelphia: American Academy of Political and Social Science, 1962.

Snyder, Richard C., and Robinson, James A. *National and International Decision-Making.* New York: The Institute for International Order, 1961.

Snyder, Richard C. et al. *Foreign Policy Decision-Making; An Approach to the Study of International Politics.* New York: Free Press of Glencoe, 1962.

Speier, Hans, and Goldhamer, Herbert. "Some Observations on Political Gaming." *World Politics* 12 (1959):71–83.

Spiro, Herbert J. *World Politics: The Global System.* Homewood, Illinois: The Dorsey Press, 1966.

Spykman, Nicholas. *The Geography of the Peace.* New York: Harcourt, Brace, and Company, 1944.

Stoessinger, John G. *The United Nations and the Superpowers.* New York: Random House, 1965.

Stone, P. J. "An Introduction to the General Inquirer: A Computer System for the Study of Spoken or Written Material." Cambridge: Harvard University and Simulmatics Corporation, 1964 (mimeo).

Tanter, Raymond. "Dimensions of Conflict Behavior Within and Between Nations, 1958–1960." *Journal of Conflict Resolution* 10 (March 1966):41–64.

Taylor, C. L., ed. *Aggregate Data Analysis: Political and Social Indicators in Cross-National Research.* Paris: Mouton, 1968.

Taylor, Charles L., and Hudson, Michael C. *World Handbook of Political and Social Indicators.* 2nd ed. New Haven: Yale University Press, 1972.

Teune, Henry, and Synnestvedt, Sig. "Measuring International Alignment." *Orbis* 9 (Spring 1965):171–89.

Thompson, Kenneth, and Macridis, Roy C. "The Comparative Study of Foreign Policy." In *Foreign Policy in World Politics*, edited by Roy C. Macridis. Englewood Cliffs, New Jersey: Prentice-Hall, 1967.

Thorelli, H. B., and Graves, R. L. *International Operations Simulation.* New York: Free Press, 1964.

Toma, Peter A., and Gyorgy, Andrew. *Basic Issues in International Relations.* Boston: Allyn and Bacon, 1967.

Tufte, Edward R. "Improving Data Analysis in Political Science." *World Politics* 21 (July 1969):641–54.

Underwood, B. J. et al. *Elementary Statistics.* New York: Appleton-Century-Crofts, 1954.

Underwood, Benton J. *Psychological Research.* New York: Appleton-Century-Crofts, 1954.

Verba, Sidney. "Simulation, Reality, and Theory in International Relations." *World Politics* 16 (April 1964):490–519.

Waltz, Kenneth N. *Man, the State, and War: A Theoretical Analysis.* New York: Columbia University Press, 1959.

Waltz, Kenneth N. *Foreign Policy and Democratic Politics.* Boston: Little, Brown, and Company, 1967.

Wert, James E.; O'Neil, Charles; and Ahmann, J. Stanley. *Statistical Methods in Educational and Psychological Research.* New York: Appleton-Century-Crofts, 1954.

Wilcox, Leslie D. et al. *Social Indicators and Societal Monitoring: An Annotated Bibliography.* San Francisco: Jossey-Bass, Inc., 1972.

Wolf, Charles J. *United States Policy and the Third World.* Boston: Little, Brown, 1967.

Wolfers, Arnold. "In Defense of the Small Countries." *Yale Review* 33 (December 1943):201–20.

Wolfers, Arnold. *Alliance Policy in the Cold War.* Baltimore: Johns Hopkins Press, 1959.

Wright, Quincy. *A Study of War.* Chicago: University of Chicago Press, 1942.

Yearbook of International Organizations, 1968–1969. Vol. 12, Brussels: Union of International Associations.

Yeates, Maurice H. *An Introduction to Quantitative Analysis in Economic Geography.* New York: McGraw-Hill, 1968.

Yuill, Stuart J. "Quantitative Information for Strategic Decisions." *Naval War College Review* 23 (November 1970):16–29.

Zawodny, J. K. *Guide to the Study of International Relations.* San Francisco, Chandler Pub. Co., 1966a.

Zawodny, J. K. *Man and International Relations: Contributions of the Social Sciences to the Study of Conflict and Integration.* 2 vols. San Francisco: Chandler Pub. Co., 1966b.

Zeisel, Hans. *Say It With Figures.* New York: Harper and Row, 1968.

Zetterberg, Hans. *On Theories and Verification in Sociology.* Totowa, New Jersey: The Bedminster Press, 1963.

Zinnes, Dina A. "A Comparison of Hostile Behavior of Decision-Makers in Simulate and Historical Data." *World Politics* 18 (1966):474–502.

INDEX